**LEBRA, Takie Sugiyama. Japanese women: constraint and fulfillment. Hawaii, 1984. 345p index 83-18029. 18.95 ISBN 0-8248-0868-1. CIP**
A study of the socialization of Japanese women into the various sequential life-cycle roles, this work is based on 57 life histories of women from different social classes. The life histories are cited throughout the volume, which is arranged topically with reference to the life cycle. Although the 17 women interviewed most intensively are the main source of examples, Lebra also interviewed men and professional women for comparative insights. The setting (introduced in a very readable first chapter) is a resort town in central Japan. The women have such varied experiences, however, that they could come from most small cities in Japan. The author skillfully applies social science concepts, primarily regarding the socialization process, drawn from mainstream sociology; she redefines them, when necessary, for Japanese life-styles. Clarity is achieved with no loss of cultural feeling for the topic. Lebra manages to convey both the ideal type of Japanese woman and the complex reality; one is not confused despite the wealth of data. The title, however, should include the term "socialization." Comparable volumes are Susan Pharr's *Political Women in Japan* (CH, Oct '81), which focuses on activist women (Lebra's study is on "ordinary women"), and *Women in Changing Japan*, ed. by Joyce Lebra, Joy Paulson, and Elizabeth Powers (CH, Feb '77), which adopts the case-study format and thus has a narrower scope than the present work. This is a fine book, highly recommended for specialists.—*J.W. Salaff, University of Toronto*

*Japanese Women*

# Japanese Women
## Constraint and Fulfillment

Takie Sugiyama Lebra

456446

**UNIVERSITY OF HAWAII PRESS**
Honolulu

**Library of Congress Cataloging in Publication Data**

Lebra, Takie Sugiyama, 1930–
    Japanese women.

    Bibliography: p.
    Includes index.
    1.   Women—Japan—Social conditions—Case studies.
2.   Life cycle, Human—Case studies.   3.   Sex role—Japan—
Case studies.   4.   Participant observation.   I.   Title.
HQ1763.L4   1984      305.4'0952      83–18029
ISBN 0–8248–0868–1

*In memory of my mothers,*
*Kimi Saigusa Sugiyama*
*and*
*Stella Welker Lebra*

# Contents

# Preface

Japan, a decade behind the United States, is now expressing its awareness of women as a major social issue. This awareness manifests itself in floods of publications, television coverage, the burgeoning of women's studies groups, court rulings interfering with sex discrimination, appointments of women to prominent positions thus far reserved exclusively for men, admission of women to such institutions as the Self-Defense Forces, police, athletics, and so on. Nevertheless, resistance to women's liberation is as widespread and persistent as ever. Only a handful of women are self-proclaimed "libbers," and they remain a source of amusement or an object of ridicule.

There appears to be little consensus regarding where women stand in Japanese society. Rather mutually opposed views have been presented. Japanese women are depicted, on the one hand, as an extreme example of sexual dichotomy. They appear strictly bound by the rule of segregation and division of labor, confined to domestic drudgery, and pitiably deprived in status, power, and opportunities. Actually or expectedly, they are demurely submissive, coquettishly feminine, and hopelessly removed from the attainment of self-fulfillment when compared with their American sisters. Feminists, both native and foreign, are thus trying to replace this extreme sexual polarity by equality and balance, at least to the extent that it is enjoyed by American and European women. Not only Westerners but also Southeast Asians, Filipino women for example, are taken as models to emulate.

On the other hand, this image of Japanese women has been refuted as a groundless stereotype or myth. It is argued that once you go beyond the surface of Japanese society and mingle with Japanese women and men on a personal basis, you realize it is, in fact, women who run men, not the other way around. We are told the Japanese housewife holds and exercises dictatorial power over the household affairs and enjoys unlimited autonomy. Rather, to be pitied is the American woman who is constrained by her husband's power and interference. To support this view, it is further contended that Japanese men have no voice or place in their homes and are fearful of their wives; it is much more difficult to find a demure, feminine woman than an invincible tigress. Japan is often characterized as a matrifocal society, alleged to be a legacy of the hypothetical matriarchy of ancient Japan. What about the exclusion of women from the public domain? Women are *not* excluded, one is told, rather they *choose* to stay or return home. Among the career women who have succeeded in infiltrating the male-dominant professions, we encounter those who exhibit little sympathy for the liberationist movement, mainly because they have not been discriminated against as women. Japanese society allows a woman, so goes the argument, to cross over the sex lines and feel like a man. The overall message is that Japanese women, housewives or professionals, are more or less contented, or could be better off if only they made the effort.

There are many more instances indicative of fundamental disagreement on the subject of Japanese women. The Japanese mother has been known as the ultimate embodiment of self-denial, totally dedicated to her child. Reflective of this is the idealized mother image held by Japanese sons and daughters. Adult men and women tend to be nostalgic about their mothers as an inexhaustible source of love and warmth. At the same time, the Japanese mother has been a target of severe attack. Her notoriety has culminated in the *kyōiku mama*, the mother who drives her child relentlessly to study. Far from selfless and single-mindedly child-centered, it is argued, the mother is actually imposing her own ambition for success upon the poor child in disregard of the child's own inclinations and welfare. The monstrous *kyōiku mama* image often appears as an explanation for juvenile delinquency and the pathological refusal to attend school. Domestic violence, which in present-day Japan has come to mean a boy's abuse of his mother, is not infrequently considered a product of the mother's egocentrism. The implication is that she deserves her son's rebellion.

Aging is another point of dispute. The Japanese woman is in a position to grow old more happily than the American counterpart, so goes one argument. She can age and die calmly, surrounded by her concerned children and grandchildren, who are grateful for her maternal sacrifice and care. This idyllic picture is dismissed as absurd by those who associate the Japanese elderly with suicide.

Which is true, which false, or are they all true? To answer this question requires a careful study based upon observations. Herein lies the rationale of the present study, which is the result of five years of research including extensive fieldwork in Japan. The life cycle approach is adopted, and the life histories of women, young and old, given in interview constitute the primary source of data. A seventy-eight-year-old woman recalling her life experience may sound incredibly outmoded to those who are sensitized to the ongoing social and technological change as reported by the media. It is my belief, however, that an elderly woman's life review, however old-fashioned, can provide valuable insights into the optimal way of life for younger women. This book is concerned foremost with an objective description of how women have lived and are living in Japan. Only at the end will I express my subjective views about the promotion of women's welfare.

Many people have participated in or cooperated with this research. Above all, I would like to express my debt to all those women and men who kindly accepted my interview requests, otherwise supplied needed information, and tolerated my interference with their usual schedules. Most gratifying was their trust in me; many confided their personal secrets. Needless to say, their anonymity is insured in the following pages by the use of fictitious names.

Among those who assisted me in the field in one capacity or another were Tomoko Inukai, Yaeko Ogo, and Yutaka Ogo. In Hawaii, Linda Kimura and Freda Hellinger helped me as research assistant and typist respectively. Dr. Edward Norbeck made helpful suggestions to improve the original manuscript. And as always, my husband and anthropological colleague, William P. Lebra, has been a professional consultant, unequivocal supporter of my commitment, and domestic coworker.

The National Science Foundation and the Japan Society for the Promotion of Science funded two periods of fieldwork in Japan. The University of Hawaii granted me leaves of absence, and the Social Science Research Institute at the university assisted me at various stages of this research. Grants from the Research Council and the Japan Government Gift Fund (both under University of Hawaii auspices) helped me at the preliminary and final phases of the project. Without all of this support and assistance, it would have been impossible to sustain my research commitment for so many years. I am indeed grateful.

# 1
# *Introduction*

I wish at the outset to spell out the objectives pursued throughout this book, objectives which have served as general guidelines for selecting and organizing data. Following this somewhat abstract discussion will be a presentation of more tangible details of where my fieldwork was carried out and how data were gathered and reached the present form.

## Objectives

A complex set of objectives are sought here. Since it is about *Japanese women* as they have lived and are living in their society, I wish, first, to present the book as an ethnography of a sector of *Japanese society*. The lengthy fieldwork in a community, as would be expected of an ethnographer, was intended to generate ethnographic details based upon "naturalistic" observations. This is not only because I am a hopeless convert to traditional anthropology but because, to my knowledge, this type of information on Japanese women is conspicuously missing even as we are inundated with either survey-based publications or popular books and articles enunciating profeminist or antifeminist ideologies. My immodest goal here is to contribute something to the tradition of Japanese ethnographies as initiated by John Embree (1939) over four decades ago. An ethnography requires that an external boundary be drawn, explicitly or implicitly, in distinction from other cultural groups. In characterizing Japanese women, I shall mobilize whatever I know about non-Japanese counterparts, especially American, as a covert reference for comparison. Therefore, when the choice is necessary, greater emphasis will be placed upon the difference than upon the similarity between Japanese and American women or societies. The culture-bound aspect, in other words, will loom larger than the culture-free aspect of women's experience.

This ethnographic bias will be somewhat controlled by a second objective, however. Focused upon *women* rather than men, this book is concerned with sex polarity, which may be observable across cultures. Sex polarity is conceived of as a continuum from an extreme polarization where there is nothing in common between the sexes to an extreme neutralization in which both men and women transcend their sexual identities or freely exchange their roles. Surveying an array of literature on women (Lebra 1979a), I have arrived at three principles of sex polarization. First is the principle of *role specialization*, assigning women to the domestic domain and men to the public domain (Rosaldo 1974). Even when a woman engages in a nondomestic activity, that activity may be secondary to or compatible with her domestic role, especially the role of mother. As pointed out by Brown (1970), a woman's participation in the subsistence economy depends upon the nearness of the work site from home, the monotony of the work dispensing with the need for concentration, and the kind of work which allows for interruptions. The second principle is *asymmetry* in distribution of social valuables such as status (as measured by esteem, prestige, honor, rights, privilege, authority, etc.), power and dominance, autonomy, role options, and the like. If women share these valuables, they would do so much less or only vicariously. More strikingly, women may play a complementary role as admiring audience for men's display of prestige, as submissive subject to male power, as men's helpmate in the maintenance of male superiority. The third principle is *segregation* by sex, which takes various forms—spatial, sensory, physical, social, symbolic. It may or may not involve the idea of ritual pollution. The institution of the "men's house" (often appearing in anthropological literature) is striking evidence of this rule, but in less obvious forms sex segregation can be observed everywhere, including the American cocktail lounge (Spradley and Mann 1975). Insofar as these three principles are in effect, women are characterized in terms of domesticity, inferiority, and seclusion. Whether such extreme polarization reflects reality or not has been a controversial issue, and many researchers have refuted this polarization model (notably, Friedl 1967; Rogers 1975; Quinn 1977; Schlegel 1977). It is more likely that a woman finds herself at various points of the polarization-neutralization continuum. The polarization model will be used in this book as a point of departure for describing Japanese women in terms of the extent to which they conform to or deviate from it. Put in a reverse order, we shall explore whether Japanese women move toward the neutralization extreme, and if so, under what circumstances this occurs and whether neutralization is facilitated or hindered by the traditional social structure and culture.

A third objective is to view our women against the temporal dimension of the life cycle. The life cycle view is unavoidable, I believe, because a woman's life pattern, role repertoire, status, and values tend to change radically over her life stages. It would be impossible, what's more, to achieve the first two objectives without taking this into consideration. There is a methodological problem inherent in the life cycle approach. Because a woman's life cycle cannot be "observed," I must draw upon a secondary source of information, her recollections of past experience. As will be shown shortly, life histories of the women living now constitute the bulk of data.

One person's life cycle becomes coupled with another's; taking a role implies hinging a certain stage of one's life upon a life stage of another role player. Becoming a daughter-in-law means coupling one's own life cycle with that of a parent-in-law. It may be through such coupling that one develops and comes to accept one's age identity. The intergenerational coupling of life cycles throws into relief two aspects of human history: repetition and change. A daughter may realize, when she becomes a mother, that she is doing the same thing that her mother used to, or it may be the mother who is amused to see in the daughter a replica of her life experience. Here the life cycle is truly a cycle. It may be speculated that a woman's life, more biologically determined than a man's, tends to be more repetitive over generations, and that, for the same reason, women have more in common with each other and across cultures than do men. This does not mean there is no gap between generations. A generation gap may stem from a difference in life stages or, more fundamentally, from social change that creates two distinct cohorts. It is the latter change that challenges us, given the seemingly accelerating transformation that Japan and its women are undergoing today.

The last point brings us to a consideration of still another dimension. A woman, Japanese or non-Japanese, is an individual person with inner feelings and thoughts, aspirations and frustrations, and an awareness of a unique self-identity. Our fourth and final objective, then, is to capture women's sense of self-fulfillment. Women do play roles and occupy statuses as defined parts of the social structure, but it is necessary to go beyond this social structure framework and see how women link or separate their role requirement and self-fulfillment. This dimension is significant particularly in view of the worldwide surge of women's movements, Japan being no exception, which seems to leave none of us unaffected. Stimulated by the liberationist ideology on the one hand, and afforded by economic affluence on the other, today's women in Japan, including staunch traditionalists, seem to have more opportunities to think about themselves and their personal happiness.

The fourfold objective will be difficult to attain, and it will be necessary, I admit, to zigzag and to shift emphasis from one objective to another within the constraint of linear writing. Particularly challenging will be the problem of how to present a coherent, meaningful picture when social structure is juxtaposed with social change, and when social structure, again, is placed alongside the individual's inner self.[1] Nevertheless, I feel compelled to accept that challenge as a testimony of my adherence to the holistic ideal.

## The Setting

The anthropological method of participant observation for data gathering is certainly old-fashioned, time-consuming, and painstaking. Nonetheless I follow this method with the conviction that it maximizes the "naturalness" and "depth" of observation. For studying the Japanese, this is an important consideration in view of their conscious distinction between frontstage and backstage behavior. There is an accidental reason behind this methodological choice as well. I happen to be a native Japanese who cannot help being a participant in the Japanese cultural context, and who can turn this ascriptive bind to her advantage as a fieldworker to produce "participatory truth."

For a participant observer it is necessary to settle down in a field site which permits access to its residents on a routine basis. I resided in a small city for a year in 1976–1977, and returned there for a brief stay in 1978 and 1980. This was a community where I had already made a series of field trips. The previously established rapports and accumulated information could thus be utilized for the present purpose.

Doubtless, this traditional method must pay its price. The question is: how and to what extent can one claim to generalize out of the findings based on such an intensive method? Is it really feasible to apply this method to a complex society such as Japan, and to a large population like Japanese women? Two interrelated issues are involved: my community may reflect a local bias not shared by other communities; the local sample may fail to reflect the depth of national-level culture or the complexity of national social structure. I shall try to meet this dilemma, first, by linking the local to the national history in the following sketch of the field site, and, second, by adding an external sample, as will be noted later.

### Shizumi City and Its Surrounding: Past and Present

A two-hour train ride southwestward from Tokyo takes one to a city fictitiously named Shizumi (Quiet Sea). Anyone who looks like a visitor, upon passing through the ticket gate at the Shizumi train station, is swarmed by a crowd of hotel agents carrying their banners and soliciting prospective customers. What one sees next are rows of tour buses waiting in the station yard. Looking through the window of a city tour bus, one further notices an overwhelming number of little souvenir shops and hotels along the main streets. It seems as if the whole city is geared for tourism, attracting visitors with its various resources: scenic views along the shorelines, beaches, fishing, temperate climate, the woods of the mountainous interior, hiking trails, golf courses, a bicycle race stadium, seasonal festivals, seafoods, bars, teahouses, geisha, and so forth. Another important attraction is the spa, and this takes us back to the root of Shizumi's tourist industry.

Located in central Japan, Shizumi is part of the land mass which emerged out of a series of volcanic disturbances lasting until ten thousand years ago. The geothermal resource of the area—hot springs—was long recognized and used by local bathers, though not for commercial purposes until rather recent times. The early part of this century witnessed Shizumi developing into a resort town for outsiders, especially for wealthy sojourners from Tokyo. Tapping of thermal waters was then mechanized, and the number of villas and bath hotels augmented. Construction workers migrated in. The next stage began in 1938 when the local railway construction was completed. The resort town, thus far catering to an elite clientele, now became a popular spot for mass recreation (SCII:707–14).[2] Not only hotels but other service industries (including bars, restaurants, teahouses, brothels, geisha houses, entertainment sports and games) prospered accordingly, despite the national government's austerity policy in response to Japan's deeper involvement in the China Incident.

Inherent in this geological accident is the fact that the area is extremely poor for farming. Except for the alluvial fan built around the mouth of Shizumi's main river, which constitutes the urban center of the city, the land is largely of mountain forests and grasslands. Within this limited condition, however, the residents tried to subsist through the maximal utilization of the tiny terraced fields for agriculture (rice and other grain crops, root crops, beans and other vegetables, tea, fruit, sericulture, etc.). The forests and grasslands were exploited for lumber, firewood, charcoal making, compost, mushroom growing, edible grass foraging. Meanwhile, the coastal residents engaged in offshore fishing as the primary means of livelihood. As of the late nineteenth century, when Shizumi was still a village containing around 1,200 households, the majority were farmers, roughly 20 percent were in fishing, with a negligible portion in commerce and other businesses (SCI:69). Although farming and fishing were simultaneously pursued by many households, it is also clear that there was a naturally conditioned division between farming and fishing districts within the village. The above occupational distribution also indicates that even such an agriculturally unsuited village shared the politically imposed national bias for agriculture, especially for rice production.

From the late nineteenth century on, change took place toward a heavier reliance upon fishing, and this trend intensified in the early twentieth century with the introduction of new fishing technology and the motorization of boats which enabled deep-sea fishing and long voyages. By 1929, the marine industry preponderated over agriculture as a household occupation (by 26 percent to 15 percent) while secondary and tertiary industries also increased (commerce, 21 percent, and manufacturing industry, 15 percent) (SCI:138). Farming itself shifted, mainly as a result of the improved transportation facilities, from subsistence crops to commercial ones, of which the tangerine was predominant.

The Second World War interrupted the further evolution of local industries first by subordinating both material and human resources to military goals, and finally devastating them. Subsequent to a period of struggle for survival during and after the war, and as Japan entered into the high-growth period which lasted from the late 1950s through the 1960s and early 1970s, Shizumi found itself more than ever committed to tourism as its specialty. No longer just a hot spring town attracting bathers—the hot springs had deteriorated in consequence of their overexploitation—it now emerged as a tourist city where enlarged and modernized hotels swallowed busloads of tourist groups. Automobiles brought many leisure consumers to the city's points of interest and entertainment. The former agricultural lands as well as forest/grasslands were increasingly transformed into lots for the construction of villas, *minshuku* inns (ordinary homes converted to cater to those who could not afford regular hotels), and extensive housing projects.

Farming households, which shrank to 8 percent in 1946, temporarily increased to 16 percent (SCI:138) due to the amalgamation of adjacent rural villages with the city, but again dwindled. By 1970, farming and forest industry households combined comprised only 6 percent. Fishing, which had once thrived as Shizumi's main industry, by 1970 had declined to 3 percent of the total number of households (SCIII: 117), in part due to industrial pollution of the bay. Conversely, tourism-related industries, including service businesses, commerce, construction, and transportation expanded. It seemed that no business would survive unless geared to tourism, as exemplified by the conversion of fishing boats into sightseeing boats.

The so-called dollar shock and oil shock resulted in replacing the high-growth prosperity by a slow-growth economy and recession in the 1970s. At the time of my fieldwork, many local residents were complaining about the slump, some claiming this was the worst that they had ever experienced. Most heavily hit was the highly invested tourist industry, which in turn was affecting all other businesses. The tourist association, hotel owners, and other interested businessmen were zealously looking for new ways of attracting visitors.

This brief sketch of the modern history of subsistence suggests that Shizumi, along with its uniqueness, has been part of, and thus affected by, national and international history. It also suggests in a general way the changing distribution of occupations of the local community. Related to the occupational distribution is the skewed sex distribution of the city's population. Since 1925 females have consistently exceeded males (as of 1950 the ratio was one hundred to eighty-nine according to SCII: 19), and female predominance concentrates among those fifteen years or older in the downtown "entertainment" districts. Furthermore, according to the national census of 1970 (SCIII:6), males predominate in all occupational categories except one, the service industry. All these point to the significance of women's role in the local hospitality business related to entertainment and tourism.

Shizumi has a population of seventy thousand, inhabiting an area of over 120 square kilometers, with a heavy concentration on the alluvial plain. Given this demographic and geographical size, it would be preposterous to refer to Shizumi as a community if the community requires face-to-face interaction among all its members. Nonetheless, the usage of this term seems warranted, as will be shown below.

Despite the enormous historical changes including the administrative reorganization, population growth, in and out migration, and in- and outflow of tourists, Shizumi residents generally share a sense of boundary, marking "insiders" from "outsiders," or residents from sojourners. During the first three months of my stay the people who recognized me as a sojourner would ask me when I had come. From the fourth month on they would say, "Are you still here? When are you going back?" The distinction between *jimoto* (local) residents and *yosomono* (outsiders) is also evidenced by the discount prices at many retail stores enjoyed by *jimoto* people only. "Unless you give a discount," said a fruit store owner, "they would never come back." The awareness of such a boundary at times encompasses the passage of many decades, as shown when an eighty-year-man who himself had migrated into the community to marry identified some of the most successful local businessmen as *yosomono*. It turns out that their businesses have existed for more than fifty years. Some of the middle-aged women I contacted

admitted to still being *yosomono* since they married into this community from outside, and some expressed gratitude for having been warmly accepted. One of the most memorable recent events in the history of
the local women's association *(fujinkai)*, I was told, is that for the first
time a *yosomono* had been elected to its presidency. *Jimoto* favoritism is
expressed most conspicuously at election time. My informants tend to
think that there is no real difference between candidates or between
parties, conservative or liberal: "No matter who wins, things won't
change substantially." What does make a difference to most voters is
whether the candidate is a *jimoto* person or not. In the 1972 election for
the House of Representatives of the National Diet, the *jimoto* candidate
received 44 percent of the total local vote. The candidate too appeals to
this *jimoto* identity by saying, as he did during the 1976 campaign, that
he was born in this city and is going to be buried in this city.

The use of the local dialect is another marker of the boundary. The
dialect is identifiable by a certain vocabulary interspersed with the predominantly standard forms of expression, by the sentence-ending forms,
and by intonations. Most people can switch between the local dialect
and the standard in response to situational demand. I was impressed
with the way this "bilingualism" was manipulated in a classroom at a
local school. Despite the general understanding that schools must teach
the standard only, the teacher of a Japanese-language class switched
from one to the other, and I began to notice that this was done deliberately for a pedagogical purpose. The students, uninterested in the
class, suddenly brightened up whenever the teacher switched from the
square, formal standard to the relaxed somewhat frivolous-sounding
dialect. Intimacy was created between the teacher standing on the
raised platform and the forty seated students. There emerged something
like esprit de corps. The teacher soon had to switch back to the standard, since this was a language course, but as soon as the students
showed signs of boredom he again resorted to the same strategy.

No one expresses hostility toward outsiders openly, but one can
detect in casual conversation a modicum of resentment or mistrust toward them as being shrewd, irresponsible, or troublesome. Among the
outsiders is a large number of migratory women employed in the hospitality industry as bar girls, hotel maids, and the like. A woman over seventy, a community leader and government-appointed social welfare
committee member, is frustrated over the fact that the right to benefit
from the government's social welfare service is not exercised by *jimoto*
people but by outsiders. Asked what is the most serious problem she
encounters as a social worker, she said: "Young [unwed] mothers. Most
are drifters from outside, such as bar hostesses."

Whatever requires neighborhood cooperation makes local residents aware of the trouble caused by temporary sojourners. Apartment dwellers in particular are identified as unassimilable outsiders. At a regular meeting of the women's association leaders, apartment residents were singled out, when the problem of street sanitation was discussed, as indifferent to the garbage disposal regulations.

A local police officer revealed that Shizumi has one of the highest crime rates in the prefecture, 80 percent of the crimes being larceny and, to my surprise, that the victims of theft are mostly tourists staying at local hotels or owners of villas—also outsiders. On the other hand, I found most households I visited unlocked, oftentimes with no one inside —a good indication that local people do not worry about theft.

On the fringe of the community are former outcasts whose residential block is still a reality in the eyes of many locals; it is alluded to in confidential tones as "inner island," or "*atchi*" (that direction). They too are regarded as *yosomono*. There is another fringe group of outsiders— Koreans. Several Korean households congregate at a tiny segment of the coastal cliff, forming what the locals call the "Korean hamlet."

The confidence the local people seem to have about one another, as indicated above, is based upon mutual familiarity. One is struck with the frequency of *tachibanashi*, casual talk while standing, of two people, especially women, either on a crowded street or in an aisle of a supermarket. When I joined a small group of women to visit a festival site, I was amazed to see how often these women were stopped on our way by their acquaintances, each time drawn into *tachibanashi*, so that it took about two hours to walk a mile. Formerly, Shizumi, as a hot spring town, had many bathhouses which were open to the public and provided important places for communal interaction on a highly intimate and daily basis. Now, the cooling of the hot spring, along with the increasing number of households having their own private baths, has put such houses out of existence. Nonetheless, there are still seventeen bathhouses attracting residents nearby and serving as spots for neighborly contact as well as for baths.[3]

Mutual familiarity stimulates, and is in turn reinforced by, the speedy circulation of information among the residents about one another. A woman of ward A was engaged to a man of ward B, and this information got around ward B, so I was told, within a few days. Whenever the woman passed along the street to visit her fiancé, the whole ward apparently was informed of this little event. She inferred this from the fact that on every such visit a package of dried fish was delivered as a gift to her from her future sister-in-law, who lived nearby and must have learned from a neighbor that she had just passed by on her way to the fiancé's house.

The sense of communal bond entails cautions to avoid offending others even when the issue is a matter of life and death. An eighty-one-year-old widow, dying, resisted switching to a more reliable physician to avoid offending her own doctor. Another widow, convinced that her cancer-stricken husband had died prematurely from an excessive injection, refused to protest to the responsible family doctor. Some people gossip about a doctor who is allegedly responsible for the muscle deformity of many local children, but no one has openly exposed this scandal to the public, let alone naming him in a suit.

Sensitivity to the opinion of fellow residents manifests itself in a compulsion to conform to conventional norms such as gift exchange. An elderly man, as a funeral host for a deceased brother, received funerary gifts (called *kōden*, usually given in cash) from his kin and neighbors and yet did not make *kōden-gaeshi* (return gifts in kind for *kōden*), which he would have done had the women's association not made a declaration to stop that outmoded, wasteful custom and imposed this decision upon everyone in the community. Soon after this funeral, another household in the neighborhood held a funeral and made *kōden-gaeshi*, disregarding the association's decision. Deeply ashamed and fearful of being accused of stinginess, this man keeps cursing himself for listening to the women's association. A woman wishes to take a trip to Hawaii, but hesitates to carry it out, she revealed to me, for fear of the enormous amount of gifts she must bring back for her neighbors, kin, and friends.

While mass media such as television and the larger newspapers are nationally oriented, information on the community is supplied by the local papers and the municipal government's newsletters that reach every household. What is more significant in light of the maintenance of communal spirit is that there are some kinds of collective activities all year around which draw many local residents together, out of their usual confinement in the home, workplace, or school and into mutual visibility around streets, playgrounds, parks, auditoriums, shrines, temples, or other public places. The most conspicuous of these are various annual community festivals conducted by wards (as will be described later), athletic meetings, and all kinds of "cultural" activities held in the fall by kindergartens, schools, the women's association, organized groups of youths, children, senior citizens, and so forth. Men and women, young and old, join these and share the excitement of the occasion as participants or spectators, ceremonial attendants or kitchen helpers, leaders or followers. Some of the rites of passage, also collectively and annually conducted, should be mentioned: the initiation ceremony (Adult Day) in January, graduation ceremonies at all levels from kindergarten to high school in March, entrance ceremonies in April, and the *shichigosan* (seven-five-three) ceremonies in November for three-, five-, and seven-year-olds. Not only the children who are the focus of the celebration but their mothers too are dressed in their best and make themselves visible to spectators.

As another stimulus to reinforce a sense of community, one should mention the municipal wired broadcasting system which chimes at 7:00 A.M. and 5:00 P.M. each day, announcing emergencies like a fire or a lost child, and urging the residents to perform civic duties such as paying their taxes and voting.

I have stressed the community boundary and tried to characterize Shizumi as a community. However, there are other aspects which do not fit this picture. I often found the sense of familiarity widely shared but exaggerated. Many people had difficulty in giving precise information on their addresses, and offhandedly told me to ask "anybody" how to get to such and such a place. If the person is identified by the house name, "everybody" can tell where it is, I was assured. This prediction was not always verified, even in the case of a locally "famous" family. The community seems to exist more in the minds of the people than in reality and this gap may be attributed to a culture lag on the part of my informants. Some are keenly aware of the change undermining the communal aspect of the city. One informant said that old houses, for example, were partitioned into rooms by removable screen doors. When a ceremony like a wedding or death anniversary rite was to be held, the whole house was converted into one large banquet hall where many guests were received. All the women in the neighborhood would come to help the host house with kitchen work, and the men would arrive to attend the ceremony. Everything was done at the host's house site and by the family and neighbors. But now the house is divided by thick walls for privacy, with no space for large gatherings, necessitating the ceremonial site to be moved to a hotel, commercial banquet hall, or temple, all of which dispenses with the neighbors' help. Ceremonies are becoming more extravagant each year, but communal solidarity is waning.

This does not necessarily mean that the traditional community has been a harmonious one. Mutual familiarity among neighbors, intense interest in one another's lives, and mutual pressures for conformity have generated the kind of conflict—as well as warm solidarity—that would be done away with under a totally impersonal, highly Gesellschaft-like social system. I was with three neighbor women chatting about one another's families in a friendly manner. No sooner did one of them leave the scene than the other two began to discuss the faults of the one absent. This was only the beginning. The two women proceeded to

identify practically everyone in the neighborhood as a source of their
frustrations and described themselves as the victims of the arrogance,
misunderstanding, or misplaced hostility of these neighbors. Each
woman had not been on speaking terms, it was disclosed, with at least
some of their close neighbors. Here is ample evidence that the Gemein-
schaft involves not only face-to-face solidarity but also back-to-back (or
face-against-face) animosity and avoidance.

What one finds here is not so much a single community as a cluster
of communities partially overlapping one another. The *yosomono* label
may be applied to a person from another ward within the city: the head
of a household who moved to his present residence thirteen years ago
from a site three miles away confessed this was the case. Yet the sense of
the city as a single community is not totally lacking, probably due to the
persistence of the reticulated system of wards *(ku)*, each of which is
divided into districts *(chōnaikai)*, which in turn are divided into neighborhood associations *(tonarigumi)*. As of 1975, Shizumi had 15 wards,
135 districts, and over 1,100 neighborhood associations. This system has
survived the war partly as a self-governing organization available to the
residents. It is one of these units which is first mobilized to undertake
some communal project such as a seasonal festival, or to provide support for an individual to run for political office. The same system serves
as the official channel for newsletters and instructions from the city government (as well as prefectural and national governments) to reach
every household. Ironically, the same system that sustains the autonomy
of the local community also integrates the community into the municipal, prefectural, and national administrations.

In formal politics, Shizumi residents are represented by a thirty-
member assembly and mayor chosen through citywide direct election.
The composition of elected officials has been relatively conservative,
corresponding with the trend of national politics. There was a time
(1958) when a communist sympathizer was elected mayor, but he had
to compromise with the predominantly conservative assembly. His mor-
alistic campaign promise to abolish the city-operated bicycle race had to
be withdrawn when he realized the budget relied heavily upon the reve-
nues from this operation. What distinguishes local from national politics is the mildness of confrontation. In one of the assembly sessions a
hike in water charge was discussed. The assemblymen were almost all
present, formally dressed in black suits; they sat facing a row of more
casually dressed administrative officials who were responsible for the
water policy. There was only one female member in the assembly, and
none among the officials. (A reporter sitting next to me whispered that
the woman was a communist.) Three men—one socialist and two com-
munists—questioned the fairness of the differential raises for household

and business uses of water. Both questions and answers were prepared in advance, and speeches were polite and unspirited. The boredom was interrupted now and then by the high-pitched, musical voice of the assembly speaker announcing the title and name of the person about to speak. The entire event had the air of a ritual. Reporters in the back seats were moving around, talking loudly among themselves as if they were not listening at all and indicating by their behavior that they expected nothing surprising to occur. Even this kind of mild "democracy" is a great advance over the prewar system, but this change must be understood in the context of a longer history, local and national.

The province containing Shizumi appears in the eighth century of national history as a place of banishment for rebels and criminals, and this is why local legends often involve heroic exiles. This isolation of the province from the political center changed little until the rise of the warriors in the late twelfth century inaugurated the long feudal age, which lasted until the mid-nineteenth century. The province then began to fall under the domination of one warlord after another.

In the course of time, the villages, which would be combined in the late nineteenth century into the core of the present Shizumi, gradually came into existence supposedly out of the settlements of fugitive warriors, refugees, and exiles, and subsequently were integrated into the late feudalistic system of the Tokugawa era (1603–1867). Integration meant, above all, maximal exploitation of peasant labor and regimentation of village peasants as compliant taxpayers to support the warrior elite. The severity of poverty among the villagers may be inferred from instances of voluntary sterility (the celibacy, for example, of younger sons who, unable to establish branch houses, remained in their natal houses unmarried) as well as instances of infanticide, as recorded in a local history (SCII:356–65).

Each village was headed and managed by local officials *(mura-yakunin)*, topped by a headman *(nanushi)*, who also served as liaisons between villagers and the delegates of the feudal rulers. Villagers were organized into *goningumi* (units of five or so households which shared joint responsibility), which constituted the lowest level of governance, functioning to expedite central control and/or to maintain local autonomy. The class distinction between the warrior elite and the peasants was duplicated on a smaller scale within a village: tax-paying, full-fledged peasants *(honbyakushō* or *osameshi)* were distinguished from partial payers *(komae)* and from untaxable "water drinkers" *(mizu-nomi)*. Village officials were recruited from among the most well-to-do *honbyakushō*. Whether there was another class, outcast, in the Shizumi area at this time is not known, and none of the government publications touches upon this subject. The local term for this class of people is *kābō*, but no informant is sure of its etymology: one associated *kā* with *kawa* (leather), and another ventured so far as to trace it to "cowboy"! Though their origin was a mystery, in the minds of local residents these people were associated primarily with butchering and related industries.

The Meiji Restoration (1868) and subsequent modernization and reforms at the national level resulted in a series of reorganizations in the local administration, including the replacement of the feudal fief *(han)* by the prefecture *(ken)*. In 1889, to meet the new prerequisites of "self-governing bodies," sixteen villages were amalgamated into four enlarged villages *(mura)*, the largest and most densely populated of which became Shizumi Village. This village was promoted to the status of town *(machi)* in 1906, and further expanded into a city *(shi)* after World War II owing to its population growth and annexation of an adjacent village. The present Shizumi City includes two more villages. The population has increased from about twelve thousand (twenty-five hundred households) in 1920 to roughly seventy thousand (twenty-one thousand households) in 1976.

Reflecting the national-level democratization of the 1890s as symbolized by the creation of a parliament, the local government came to involve citizen participation in the election of the mayor and assembly-men, though it was not until 1925 that universal male suffrage came into effect. Former class barriers were largely removed. Yet, democratization in general was circumscribed by the sanctity of the emperor's sovereignty, to which all institutions, including the parliament, were subordinated. Even the pre-Meiji class system was not completely eliminated. The former elite class (Imperial Court nobles, *kuge,* and the highest echelons of the feudal governments, the *shōgun, daimyō,* and administrative chiefs), together with those lower-ranking samurai and commoners whose meritorious service was recognized, was reorganized into a newly created nobility called *kazoku.* The *kazoku* constituted a stratum directly below the Imperial House and its collateral princely houses forming the very top of the national pyramid. Below the nobility was a class of gentry *(shizoku)* consisting predominantly of common-ranking former samurai. At the very bottom of the pyramid was the greater portion of the population classified as commoners *(heimin).* Within the commoner class was recognized a subclass identified as new commoners *(shin heimin)* which referred to the former outcasts. (The local residents seemed to have little to do with such class distinctions. In interviews or casual conversation, however, many claimed *shizoku* ancestry and many more unwittingly revealed the tenacity of elitist orientations quite consonant with this class system, despite that the system itself was abolished early in the Allied Occupation.) More significant in terms of daily living was the survival of the economic classes based on the ownership of land and other properties, although the hierarchical distribution of wealth seemed somewhat compensated for by a large number of communally owned areas of forest and grassland for the villagers' equal use—a characteristic of the Shizumi area.

The militarism of the 1930s, the China Incident, and World War II affected the local community, like the nation as a whole, toward a reversal of earlier liberalization. The pre-Meiji villages comprising Shizumi had been retained as Shizumi's wards *(ku)*, and these were subdivided into districts and neighborhood associations, reminiscent of the five-household-group system of the Tokugawa era. This reticulated system, whose vestige in today's Shizumi was discussed earlier, served as an effective means for insuring the regimentation of the most peripheral strata of the people. Many local men were drafted into military service and many died overseas. Women were organized into the nationally united women's association (absorbing the Patriotic Women's Association and others) with a renewed mission to cooperate in the war effort. They participated in air raid drills, saw off the draftees, sent gift packages to soldiers, solicited donations, and visited the wounded at the national hot spring hospital located in Shizumi Town. Young women and local high school girls were mobilized to work in military factories. Many of the local hotels were turned over for military use.

It was only through the devastating end of World War II and the postwar reforms enforced by the Occupation forces that democracy and equality became established. Among the numerous changes were the truly universal suffrage for men and women along with the established supremacy of the National Diet and the legalization of all political parties. The latter triggered the activation of the local cells of the Communist party, which led to its success in sending one communist, together with three socialists, to the city assembly in the first postwar election of 1947. Economically, the postwar agricultural land reform benefited tenant farmers, and the overall standard of living rose, particularly in the formerly impoverished rural districts, partly as a result of the release of communal land for private ownership and the rise of land values.

Western-style hotels in and around Shizumi were commandeered by the Occupation, employing local people and providing direct contact with American servicemen, sometimes resulting in international marriages—something unprecedented and previously inconceivable in this community. In 1952, the previous year's peace treaty came into effect to put an end to the Occupation. As Japan reemerged as a world power, as television infiltrated every household with overseas news, and as affluence came to permit traveling abroad, even this provincial city began to accept its contact with the world beyond the national borders as inevitable. In 1976–1977, I found one in every three households with some kin, close or remote, permanently settled or temporarily sojourning abroad—a remarkable change since the time when this province was an enclave for native exiles.

As the local government plays a mundane role in maintaining Shizumi as a community, so does religion play a symbolic role in doing the same. To be sure, the TV generation is less involved in traditional religions, and local priests—both Shintoist and Buddhist—deplore the decline of faith in gods and buddhas. Nevertheless, one still finds signs of communal solidarity as symbolized by ritual action. Some aspects of the local religion, targeted by the tourist industry as attractions for visitors, are actually being revitalized. The most notable is an annual festival held by each ward according to its schedule, design, and tradition. One of the main attractions is the wild parading of the *mikoshi*, a palanquin shrine containing the god body temporarily removed from the regular ward shrine, through the streets of the ward. The *mikoshi* rests on crisscrossed poles which are supported on the shoulders of as many as thirty or more men jointly, facing in all directions. In consequence, no individual is in control of his movement, rather all the carriers move back and forth or sideways more or less blindly. The *mikoshi*'s movement thus can get out of hand. The whole display is a dramatic reminder of a "communitas" (Turner 1969), where individuals are totally submerged in the unpredictable will of the group (or of the god in the *mikoshi*). An older group of men who have carried the *mikoshi* in the past surround it to control and guide its movement. Further away from the *mikoshi* is a procession of elders who, in formal black kimono with family crests, embody the traditional authority of the community. Among the latter are the representative of the ward shrine members *(ujiko)*, ward chairman and councilors, and district officers.

There has been no change in this traditional form of festival, I was told by one of the elders participating in a shrine procession. I did notice, however, a member of the guiding group serving as an automobile traffic controller. It was amazing to see how the cumbersome, potentially destructive shrine was handled amidst the heavy street traffic. Another "innovation" was the placement of the shrine on wheels when it had to go through heavily congested streets. These nontraditional accommodations did not interfere with the participants' enjoyment of the affair however. Contrary to my assumption, the carriers were all volunteers, I was told, and had not been forced into this as a part of a young man's obligation. A leading member of the guiding group said,

"Everybody wants to be near the god once in life." He continued to say that, though young men do this sort of thing only once a year, the experience really ties them together. And this solidarity is necessary, he said, for the fire brigade to work effectively since "fire fighting is not a matter of technique but high-spirited cooperation." It now becomes apparent that many of the shrine carriers and guides were also members of the ward fire brigade. It was further learned that these young men all used to be organized into young men's associations *(wakamono-gumi)*, and required to sleep in the association's dormitories.

The show climaxed when the shrine plunged into the water, drifting out to sea, finally disappearing from view between the waves. The beach was now covered with excited spectators. The majority of the spectators—other than tourists—were women and children. Women and children had no part in this shrine show, and yet practically the whole show was addressed to them as an audience. Women also prepared food and drinks, entertained the male "actors" wherever they stopped to rest, and received visitors from other wards. The children, accompanied by their mothers, participated in pulling the floats, another attraction, which carried performing dancers and drummers under the guidance of adult male "presidents" of children's associations. Everyone seemed affected in one way or another by the two-day festivity. Each household in the ward was solicited to make donations for the event; some people complained but few would refuse. The sound of drums permeated the whole area.

The *mikoshi* belongs to the ward, as does the stationary ward shrine generally called *ujigami*. The *ujigami*, also denoting the lineage god, evolved historically into a communal god or shrine worshipped and sustained by the villagers. The communal activity of the villagers, centering around the *ujigami*, has been the local representation of Shinto.

As Shinto emerged after the Meiji Restoration virtually as a state religion to embrace the "restored" emperorship in its mythology and mysticism, adherence became de facto compulsory. New national shrines were built, and attempts were made to reorganize old local shrines as well in a standardized hierarchy of official ranks and titles, at the apex of which was the Ise Shrine of Amaterasu (the Sun Goddess). The priest of a Shizumi *ujigami* shrine recalls how well off the Shinto priests were under the state's protection before the war, and that even the lowest-ranking local priest received a government-funded salary of sixty yen while the schoolteacher's salary was forty-five yen. Postwar reform abolished this privilege, leaving the shrines and priests impoverished. Nonetheless, *ujigami* shrines in Shizumi continue to provide local foci for residential identities. Those who usually pay no attention to religion become aware of their *ujigami* affiliation at the time of life transition rites, particularly those of weddings and childbearing.

Most Shizumi residents are Buddhist as well, belonging to one of the Buddhist sects and one of the local temples. Even a prominent communist politician is a devout Buddhist who recites sutras every morning. Each family has a Buddhist affiliation, supposedly handed down from their ancestors. This, of course, is a survival of the compulsory Buddhist registration politically imposed upon every household during the Tokugawa era. The retention of the old parishioner identity is mainly because the family cemetery is in the temple compound and death rites are presided over by the temple priests. In other words, Buddhist identity for Shizumi residents, as for most Japanese, is inseparable from the cult of the dead and ancestors of the family.

The Buddhist affiliation is by the family not by wards as is the *ujigami* membership, and thus could be communally divisive rather than integrative. Nevertheless, in Shizumi there is a rough correspondence between residential areas and affiliated sects as far as the dominant sects (the Nichiren and Sōtō Zen sects) are concerned. Moreover, there is little evidence of animosity between sects. Mutual tolerance and acceptance are also seen between Buddhism and Shinto. A Shinto priest belongs to a Buddhist temple as a parishioner, and a Buddhist priest acknowledges his membership in one of the *ujigami* shrines. (This flexibility in religious adherence may be attributed to the long history of Shinto-Buddhist syncretism prior to the Meiji Restoration. Locally it was the Buddhist priests who were in charge of the shrines and services of Shinto, while the Shinto gods were regarded as guardians of the Buddhist temples.) Furthermore, as far as Shizumi tradition goes, when death strikes in a family, the whole neighborhood (usually the neighborhood association) is involved in conducting the funeral and hosting the attendants regardless of sectarian differences, although the funeral is *ritually* presided over by Buddhist priests. In sum, both Shinto and Buddhism tend to reinforce communal solidarity.

The promulgation of freedom of religion in the Meiji Constitution brought Christianity to the surface again after more than two centuries underground. But as Japan entered into the chauvinistic era of the 1930s and early 1940s, it again became a victim of political control. Shizumi witnessed its first missionary work—organized by a Scandinavian group in the 1890s—which led to the emergence of local ministers and later to the establishment of a church. After experiencing its share of wartime suppression, local Christianity enjoyed a sudden boom in membership and church attendance, and a proliferation of several denominations including Catholic, Seventh Day Adventist, and Holiness. This pro-Christian enthusiasm turned out, however, to be little more than a postwar fad which reached its peak around 1948–1949 (SCII: 1048). Or the Christian faith, if any, tends to be as superficial as suggested in the caricaturized Japanese religious career: "Born Shintoist, marry Christian, and die Buddhist." To be sure, this is an indication of the tenacity of traditional and nativistic religions, but the failure of Christianity may have much to do with its inflexibility, which is disruptive of the communally based flexibility of the Shinto-Buddhism complex. Most of the households I visited in Shizumi were furnished with both a *kamidana* (god shelf associated with Shinto) and a *butsudan* (ancestral altar symbolic of Buddhist affiliation).

Nonetheless, the traditional religions have not remained immune to the encroachment of "new religions." In Shizumi, along with more than ninety traditional temples and shrines, there are several nontraditional sects including Tenrikyō, Konkōkyō, Reiyūkai, Seichō-no-ie, Gedatsukai, and Nichiren Shōshū. While most of these share the nonexclusiveness and flexibility of the traditional religions and thus are regarded as harmless, the exclusive and militant sects like Nichiren Shōshū, more commonly known as Sōkagakkai, do upset the adherents of traditional religions. Since sectarian loyalty precedes all other loyalties, some member children do not even bother to attend school, a schoolteacher complained to me, when there is a major sectarian ritual. The strength of Sōkagakkai is estimable from the success of the Komei party (the sect's political arm) in gaining three seats (1975) in the thirty-member city assembly.

What is interesting about the nontraditional religions is the role women play in them. Traditional Shinto and Buddhism either relegated women to a secondary position or excluded them from public rituals due to the pollutions ascribed to their sex. This androcentrism is peculiarly lacking in nontraditional religions. Tenrikyō, for example, emerged in the late Tokugawa era under the leadership of a female shaman, Miki Nakayama. Postwar Japan has witnessed a series of "living goddesses" founding new sects. To mention a few conspicuous female leaders: Kimi Kotani of Reiyūkai, Toshiko Nagaoka of Jiukyō, and Sayo Kitamura of Tenshō-kōtai-jingūkyō.

A smaller version of female dominance is observed in Shizumi's branches of nontraditional religions. The ward branches of Gedatsukai, when I studied them in 1970–1971 (Lebra 1974a, 1976a, 1976b, 1982), were headed by elderly women; the local cell of Tenrikyō was established by a woman; Sōkagakkai has several female leaders in its local branches; and so on. Among the rank and file, too, female members are much more active and aggressive in these sects than in the traditional ones. It seems that the new sects, unhampered by the traditional sex polarization, harness the energy of women which has been pent up in their mundane lives. These sects also mobilize and use as a resource the women's receptivity for supernatural communication. Indeed, one of the Gedatsukai branch leaders was known as "always talking or listening to gods."

## THE DOMESTIC INSTITUTION: THE *IE*

The average woman is assumed to orient herself primarily to her family and kinship, and her life to center in and around the domestic realm. It would therefore be useful to outline the structure of the Japanese domestic institution.

The Japanese domestic structure is built around the unit called *ie*. In my view, the *ie* has two major elements: genealogical and functional. Viewed genealogically, the *ie* may be translated as "stem family," and defined as "a vertically composite form of nuclear families, one from each generation" (Morioka 1967:597) or a "series of first sons, their wives and minor children" (Johnson 1964:839). These definitions set forth, first, the transgenerational perpetuation of the *ie* unit. An *ie*, observed at present, may look like a typical nuclear family, but it potentially or ideally expands into a three-or-more-generation family. Along with this genealogical continuity is, secondly, the rule of unigeniture whereby one child, not more, inherits the house assets (house property, house status, headship, etc.) and becomes the sole link between generations while all the other children must leave the house. Ideally, the successor is the first son but exigency may dictate succession by a younger son, a daughter, a daughter's husband, or an adopted son. Marriage requires the bride to move into the groom's household if the latter is the successor. The roles are reversed if the groom is to be a *mukoyōshi*, the adopted son-in-law who assumes the wife's family name. Marriage between nonsuccessors is neolocal.

Viewed from its functional standpoint, the *ie* means the household characterized as a corporate body of coresidents, each performing his/her role to maintain it. The genealogical and the functional aspects of the *ie* merge together in many cases, but discrepancy does occur. A functionally indispensable member may happen not to be a member of the stem family, as in the case of a competent servant or household employee. It is this coresidential and functional aspect that is stressed when anthropologists like Nakane (1967) distinguish the *ie* from the family. The *ie*, then, is characterized in terms of the precedence of occupational or economic continuity over descent and bloodlines. This view is supported by the frequency of *mukoyōshi* and virtual bilaterality or even matrilineality. A Shizumi informant underscored this point by saying, "There are two kinds of blood: the blood in the body and the blood in the *ie*." For him the latter claimed priority.

I think that neither the genealogical nor the functional view of the *ie* can be ignored, and would rather argue that this dualism is the very essence of the *ie*. The genealogical, stem-family principle concerns the legitimacy of succession which is biased for patrilineal, patrilocal norms, whereas the functional viewpoint throws into relief the economic efficiency and day-to-day operation of the *ie* unit. It is in light of this dualism, I believe, that women's role and status should be understood.

Although the above depiction of the *ie* with its structural emphasis might give the impression of its timelessness, the actual impact of *ie* ideology for the majority of Japanese was of recent history. Through the feudal period the *ie* became established as a distinct unit commanding loyalty among the privileged classes, but it was not until the modern era beginning in 1868 that peasants, who constituted the majority of the population, became committed to the *ie* ideology as mandatory. This is one of the paradoxes witnessed during the Meiji period (1868–1912), when the official dissolution of the samurai class resulted in encouragement of the peasants to absorb samurai values and styles.[4] There is little doubt that the permeation of the *ie* ideology was significantly due to the Meiji democratization, including the government's "permission" in 1870 for commoners to assume family names, and the 1871 house register law prescribing every household to be registered in the local government's file. Consequently, the *ie* became the most basic, indivisible unit, and individuals were submerged in it or were regarded as representatives of an *ie*. This can be illustrated by the usage of a collective term to identify both the household as a whole and its members. In addition to the newly acquired and legally registered family name, many households retained an old *yagō*, the legally unrecognized but often better-known house name, derived from the household occupation, kinship status, location, symbolic property, the abbreviation of the house head's full name, a combination of these, or many other accidental sources. Yamacho, for example, may be the *yagō* of the house headed by Yamamoto Chotaro; Taiyomaru may be a *yagō* named after the fishing boat owned by the so-called house. Yamacho-san refers either to the household as a whole or any member of it.

Two or more *ie* units are organized into a kin group recognized as *shinseki*, *shinrui*, or other local terms. Once two households, A and B, form a *shinseki* relationship, another household, C, which happens to be A's *shinseki* through another liaison person may form a *shinseki* alliance with B. Kinship thus may widen extensively, and this is particularly the case if one member house is wealthy or influential and thus regarded as a useful ally. All that is required to establish a *shinseki* relationship is to identify a chain of departures and entries of liaison persons from house to house. A Shizumi informant described house Kadoya *(yagō)* as his *shinseki* "because my elder sister entered house Shimakyu as a bride and from that house came the mother of Kadoya." How the two linking women relate to each other in specific kin terms is not questioned; what matters is the fact that the three houses have become *shinseki* through the departure and entry of the two women.

Some *shinseki* households form a tightly organized group which has become identified in Japanese ethnology as "*dōzoku.*" In characterizing the *dōzoku*, I follow Befu (1963) in large measure, although I have some reservations in agreeing that *shinrui* (or *shinseki*) should be contrasted as personal kindred to *dōzoku* as the patrilineal descent group. (I think rather that the *dōzoku* is a subset of *shinrui* or that, at least, there is a large amount of overlap between the two sets given the native's indiscriminatory usage of the latter term.)

A *dōzoku* begins to be formed when a nonsuccessor son, upon marriage, leaves his natal house and establishes a *bunke* (branch house) in relation to the *honke* (main house) from which he has branched out. A series of such branchings by nonsuccessor sons will give rise to a number of satellite *bunke* organized under the leadership of the *honke* and bound by reciprocal obligations.

The *dōzoku* as a corporate body sometimes claims its historical continuity over generations, traceable to a remote ancestor as its founder. Implicit in this claim is the assumption that branching has taken place more than once over two or more generations, differentiating a senior branch house from a junior branch house with respect to the time of branching. Historical continuity further implies the proliferation of branch houses out of a branch house, the latter being regarded as the *honke* within this segment. The original main house, then, will be identified as *sōhonke* (supreme main house), which in turn regards its *bunke*'s *bunke* as *mago-bunke* (literally, grandchild branch house). Legends may accrue to the first ancestor and to the continuous line of the main house, although in fact such continuity tends to be less than real. What holds the *dōzoku* together ideationally is the shared belief in the common ancestry.

The *dōzoku* structure is further characterized as a simulation of patrilineage, a descent group linked by males, or more correctly a group of the main-line and collateral-line households headed by blood-related males. Some cases may approximate a real patrilineage in that all *bunke* are headed by male offspring of the *honke* head. What distinguishes the Japanese *dōzoku* from the Chinese lineage, however, is a propensity for symbolic simulation of patrilineage while actual fidelity to the model is often violated. A *bunke* may be established by a *honke* head's daughter or sister whose husband moves into the *bunke* house, assumes the wife's surname, and becomes the head of the *bunke*. Furthermore, a *bunke* may be headed by a non-kin, unrelated in blood to the *honke* head but recognized for his loyalty and ability. The *honke* head may grant the right to establish a *bunke* to his foster or adopted son, his servant, tenant, or employee. In a rural ward of Shizumi I met a man who claimed that his house was a member of a tightly organized *dōzoku* which had existed for hundreds of years. His was one of four *bunke* houses linked to a *honke*. He did establish a blood link between his house and the *honke*, but was unable to do so with regard to the other three *bunke*. "I really wonder, and nobody can tell, why they became our *bunke*."

Because of the above variation and the simulative nature of patrilineage, different views of *dōzoku* have been proposed. Brown (1966) calls the *dōzoku* a cognatic descent group, while Befu (1963) regards it as a corporation of "families patrilineally related (fictively or otherwise)." Nakane (1967), on the other hand, goes so far as to rule out the idea of *dōzoku* as a kin group and to emphasize the economic, functional nature of the nexus of its components, independent of descent.

Despite these points of disagreement and the possibility of the daughter-*bunke*, it may be safely assumed that the *dōzoku* is symbolically male biased whereas the *shinseki* is more bisexual or, relatively speaking, female biased in that it is a woman more often than a man who leaves the natal house and marries into another house, serving as a liaison for *shinseki* formation. Regardless of the sex bias of either *shinseki* or *dōzoku* in terms of their organizational principles, it may be hypothesized that a woman more than a man tends to be bound by kin obligations as well as to rely upon kin ties simply because kinship roles are an extension of domestic roles.

The implication of ideological and institutional postwar changes for this "traditional" structure of family and kinship is far-reaching. The new ideology pronouncing the values of individual autonomy and equality has replaced the *ie* ideology characterized by the corporate unity and hierarchical order of *ie* members. Under the new ideology there should no longer be an impersonal entity called *ie* which is beyond the individual's control and which has its own will and power over individual members. The principle of equality, combined with that of individuality, has amounted to the abolition of the legal status of the house head: the family is now simply a collection of individuals or a multi-cephalous group, not a unicephalous structure. Derogation of the house head is accompanied by that of successor status, now that all the children regardless of birth order are regarded as equal and can claim equal shares of the inheritance. Likewise, equality by sex—whether between husband and wife or brother and sister—has been established in law, if not in practice.

Implied in the above direction of change is the replacement of the *ie* unity by the dyadic conjugal bond. The precedence of marital solidarity over other relationships as the core of the family, once thus established, inevitably leads to the breakdown of the traditional ideology advocating the overgenerational perpetuity of *ie*. Each and every couple in every generation attains independence and achieves *discontinuity* from another couple in the preceding generation or subsequent generation. The idea of lineal continuity has lost its legitimacy. This change is implemented by the revised house register law which prescribes one register unit for one couple and their unmarried children, and no more. Every marriage is thus marked by the departure of both parties of marriage from their respective registers and the creation of a new register of their own.

Independence and priority of the conjugal bond are further linked to *the desirability of personal choice* of a marriage mate. Love marriage has thus gained legitimacy, whereas arranged marriage has been stigmatized as a sign of outdatedness or personal inadequacy.

Whereas the old system of the *ie* allowed or necessitated the inclusion of non-kin as members of the *ie* under the approval of the house head, the new family ideology, independent of the *ie* concept, stresses the importance of actual kinship. This means that the traditional ease with which the Japanese could play and simulate a kin role has lost ideological support and has given way to the idea that actual kin can claim his or her right, irrespective of his/her role performance, by virtue of kinship. The egalitarian ideology further has undermined the authority of *honke* over *bunke*, leading to the decline of *dōzoku* solidarity. All these changes have been accelerated through the recent high growth economy of Japan and its generation of an unprecedented labor shortage and affluence.

## Data Collection

The data for this study were generated from several, instead of a single, modes of information in order to accommodate my methodological choice. Information is conceived of here as a product of interaction between an information-giver and the information-receiver. First, the interaction situation may be such that the informant is fully aware of being an informant and does or does not give information accordingly, or conversely she may be expressing herself without being conscious of an informant's role.

Secondly, the informant's expressions vary in releasing information: the expression may be verbal or nonverbal, and if verbal, it may be oral or written. The interview situation, for example, stimulates the informant to be role conscious and to release oral information, but it also generates a role-unconscious response (e.g., spontaneous conversation between the informant and her family which is heard by but not addressed to the interviewer) and nonverbal information (e.g., posture, eye direction) as well. As will be shown below, data collection relied upon all possible modes of information, with a bias for the role-unconscious mode.

## THE LOCAL SAMPLE

Of foremost importance is a set of life histories collected from Shizumi women. Fifty-seven women were selected by various criteria within a limited extent of accessibility. The first criterion was maximization of variation: the sample varies in age from twenty-eight to eighty; in the rural versus urban residence within the city limits; and in socioeconomic status (from a live-in housemaid to the wife of an M.D., from a woman with no schooling to university graduates). Twenty-one women have had no extradomestic occupation of their own but many of them have participated in their husbands' occupations as assistants, or as successors to their husbands when widowed. This reduces the number of full-time housewives to thirteen.

Secondly, women with occupations were selected so as to correspond to some degree with the occupational distribution by sex as appeared in the prefectural volume of the 1970 census (Sōrifu Tōkeikyoku). Thus, women with typically or exclusively feminine occupations such as health professionals (nurses, pharmacists, and a dietician), midwives, educators of small children (kindergarten and primary school teachers), secretarial clerks, a hairdresser, a koto teacher, domestic workers (housemaids, baby-sitters), and a dressmaker, were included.

The third criterion concerns the sample's reflection of the local industries. To represent the industries of tourism, leisure, and entertainment that predominate in the current local scene, the sample included owners and employees of hotels, bar hostesses, a bicycle race stadium employee, a bathhouse operator, a brothel keeper (prior to the antiprostitution law of 1956), and restaurant operators. A former geisha was included, although it turned out that she had been one in Tokyo before moving to Shizumi. To these occupations were added farmers and fish-processing workers to reflect the major industries of the past.

The husbands' occupations appeared to vary as widely: highly skilled professionals (a gynecologist, a pediatrician, dentists, and an engineer); businessmen (executives of local companies and banks, stock-brokers, dealers in lumber, construction materials, or dry food); white-collar workers (schoolteachers, bank employees, city government employees); manual workers (fishermen, farmers, a woodworker, a floor mat maker). In the younger age bracket we find cab or bus drivers overrepresented. Most of the house-attached businesses, such as hotels and shops, are or have been run by husband-wife teams.

Working women are either active or retired, either full-time or part-time, with single or multiple (sequential or simultaneous) jobs.

Of the total of fifty-seven, fifty-four women have had marital experience: thirty-two are still married to their first husbands, sixteen are widowed, one is divorced, and the remaining five involve various combinations of divorce, widowhood, and remarriage. It was found that twenty-four out of the fifty-seven had been born and reared outside Shizumi, including three from Kyushu and two from northern Honshu, which gives some balance against the local bias.

These women were identified and reached either with the help of several women whom I already knew and who are knowledgeable about the community and popular among the local residents, or through a chain of acquaintanceship from one informant to another. I also made contact with possible sample candidates in a haphazard manner at meetings of the various groups and associations I attended. Reactions to my request for an interview appointment were well patterned. "Are you sure a nobody like me is all right?" "My life is so commonplace that I don't think you will find it useful." "I am no good with my mouth [cannot talk well]." "I am so far behind the times. Why don't you ask somebody else who is more up to date?" But most of them were persuaded to accept the request.

The interviews were conducted mostly at the informants' residences (otherwise in my apartment) soon after an appointment was made. The desired privacy was not always easy to obtain: the children or grandchildren, sitting around, demanded attention from the informant and screamed into the tape recorder; some adult members of the family, present and within hearing distance, inhibited the informant; some informants, not confident about what they were going to say, had invited their friends over to have a collective interview for which I was not prepared. Most disastrous was the unsolicited participation by the husband, not only because it inhibited the wife's response but because I felt compelled to address my questions more to him as the head of the house than to her. In one case my cautious request to interview the woman alone, which she had accepted, was ignored: upon my arrival she called to her husband upstairs, "Sugiyama-san is here!" The husband, of course, was convinced that I had come to see *him*. These disruptions, while ruining my original purpose, did provide a clue to the family relationships.

Each informant was solicited to produce an oral autobiography in response to my questions. The interview situation, with a tape recorder in front of the informant if permitted, raised the level of role consciousness on the part of the informant as measured by her nervousness and inhibition. In order to overcome this initial obstacle and to induce trust and relaxation, it was invariably necessary to give a brief but highly personal account of my own life. To encourage spontaneous response, questions were put in a vague form analogous to a projective test. I would say, for example, "Please start from your birth," or "What kind of family were you born into?" Some cautious informants would demand the question to be more specific, but most would have no trouble and begin right away to talk about a remote ancestor who founded the *ie*, the father's occupation, or the family status, depending upon the informant's values and identity.

The duration and intensity of contact varied according to the interviewee's hospitality and informativeness. The total contact time ranged from two to fifteen hours. While the majority were contacted only once or twice within the first year (1976–1977), some were interviewed more often over the four-year period up to 1980. The age is frozen at the time of the first interview, and it is this age that will be used here unless otherwise specified. The mean age of the sample was 55.2. Reliance upon a questionnaire having been dismissed as inappropriate, quantitative data are not substantial. But whenever I mention some quantity like "three," "every," "more than half," "80 percent," I am referring to this "primary sample" of fifty-seven women as the total.

One and the same life stage belongs to the past to be recalled, to the present to be described or observed, or to the future to be anticipated, depending upon the informant's contemporary life stage. Needless to say, earlier stages will be filled more with retrospective information, while later stages will abound more with contemporaneous or anticipatory information. Recollections are admittedly full of distortions, and yet I would argue that how recollections are made is culturally significant since that is how one's experience is transmitted and incorporated into a cultural legacy. Nonetheless, I have made some attempts to counteract gross distortions: intensive interviews were conducted, sometimes lasting five hours at a time; post-interview telephone conversations and interviews with the husbands of some women hopefully improved the veracity of recalled information. Inevitably, there will be tense fluctuation between past and present. The present tense will be used when I am making a generalized inference from my overall observations of contemporary Japanese women or when I am referring to an episode which a particular informant was experiencing or had continued to experience at interview time.

The seventeen most intensively interviewed women are listed below by the alphabetical order of first names, and identified by age (as of the first interview time), marital status, and primary or most recent occupations: what these women confided to me will appear most often, with or without their names, in the following chapters.

| Name | Age | Marital Status | Occupation |
| --- | --- | --- | --- |
| Ayano | 56 | Married | Kindergarten teacher (Retired) |
| Emi | 71 | Divorced/ remarried/ widowed | Restaurant operator (Retired) |
| Hamako | 53 | Widowed | Farmer |
| Hanayo | 54 | Married | Pharmacist |
| Harue | 57 | Married | Housewife |
| Harumi | 36 | Married | Dress shop keeper |
| Kumiko | 47 | Married | Housewife |
| Kuniko | 60 | Widowed | Dry food processer/dealer |
| Naomi | 45 | Married | Dress shop keeper |
| Rin | 78 | Divorced | Amusement-sports shop keeper (Retired) |
| Sayo | 77 | Married | Housewife |
| Suzuko | 28 | Married | Housewife |
| Taeko | 46 | Married | Nurse |
| Toshiko | 67 | Widowed | Saleswoman (Retired) |
| Tsuruko | 66 | Married | Housewife |
| Wakako | 68 | Divorced/ remarried | Geisha/bar hostess (Retired) |
| Yoshimi | 47 | Widowed | Restaurant operator |

The so-called generational gaps do not necessarily match age differences, but when social change is in question we shall look at the generational breakdown arbitrarily in terms of three age brackets: sixty and above, forty-five and above, and forty-four and below, which are meant to stand for prewar, wartime, and postwar generations respectively. My primary sample includes twenty-one members of the prewar generation, twenty-four wartimers, and twelve postwar women. To the primary sample is added a scattered sample of women who came into contact with me in a variety of contexts and released information on one or another segment of their life courses including the contemporary phase. Casual conversations on the street, for example, were an important source of information generated without the informant's role consciousness. The contemporary life-styles were directly observed primarily through participation in group activities which ranged from studies, ceremonies, entertainment, sports, to trips.

Some activities were sponsored or aided by agencies such as the board of education of the city, and others were organized by the participants themselves. Some groups were exclusively female while others included male participants. My strategy as an observer was to remain as unobtrusive as possible and thus to avoid stimulating the informant's role consciousness. In this I could take full advantage of being a native. However, even for a native it was not easy to be unobtrusive and anonymous unless the group activity was addressed to the general public. If the activity was exclusive to the group members, unobtrusive observation would not only be practically difficult but ethically impermissible. Either I had to identify myself and become an obtrusive observer to some participants' discomfort, or to join them as a participant, as I did in a small haiku group. Even when I was in the general audience, I was sometimes spotted by someone in the group, formally introduced to the whole assemblage, and asked to give a talk. Although anthropologists refer to participant observation as if it were something natural to them, participation and observation for me were not always easily combined. In order to be fully accepted by a group, one has to do a good job as a participant. Sometimes I became so carried away in performing my participant role, as I did in a leatherwork group, that I neglected my observer's role.

In addition, group interviews were conducted with peers. Data collected from groups of classmates, neighbors, or co-workers, for example, supplemented that of the primary sample.

A case may be cited either from the primary sample or this scattered sample without indicating the sample origin unless it is necessary to do so. But whenever personal names (that is, pseudonyms) are used, it should be understood that they are of primary-sample women, although the latter are not always so identified.

In order to tap ideas and values held by teenagers, some in-classroom tests were administered to local schoolchildren from primary up to secondary high school. Particularly to be noted here is a collection of "future-autobiographies"[5] solicited from high school students. Male and female students aged seventeen to eighteen were asked to write about their future careers from the time of high school graduation, which they were then facing. The result turned out to be interesting and informative, and will be used within the limits of space.

As an implicit, if not explicit, reference for comparison with the female sample, I will be using a male sample consisting of thirty-two men in various occupations whom I have interviewed over the years for a series of different purposes. This sample includes a diversity of occupations: construction workers, schoolteachers, city government workers, politicians, priests, a chef, a fisherman, a camelia oil manufacturer, a footgear maker, a navy doctor, a pediatrician, an obstetrician. Three of these men are the husbands of the primary-sample women. The male sample provides insight into women's roles and life cycle, first, in terms of the male-female contrast, and second, because some of the professions represented in the male sample are addressed to women as the exclusive or predominant clients (note the obstetrician, pediatrician, some government workers such as the one in charge of government pensions for the aged).

AN EXTERNAL SAMPLE OF CAREER WOMEN

Between October 1978 and January 1979, interviews were conducted in Tokyo, Yokohama, Kyoto, and Osaka with ten women who might well be classed as prominent career women. The occupations range widely: two national government officials, a semi-governmental corporation official, a judge, a producer for national TV, a women's college professor, a tenured assistant at a national university, a journalist, a research corporation president, and a businesswoman (company president). Ages ranged between thirty-two and sixty-four. This group of women play a central role in the chapter on occupational careers. Hopefully, this sample will serve as a balancing weight against the limitation and bias of the local sample.

The following six chapters are organized around a combination of life cycle and roles. The life cycle is first divided into the premarital and postmarital stages. Chapter 2 takes the premarital stage, covering the whole spectrum of roles, both domestic and public. Marital candidacy and commitment as a major transition is the topic of the third chapter. The prime of life is divided into three roles in parallel rather than in sequence: marital, maternal, and occupational. The postmarital involvement of chapter 4 refers to the woman's role as a wife and daughter-in-law. Her role as a mother is a separate topic discussed in chapter 5. A variety of occupational careers involved in the public domain is the topic of chapter 6. The seventh chapter focuses on the last but long stage of life extending from middle age through old age and death. This final stage, like the premarital stage, covers all roles—domestic and public. The concluding chapter is an attempt to draw together some generalizations focusing on social structure and self-fulfillment.

# 2
# *Premarital Constraints and Options*

The premarital stage covers a time span stretching from childhood, possibly the remotest past one can remember, to early adulthood immediately prior to circulation in the marriage market. The informants will be placed, first, in the premarital domestic sphere, namely, their natal households. The individual is born into the natal family without choice and spends her earliest, most dependent life stage there. It is assumed, therefore, that it is the natal family with its adult caretakers that imposes the heaviest constraint, conscious and unconscious, upon the conditions and goals of her life. The women will be further placed in public spheres which involve the later phases of the premarital stage. Here there are more options, the assumption goes, and the individual exercises her choice more in determining the course of her life.

## The Natal Household

The premarital experience in the natal household is reconstructed with reference to the significant members as socializing agents as well as to modes of socialization.

### Parents and Surrogates

Every informant holds that the parents are the most desirable persons for childrearing and assumes that both parents should normally participate in this task, each playing a sex-appropriate role complementary to and balanced with that of the other. However, the recalled reality deviates more from this ideal than conforms to it. Many informants do contrast father and mother, but the contrasts tend to be strikingly imbalanced, or reversed in sex roles.

> My female parent [some informants prefer this term, *onna-oya*, for mother] was a very smart woman, strict with us children. . . . My male parent

[*otoko-oya*] was only interested in his work. It doesn't matter, I think, whether the male has a good mind or not. As long as the female has one, the children will be smart.

My father was like a shadow, but my mother was a strong woman.

I was always conscious of my father, his feelings toward me. I tried to do my best in everything just to please him, to get praise from him. . . . Probably that's why my impression of mother is rather thin.

We were scared of father [a navy officer]. If we didn't obey him, if we entered the house without washing our feet, he would force us to stand still out in the yard even in midwinter. . . . Mother? She was absolutely obedient to him. Even if she felt sorry for us, she simply told us to apologize [to father].

These remarks suggest that one parent tended to overplay and the other to underplay the role of a socializing agent or a supporter. Some cases of such imbalance are accounted for by a sudden decline in the family status. Sonoko, thirty-six, told about her father, who had at one time had a food processing factory in China in connection with the Japanese government. He had lived like a "millionaire" there, she said, and was unsettled with anything he undertook after he repatriated. Demoted to the bottom of the scale after the war, he switched from one odd job to another. To make matters worse, he was crazy about women and had a new affair every few months. This caused violent fights—"knock-down-drag-out-fights"—between the father and mother. The father's folly also drained the family's revenue and made it necessary for the mother to work as a nurse.

Some informants were extremely willing to talk about one parent and showed strong attachment to or respect for him or her, but preferred to remain reticent about the other parent, or showed indifference to or disdain for him or her. Why such imbalance? It may be that imbalance is inherent in the marriage itself: two contrasting personalities may attract each other to begin with, or such differentiation may develop in the course of married life. It is also possible that the child plays a significant part: the child may become more sensitized to the influence of one parent than to the other and the parents react differentially to this, which in turn further intensifies the child's skewed receptivity. In addition to such interactional dynamics, the domestic structure also has to do with this imbalance, as will be shown later.

What is interesting is that, contrary to what might be expected, it is not predominantly the mother who plays a superparental role. There are almost as many fathers who are recalled with love, warmth, respectfulness, or admiration, and there are as many mothers who, in contrast, are disapproved of. This finding does not conform to the generally shared image of the Japanese mother as a supermother.

Ayano, in her mid-fifties, recalls her father, a gold-mining engineer, as hardworking, intelligent, innovative, well mannered, and loving, and described herself as a daddy's girl "because he loved me most as I was born right after my elder brother died." The informant would have avoided talking about her mother if I hadn't pressed her. Unlike most mothers, she said, her mother was not disposed to take good care of the children because she was self-centered, and the children, to their dismay, often found her lying in bed when they returned from school. Ayano and her elder sister congratulate themselves for resembling their father more than their mother.

*The perfect mother as a cultural type.* Some recollections thus contradict the generally shared image of the Japanese mother as a perfect supermother. Is the perfect mother a groundless myth after all? To answer this question, we must depart from the mere frequency pattern of positive versus negative ratings of the parents and go into the quality and intensity of each rating. When the mother is favorably recalled, there tends to be a characteristically emotional tone in which she is described as having had enormous hardship and suffering in one way or another. This tendency is accentuated in the cases where the mother was widowed early, as early as before the informant's graduation from the six-year primary school. In the primary sample, I found eleven instances of the early death of a parent (five fathers and six mothers) and one case of parental divorce, also early. It turns out that all of the widowed fathers remarried while none of the mothers did—a strikingly faithful representation of the traditional sex dichotomy. All but one of the widowed mothers are recalled with warm empathy in association with their extraordinary hardship and sacrifice for the children.

In some cases the mother became the sole breadwinner as well as domestic caretaker. Fukiko, forty-nine, claimed that the family had been wealthy enough to hire several maids to help her mother until her father, a bank employee, died when Fukiko was five. The mother then had to support the family by picking up all sorts of jobs—sewing, working in a cannery, doing laundry for hotels, and whatnot. Kumiko told of how her mother supported nine children by selling things like dried fish after the father was struck with apoplexy and became bedridden. And yet the mother was a perfect caretaker and educator of the children. "I absolutely worship my mother," said the forty-six-year-old daughter. Indeed, these mothers seem to have overcompensated for their handicap by caring for the children more compulsively than more fortunate mothers would have. The widowed fathers and their second wives, on the other hand, are recalled with animosity or indifference, or are totally omitted from the daughters' life histories. Rin refused to call her stepmother "Mother," and kept saying: "My mother is dead. What's the name of this woman? Where is she from?" She then yelled the stepmother's first name. Needless to say, Rin was intensely hated by her stepmother.

The positive recollection of the father tends to lack this reference to hardship and this emotional intensity of empathy, but is made with more distant appreciation and respect. Illustrative of this contrast are the results of the sentence-completion test administered to high school students (twenty-five boys and twenty-three girls) sixteen to seventeen years old. They were asked to complete the sentence fragments: "When I think of my father, I . . . " and "When I think of my mother, I . . . "[1] Both boys and girls indicated intense empathy toward the mother while the father appeared to be more respected, admired, or thanked for his ability, character, or diligence. It is also interesting to note the respondents' sex difference in expressing empathy toward the mother. The typical female response stressed the mother's *kurō* (hardship and suffering) and described her life as *taihen* (extraordinarily hard). The typical male response revealed even more subjective, intense emotions expressed as guilt feelings: "Usually cannot help feeling guilty. It may be because she works so hard everyday to the point of disintegration of her body." "Find my heart broken." "Feel tears in my eyes."

The Japanese supermother is indeed a stereotype, but I contend that this stereotype is bolstered by such emotionally intense empathy and guilt toward the mother that it overrides the statistically more random distribution of pro-mother and pro-father attitudes. The emotionally invested mother figure, in other words, is more likely than the respected but distant father figure to crystallize into a collective memory and thus become an essential ingredient of culture.

*The disqualified mother.* The mother who has had *kurō* thus represents a model mother. By contrast, a woman who has had an easy life is regarded by my informants as worthless as a mother and a human being. This argument came out often in connection with the type of marriage which involves uxorilocal residence and the husband's assumption of the wife's family name as a *mukoyōshi* (adopted son-in-law and husband). Six informants indicated that their fathers were *mukoyōshi*. In such marriages, the informants claimed, the mother continued to be protected and indulged by her parents, had no exposure to the severity of life, and was thus disqualified as a mother. On the other hand, the father as a *mukoyōshi* was in no position to assert himself as an authoritarian figure. The informants were apparently unhappy, resentful, or embarrassed about such parents, the mother for being *kurō shirazu* (unaware of *kurō*) and the father for being *otonashii* (subdued). Yone, seventy-six, recalled how her mother, the only daughter and *uchi-musume* (house daughter who brings the husband in), would sit around the house all day long doing nothing. "Why is it," asked Yone, "that this house has had only a daughter [never a son] generation after genera-tion?" The mother speculated that heaven had punished the house for the sins committed by her ancestors, who were notorious "head slayers" (meaning samurai warriors). Commenting that her mother was useless because she did not know any hardship, Yone exclaimed: "A human being with no experience of hardship is a failure!" Association of the mother's inadequacy with *mukoyōshi* marriage is further substantiated by a case of neolocal marriage. An informant attributed her mother's easy going disposition to her father's employment in her mother's natal family business which placed him in a *mukoyōshi*-like status.

To mature into a well-qualified mother, a woman should marry virilocally, it was contended by several informants, so that she will suf-fer under a mother-in-law. The underlying postulate is that suffering is a necessary condition for an individual to develop empathy for others— the ability without which a woman cannot be a true mother. Both the positive and negative recollections of mothers are thus derived from the same standard of ideal motherhood. Suffering and empathy are at one pole, and easy living and self-centeredness are at the other.

In addition to hardships, a model mother is supposed to have a degree of mental autonomy from her husband. The mother who obeyed her husband unquestioningly, who was unable to provide a buffer be-tween the autocratic father and the frightened children is a countermo-del. The mother who is like the father's shadow is no more acceptable than the father who is the mother's shadow.

*Grandparents, siblings, and* dōzoku *extension.* There were other significant persons in the natal household whose presence interlocked with the quality of the parents' role performance. Particularly indica-tive of the *ie* structure was the presence of grandparents. A grandmoth-er, if young enough, was the likely surrogate mother for a motherless granddaughter. Some informants claimed that it was the grandfather who disciplined the children with utmost strictness. The grandfather's active participation in socializing the children appeared to have a dou-ble implication: he played the role of a surrogate father when the father was not disposed to take a paternal role; by stepping into the father's role, the grandfather undercut the father's (and/or mother's) authority. Yasu, in her seventies, remembers her grandfather always scolding everybody else in front of the children, not just the grandchildren but Yasu's father and mother as well. Her mother was inhibited from openly taking a maternal role by this grandfather, as long as he remained active. Mari, twenty-eight, coming from a fishing-farming family, recalls her mother suffering under her domineering mother-in-law (Mari's grandmother) and being frustrated with her inability to play the role of a mother fully. "Suppose I wanted five yen, my mother could not give it. It was Grandma who held the money. That must have been the hardest thing for Mother. Yet I kept demanding, 'Buy this, buy that.' "

This double grandparental role—supplementary to and inhibitory of the parental role—may give a clue to the merits and demerits of the extended family structure in contrast to the nuclear family. Furthermore, a grandparent undercutting parental authority and privilege may offer one of the explanations for the previously described asymmetry of the parents. Indeed the woman who characterized her father as "a shadow" and her mother as strong also had a grandfather who ran a hardware store and held "all the power" in the family. The father may have become a shadow in reaction to the grandfather, and the mother may have developed a strong character in defense against her father-in-law.

For Tama, seventy-seven, it was the mother and grandmother who disciplined the children "because both father and grandfather were *muko*" (*muko* can mean either groom or adopted son-in-law, namely, *mukoyōshi*, and in this case, it meant the latter). This again illustrates the handicapped status of a *mukoyōshi* as a father.

A lonely old couple may "borrow" a grandchild to live with them. Hanayo was taken as a child to her mother's parents and alternated between the two residences until her marriage.

Children also may find surrogate parents in their siblings. The number of siblings of the primary-sample women ranged from eight to none, excluding those who died in early childhood. It was an elder sibling who often substituted for a parent when the latter died prematurely or was ill, too old, or otherwise incapacitated. For Sayo, the youngest of eight children, it was an elder brother rather than the old father who lavished paternal love on her. Again, it may be hypothesized that a *mukoyōshi* father tends to concede paternal authority to a son, unless he has already been pushed aside by his father-in-law. We have only one such case, but this tentative generalization was confirmed by a local man when he said that he used to consult his brothers for advice on whatever mattered to him "because our father was *muko*." Three women confided that there was mutual attachment between themselves and particular brothers and that the latter had an autocratic voice in their sisters' marriages.

An eldest sister might become a surrogate mother, as in the case of Emi, whose mother died giving birth to her. She was brought up, loved, and trained by the elder sister, and when the latter was to marry she moved out with her instead of staying with the father and stepmother. An elder sister may have to substitute for the father as well, as in a case where the elder brother's death was followed by the father's, and yet the mother remained as dependent, lazy, and spendthrift as before. When all the savings were exhausted, Ayano's elder sister worked to sustain the mother and three younger siblings. The informant feels at once grateful and guilty toward the sister who thus sacrificed her life and has remained unmarried.

Two cases involved an uncle taking a surrogate role for the deceased father. In one of the two, the father's brother moved in bringing his family with him. The understanding was that he would step down when the successor son, the informant's brother, attained adulthood. When the family sat at the dinner table, "this uncle took the top seat, followed by grandmother and elder brother, the two being about equal to each other," and close to the door (the lowest seating area) sat the rest of the family including the widow and her dauther, Yukie. Here one can see a temporary fusion of the *honke* and a *bunke* of a *dōzoku* system.

The family size ranged from two (mother and daughter) to more than ten (some informants are uncertain about it). Together with the wife and children of an elder brother who succeeded to the house, the family could become quite large. "Our family was about thirteen," said Sachi, seventy, who is from a fishing and farming family in a rural ward of Shizumi. She was not only a daughter and sister, but a sister-in-law to the brother's wife and an aunt to her brother's children.

*Foster parents.* There is a wide variation in the forms and functions of fosterage. What is locally called *moraikko* usually refers to a child who has been given away by a family with too many children to feed and picked up by a family that needed cheap labor. A ward of Shizumi with a concentration of fishing households is known for having received many such *moraikko* as future fishermen. The foster child is reared as such, not as a full-fledged member of the family, but as a sort of servant. As future laborers more males than females seem to belong to this category. This type of fosterage is no longer practiced. The other and still common extreme is the adoption (*yōshi* for a male, *yōjo* for a female) of a baby boy or a baby girl as a full member of the family, taking every precaution to keep the child's origin a secret. Four of the five adopted daughters in my sample belong to the latter category. They all emphasize how much they were loved by their adoptive parents. Yuri was initially taken to the foster mother to be nursed as her own mother did not have enough milk. The wet-nurse became attached to her, which resulted in her adoption. These adopted daughters were ignorant of their being adopted until the two families involved, for one reason or another, had to revive ties, or the official house register or schoolmates' gossip revealed it much later in their lives. Even when they discovered their origins, they accepted it calmly, they said, since they knew their natural parents could not have indulged them as much. This is contrary to the culturally stereotyped obsession, as depicted in popular films, with blood parentage and the trauma experienced upon reality disclosure.

*Personal servants.* Before the wartime food shortage and air raids had forced the dispersal of household coresidents, most upper-class and many middle-class families had live-in servants who participated in childrearing for the master's children. While most servants were of the generalized type in that they did all domestic chores as well as baby-sitting, some were assigned exclusively to the children as nurses or attendants. Some of my local informants recall having been looked after by their housemaids, but only of the former type. The latter type was afforded only by upper-class families, the *kazoku* (nobility) being at the top of this social stratum.

## SOCIALIZATION

How a parent or surrogate parent treated the daughter is conceived of by the informants in two contrastive ways: he/she treated the child with loving care and indulgence, and/or disciplined her with various degrees of severity. These variables somewhat overlap with the ideas of Whiting and Child (1953), but I am applying these not only to early but to late childhood as well. Generally, the informants tend to adore or resent a parent because of his/her ability or inability to embrace the child with love and nurturance, and to train her in the rules of conduct or character development. Except for an only daughter, the child is exposed to co-socialization with her siblings.

*Indulgence: being fondled.* When informants stated that they grew up being "fondled" *(kawaigarareta)*, different aspects of indulgence were emphasized. First, extreme intimacy is equated with fondling, as expressed through physical contact. The adoptive mother used to stroke Yuri's face all the time to show her love; "everyone" in the house loved Sayo, the last-born child, and showed it by carrying her around on their backs even when she was of school age; the daughter was allowed to sleep in the mother's bed in her late teens. Here again, parental asymmetry is noted. As Rin recalled, "Mother carried me around on her

back, without paying much attention to the other children. But Father
beat me all the time."

Second, indulgence, particularly among older generations and
well-off families, involves the parental protection of the child, the
refusal to expose her to external influence: "My mother would not let
anybody touch me." A child so protected was often described as *hakoiri-
musume*, a "boxed-in daughter." Third, in contrast to such protective-
ness where the child's autonomy was suppressed, indulgence can also
mean parental confidence in the child which allows her to enjoy freedom and pursue her interests without penalty: "We children could do
anything we wanted; our *oya* [parent—mother or father or both] somehow trusted us." Fourth, the parental leniency implied in the above
may go so far as to hamper the child. Such leniency is often combined
with the gratification of *amae*, dependency-wishes.[2] Yoshimi regrets
how much *amae* she was allowed to enjoy throughout her school life, to
the extent of having her mother do all her homework. Fifth, the child
felt indulged when her parent, usually the mother, underwent hardship
and sacrifice on her behalf. The combination of sympathy for the
mother and feeling her indulgence thus expressed makes the mother an
unequalled object of intense emotions. Sixth, indulgence is expressed by
a parent's identification with the child, as when the father, excited over
the daughter's successful performance in school, would brag about her,
and would wish that she were a boy who would have a great career.

It may be noted in passing that one of the Japanese ethnotherapies,
called Naikan, mobilized the client's memory of those individuals who
participated most significantly in the client's childhood life, notably the
mother. The client is supposed to recall all the unpaid debt he incurred
to this person (Lebra 1976c:201–14). Considering the wide range of
meanings attached to indulgence that we have seen above, one can see
how this therapeutic method works—it would be difficult to find a parent who was not indulgent in any one of these senses. "*Kawaigarareta*"
is indeed a culturally stylized self-portrait among Japanese, just as
much as *kurō* is a culturally shared theme. The recollection of *kawaigarareta* often sustains the self-identity of the Japanese individual, male or
female.

The particular expression and amount of indulgence is determined
by the birth order and sex distribution of the children. The last-born
child, regardless of sex, is the most indulged and tends to be spoiled.
Sibling rivalry thus aroused in an older brother or sister may survive
long after the parents' deaths: Sayo at seventy-seven years of age is still
the target of her elder sister's jealousy for being a special child as the last
born. Special attention also goes to the firstborn in a different form of
indulgence, but in this case sex counts: the eldest son *(chōnan)* holds

a privileged status as the successor and is treated with special care, whereas the eldest daughter *(chōjo)* does not enjoy such distinct privileges in contrast to younger daughters. However, if there are no sons, the *chōjo* as the heiress is treated like a *chōnan*. For this reason, a twenty-six-year-old informant's elder sister was extremely fondled by the grandfather while "I was brushed off or maltreated." This younger daughter hates the grandfather. It should be noted that the Japanese reckon birth order within the same sex so that two birth orders—one for sons and another for daughters—are identified. It is, therefore, possible that the *chōnan* might be younger than the *jijo* (second daughter).

The only daughter among many sons, or the only son among daughters invariably become the target of overwhelming love and attention. Maki, an only daughter, became a favorite topic of conversation at mealtime, and thus "I grew up *wagamama* [self-centered or unruly]." If one is both an elder brother *and* the only brother among sisters, his privilege will be overwhelming. Kuniko, sixty, recalled that her brother had had a seat next to the father's around the fireplace and had always been the first to receive candy and other goodies. If someone brought *yōkan* (sugared bean paste candy) as a gift, half of it went to him and the rest was divided among the six sisters. When the family could not afford enough fish for everyone at a meal—her family was poverty-stricken in her childhood—the father and brother alone enjoyed it. "We sisters were not allowed to take a bath before brother."

If the informant had not grown up as an only daughter, or *chōjo*, or as the last-born, she would not pay much attention to her birth rank as a basis for her life history, whereas every informant falling into any one of these categories stressed this ascribed identity as if it determined her life course. Kumiko, when asked about her birth rank, said: "Of the nine siblings, I was, let me see, what rank was I?" turning to her daughter sitting nearby. "Eighth child," answered the daughter, chuckling. This was meant to be a joke to dramatize the insignificance of her sib-rank. Because of the distinguished status of *chōnan*, sib-rank discrimination seems resented more by a younger son than by a younger daughter. A local male informant, a Buddhist priest, described himself as a *sannan* (third son) and "therefore *doko no uma no hone ka wakaranai* [of totally obscure origin]." A younger son is also designated *"hiyameshi"* (cold rice eater) or *"kerai"* (retainer or vassal). It is my impression that discrimination in indulgence is determined more by sib-rank and imbalance in sex distribution than by sex per se and that when sex counts, it is only in combination with the other two variables. In other words, sex dichotomy is blurred by the structural emphasis upon the hierarchy by birth order as well as by scarcity value.

*Discipline.* Indulgence is often distinguished from "true love" as the latter, informants stressed, contains discipline. Indeed, the parent or surrogate parent to whom the informant is the most deeply attached is seen to combine indulgence and discipline, or *yasashii* (tender) and *kibishii* (severe), in one person. The parental asymmetry in its extreme form is expressed in one parent combining the two qualities, and the other having neither.

One cluster of disciplinary measures is oriented toward what might be called the "exterior." Involved herein is training in manners and comportment according to the culturally standardized codes of propriety. While some codes are imposed upon both sexes, most codes are addressed more readily or exclusively to girls as expressions of femininity. We might be justified, therefore, in labeling this aspect of discipline *femininity training*.

Femininity training first concerns *modesty*, the specific forms of which vary from culture to culture. The prewar or wartime Japanese woman was trained in subtle codes of exposure avoidance, whether it related to her posture, movement, manipulation, or speech. Such training was stressed in late childhood through early adulthood, but was started in rudimentary forms at the preschool stage. Particularly important was the sitting style, indicative of the traditional living on the tatami floor. "If I sat with a foot sticking out [instead of it neatly folded underneath the torso]," says Yone, "my mother would strike it with a yardstick relentlessly, interrogating: 'Why do you sit like that?' " For the woman, sitting with legs crossed in front *(agura)* or stretched out would be the worst offense. The male was not expected to conform to this code, and yet if he did he would likely be praised. Ayano praised her father for having been well mannered, never having appeared in *agura* posture. Mealtime in particular demanded postural propriety, ruling out leg-stretching or elbow-resting on the table. Exposure control also had to be exercised for body movements like sitting down, standing up, moving forward, backward, or sideways. Vulnerable states like sleeping and bathing, insofar as these involved co-sleepers and co-bathers, also were subject to the modesty code, and co-sleeping and co-bathing did provide opportunities for a mother to train a daughter in this respect.

As for speech, modesty demanded overall reticence, a soft voice, the polite and feminine style of speech, and avoidance of exposing the oral cavity (the wide-open mouth should be covered with a hand). "I was a tomboy, and used to talk loudly [the informant still does]. Mother scolded me, saying: 'Neighbors will hear. It's embarrassing.' " Yukie, forty-six, is grateful to her widowed mother for having strictly trained her in, among other things, *o-gyōgi* (manners and comportment) "probably because I was a girl." Unlike her brother, she also was taught to speak standard Japanese, thanks to which "people do not believe I was born here."

The code of silence was particularly emphasized during mealtime. "You must not talk while eating" was the most frequently mentioned rule; some informants could recall no discipline except this one. Talking while eating was permitted for Hanayo only if speech was addressed to the father. "We children were forbidden to talk to one another, allowed to talk to father only." Also, the father encouraged the children to speak as succinctly as possible, to avoid long-winded sentences.

As far as reticence training is concerned, it had nothing to do with femininity but applied to both sexes, or more to males. Suzuko, of the postwar generation, remembers being indulged but not especially disciplined by her parents. When I pressed her about not speaking at mealtimes, she said, "No, I was not told so, although I am the loquacious type. But if my brother talked too much, father said, 'A male should not talk.' " Probably because of such differentiation by sex in socialization for reticence, most informants recall male members of the family to be less talkative than female members. In the above case, the brother, now in his twenties, has come to refuse to express his thoughts so that the family is nonplussed, totally unable to predict what he will do the next moment. In a questionnaire asking high school students (sixteen and seventeen years old) what they want from their fathers (and mothers), a couple of male respondents wished their fathers would communicate more with them, whereas there was no such response with regard to mothers. Interestingly, one female student wrote, "I wish he [father] would not talk so much like a woman but sit quiet and composed."

Closely related to modesty is feminine *elegance* in handling things. Again an oldtimer had to learn how to manipulate things or set them down without making noise. In addition to oral silence, table manners included handling the dishes and chopsticks quietly (foreigners might wonder why such a strict code of quietness did not include the prohibition of soup slurping—an instance indicative of cultural relativity in expressions of elegance and crudeness). Considered crude and unfeminine would be such actions as banging the door, and throwing or dropping things. Elegance training further involved encouragement of smoothness in the motion of the body or hands and discouragement of awkward or jerky manners.

A third subset of femininity training concerns *tidiness* or neatness. A daughter was disciplined much more strictly than a son to be well groomed with regard to her face, hair, and dress. Putting on a kimono in such a way that it would never become loose regardless of one's motions was an important part of learning tidiness. (It might be noted that young women today, having had no home training in kimono wearing, must go to special schools to learn it so that they can wear kimonos on special occasions without relying upon an expensive, professional beautician each time. Hence the nationwide proliferation of kimono schools which teach how to "wear" a kimono. For a detailed case study of kimono schools, see McCoy 1979.) A model mother was characterized as neat in physical appearance: "My impression of my mother is that she had her *marumage* hairdo [symbolic of postmarital status] always neatly fixed and her kimono tightly bound by a black satin obi. She never looked as if she had just gotten out of bed." A countermodel mother, as another informant recalled, would receive the children, coming home from school, in her nightdress. "Sometimes," continued the same informant, "Mother was found well dressed, and even had her face made-up. We children rejoiced."

Tidiness training extended from one's physical appearance to environmental appearance. Whatever had been displaced had to be returned to its original place, whatever had been used needed to be put away, so that a room, a hallway, or a desk would look neat and tidy. After wearing a kimono, the daughter was told to fold it properly and put it away. When she was about to go out, she was supposed to put her slippers in the right spot, and when she came home, her outdoor shoes had to be placed on a shoe shelf. If she opened a door, it had to be closed. And so on. Sloppiness in leaving things about invited punishment. (This aspect of training seems to be often ineffective, as some of my informants admitted that their husbands are much more fastidiously tidy, "like a woman," than they are.)

Training in modesty, elegance, and tidiness all pertains to the exterior of the person or the environment, and thus is primarily oriented toward the kind of audience with whom ritual propriety must be maintained. Within the family, the presence of the father, grandparents, or anybody else who would deserve special respect called for conformity to propriety codes. This is why strict manners were prescribed during mealtimes when all of the family, the father in particular, were present. Of greater significance, however, was the occasion when interaction with an outsider took place, particularly in a host-guest relationship.

Femininity training thus involved *courtesy*, as expressed in modest, elegant, tidy manners. If the family was hosting a guest, the daughter would be called upon, either as part of the training or to display her already accomplished femininity, to serve tea and offer *aisatsu* (formal greeting), which included bows and stylized polite speech. When she received or saw the visitor off at the house entrance, the mother would teach her to half sit so that her eyes would come down to the same level as those of the visitor who stood on the floor, which was at a lower level. The same logic applied when the guest was sitting in a room: it would be rude to open the sliding door while standing; to be at the same height as the guest, the hosting woman would have to open or close the door in a sitting position. When the situation was reversed and the girl visited someone else, she was supposed to be able to follow the codes for guests, including proper ways of accepting tea, a *zabuton* cushion, and so forth.

There is an exaggeration in the informants' claims to such training, since they do not necessarily verify in their actual behavior what was supposedly taught. But the word "discipline" *(shitsuke)* seems foremost associated in their minds with exterior training, which may explain such an emphasis on this aspect of training. Furthermore, femininity training is largely conditioned by the domestic architecture and dress style. What was required from a resident of a house with raised tatami floors and privacy-inhibiting sliding paper doors would prove either irrelevant or unteachable to a dweller of a more westernized house with chairs and fixed, thick walls partitioning rooms. Femininity conditioned by the kimono must change into what is more suitable for Western-style dresses or even blue jeans. It is in this aspect that we can see a remarkable generation gap, and this change has affected our older informants as well, even though they complained about the mannerlessness of the younger generation.

Another factor is that, despite exposure to femininity training in one form or another, several informants described themselves as having been rough, unfeminine, or masculine and appeared to take pride in it rather than be embarrassed about it. This may indicate the primacy of masculine qualities, accepted by male and female alike, which drives some women toward gender neutralization.

For young children today, discipline seems to be focused upon verbal courtesy. In classrooms one sees posted a weekly slogan, such as "Let us say, 'Good morning!' " I observed two-year-olds being trained by a nursery teacher to say *"konnichiwa"* (hello) with a bow in response to a hand puppet manipulated by the teacher. Bank employees are also trained to offer proper *aisatsu* to customers. A retired school principal observed:

> I believe external forms are important. My instruction is "Say 'Good morning' to everybody, and say 'Thank you' to anybody who deserves it." This may sound formalistic, and people may object, saying that unless it is accompanied by true feeling it would mean nothing. But I believe the

opposite is true. By following a form one tends to feel the way the form dictates. By offering *aisatsu*, we become respectful of others.

This comment suggests that courtesy is still a vital part of child training and it is so for both sexes, although I claim it is more strictly prescribed for women as part of the femininity code. It also implies that courtesy does not remain on the exterior of the person but can penetrate the inner world, which leads to the second aspect of discipline.

Severe discipline extends to the "interior" of the trainee and this aspect will be termed *moral training*. Moral codes, like propriety codes, may well be addressed to an audience, but are meant to be internalized so as to become building blocks for personal character. I assume this aspect of training to be more sex-free and more culture-free than exterior training, and therefore to warrant only a brief discussion.

The first code to be noted is that of *compliance*. The daughter in the prewar/wartime generations was supposed to respond with the compliant utterance "Hai!" to whatever a parent or any authoritative figure told her. Emi attributes her father's severity in this respect to his *shizoku* (warrior class, see p. 14) origin: "So my family was feudalistic." It was inconceivable to some informants to talk back to their parents, and this resulted in their inability to say no under any circumstances.

Related to compliance is the training of a small child to be *otonashii* (subdued), particularly in the presence of guests. A young informant clarified the word as meaning "being around but appearing as if you didn't exist."

Compliance is an umbrella code under which all other codes are subsumed. One of the most frequently mentioned imperatives was to come home by a fixed time, before dark. This protection-oriented rule of punctuality was enforced upon daughters more than on sons. Yet, compliance does not necessarily imply dependency. In fact, there is a strong emphasis upon discipline for *self-reliance*. "My mother would never help me; she was really severe, training me to do everything by myself, not to rely upon anybody." The need for self-reliance was discussed in conjunction with one of the most sacred cultural codes, the avoidance of causing *meiwaku* (nuisance or trouble) to others. Dependency was disapproved of mainly because it makes one a *meiwaku* for others.

*Diligence* is another value stressed by many trainers. The grandfather used to tell a story, Yasu, seventy-three, recalled, about how a neighbor house became prosperous by working hard from early morning to late at night. "You won't be able to have a good life since you stay in bed till so late." To bring about prosperity, work must be accompanied by *thrift*. The virtues of frugality and saving were inculcated with regard to any household consumer goods, and rice in particular. "Mother taught me how to wash rice. If I poured out a few grains with the rinse water, she would spank me saying, 'You must not waste even a single grain.' " "I was told not to leave a single grain remaining in the rice bowl."

*Endurance* was also stressed as a necessary step toward character development, which underscores the desirability of hardship experiences. If the family was well off, especially if it was wealthy enough to have hired hands, it could be difficult to impose the hardship necessary to train the children in endurance. The opportunity may not have come until the daughter's marriage. Even so, verbal instruction was given on the virtue of quiet endurance. There seems to have been a sex difference in endurance training. While daughters were more or less protected, as much as the family economy permitted, from exposure to hardship outside the family, many sons, including those from wealthy families, were sent away to "eat a stranger's rice" just to experience hardship and thereby learn to endure. It may be that daughters were believed to be obedient to their parents whereas sons were beyond family discipline and therefore in need of nonfamilial discipline.

This does not mean that the value of endurance was stressed more for boys than for girls. As a matter of fact, a mother would say: "What is most important for women is endurance [*shinbō*]." Indeed the mother who had suffered under poverty, a domineering in-law, or her promiscuous husband embodied this virtue. A main sex difference seems to be that endurance for a daughter was a component of "anticipatory socialization" (she would be told over and over again that once she married she would have no choice but to endure hardship), whereas it was to be learned by a son through "participatory socialization" (he would have to live with a master-employer, for example, to have a taste of the deprived status of an apprentice).

*Task assignment.* Femininity training and moral training went together with work assignment, which usually involved assistance with housework. Since work assignment is not exclusively meant for child training but is more likely to combine teaching in domestic skills with securing auxiliary domestic labor, it is best dealt with under a separate section.

Assigned tasks included running errands, yard sweeping, housecleaning, table setting, kitchen work, laundry, fabric starching (using starching boards), ironing, sewing, bed making, and baby-sitting. Yukie, forty-six, said, "I had to help my mother with all sorts of routine work, although we had many servants. Mother had me prepare meals with her and assist her with all other housework. Grandmother, too, was very strict. With her I had to wash and board starch kimono fabric, to refresh cotton for *futon* bedding. I learned all those necessary things in my family." "My mother inspected my starching job and had me redo the whole thing unless it was flawless." Emi, seventy-one, claimed she learned everything about childrearing, including home medicine, by helping her sister rear her child. Some domestic skills, like sewing, were regarded as doubly important, not only for bridal preparation but because they might help women as a means of earning their livelihood should an unexpected misfortune strike and require them to be self-supporting.

Brothers were exempted from domestic tasks, kitchen work in particular. When I asked if her brother had worked in the kitchen too, Kuniko exclaimed, "Heaven's no! If he did, we women would have been criticized as slobs." The only brother with many sisters depended upon their caretaking service, such as folding up his *futon* bedding.

Where the father's occupation was attached to the house, daughters (as well as sons) were mobilized to render assistance in the family business, and this was particularly true with agriculture, retail or wholesale businesses, and hotel management. Tama, a farmer's daughter, seventy-seven, said she was lucky to have been the second youngest child, too young to be assigned to a baby-sitting job, whereas most of her little neighbors were always tending their younger siblings. Instead, she helped with the farming, particularly in the processing of the harvested rice, assisting with such tasks as hulling the rice by pushing a heavy stone grinder. Some other daughters from farming families were periodically mobilized for sericultural work (many of the local farmers used to engage in the silk-raising industry as a side job), which interrupted their bridal training in sewing. A hotel owner's daughter like Yoko was expected to work as one of many maids, and thus could devote much less time than her classmates to schoolwork.

Some informants took over a parental role—not just an auxiliary one but a primary role—to substitute for a mother as a housekeeper or for a father as a breadwinner. This happened where the parent was dead, sick, or inadequate and the informant was the eldest daughter. The importance of sib-rank in the assignment of surrogate-parental role has been previously discussed as taken by some informants' elder sisters, but here it is the informants themselves who as elder sisters were put into that role. Even before they had graduated from the six-year primary school, some informants had learned to prepare complete meals, including making a charcoal cooking fire. Hiroe, the eldest daughter of a wealthy farmer, became the sole caretaker for four younger siblings when her mother died, and this responsibility tied her down to the house all year around. Fuyuko used to wash her baby half-sister's diapers early in the morning before school. When she grew older, she became the mainstay of the family economy as the hardest-working and most skilled seamstress in the clothing store run by her father. She supported the stepmother and four younger half-siblings, and for this reason her parents did not let her marry for a long time. Some mothers came to depend on their daughters when their life conditions suddenly took a turn for the worse. One such mother had had a luxurious life in her childhood, pampered by her indulgent grandmother and waited on by as many as four maids. She continued to enjoy this easy life after she married until two tragedies occurred. Her husband, a brilliant graduate of the Imperial University of Tokyo, after having held a series of high official positions in the government and executive positions in lucrative businesses, quit working and eventually died. Meanwhile, they found out that her youngest son had cerebral paralysis. Toshiko, as the eldest sister, nursed this brother and went to work to support the family.

Task assignment in these cases involved an element of exploitation of the daughters by adults and thus is generally resented as extracting sacrifice rather than being appreciated as designed for discipline. The worst case of exploitation is that of Rin. Rin, seventy-eight years old, unreservedly denounces her father as *rokudenashi* (worthless). The father played around, drank all the time, and spent whatever money the mother had earned from farming and running a variety store. As soon as the mother died, the "male parent" sent seven-year-old Rin to work as a baby-sitter so that he could obtain the wages paid in advance by her employer. Interested only in squeezing money out of her, he forced her to move from one family to another in order to extract as many advance payments as possible. Rin finally ran away and escaped from his control, but he somehow managed to keep track of her whereabouts until he died when she was twenty-four. She ended up with no formal education.

Because of the possibility of such exploitation, premature training of a child in adult work roles may arouse gossip from neighbors. Wakako, sixty-eight, recalls that the neighbors suspected that she was either a *moraikko* or a stepdaughter. As early as eleven years of age, she was fetching water from a well and cooking rice and miso soup every morning. This was because she was an only child and the mother wanted to prepare her to be useful as a woman in case the parents should die. (A later interview revealed that Wakako was indeed a foster child, born out of wedlock.)

Work experience of women in the premarital stage is not confined to their own homes. A later section of this chapter will, therefore, take up work outside the natal family.

## The Public Domain

Both daughters and sons begin to participate in the domain outside home prior to school age. For the sake of convenience, however, we shall discuss the educational subdomain first.

### EDUCATION

School experience comprises a major portion, equally or more important than family experience, of a woman's premarital stage. If one asks a vague question such as, "How was your childhood?" some women would immediately place themselves in a school setting. Furthermore, a particular event or experience was recalled more often in association with the recaller's school year ("It was when I was in the fourth year of primary school") than with her chronological age.

*Opportunities.* To estimate to what extent school education has been open to girls, let us trace the educational pathways through which our primary sample has gone. In the prewar system, the six-year elementary school was compulsory,[3] and was attended by every woman except seventy-eight-year-old Rin, whose father had kept her from school. This is consistent with the fact that by 1902, the year my oldest informant, Kayo, had reached school age, elementary school enrollment in Japan had risen to 90 percent of all the eligible children (Education Ministry Annual Report, cited in Ito, Sato, and Hisahara 1967: 124).[4] At the time of graduation from primary school, a choice was made as to whether to terminate education there or to go on to a noncompulsory, more advanced level. Surprisingly, all primary school graduates went on, as if there had been no other choice. The real choice, however, was between the two-year upper-grade primary school (generally called *kōshō*) and the four-to-five-year girls' high school (called *jogakkō*). It was found that of the forty-five primary school graduates under the prewar system, seventeen (38 percent) went to *kōshō* to continue basic and practical education whereas twenty-eight (68 percent) chose to go to *jogakkō* for a more academically oriented, intermediate-level education. Of these, twelve graduated from *kōshō* and twenty-two from *jogakkō* without further formal education, while the rest (eleven) went on to still higher education at either a short-term (one-to-two-year) vocational school or a full-term (three-to-five-year) professional college. (The above figures include one dropout from *kōshō*, two from *jogakkō*, and one from a professional college.)

In the postwar system, the six-year elementary school and the three-year junior high school together comprise compulsory education. Only one informant received no education beyond the junior high school level, six terminated their education at the senior high school level, two went on to a two-year vocational college, and two graduated from a four-year university.

Several variables are involved in determining educational pathways. One is the historical change in the significance of education for girls. It is thus assumed that the younger the person is, the greater her opportunity for advanced education. This assumption was confirmed by the age difference of the graduates from the different kinds of educational institutions. The average age of the twelve *kōshō* terminals is sixty-seven while that of the twenty-two *jogakkō* terminals is fifty-five, twelve years younger. A similar age contrast is found between short-term vocational school graduates (sixty-five) and full-term professional college graduates (fifty-four). For the postwar generation, however, the above assumption is not borne out.

Educational opportunities for women have not simply expanded linearly and smoothly over the course of time. The Second World War in particular affected the educational careers of some women not only economically but ideologically as well. This was a generation subjected to a shortage of teachers, reduction of class hours, cultivation of school grounds for crops, and students' mobilization to farms or naval factories. The deletion of the "enemy language" from the school curriculum blocked one high school girl's ambition to enter college and specialize in English.[5] The result of these wartime restrictions on education is that a gap has been left irreversibly unfilled. This roughly corresponds to the generation which is identified as "the one-digit generation of the Showa era" (those who were born between the first and ninth year of Showa, that is, 1926–1934). This generation is characterized, in contrast to the two-digit generation (1935– ), as awkward in coping with the highly complex, mechanized, affluent, contemporary world.

A second important variable was place of residence. The crucial question was whether one lived in or near a big city where a girls' high school or a women's college was accessible within a limited transportation system. This was particularly important for girls because it was inconceivable for many families to allow their premarital daughters to live alone away from home, though such domestic protection was dispensed with for sons. Most high school students away from home had

relatives in a city to live with and to supervise them. This, together with
the first variable, explains why high school enrollment increased sharply as soon as the local girls' high school was established in Shizumi
(1933) and before long came to absorb the majority of female primary
school graduates.

A third, and perhaps the most important, variable is class background. Since intermediary and higher education, particularly away
from home, was expensive, the family's wealth determined educational
opportunities to a large degree. "We were well off [by village stan-
dards]," said Yoko, a prewar-timer. "In those days there were only one
or two in the whole class [in primary school] who could go to a *jogakkō*,
and I did." As far as the older-generation informants were concerned,
the *jogakkō* was attended by daughters of landowners, hotel owners,
businessmen, a teahouse operator, a naval officer, an engineer, and a
wealthy farmer-politician, while only the *kōshō* was open to daughers
of farmers, fishermen, a *geta* maker, and a bankrupt shopkeeper. However, closer examination brings out more than the difference in wealth.
"Class background" means not only the financial capacity to pay for
higher education, but the status appropriateness of receiving an advanced education in terms of either worthiness or need, regardless of
actual solvency. "In those days, no one thought of leaving home for education unless the family had a special status of honor." Yoko meant the
traditionally established family reputation. For a boy, family prominence imposed higher education without choice. A man from a family
of distinction in rural Shizumi with both huge real estate holdings and a
background of hereditary village headmanship plus *honke* status said:
"My family had to sell one forest after another to pay for each son's university education. What a stupid thing to do! And I did not want to go
to university. But with that family status, we had no choice but to go."

A farmer's daughter, fifty-five, wanted to go to a girls' vocational
public school after *kōshō* since *jogakkō* was out of the question. She was
told by the family: "Even the daughter of *honke* [of their *dōzoku*] did
not go. It would be embarrassing if a branch house like ours would let a
daughter go." So Mutsuko was sent instead to a more modest, though
one-half-yen more expensive, *juku* to study sewing. (*Juku* referred to an
informal, small class usually held at the teacher's residence. Girls who
could not go to a formal girls' high school were sent to such *juku* for
bridal training. In today's usage, the same term, *juku*, refers primarily
to cram schools for entrance examinations, as will be described in a later
chapter.) Another daughter of a farmer, Tama, liked to study so much
that she would sneak out of the house to attend a little neighborhood
*juku* after regular school hours. Even so, Tama did not question that she

was, like everyone else in the village, going to become a farmer and therefore would make no use of a *jogakkō* education. One decisive factor, embedded in class background, was whether the family already had a well-educated member or relative whom the daugher could follow as a model. Fusa, seventy-six, explained her education at a temporary teacher training school after *kōshō* in terms of her uncles, who were all in the military and thus well educated, and her mother who had been educated at a *terakoya* (private schools available to commoners prior to the Meiji reform). Hanayo, a pharmacological college graduate, referred to her uncles as having "the Imperial University pedigree."

The assumed correlation between educational opportunity and class and/or residence is well confirmed by my sample of "career women," all but one of whom are university graduates. Most of them came from upper-middle- to lower-upper-class background and lived in Tokyo, Kyoto, or other major cities. Many of their families were mobile, moving from place to place in accordance with the father's job assignment. The families which happened to be in a rural town moved to a large city for educational purposes when a daughter reached school age.

Fourth, sex influenced educational opportunities in that higher education was considered desirable for a son while intermediate education was taken as the most that a daughter would need. Also, a daugher's education was made contingent upon such factors as class and residence whereas arrangements were made to overcome these problems for a son's education. Fukiko had to go to a *kōshō*, unlike the majority of her primary school classmates, who went to *jogakkō*. Her elder brother and sister, on the other hand, graduated from a professional college and *jogakkō* respectively. This was because her father had died. But when her younger brother reached intermediate school age, the whole family moved to a city where a reputable prefectural boys' middle school was available, as if, it seemed to me, the economic hardship of the family had suddenly ceased to exist. A much narrower range of fields of specialization was considered appropriate for girls than for boys. Advanced education was denied to a daugher if she chose the wrong field. "I wanted to go to the Women's Art College," says Yasu, seventy-three, "but was told, 'What on earth is a woman going to do with art?' " Even a postwar coeducational high school graduate, Shoko, now thirty-eight years old, was denied her wish to go to an athletic college because athletic training had "nothing to do with womanhood."

The last to be mentioned is the status of the daughter who was destined to have a *mukoyōshi* marriage. It was observed that such a daughter—the only or eldest daughter without a brother—received a better education with the parental hope that she could thereby bring in "a nice man" to succeed the house. It is not clear, however, whether it was thought that a well-educated woman would make a desirable bride, as implied in the above statement, or whether a woman who was to marry a *mukoyōshi* should be well educated so that she could support the family in case the husband could not. In any event, of the six *mukoyōshi*-married informants, two had a professional college education, one attended vocational school, and two graduated from *jogakkō*.

*Aspirations.* In the above section we have seen the objective conditions which opened or blocked educational opportunities. Now attention is turned to the subjective world of the young women facing educational choices or receiving an education. As education for girls beyond the *kōshō* or *jogakkō* among old timers was less than common, one would expect to find a strong career commitment in a girl who was so educated. To my surprise, most of the professional college women turned out to lack such career aspirations at the time of college entry. Asked what her thoughts were on her future at the time she entered college, Hanayo, fifty-four, answered that it was mainly her father's idea, not her own, that a woman too should have an occupation. The reason she chose a pharmacological college was because there were doctors and a drugstore keeper among her *shinseki* (see p. 21) and also because her father decided that all the daughters should specialize in a medical, therapeutic field in order to help the sickly son. "Frankly, I did not like science," but she could hardly say no to her father. The four years of dormitory life were trying, and course requirements were often hard to bear. But not once did she think of dropping out because, "If I had returned home before finishing college I would have been expelled by my father."

In this case it was compliance, not career aspiration, that carried the woman through her professional education. Motoko, sixty-three, another graduate from pharmacological college, was likewise expected by her father to major in that field. She recalled that as a small child, whenever she stumbled and was injured, he would warn her: "With such carelessness, you will never be able to become a pharmacist." But she resisted and entered a girls' high school known for its training in sewing, which was what she wanted to do most. After graduation she tutored *shinseki* children in sewing. Her father had not given up, and prevailed on her to go to a pharmacological college. Why was he so insistent? "I asked that question too. It was because I was the elder of the two daughters and should have an occupation, he thought. Nothing of the sort was expected of my younger sister." Motoko was to marry a *mukoyōshi*. As a student she remained uncommitted, reluctant to attend classes, often tempted to quit, and her wish to drop out was supported by her *shinseki*. But her father alone was adamant. "That's how I finally graduated, thinking of quitting until the very last day."

It was the father, elder brother, and, occasionally, the elder sister who decided on the career for the daughter/sister, imposed it on her, or helped her pursue it. Yoko, however, was pushed into a professional career by a schoolteacher instead of by her family. Her mother had already prepared her to enroll in a sewing school when the woman teacher talked her into taking the entrance examination for the prefectural normal school and persuaded her reluctant parents to go along with this. "I had a weak will, no idea what I wanted to be. I just did not want to leave home. . . . But the teacher was so enthusiastic, and she loved me like her own daughter." She took the examination unprepared and was surprised that she passed while some of her well-prepared classmates had failed. Living in the dormitory, she became homesick and cried in the evenings. Even five years of normal-school life did not convert Yoko into a zealous schoolteacher with an educational mission.

Shinobu, forty-four, was an exception in that she took the initiative in the choice of a career in nursing and pursued it despite her parents' strong objections. It was not that she was committed to this profession from the very beginning, but that she found it absolutely necessary to be self-supporting when her parents fell ill and the air raids reduced the family property to ashes. She regarded nursing foremost as a skill for survival, held no romantic dreams about the white uniform, and had thought of dressmaking as another alternative. While at nursing school, she was about to quit, partly due to the inadequate dormitory food, but her elder brother and sister dissuaded her.

A clear pattern emerges from these accounts. The girls who were fortunate enough to enjoy an opportunity for advanced education were not so much personally motivated for a professional career as compelled to accept the opportunity as a matter of either the obligation to comply, or the wish to maintain good relations with a persuasive adult, or the inclination to avoid a less desirable option. It was the father or elder brother more often than the mother who took the initiative or exercised influence upon the daughter's education. In some cases vicarious career aspirations seemed to be involved in that a father or brother insisted that a daughter go to college to fulfill the career ambition he himself had been prevented from carrying through. Also, some fathers demonstrated themselves to be very up-to-date by suggesting that from now on women, too, should have an occupation. After being told this by her father, who had started making leather shoes with the conviction that they would replace wooden clogs in the new age, Yaeko, fifty-seven, decided to become a (permanent wave) beautician and entered a beauty school in Tokyo. Her own original idea had been to have some "bridal training like sewing." Relatively more of the students who attended vocational schools for two years or less had stronger career motivations than those with three or more years of college education.

Discrepancy between opportunities and aspirations for education has continued into the postwar era when institutional emancipation and then economic affluence opened up educational opportunities for women. Female college enrollment did rise sharply. For thirty-six-year-old Harumi, it was her mother rather than a male figure, as in most other cases (her father being a *mukoyōshi*), who "built the railway for her to ride on" toward a career goal. It would be difficult to pass an examination for a good university if one were educated up to the senior high school level in Shizumi. The mother arranged everything so that the daughter could move to Tokyo and enter the junior high school of one of those elite private school systems which include all grades from the elementary to the university level. The mother hoped thereby that Harumi would have a painless ride on an "escalator" through the university. What still bothers Harumi is that she herself was not particularly interested in higher education. Sakiko, thirty-one, a graduate of two universities including the top national university of music and the arts, studied hard to pass the difficult examination primarily with the idea of pleasing her father. A twenty-eight-year-old woman could not recall any motivations for going to a junior college other than "I would rather be in college than sit around home doing nothing." We will return to the problem of career motivations in a later chapter on "Occupational Careers."

There are women who reported having a strong desire for education and a career but who could not carry it through for economic or ideological reasons. Many such instances were mentioned in the previous section with reference to the variables blocking educational opportunities. We might add a few more. Ayano had applied for admission to a national women's higher normal school—one of the very best educational institutions for women in the prewar era—when her father fell ill and died. Her wish to major in the academic field of child education thus remained frustrated. Yuri wanted to become a midwife, and with the encouragement of an older brother she moved to Tokyo. But before she had a chance to go to school for midwifery she had to succumb to her oldest brother's forceful order to return home immediately to marry.

It would appear that the well-motivated women remain frustrated while those who have options lack motivation, or that frustration creates, intensifies, or maintains motivation whereas the fulfilled motivation is destined to lose force. Whether this simplistic frustration hypothesis holds will be seen later.

At this juncture, let us look into the educational prospects held by contemporary youth. In the future-autobiographies written by seventeen- to eighteen-year-old high school students (fifty-six males and fifty-two females), one finds a clear sex polarization regarding their educational commitment. For male students, admission to a good, hopefully prestigious national university is the absolutely indispensable foundation upon which to build a career identity. They are obsessed with the hurdle of the "examination war" and write about attendance at cram schools (*juku, yobikō*), a miraculous success in passing the exam in the high school graduation year, studying as a *rōnin* (examination candidate who is not enrolled in any regular school, a position analogous to that of the masterless samurai) year after year until final success comes, or rejoicing over the notice of passing. Some are too unsure of success to continue to write anything beyond this initial stage of a career. The names of specific universities they aim at, including the University of Tokyo, are often identified. By contrast, female students reveal much less of such myopic obsession with the examination war, choose two-year colleges more often than four-year universities (they specify such numbers of years while no male respondent does so), and specify no college names. With regard to fields of specialty, there is some overlap between sexes in such fields as pharmacology, English language or literature, and agriculture, but for the majority there is wide divergence. Most males identify specialties such as "science" or "humanities" because these categorizations determine the kinds of examinations to be taken. Narrowly defined areas tend to concentrate in engineering, law, business administration, and archaeology. Female autobiographers present two polar types: either they do not bother to identify their fields at all, or, if they do, the fields tend to be narrow, practical, and directly linked to specific vocations, particularly "pink-collar" jobs, including dietician, health worker, clinical technician, nursery schoolteacher, primary schoolteacher, teacher of handicapped children. They are more concerned with obtaining a professional license and less with academic training than are male respondents. One girl, for example, wants to major in economics in order to acquire a "public accountant's" license. I hypothesize that this interest in a professional license is because women tend to be prepared for taking up a job only when it becomes necessary, as in the case of being widowed or when time becomes available as at the postparental stage. A professional license could be invoked at such a time as if it were savings to be withdrawn in an emergency.

*Academic performance.* While generally lacking in strong career aspirations, many informants have cherished memories of distinguished school performances. After expressing embarrassment at bragging, they talked about how teachers called upon them only after exhausting all responses given by other less able students; about their class ranks and report cards; about their end-of-school-year awards. Most of all, academic excellence was demonstrated by admission to a school difficult to enter. Ayano recalled how excited the whole village was when she passed the entrance examination to the *jogakkō* of the highest reputation in the area. She described the event as like a festival—she was the first village girl admitted. Above all, her primary schoolteachers were proud and pleased. The daughter's academic distinction gratified the family as well. But regrets were expressed that she was a girl, not a boy.

Everyone had an opportunity even in prewar times to observe boys' performance in comparison with girls' since the primary school or at least its first three years were coeducational. Informants tend to agree that at first little difference by sex showed but that as years progressed the gaps in competence widened. All informants stated without hesitation that boys have better brains, are smarter, that girls are no match. While older women attribute this to an innate difference, younger women tend to interpret it in terms of expectations on the part of surrounding people. A university senior said:

> In the elementary school I found no difference. By the third year of junior high school boys were way ahead in study efficiency, especially in math and natural science. Girls do not try hard in these subjects because they are told all the time girls are no good at them. In high school, girls have no idea what they are doing in the classes of physics and chemistry.

*Bridal training.* One of the major characteristics of prewar education was sex segregation. Although *jogakkō*, the girls' high school, was formally equivalent to *chūgakkō*, the boys' middle school, it was distinctly oriented toward the cultivation of qualified brides and mothers. Not only domestic skills such as sewing and cooking but manners too were an important part of the curriculum, along with academic courses. The whole school system may well be labeled a "bridal school" (*hanayome gakkō*) in this sense. The postwar coeducational high school, free from sex segregation, looks totally different, but the label of bridal school remains, having been transferred to the women's junior colleges.

Apart from the regular *jogakkō*, there were, before the war, small private schools, or *juku*, licensed and unlicensed, exclusively specializing in bridal training which were attended by graduates from *kōshō*, *jogakkō*, and even from higher institutions. The most prevalent was training in sewing. Older women learned to make Japanese clothing, and younger women went to Western dressmaking schools. Sewing school attendance cut across class lines. Here the girls themselves were generally motivated, but many were pushed, this time by their mothers, who were convinced that sewing was inherent in womanhood. Dexterity for women referred to sewing skill. Cooking might be considered as important for bridal training, but none except two young informants attended a cooking school. It never occurred to the rest or to their mothers to learn cooking at a special school; it was assumed that it should be built into home learning. In fact there were no cooking schools in prewar and wartime days, the informants claimed. Obviously, home learning was less than adequate, for I found a surprising number of women well trained in sewing but with no confidence in their culinary skill, even after many years of kitchen experience. Today, cooking schools are ubiquitous and thriving, being attended by wartimers as well as bridal candidates.

Less prevalent and more class-bound than sewing in the prewar/wartime era was a set of expressive specialties intended for femininity training, such as flower arrangement, tea ceremony, koto and *shamisen* music, classical dance, and calligraphy. Although these were considered a core of bridal training in those days, women seldom used these skills to entertain their husbands. The general goal was not so much to learn the specific technique of an art as to internalize proper manners and comportment *through* the art. A woman confessed that she did not realize how crude her manners were until she began to attend a tea school, where she learned how to handle things like bowls without making noise. It seems that these expressive arts were considered the best way to cultivate modesty, elegance, tidiness, and courtesy. And this is not limited to old timers. While not a few Japanese, female and male, dismiss such training as useless, its popularity still persists. Even a national nursing school, I was told by one of its postwar graduates, had tea ceremony, flower arrangement, and manners in its curriculum. The younger the trainees, the more variable their motivations are. Young women today simply enjoy tea ceremony, find its theory sensible and intriguing, or participate in it only because they want to wear kimono. The persisting popularity of bridal schools is shown by the fact that seven out of fifty-two female future-autobiographers have consciously chosen to attend one.

In an old-style bridal-training class, a teacher trained a small group of students, often on a one-to-one basis, at her own residence. Intimacy thus developed, and the teacher, usually female, could give the student not simply technical instruction but also moral guidance, and play the role of a premarital counselor. Tsutae, fifty, cannot forget what her tea teacher had told her before she got married: "Once you marry, no matter how hard you work it will be taken for granted. So marry only after you think it over long enough. However faithfully you serve your mother-in-law, you will not be specially appreciated." If endowed with an inspiring personality, a teacher of tea, flower arrangement, koto, or sewing could socialize a young woman and have a lifelong impact on her.


WORK EXPERIENCE

Work may or may not be characterized as a career-oriented occupation. Where the career-oriented occupation is concerned, a very narrow range of options has been open to women. In addition to the question of compatibility of an occupation with the housewifely role, stigmatization of working women as "low-class" has blocked women from occupational careers until recently. Even a distinctly feminine occupation like nursing was spurned by parents for this reason. A public health nurse, now fifty-five, employed by the city government, took the risk of being disowned by her parents when she entered a nursing school. Her family, descended from a samurai vassal who had lived in a castle, was endowed with a *kafū*, house style, which would not accept a daughter working as a nurse.

Given the limited occupational opportunities, the general lack of strong academic aspirations among women that was shown earlier is hardly surprising. Discrepancy between academic training and employment for female college graduates was demonstrated by Sekiguchi (1973). The conversations I have had with college students make me suspect that they anticipate or accept such a discrepancy, particularly if they major in liberal arts.

The limited occupational options and the anticipated discrepancy between educational specialization and occupation result not only in women's frustrations but in their sense of options for nonoccupational careers. A university senior majoring in history, with no prospect of finding a related job, is thinking of going home after her graduation to remain the father's dependent until marriage—an option allowed her but not her brother.

*Motivations for employment.* Despite the limited occupational opportunities and the education-employment discrepancy, many women in our sample worked before marriage. We shall first explore how and why the women became involved in work in terms of their initial motivations. The following kinds of motivations are not necessarily mutually exclusive. As far as the graduates from professional or vocational schools were concerned, it was primarily *educational investment and exposure* that made occupational engagement necessary or desirable. Despite the initial weakness of motivation, most of the students developed occupational identity and pride before graduation as a result of investment in their education and their exposure to training. Graduates from professional or vocational schools did manage to find occupations related to their training. So the pharmacological college graduates found employment as pharmacists in a hospital or drugstore; the nursing school graduate started her career at the clinic of an industrial corporation; the graduate from a nutrition school was employed at a hospital as a clinical dietician; the trainees in teaching began to teach at primary schools; a similar commitment to employment was made by the graduates from a beauty school, midwifery schools, and an accounting school.

Career identity seems to have crystallized through strenuous study, particularly toward graduation time in preparation for the national licensing examination. Some informants proudly told how they cut down on sleeping hours and how they passed the examination while many classmates failed. Also supportive of career commitment was the kind of human interaction on campus which the informants claimed could not be replicated anywhere else. Shinobu recalled the dormitory life at the nursing school where each room had fifteen roommates with as many beds and desks. Through this intimate co-living, an everlasting bond developed which she can fall back on still today, professionally and otherwise. The beauty school graduate, initially disturbed by the commonly shared idea that the occupation of hairdressing was not respectable, emerged with the conviction that beauticians have an important mission. Contributive to this conversion was the impressive personality of the school principal, who had returned from America and who not only taught the techniques of the profession but, as a devout member of the Seicho-no-ie sect, held a religion class every day.

That occupational commitment resulted from educational investment and exposure suggests the limited plausibility of the frustration hypothesis to account for motivation. Many people, particularly the young, may come to know what they want for their lives only after being exposed to it and expending energy for it. The initial lack of career motivation on the part of many women, therefore, does not justify or necessitate sex-role polarization.

The above comment, however, does not preclude the possibility that exposure to higher education may fail to arouse professional commitment. Five years of normal school and dormitory life failed to turn the daughter of a hotel operator into a career teacher. After teaching for three years—the minimal obligation of a normal-school graduate—she quit and returned to work in the family business. The two university graduates married before having had a chance to engage in an occupation related to their specialized field, and have had none since. A more systematic analysis, with more data, of career professions will be given in chapter 6.

A proportionately large number of women became employed for *apprenticeship*. If the family was too poor to send the daughter to intermediate school, she could opt to work for little or no wage in exchange for training of some sort. Tama, a farmer's daughter, started to baby-sit for a neighbor family in exchange for learning weaving skills from the baby's mother. All the other cases involved the live-in apprenticeship, where free room and board as well as training compensated for the negligible wage. Living with the employer family meant that the primary work assignment was that of a housemaid and that the educational benefit was whatever accrued from that assignment. Since ideally the training should include not just domestic skills but discipline in ritual propriety and femininity, such employment was sought in an upper-class family, where ritual propriety was believed to be a matter of routine. Hence, this kind of employment was often called *"oyashiki-bōkō"* (apprenticeship in a mansion). "In my days," said a seventy-eight-year-old woman, "you would not have been wanted as a bride, no matter how rich you were, unless you had done *oyashiki-bōkō*." This woman served as such for five years. The *oyashiki-bōkō* of my informants was done at the homes of high government officials, an army officer with a noble title, a company president, and a film engineer, all in Tokyo. Work included baby-sitting, housecleaning, kitchen work, and—what was regarded as the most desirable—personal attendance to the master or lady of the house. One of the informants was hired as a tutor, "not as a maid," for the children, but she had to escort the children to and from Gakushuin (the Peers' School) every day as part of her assignment.

It might be noted that, given the prewar system of stratification, this work-apprenticeship arrangement was probably the only avenue for personal contact and mutual influence between the upper and lower classes of women. Cross-class transmission of culture was indeed mutual —both upward and downward: some of the *kazoku* (see p. 14) women I have met stress how much they learned from their servants, while the *oyashiki-bōkō* apprentices also went into service intending to learn something of upper-class culture.

Training in *gyōgi* (manners) was supposed to be acquired through waiting on the master, his wife, and their guests, mostly by watching their behavior as well as the manners of a model senior maid. Hence this kind of working-learning was called *gyōgi-minarai*, *minarai* literally meaning "look and learn." Some *minarai* servants had exposure to bridal training in tea ceremony, flower arrangement, calligraphy, and other arts, but this too was mainly through *minarai* (or as one informant put it, through *nusumi-narai,* "learning by furtive glance") from the way the daughters of the house were tutored in these arts.

Again, some parents chose *oyashiki-bōkō* for their daughters, along with training in skills and manners, so that they could learn to endure hardship, or to "eat a stranger's rice." This kind of employment was usually undertaken with the parents' encouragement or even orders and against the daughter's wishes. One case was exceptional, however, in that the daughter arranged the employment by herself in secret and left home without her parents' approval—she wanted to escape from farming, the family occupation, and was enchanted with the idea of living in Tokyo and learning tea ceremony and flower arrangement.

Three cases involved live-in employment in exchange for vocational training: a live-in apprentice *(uchi-deshi)* at a beauty parlor, a midwife's apprentice, and a cook's helper in a company dormitory.

Since professional cooking had traditionally belonged exclusively to males, a woman's commitment to this career would have required some explanation. Without being asked, Sachi indicated that she had been born in the year of *hinoeuma* (a certain year of the horse in the Chinese zodiac system which returns in a sixty-year cycle). The *hinoeuma* year is associated in folklore with the birth of husband killers and known, therefore, in Japan for an abrupt drop in birth rate which has intrigued demographers. Not that Sachi accepted this belief as being true, but nonetheless she felt her life doomed by this prejudice, since "no man would like to have a *hinoeuma* woman for a wife." To be self-supporting was the main goal she had set herself since childhood. There are suggestions that she unwittingly fell into the trap of believing the folktale, considered herself to be more like a male than a female, and wished to outdo male rivals in whatever occupation she would undertake. It is purely a matter of speculation whether she chose to become an apprentice in a male profession because of such confusion about her sex identity. But what she did say was: "It would be best to hold a *hōchō* [a sharp knife symbolizing the Japanese culinary art], I thought, because I am a shrewish *hinoeuma.*"[6]

The above two kinds of motivation for employment are mutually exclusive in that one involves employment as a career occupation which has been invested in through obtaining advanced education, whereas the other is for temporary employment with the prospect of "graduation" from the *minarai* training. Since formal education has become widely open to women, apprenticeship is no longer an attractive alternative.

Some had to or wanted to work for *survival* or *income.* Life was so hard, I was told, that there was no time to stop to think about what one wanted to do. "Struggling to survive was all I was concerned about," and this was often partly due to the family's condition and partly to a societal disaster such as war. Kumiko, a *jogakkō* graduate, started to work at a local bank at the time of the economic disaster of the postwar era. Her monthly salary of three hundred fifty yen was not enough to buy a pair of shoes. Working for income was necessary for some informants as a burden of sib-rank, of being the oldest sister and expected to support the family and to educate the younger siblings. Toshiko, the sister of a victim of cerebral paralysis, thinking that an ordinary woman's job would amount to little, decided to take the lucrative job of peddling door-to-door a newly manufactured food item in order to support the family. From the very outset she proved to be a very successful saleswoman, which made the family more dependent upon her. Rin, while cursing her exploitative father, spent her childhood as a live-in baby-sitter, moving from one house to another. As she grew older, she moved away to be free of her father and worked as a live-in maid mainly doing "low jobs" such as cleaning, laundry, or kitchen work; the "high job" of serving the master in the inner room was reserved for "educated maids." Her father died when she was twenty-four, which was a relief to her. "But didn't you feel sorry for him?" I asked. Her answer was an unequivocal "No." In fact, she wished he had died much sooner. She seems to be obsessed with protecting herself from exploiters and parasites.

In contrast, another woman volunteered at thirteen to drop out of the *kōshō* and work for money to help her parents, convinced that no one but herself would be able to deliver the family from utmost poverty. Her father, proud of his samurai ancestry, was upset. One night he dragged his daughter out of the mosquito net and slapped her because he had just learned of her quitting school and going to work at a geisha house—the quickest way of getting money in advance. By then Wakako knew the secret of her birth: she was born out of wedlock and reared by the foster mother whom she had never doubted to be her real mother. Although she did not explain so to me, my hunch is that her decision to become a geisha was derived from her birth identity and a sense of debt to her foster mother. Also, her natural mother may have been an entertainer. In any event, the school dropout became an apprentice geisha, and after a year of training, began to entertain male customers.

Still other women came to their occupations for *accidental reasons* rather than because of economic pressures or professional commitment: the parents found a teaching job for their daughter just to distract her from her frustrated wish for a college education over which she was "sulking"; assistance with midwifery was chosen only because all the other alternatives were less attractive—housemaid, factory worker, or student at a *jogakkō;* the village school needed a teacher and asked the informant to take the job; and so on.

Whatever job was taken, there was general concern that it should not draw the woman too far away from the "right track" of womanhood. One can tell this from the kinds of jobs taken—those proper to the female sex (with the exception of professional cookery). This concern was also expressed in the choice of the location of employment: many found a job in the proximity of the natal family so that they would remain under domestic protection or would not lose touch with domesticity. If one had to move away from the natal home, the work situation should replicate a home, and this was why *oyashiki-bōkō* was endorsed by parents. To live alone and work at a factory, for example, would have been the most undesirable choice for a premarital woman. For postwar women, it is often necessary to live away from home for higher education or premarital employment. Still their families try to exert "remote control" by frequent telephone calls or visits.

*Occupational involvement and professionalization.* Regardless of the initial motivation, the new jobs challenged the workers and drove them more and more, in the course of coping with the challenge, toward professionalization. This was particularly true where a woman found herself a pioneer in her job. Without thinking about what was involved, Ayano accepted a job offer to teach in a public nursery school, a new job created for the first such institution in town. A *jogakkō* graduate, she had had no special training; all she knew was that she loved children. She was immediately put in charge of two dozen children. At a loss, she told them simple stories like "Peach Boy," and cried. There was no one to turn to for advice: young male schoolteachers who might have had some ideas were inaccessible under the rule of sex segregation, and older teachers only instructed her to let the children kill time or not to spoil them. As she read a few books on child education, she was horrified at what an incredible responsibility she had undertaken. Now she devoted her time to studying her profession and used her imagination to invent methods and tools for "what people today would call 'audio-visual' education."

Two women, in the course of helping midwives, became interested in the profession, and decided to enroll in schools specializing in midwifery. As far as as they were concerned, they had made an unconditional commitment to the occupation before entering the school. Maki, as soon as she finished her education, opened a clinic as the first licensed midwife in her home village. She had to begin by educating the village women on the idea of sanitation: the use of sanitary cotton, washing bowls, and so on. To visit the patient's house quickly and frequently enough, she became the first woman bicycle rider in the village, where there was no transportation system and no telephone. Experience taught her that each and every woman had a unique body structure and that the textbook instructions thus needed to be adapted each time.

Likewise, Hanayo and Shizuyo both found themselves the first licensed professionals in their respective fields to be employed in the hospitals. Their problem was how to cope with the old unlicensed staff who had been doing the job. Hanayo, a pharmacist, recalled how embarrassed she was to reveal her ignorance in front of an uneducated but experienced nurse. "I felt fire on my face." But she now appreciates the fact that this kind of experience did help her develop real expertise, as college education alone would get one nowhere. Shizuyo, a dietician, immediately realized it would be impossible to apply the theory she had learned at school. She worked in the kitchen with an older woman, her predecessor, who had been preparing meals without any idea of a nutritional plan, and under the supervision of the hospital director's wife and mother. It was only after the national government imposed the minimal criteria for nutrition upon hospitals that specialized expertise became necessary and "supreme authority" was transferred to Shizuyo.

As pioneers, these women had no model to follow and so had to establish themselves as specialists through a combination of their creativity and social sensitivity to what the clients expected of them. It was participatory more than anticipatory socialization, more exploratory than planned, that characterized their learning. Furthermore, they were charged with a sense of mission as pioneers. All of these elements seemed to contribute to the evolutionary process of professionalization.

Even temporary or nonprofessional workers became so involved as to develop pride or to extract satisfaction from their work. Some of the *oyashiki-bōkō* maids, too, by and large felt generously rewarded with training in manners, speech, or "fancy" cooking, and with a high standard of living allowing access to luxurious goods and foods, (such as imported fruits) which were inconceivable in the natal family. The personal attendant to the master might overhear his conversation with his colleagues and thus share the privileged information determining the destiny of the country. One of the maids found herself totally in charge of the household affairs "as if I were the the lady of the house," because the real lady was an actress and paid no attention to housekeeping. Most of them were gratified that the employers became so dependent on and fond of them that they were reluctant to let them go and only did so with an extraordinary amount of farewell pay.

What appeared trivial to outsiders turned out to be important to the worker in maintaining her pride and identity. Being a hotel maid used to demand rigorous training. For Mutsuko, a wartimer, the most challenging task was to climb the stairway carrying single-handedly over her shoulder a stack of individual trays loaded with food. She worked hard to learn this skill until she emerged as the hotel's carrier of the largest number of trays—as many as twelve. At long last she felt she had become a fully qualified maid. Eventually she was promoted to the status of head maid, paid the highest salary, and endowed with the power to supervise all of the maids and to make decisions on work schedules. Kumiko, as a bank clerk, took pride in being the first to get to work in the morning in order to clean the office so that senior colleagues could start working immediately, and felt self-satisfaction in always being ready to answer the phone, serve tea to guests, and so on.

Toshiko began her career as a saleswoman with the trepidation of "a lone sailor about to launch a boat in the vast Pacific Ocean." Untrained, she was sure of one thing: a strong conviction is the key to success. Every day she changed her underwear to feel refreshed, and stopped to bow to every Shinto shrine on her way. Somehow affected by her faith thus nurtured, the customers were unusually receptive to her. She soon topped all of the sales personnel and was given the flattering nickname "Dollar Box," meaning the best salesperson in the company. Her income rose as high as that of any executive, and was more than enough to support her mother and bedridden brother. This was how she overcame the inferiority complex she had held in relation to her "brilliant" elder brother and "beautiful" younger sister.

The geisha apprentice quickly learned a whole repertoire of music and dance, which she loved, by studying all day and every day under different teachers. Wakako was well cared for (unlike many others who were exploited) by the geisha-house mistress, her employer (called "*nee-san*," elder sister), who housed and fed her, as well as by the mistress's nonlegitimate husband (geisha-house mistresses were concubines). After a year's training, she was promoted to the status of *hangyoku*, assistant geisha, with a professional name, Hanachiyo, by which she was to be identified from then on. As a *hangyoku* she was taken by her mistress to every *ozashiki* (parlors or customer rooms of teahouses, hotels, etc.), where she was hired to entertain and danced to the *shamisen* music played by her mistress. It took one-and-a-half more years for Hanachiyo to become *ippon*, a full-fledged geisha able to perform independently. Usually, and most desirably, the *ippon* status was associated with a woman being "fortunate" enough to find a patron and have her own house or shop as his concubine. It was the patron who financed the enormous cost of the ceremony to announce and publicize the woman's new status as *ippon*. Even fifty years ago it cost as much as one thousand yen (roughly five hundred dollars at the prewar rate) to cover the expenses for a whole new wardrobe (in which the promoted geisha made publicity visits to all the geisha houses and teahouses in the area) and for the gifts she took with her on these visits. By the splendor of the wardrobe and the generosity of the gifts one could tell what kind of master the geisha had obtained. This ceremony certainly marked a peak of a geisha's career, and "catching" a good master was a key to her success. Hanachiyo, however, did not have such a master partly because she had been discouraged by her mistress from becoming a concubine. (The mistress herself eventually ran away to put an end to her misery as a concubine.) This meant that the *ippon* ceremony was funded by her mistress and that she continued to live with her.

Thus, Hanachiyo was not a success in the conventional sense, and yet she had her own professional pride. She was widely known among her colleagues and customers as sexually inaccessible, despite that she lacked the patronage of a master. *Mizuten* (literally "tripping without even looking," that is, the geisha who sells sex indiscriminately) or "pillow geisha" were scorned by colleagues. With a wealthy patron, a geisha would be protected from the need of being a *mizuten*.

The geisha's professionalism seems to lie in two kinds of skills. One is, obviously, expertise in the geisha arts of dancing and music. Wakako, formerly Hanachiyo, proudly told of having mastered a wide repertoire so that she had no difficulty in playing and performing whatever a customer demanded. "Look at young geisha today. They say without shame, 'I can't play that.' We were not allowed to be that way." The other skill is to manage the ambivalent role of a geisha—to maintain sexual chastity and autonomy while appearing hospitable to every customer. To be a professional geisha, one needs to master the subtle skill of "slipping" away from a solicitous customer without offending him.

There was something else that made the former Hanachiyo proud of her geisha profession. She was one among about six hundred geisha of the Akasaka district of Tokyo. Akasaka geisha—known as the most refined, elite geisha in the country—could look down upon all other geisha including their neighbors, Shinbashi geisha. According to Wakako, Akasaka's prestige derived (and still does) from its elite clientele, primarily government officials, politicians, and military officers. In the district there was a famous teahouse called Kōyōkan, where highly selected geisha, the best of all Akasaka geisha, were invited. Hanachiyo, together with her mistress, was one of around thirty geisha out of six hundred who were regularly invited.

Around four o'clock we go to Kōyōkan. There we take a bath, do makeup, and get ready by six. Customers begin to arrive one by one. Cabinet ministers are unpunctual, but military officers always come on time, fully

> decorated with golden braids. To kill time until everybody shows up, entertainers such as storytellers and magicians are hired to perform. We geisha entertain the waiting customers by playing *go* and *shōgi* [two kinds of Japanese chess] with them.

She could hear these leaders of Japan loudly and heatedly arguing over national issues, "although we did not understand." Kōyōkan's status was such that even the maids were carefully selected from "good families."

By a sociological standard, my informants varied widely in occupational status, but subjectively they were alike in terms of occupational identification and pride. The bases of their occupational identification can be largely grouped into two classes. One is the acquisition and mastery of *professional expertise* itself, which fulfills one's need for achievement and fosters one's self-confidence. The other refers to the *social relationship* with the employer, co-workers and colleagues, clientele, and the public in general. This is threefold. The worker may, first, enjoy the status or power that her occupation brings her vis-à-vis people involved in the occupation in one capacity or another. To be noted here is the fact that the status or power obtained by a woman tends to be within a group consisting of women only (e.g., the head maid's power over other maids); to be of a backstage kind (the *oyashiki-bōkō* maids power over the employer's household matters); to be vicariously assumed through identification with the high position of one's employer or customers (the Akasaka geisha's elite status coming from the status of their clients). Second, the social relationship involves identification with the community which the worker serves. One may take pride foremost in being useful and indispensable to the welfare of the community through one's occupation; this aspect was emphasized by schoolteachers, kindergarten and nursery teachers, midwives, and health workers. Third, occupational commitment may be a product of mutual respect, trust, and love between the worker and employer, co-worker, or clients.

Overall, the social reward seems very important in encouraging occupational commitment. This was confirmed by the cases of those women who failed to develop an occupational identity. Some were disillusioned, some quit, shifted from one job to another, or hardly got involved, primarily because of social disappointments. Sonoko, a postwar junior high school graduate, quit one job after another because she was disappointed each time by the moral sluggishness of the female employer-teacher or co-workers. Sexually undisciplined women in particular upset her because her father had extramarital affairs and thus served as a countermodel for her. Work peers do not always form a cooperative, friendly team. Ikuko, while she was a hotel maid, was a victim of the jealousy of her female co-workers because, for example, she had a number of regular customers who would always designate her as the room maid to wait upon them (Japanese-style hotels used to assign a maid to a room around the clock). There is a general tendency to criticize female colleagues, more than male colleagues, as jealous, competitive, or mean, precisely because workers of the same sex compete in the same labor market.

Two dropouts from *oyashiki-bōkō* deserve mention. The farmer's daughter who ran away from home to become an *oyashiki* maid found herself hungry all the time because the master's mother was stingy with food. She had to have food sent from home. Besides, the promise of bridal training—the very reason she accepted the job—was never carried out, and she had to clean the house every day and all day. One year later she returned home. The live-in tutor found herself stuck with an unruly, unwilling, and stupid child to teach. She came to the conclusion that to try to educate just one such hopeless child was a waste of her time. She too quit in one year. In both cases we see class-bound injustice. Even in those cases where the workers felt gratified by the generosity of the employers, *oyashiki-bōkō* was more or less accompanied by class resentment. Kuniko was infuriated when she overheard the lady of the house refer to her as *"gejo"*—an old, derogatory term for a maid servant. The same lady refused to respond when addressed as *"oku-san"* instead of the more respectful *"oku-sama."* Despite such pretentiousness, Kuniko further recalled the couple quarreled "as roughly as any lower-class couple." Thus her resentment was mixed with disdain, while, at the same time, she vicariously enjoyed the employer's upper-class status.

Wakako also quit her job mainly because she did not feel like working for a new mistress after her previous mistress withdrew from the geisha world.

Many premarital workers, including some with career occupations, became disengaged from occupational involvement and withdrew temporarily or permanently as they approached the marital stage. This, however, belongs to the topic of the next chapter.

## PEER GROUPING

Life experience at the premarital stage generates intimate friendships primarily with age peers. Peer interaction begins in the neighborhood at preschool age. But most informants, although they did have neighbor playmates, do not recall their identities. The strong, everlasting peer solidarity is associated foremost with school life. Neighbors too are recalled only if they were also schoolmates. Specifically, two or more classmates developed ties through years of co-experience. For a local woman, peer grouping is often based on many years of shared school experiences from primary school through higher schools. The priority of classmating over neighboring for a peer bond is shown by the fact that the girls who chose to go to a distant high school instead of a local one ended up friendless in the neighborhood. This schoolcentric tendency has intensified over the years. The strict age-peer grouping of classmates, coupled with the seemingly rapid sociocultural change, accounts for a strong sense of age gap that even a young adult seems to hold vis-à-vis anybody a few years younger.

*Sexual identity.* The informants who do remember playing with neighbor age-mates describe the play groups as heterosexual. Although there was a degree of sex specialization in playing and games such as playing house for girls, tree climbing for boys, the informants tended to characterize themselves as having been tomboys always mixing with boys and enjoying rough games. Emi, seventy-one, remembers having played with a bunch of boys only. She had to wear a formal kimono to attend her koto lesson, but just to have fun with the boys she would take off the outer garment of her kimono and wrap up her head with the loin cloth. A tomboy also tended to be a *gakidaishō*, boss in the kids' group. For these women, childhood freedom appears associated above all with being unfeminine.

Once in school, girls, as far as old timers were concerned, began to congregate among themselves. For the first few years of primary school classes were heterosexual. Some teachers made special efforts to mix boys and girls through seat arrangement, and they did play together. But from around the third year on, classes were segregated, and cross-sex intimacy was discouraged or teased about. Ayano gave an account of herself, as class vice-president, being paired with a male class president. Classmates teased the two by addressing the boy by the girl's name and vice versa. One day, the boy stopped responding to her call, which was the beginning of her realization that a boy and girl should not be friendly.

Sex segregation became further regimented after primary school graduation. Girls now lived in the world of girls, with the exception of schoolteachers. Young male teachers in girls' high schools were the objects of concentrated attention. Furthermore, some girls found a substitute for heterosexual relationship in intimacy with other girls. This kind of "sisterhood" was illicit, of course, as much as a heterosexual adventure was.

The postwar coeducational system has liberated sex. Heterosexual intimacy in class has become a common phenomenon which no longer arouses curiosity or embarrassment. A postpubescent boy and girl, sitting next to each other, exchange messages of love in notes or diaries, I was told. Particularly generative of heterosexual pairs are extracurricular activities, such as school study tours and after-school preparations for the school's "culture festival." Instead of concealing the information, girls now proudly announce having boyfriends, and let other girls read the love letters they receive. Some of such heterosexual pairs continue or revive intimacy and end up as husband and wife. Despite such legitimate access to boys, however, for the majority of girls, truly intimate peers are exclusive of the opposite sex. The two sexes join for formal group activities such as Christmas parties planned by classes, but more personal co-activities are only among girls. This indicates another aspect of cultural continuity.

Among the prewar/wartimers, the relationship with opposite-sex peers, even when it took the form of sex segregation, contributed toward the establishment of sex identity. The girl's sex identity was further reinforced through menarche. The knowledge of menarche, together with other facts of life, usually circulated among same-sex peers. Rarely was the mother the first source of information. As far as my sample goes, menarche was experienced between ten and sixteen years of age. The later one encountered menarche, the better prepared one was, thanks to the information from "mature" classmates. Even this anticipatory socialization contained a dramatic experience. A woman in her late fifties vividly recalled:

> You know the old-style toilet shows what's inside. I was shocked. I was in the first year of *jogakkō*. For heaven's sake, there you saw blooded cotton. We immature girls exclaimed, "Look, something horrible is here! Somebody must have been seriously injured." Big classmates said nothing, but one of them taught us, "Don't make such scenes. This is what all women have."

Such ignorance and shock are no longer shared by young girls today. Anticipatory socialization is taking place more smoothly and much earlier through media exposure and sex education at school.

The "late" girls and their mothers worried about their normality, waited eagerly for the onset of menstruation, and celebrated its arrival with a *sekihan* (red-bean-mixed rice) meal—symbolic of a happy event—often without telling the male members of the household what was being celebrated. Too "early" girls had their own suffering. They received no sympathy for their monthly problem from their classmates, or worst of all from male gym teachers.

Black panties together with G-strings were worn, and girls were embarrassed at hanging them over a laundry-drying bar. To protect the menstruating girls from conspicuity, some *jogakkō* forced black panties upon all the students. Nowadays, menstruation is much less burdensome due to the widespread use of sanitary belts, napkins, and tampons.

*Social class identity.* Girls began to learn social class distinction between families mainly though peer interaction or peer identification. Groups were formed much along class lines. Hanayo, a naval officer's daughter, observed:

> There were children of peasants, of shopkeepers or of doctors. This group was separated from that group by family backgrounds. People went to the group of their own when they needed help. We still do the same.

Sayo, daughter of a landowner, learned in school that many of her classmates were not available to her as friends because they were to become housemaids after graduation. She does not remember a single *shinheimin* (new commoner, see p. 14) enrolled in her class "probably because they did not bother to send kids to school those days," but does remember a *moraikko* boy who was smart and the top student in class but, once at home, was subordinate to the "stupid" children of the house. One of the biggest events that impressed the idea of class difference upon the children's minds was the choice of a post-primary school course of life. Only those from "good families" went to *jogakkō*. How the lower-class children felt toward the more fortunate children was revealed much later. Sayo learned at a class reunion when she was twenty that one of the boys had been watching the way she left for Tokyo for *jogakkō* education:

> "Everybody was saying," he said, "you are going to Tokyo. An automobile was waiting at the entrance door to take you to H village. To H village I have always walked. And then someone said you were to transfer to another automobile there to go further to O town, and then to take a train to Tokyo. I was watching you from a distance."

This classmate, like many others, was restrained by class barriers to keep his distance from her.

There seemed to be two directions in which, in prewar Japan, the sex variable was affected by the class variable in peer grouping behavior. First, as the last episode suggests, the rule of sex segregation was more rigorous for relatively upper-class women than for lower-class women, and chaperonage was a common practice for the former. Second, a high-class position permitted a woman to transcend her femininity while a lower-class woman had to submit to the rule of feminine inferiority in relation to men. No higher-class girls remember having been bullied by boys as lower-class girls do; on the contrary, they dominated boys, protected other girls from boys' abuse, or even defended poor, helpless boys from other aggressive boys. In short, class contaminated sex in both an inhibitory and an emancipatory direction. Whichever the case, one should note the importance of social class in determining cross-sex interaction. As the children grew older and revived friendships at a class reunion, for example, they discovered themselves free from the class boundary based on natal family background and replaced the old distance with equality and intimacy appropriate to true peers.

The above statement suggests a paradox inherent in peer alignment involved in school affiliation. By being placed in a peer relationship at school, the children became more conscious of their differences in family backgrounds. Yet, at the same time, perhaps at a less conscious level, a sense of equality must have overridden that of class hierarchy. Egalitarianism was encouraged under the Japanese school system with its centralized regimentation throughout the country. Not only was the curriculum basically controlled by the Ministry of Education but material and physical uniformity (e.g., school uniforms, hair styles, stationery, etc.) were enforced by each school upon all the students.

The school-based peer grouping would continue to play a prominent role throughout one's life course, and this is also true with the postwar generation. Discussing boys and girls in general, Chodorow (1974: 57–58) mentions sex difference with reference to peer solidarity and lineal bondage: girls participate in an intergenerational world with their mothers, aunts, and grandmothers, while boys get involved in a single-generation world of age-mates. As far as Japanese women are concerned, school-affiliated peers accompany them like "convoys," as put by Plath (1980). Particularly important is a small group of same-sexed classmates who are ready to respond to calls for intimate, free interaction, as observed by Salamon (1974) among urban executive wives. Such peers may sustain a woman who would be otherwise subjected to the lineal order of the domestic domain. This prospect will be documented where later life stages are dealt with.

In this chapter I have explored the women's experiences at their early life stage primarily as recalled by themselves. Sex polarity was highlighted by the "first-son syndrome," the femininity training that daughters have undergone at home, sex segregation at school, the limited educational opportunity for a daughter in contrast to a son, and the maid-apprenticeship as one of the few accepted options to fill the interval between school graduation and marriage. We have noted that former tomboys later became constrained by the code of feminine modesty. In this respect the sequence of "constraints and options" of the chapter title should be reversed. Indeed the early childhood was recalled in association with total freedom, which meant freedom from femininity.

There is nothing particularly unexpected in this finding. What does surprise us is that the mother image depicted by the daughters was not infrequently a negative one. It turned out that the mother disapproved of by an adult daughter had typically led an easy life made possible by her marriage with a *mukoyōshi* husband. Implicit in the daughter's critique is the idea that a woman should have hardship, preferably under a domineering mother-in-law. Her embarrassment at her *mukoyōshi* father suggests that she, the daughter, wished to have had a strong, manly father. This indicates that socialization was quite successful in instilling the sex-typed role identity and patricentric norm in the daughter's mind.

The same holds for career motivations. Contrary to my expectations, the women who went on to higher education and entered professional careers did so, in most cases, against their wishes or without a clear notion of what they wanted to do. Many were forcibly dragged into that alternative of life course by their fathers, not by their mothers. This, too, shows the depth of the women's internalization of gender identity.

The father's role in determining the daughter's nondomestic career is symbolic of the fact that the Japanese domestic structure did not necessarily support sex dichotomy. The *ie*, while entailing male superiority and role division by sex, also found a son substitute in a daughter and demanded her to transcend her feminine identity.

However successful the sex-role socialization was, many women did not remain adherent to what they had learned earlier. As they were exposed to specialized training and became engaged in one profession or another, they were gradually transformed into firmly committed professionals. This was especially the case with the "pioneer women." Experience rather than the initial motivation opened up the unfolding of potentials.

At this initial stage, we have already encountered the complexity of relationship between structural norms and a woman's self-fulfillment. On the one hand, we have seen how narrowly limited a girl's life options were, how the rigid order of sex polarity frustrated a daughter's aspirations. On the other hand, the same structure turned out to have rescued some women, even against their own wish, from an ordinary female career confined in the domestic realm, and pushed them toward their self-fulfillment through professional commitment.

Similarly, sex segregation, structurally imposed in schools, indeed suppressed the sexual emotions of adolescent girls, involving some with "sisterly love," and made them nostalgic about the heterosexual freedom of preschool days. The same rule of segregation gave rise to the peer solidarity usually based upon same-sexed classmates, which would provide a woman throughout her life with emotional sustenance and a sense of autonomy in counterbalancing another structural order, that is, the vertical pressure of kinship and domestic life.

The postwar change has been noted first with regard to femininity training. The standard of feminine beauty itself has changed from modesty to body exposure, as symbolized by the contrast between the kimono concealing the body contour and the bathing suit to outfit a beauty contestant. This change has taken place, of course, hand in hand with an end to the rule of sex segregation, as brought into effect by the coeducational system. The latter links to another remarkable change, namely, a greater opportunity for higher education. How irreversible these changes are has yet to be examined against the challenge of candidacy for marriage.

# 3
# *Marital Transition*

## Views of Marriage

### THE *IE* AND MARRIAGE

Marriage, conceived within the framework of the traditional social structure, is necessary for the maintenance of the *ie* (p. 20). First, from the point of view of the household, marriage is a way of recruiting the personnel to occupy key positions in it. As a bride, a young woman is to fill the position of *shufu*, house mistress, whereas the bridegroom is to take the position of *shujin*, the house master. If the household runs a business of its own and must mobilize its entire labor force, the incoming spouse will be counted upon as an additional worker. Second, from the point of view of the stem-family structure, the *yome* (bride or daughter-in-law) or *muko* (groom or son-in-law) is needed as the successor to the mother- or father-in-law to take over her or his responsibility immediately or later. This view of marriage ties in with Kitaoji's (1971) delineation of the Japanese family in light of "positional" succession. The imperative of positional succession further involves securing the offspring as a blood-linked successor for the next generation; marriage is, then, foremost a means for procreation. Eligibility for marriage is, from this point of view, measured by the candidate's aptitude and competence—physical and mental—to perform these responsibilities. Entailed in the function of procreation in particular is the uncertainty of the status of a spouse, particularly a wife, until her fertility is proved. Less crucial than the above function in most cases and yet possibly more important in some cases is the instrumentality of marriage to the formation of a desirable alliance between the two *ie* involved. By giving and receiving a bride or bridegroom, the two families become *shinseki* to each other and expect thereby to benefit from this bond. This is a common theme of the politically engineered marriage among the elite class observable in modern as well as feudal Japan.

## THE LIFE CYCLE AND MARRIAGE

Marriage can also be viewed in the light of the individual's life cycle as a key stage which the Japanese believe everyone must go through. Everyone must, because marriage is a necessary, if not sufficient, condition for making one an adult *(ichininmae)* and a human being in the full sense of the term. It appears that the Japanese see in marriage not only the culturally prescribed norms and obligations as implied above in connection with the institution of *ie* but also the natural unfolding of human existence. I remember, at an international gathering of scholars, a Japanese professor asking a middle-aged American scholar, apparently to the latter's annoyance, why he was unmarried. "It is inhuman not to marry," commented the Japanese.

This view of marriage is imposed more heavily upon women, so much so that a woman without marital experience is considered deprived of meaning in her life, whereas men are seen as able to enjoy their lives at least through their work. A government survey (Naikaku Sōridaijin Kanbō Kohōshitsu—hereafter, NSKK—1973:83) indicates that the majority of the female respondents, in answer to the question "Why is marriage desirable?" selected one of three alternatives in this order of frequency: "Marriage brings happiness for women." "Marriage is something to be taken for granted." "Marriage gives mental stability."

Women must marry and do so at the right time, or during the period called *tekireiki*, marriageable age, which according to the above survey (p. 89) is around twenty-two to twenty-five years of age. External pressures for a girl of marriageable age to marry could be undisguised. A middle-aged woman in the neighborhood may ask the girl how old she is, and warn, "So, it's time you married." Subtle pressure may come from her mother, who devotes herself to sewing a wardrobe of many sets of kimono obviously for the daughter to take with her as a dowry. The most devastating is to witness one's peers, especially the closest classmates, marry one after another.

Throughout my fieldwork in Shizumi, I failed to encounter even one woman who was proud of being single or ideologically committed to staying unmarried. However, younger women, as represented by our future-autobiographers, project another view of marriage. As expected, more female (76 percent) than male (57 percent) students refer to marriage as a life stage, but 21 percent of the girls who mention marriage deny a married life to themselves while only one of the male counterparts does so. Two of these girls opt for suicide, and the rest want to remain unmarried as a matter of principle with the apprehension or conviction that marriage will thwart their pursuit of a career or freedom. Moreover, more girls, even when they choose to marry, tend to see troubles in the marriage, and more boys project marital satisfaction.

Should these findings be interpreted as a sign of change in views of marriage? Do they merely reflect young girls' fantasies having little to do with their projected reality? Another possible interpretation is that, without the pressure of urgency, young girls are freer to announce their principle of celibacy or to see marriage as "the end of a life." Indeed, women below the marriageable age, particularly those who enjoy their occupations, tend to see options other than marriage for their future. But, once over twenty-five, marriage becomes an unconditional necessity. A twenty-eight-year-old single woman, like her classmates also unmarried, confessed she is eager to marry even though she does not expect marriage to be a happy experience. A woman unmarried beyond the marriageable age is a source of gossip for neighbors. "But that's understandable," said a twenty-eight-year-old single woman in a group interview with college graduates. "We too gossip about anybody older than we are." The group voiced agreement. For the woman and her family the situation is a cause of embarrassment.

Akemi, one of the three unmarried women in the sample, is forty-five years old and a victim of the mother's irritability, stimulated by the neighbors' gossip. The daughter's life is incomplete without marriage, but the gossip goes still further: she cannot marry because there is something wrong with her. The totally groundless rumor that upset the mother and daughter most is that she has enuresis nocturna. The suspicion of physical abnormality is the very reason why another woman of twenty-seven, Hamako's eldest daughter, is thinking of marrying with the proviso that immediate divorce shall take place. She hates the idea of marriage, but feels compelled to marry once so that she can demonstrate her physical normality. Given this cultural climate, it is also understandable that late marriage can cause exaggerated excitement. While I was in the field, a fifty-year-old woman became engaged and this news was quickly circulated and drew excited congratulations from many people—kin, friends, and others in remote areas—who until then had not bothered to contact her. Their congratulatory remarks, though well intentioned, bluntly conveyed the belief that the woman had become a normal human at long last.

## Candidacy

Premarital training in the family and schools was aimed, as we have seen, primarily at molding girls into future "good wives and wise mothers." One of the conventional verbal sanctions against deviancy was: "If you act like that, you will not be wanted as a bride." As a woman approached the marriageable age, she was driven into the marriage market by internal as well as external pressures.

AVAILABILITY

It was first necessary to become available as a marriage candidate in the eyes of possible suitors or matchmakers. A concerned mother or other relative would circulate copies of the daughter's picture as a definite sign of availability. Some of my informants claimed that such a candidacy picture was sent to a future husband without their knowledge.

Availability did not necessarily mean visibility. In fact, the younger and more qualified in age the candidate was, the more sheltered she was supposed to be to signal her availability. Overexposure to the nondomestic world made a woman undesirable as a spouse, and was even taken as a sign of unavailability. Involvement with a career occupation would alienate a possible suitor or mediator as much as would unrestrained circulation in the male world. This explains why the majority of the premarital women in the sample stayed home either as assistant housekeepers or helpers with household occupations, worked where they could commute from home or, if working away from home, returned home as they matured into marriageable age in order to restore domesticity before it was too late. Yaeko, a wartimer and trained beautician, was working at the parlor of a *senpai* (senior graduate) from her alma mater, but seeing her co-workers quitting one after another, she too decided to go home. She gave a retrospective explanation for why she quit after only six months of work: it was the period when chauvinists attacked the permanent wave as being a sign of a traitor. "That may have been why, as I look back." Also she said: "I must start to prepare for marriage, I thought. If I continue to work like this, I worried, nobody will want me as a bride." She was still twenty. It was four years before she finally got married, during which time she stayed with her natal family. Sachi, a prewar-timer and live-in cook who moved from one place to another, caused her family and kinfolk to worry that she was "running around" by herself. "In those days people would speak ill of a woman like that. They thought she was having a wild life, mingling with menfolk." She succumbed to family pressure and returned home to accept a marriage proposal (her *hinoeuma* birth turned out to be surmountable after all). Wakako returned home from the geisha house at eighteen to prepare for a proposed marriage with a second cousin. Once she was back home, her father reinstated his authority to remold her into a "lay" woman, and prohibited her from being out at night without the mother as a chaperone.

Fukiko, still unmarried at forty-nine, exemplifies how a woman may squeeze herself out of the marriage market. Having graduated from *kōshō* during the war, she found a clerical job at a naval technology institute. After the war she worked as a maid at a hotel commandeered by the Occupation forces and inhabited by families of American servicemen. The situation changed radically when she switched to a job on an American base, which necessitated her departure from home. Until then she had always commuted. She accepted the job offer, overruling her family's objection. She worked, first, as a housemaid for one family after another, and then as a PX clerk. Meanwhile, she had dates with GIs and fell in love with a sergeant. The couple became engaged, but before they applied for a marriage license, the boyfriend was sent back to the United States. He continued to write to her for a while, but then stopped. "Somehow nothing came of it. Why? I don't know." Deeply hurt, she was at a loss for a long time thereafter. Although she had more dates, she never found herself as involved and became resigned to remaining unmarried for life. Once she lost hope of marriage, the American base suddenly struck her as being an alien country where she would remain rootless. After twenty years of work there, she returned to her hometown, Shizumi.

The subjective explanation for her being unmarried seems to be that her amorous energy had been exhausted on the sergeant, who unfortunately stopped reciprocating. Indeed, her identification with an American(s) is evidenced by a dream she still has—a nightmare of an air raid scene from which she is running, holding hands with an American. The dream associates the American both with the aggressor (in the air raid) and with the supporter, and the dreamer is both victim and ally. The woman's identification with American friends is justifiably an ambivalent one, but the interesting thing is that no Japanese appears in this dream. Her energy exhaustion on the American sergeant means, I think, that all other males, including Japanese, have ceased to appeal to her as possible mates.

An objective explanation may be offered as well. Fukiko excluded herself from the conventional marriage market by overexposure to the predominantly male world away from the home base, and, even more seriously, by exposure to the exclusively American world. She was out of circulation in the Japanese market not only because she was inaccessible to Japanese suitors or mediators but because her intimate contact with American males ruled her out as a desirable wife. Intercultural exposure like this was not necessarily associated with sexual laxity, but it was believed, at least until very recently, to undermine traditional virtues including the expected feminine compliance or endurance. Furthermore, Fukiko and her generation happened to have matured at the time when both marriage and job markets were constricted: many males some years older had been drafted, killed, or were yet to repatriate; jobs were open only in the military area—first Japanese and then American.

Attendance at a school for bridal training was and is a positive signal of availability. Some of the women—including the beautician, who had had no chance before—began to attend one of these schools just before they married. Bridal school attendance, therefore, may have a double purpose: to obtain the training itself, and to display one's marital candidacy. For an upper-class (by the local standard) daughter like Sayo, even bridal school attendance required chaperonage. This was not so much from the concern about a male's access to her as with an intent to display her premarital chastity and, thus, her qualification as a bridal candidate.

All this implies that availability was communicated through a mediator rather than through direct contact between woman and man. Even a bridal school did not reveal a candidate to a male audience directly, but only to possible mediators including the female instructor. The marriage market was not totally controlled by mediators, however. Some women had contact with male candidates without mediation. This was true more with younger informants, and those who could not afford or did not have to be sheltered for economic or professional reasons, as will be shown below.

## SOCIAL NETWORK

Access to a spouse was obtained through activation of a social network within which a mediator or a candidate happened to find her/himself. A mediator here means anybody who participates in linking two individuals as husband and wife, either by taking the initiative or by passively transmitting a message from one person to another. Two or more mediators may be involved for one match, thus forming a chain of links between the two principals. The social network may include relationships that have always been active or that had been forgotten and then rekindled in conjunction with the marriage candidacy.

Several kinds of relationships were found to constitute basic units of such a network. The first and most frequently mentioned was *kinship*. It was the father or older brother who took the most active role as mediator. They were followed by the mother, sister, uncle, aunt, or cousin in a more passive capacity. A long chain of kin could be involved, such as the candidate's "sister's husband's aunt's husband," although actual initiative was likely to be taken by one or two kin at the end of the chain. Kinship may connect not only a candidate with a mediator or one mediator with another but the two principals themselves. In my sample, I found three instances of first cousin marriage and four of more distant kin marriage. There seems to be neither special preference for nor aversion to marriage with a cousin either on the paternal or maternal side. Some cases of cousin marriage involved the woman's compliance with the parents against her personal inclination, and in some others the woman's own decision overruled the parental objections.

Coupled with kinship was a second type of relationship, *friendship*, which largely involved age peers from the same school. For instance, a man and woman became husband and wife through the friendship of their fathers, who had been classmates, or a woman was introduced to her brother's classmate. Wartime friendship between soldiers in the same squadron could also determine the destiny of a woman's marital career. A local woman had to marry her brother's wartime buddy because he had promised to "give" her as a consummation of their brotherhood. Again, friendship may connect two principals directly. My sample includes two pairs of former classmates, and one couple of dating college students who are in a younger age bracket.

A third important relationship was embedded in *employment*. Here we find co-workers, colleagues, employer-employee, or boss-subordinate in a chain of mediation or in direct contact. Five secretarial or clerical workers found marriage mates among higher-ranking co-workers, and one was "lucky" enough to marry the manager of a firm where she was hired as a clerk. Most notable in the interlocking between marriage and employment was the case of schoolteachers. It appears that schoolteachers have had a tradition of marrying among themselves and that marriage has often taken place between teachers on the same campus. In a group interview with female teachers at a primary school of Shizumi, it was claimed that "many couples" had been "born" from this school. My sample includes two cases of such marriage. The role of mediator was crucial if the candidates taught in different schools. (In the prewar era the occupational burden of a schoolteacher as a moral example for pupils necessitated a mediator even when the two saw each other every day in the same school.) Colleagues might volunteer to mediate, but more important was the school principal, who considered himself responsible. Fusa and her husband, both teachers, were introduced to each other through an arrangement by two principals, one at her school, the other at his. It seems that schoolteachers have enjoyed relative equality between the sexes based on a shared occupation.

Less frequently, a fourth kind, the *neighborhood* relationship, made candidates or mediators accessible to one another. A midwife married a fellow-villager in her neighborhood. Living in the same community, two prospects may have seen each other with no thought of marriage in mind, but after a marriage proposal was made, through a chain of kinship and friendship for instance, they might begin to look at each other in a totally different light. In any event, marriage between neighbors is reminiscent of the village endogamy which used to be customary among peasants.

Lastly, marital opportunity might have been opened up through *clientage*. Examples include a customer of the candidate's natal family business, and a private tutor for the candidate in preparation for a college entrance examination. Clientage and neighborhood combined in the case of Suzuko. She dropped by a snack bar for a soft drink to find that it was run by a former neighbor. Surprised, the latter welcomed her and asked her age, which triggered a whole process of matchmaking.

In the contemporary scene, the network seems to rely increasingly upon employment and friendship, and less upon kinship and neighborhood. Moreover, one witnesses the role of the matchmaker being taken over by private or public agents specializing in matchmaking. During my fieldwork, the Shizumi government opened a marriage counseling office that served as a mediator.

## Structural Constraints

Naturally, there are many variables involved in selecting a mate in addition to his or her aptitude and competence to assume the role of a spouse. Here we shall discuss two such variables which have to be considered at the stage of candidacy.

*The stem family structure.* One was the stem family structure, involving residence and succession, that determined the individual's marital option. Generally, residence and succession were inseparable. If neither the groom nor the bride was successor to the natal house, the couple was free to establish a neolocal house. But if one was a successor, the union by necessity was asymmetrical; the other not only could not be a successor but had to move to live with the spouse's family. The first question that the woman or her family was likely to raise about a proposal was whether the groom-to-be was *atotori* (successor), and if so, how many in-laws of what type the bride would have to live with. A large family thus handicapped a successor as a prospect in the eyes of a female candidate. We have cases where women or their parents resisted or turned down marriage proposals primarily because there were "too many relatives."

The liability of being a successor applied to a reverse case also. If the daughter was *atotori*, she would have a *mukoyōshi* marriage and have to accept this status as a liability in the marriage market. This status was more of a liability for her than for a male heir because of the ideological bias for patrilineality. As acceptance of such a disadvantageous status could not be achieved overnight, the *atotori* identity had to be internalized through careful socialization from childhood on. Probably as a result of successful socialization, none of the six *atotori* women in my sample questioned her obligation to have an uxorilocal, *mukoyōshi* marriage. On the other hand, in two other cases where the daughter was considered a possible *atotori* (in one case it was because the elder brother turned out to be a playboy and thus was disqualified in the eyes of the parents), the idea was rejected unambiguously. This suggests that a woman's *atotori* status, if it was a matter of choice or late development rather than predetermined destiny, tended to be repelled.

While preference for patrilineality existed prior to the Meiji era, particularly in the upper class, its preponderance among common people seems to be a more recent phenomenon (p. 21). Older informants recall the prevalence of succession by the oldest child regardless of sex. Fusa, born in 1900 (the thirty-third year of Meiji), said: "In those days, if you were the first-born daughter, it was customary that you succeed the *ie* even if you had a brother. It was long after the Meiji Restoration that it became the male line only." She herself, as the first born, was nominated as *atotori*, and her parents were adamant on this decision even when a younger brother was born.[1] This custom worked only if there were enough candidates for *mukoyōshi*. Fusa underscored this point when she said: "In those days, even the wealthiest families tried to get all the younger sons married out as *muko*." Nevertheless, the patrilineal value must have eventually permeated all classes and Fusa's own thinking as well. She was embarrassed to say that her mother too was a *mukotori* (*mukoyōshi* taker). Furthermore, Fusa knew that it would not be easy to find a man who would come to her house because, "We were a big family—many siblings, our parents, and grandparents—and we were not rich."

*Mukoyōshi* marriage usually went hand in hand with daughter succession and uxorilocal residence, but not necessarily so. A daughter, even though she was not *atotori*, might become a *muko* taker and live in a neolocal house as part of her *dōzoku*. This is what is called *musume bunke*, daughter branch house, carrying the name of the *honke* (main house), namely, the wife's natal house, into which the husband must be incorporated. Sayo had such a marriage "probably because my family thought I wouldn't be able to carry out the duties of a *yome* [daughter-in-law]." Also, her older brother was attached to her and wanted to keep her within a few blocks of his house. Yoko was a temporary *atotori*. She married her *mukoyōshi* husband and lived with her parents until her younger brother grew old enough to take over the household responsibility, whereupon she and her husband were allowed to establish a *bunke* nearby. Both women came from wealthy families.

It is interesting to find that partners in *mukoyōshi* marriage are overrepresented among schoolteachers: among the seven such couples (including the daughter branch house), three husbands and four wives were schoolteachers, including two couples where both partners were teachers. It was noted previously that a daughter destined to marry a *mukoyōshi* tended to be well educated. This may have resulted in her taking a teaching job, one of the few respectable occupations for women. As a schoolteacher, she had a greater opportunity to marry a colleague.

Uxorilocal residence did not always entail *mukoyōshi* marriage any more than the latter does the former. My sample includes a couple who lives in the woman's natal house with her widowed mother without the husband assuming the wife's name. Such separation between residence and succession is coming into vogue, and more and more daughters are bringing their husbands into their natal house without imposing a *mukoyōshi* stigma on them.

The greater part of the above discussion underlines the general desirability of neolocal residence with a nonsuccessor husband. However, it was discovered that this was not always the case. Virilocal residence with the successor husband was sometimes considered to have advantages that more than compensated for the price the bride had to pay. The inheritance of the bulk of the property from the husband's parents was the most notable advantage. The main reason why Tsuruko found her family opposed to the man of her choice was because he was a second son. Several informants, married to nonsuccessors, expressed resentment over their deprivation and the monopoly of the inheritance by the main houses. In addition to their material plight, the younger sons' wives might have had to take a secondary position vis-à-vis the successor sons' wives, subject to their authority if these two lived in proximity. (This point will be detailed more in the next chapter where pertinent.) Suffice it to note that the status of a successor's wife was not prized by herself but only envied by a nonsuccessor's wife, probably in much the same way as "the grass always looks greener in the next pasture."

*Ethnicity and class*. Probably the most insurmountable barrier which constrained the marriage market was the ethnic barrier. As far as my informants were concerned, it was inconceivable for them to marry a non-Japanese. This ethnocentrism was and still is more rigid toward non-European than European foreigners. It may be mentioned in passing that two male future-autobiographers projected marriages with American women. The second most rigid barrier was that of class, especially of ascribed family status. The outcast status, above all, was a constraint which, in the prejudiced mind of an average Japanese, combined class with alleged ethnicity. While endogamy prevailed, crossing this barrier was a conceivable possibility to the local informants. I was told that the inspection of a candidate through a hired detective—a common practice—was primarily to discern his or her outcast ancestry. Such inspection would be necessary, I was further informed, only if the candidate was a *yosomono*, outsider. Crossing did take place, but at a price. A sixty-seven-year-old informant referred to a neighbor woman whose marriage was strongly resisted by the groom's family and *dōzoku* because of her *shinheimin* status. Marriage did take place nonetheless. "She must be glad," said the informant, "to have raised her status by marrying a son of a regular family," one belonging to a locally established *dōzoku*. The husband was physically handicapped, and it was the wife who supported the family.

I was often warned that one should not use discriminatory words like *eta, burakumin, shinheimin,* and the like when referring to former outcasts. Many Japanese have declared to me that they have no prejudice, and that such people no longer exist. But when it comes to marriage, the old prejudice dies hard. This persistence is strange in view of the local consensus that the former *shinheimin* are generally more wealthy than the rest of the local residents. It should be noted, however, that the content of the stigma is changing: no longer associated with pollution, the former outcasts are feared and avoided as "troublemakers" allegedly taking advantage of their group power to force their demands on the majority. This change may be a sign of eventual dissolution of this particular class barrier, but for the time being they seem to remain caught in a dilemma where their visibility in the public arena as active participants in the liberation movement perpetuates, if not intensifies, prejudice in the private, covert domain where marriage is involved.

## Proposals and Reactions

Our informants, in the course of circulation in the marriage market, encountered marriage proposals. Let us look at how a proposal was made, considered, accepted, or rejected.

MEDIATED PROPOSALS: COMPLIANCE AND AUTONOMY

First, we find a great majority of proposals to have involved mediation by a third person, whether a relative or nonrelative, who happened to be in the social network delineated above. We further discover that the mediated proposals encompassed a number of widely varying patterns. In connection with this point one should note that, given this variety, mediated marriage was not necessarily identical to the *miai* marriage, although the latter is often translated as "arranged marriage." Nor were *miai* marriage and *ren'ai* (love) marriage mutually exclusive. Reality was more complicated than such a dichotomy, as has been perceived by Blood (1967), and confirmed in my previous paper (Lebra 1978). All the observed (recalled, more correctly) reactions to the proposals which involved mediation in one way or another are classified into the following four types along the compliance-versus-autonomy variable.

*Unquestioned compliance.* This first type appeared where the female candidate accepted the proposal out of total compliance with the mediator. This was an extreme case of 100 percent compliance and zero autonomy on the part of the proposal recipient. We have five women, all but one in their seventies, falling into this type. For Sayo, it was her elder brother who went to meet her future husband and was favorably impressed. The brother then told her to marry the man, because "a man he liked could not be bad for me." It never occurred to her that she too must check on him, or that such matters should be within her jurisdiction. She never doubted her brother's good judgment. To comply was a woman's way, she thought. Until the very day of the wedding ceremony, Sayo had no glimpse of her husband-to-be, not even his picture. Another example: the mother decided to marry her daughter to an employee of the house business, turning down all other proposals. "Being old-fashioned, I could not say no, if they told me, 'Marry this man.' " So Yone married the man, though she had no particular reason to like him. In a third case, the mother had arranged a marriage for the daughter long before the latter knew about it. "So nothing could be done," said Ai, "no matter whether I liked him or not." The forcefulness of the mother in the last two cases seems to have derived from her being widowed and thus responsible for the children's marriages. Another case involved a foster mother to whom the candidate felt indebted, so much so that it never occurred to her to resist the mother's proposal for her to marry her relative. In this type one finds the clearest evidence of success in compliance training throughout childhood.

*Coercive compliance.* Four other women, younger on the average than the women mentioned above, finally accepted the proposal under the condition of coercive compliance. Unlike the first type, this involved some autonomy on the part of the woman in that she resisted and even strongly protested, only to be defeated by the mediator. At eighteen, Yuri was forced to come home from Tokyo, where she was expecting to enroll in a school, and to marry a man of her brother's choice. She expressed her protest by crying. The brother overruled not only the sister's reluctance but also the parents' objection that the groom's family had too many in-laws—as many as ten—including the mother-in-law whose meanness was well known among the neighbors. (This is one of several instances where the brother's authority exceeded the father's. This often happened when there was a wide age gap between brother and sister and when the father was too old to exercise his authority. Given the much shorter life expectancy and a longer period of fertility in prewar days, one may suspect that there were as many cases of fratriarchy as of patriarchy, particularly if we add the instances of *mukoyōshi* fathers.) The brother's insistence was due to the fact that the proposal came from a *shinseki*—the brother's wife's mother's sister's grandson. I was often told that a proposal from *shinseki* was hard to turn down.

Motoko objected to the idea of marrying a man she had never met, but the father would not relent, insisting that no parent could possibly choose anybody undesirable. She reluctantly complied, not because she trusted her father but "because he would have gotten angry with me otherwise." Fumie resented the offhanded as well as unilateral manner in which her marriage was arranged. There was a proposal for her, and her father took a trip to inspect the prospect and his family, but on the way he stopped at his nephew's house overnight. Learning of the purpose of his journey, the nephew's wife proposed: "Why don't you give her to *us* instead?" "Oh, you mean it? Okay, let's do so," agreed the father without a second thought. Fumie was not opposed to her husband-to-be, but to the way her father handled it. The mother was at a loss, torn between her stubborn husband and her rebelling daughter, but persuaded Motoko to comply first and to come home if the match turned out to be a mistake.

Mutsuko was more adamant in her protest. A farmer's daughter, she had ruled out farmers and fishermen as prospects, but a proposal came from a fisherman. "God damn! I hated it, I hated it. I cut my long hair short and got a permanent," which of course infuriated her father, who had already promised to "give" her to the fisherman. On the day the matchmaker came to her house to meet her, she was still working as a live-in hotel maid. The family finally called the employer, who then asked her to go home "because your dad scares me." She had no choice but to go and serve tea to the matchmaker. She did so with her maid's apron on instead of being more formally dressed as required by the occasion.

These four cases show increasing degrees of resistance and autonomy. All ended in compliance, but the degree of resistance corresponded to a decrease in the informants' age from the seventies to the fifties.

In the total sample there are six women who never had a chance to see their grooms prior to the wedding, and all except one were found to belong to one of these two types: unquestioned compliance or coercive compliance.[2]

*Rationalized consent.* Many more women persuaded themselves, in response to a mediated proposal, to go along with the mediator on the basis of some rationale. The rationale largely involved the woman's recognition, in one way or another, of her liability. First, many informants referred to what might be termed *timing* as a persuasive rationale. Particularly important was the candidate's age. Harue had rejected a series of proposals until she passed the age of twenty-five. Her father, in tears, persuaded her to accept the last proposal, warning that unless she compromised at a reasonable level she would soon be too old. She agreed.

The idea of *tekireiki* (marriageable age) thus limited women's bargaining power. Kumiko, who also married at twenty-five, quoted a tea ceremony instructor's counsel that where marriage is concerned a woman must retract one demand for each year she adds to her age. In such a marital strategy, twenty-five seems to be a turning point. The marriage age for my informants ranges from eighteen to forty-three, and concentrates between nineteen and twenty-six, but those who married at twenty-five or twenty-six tended to mention age as a factor pressing them to accept the proposal. This sense of urgency would in a few years turn to despair. Masako, passing *tekireiki*, moved to Manchuria and worked as a bank employee. Her father asked her employer, his friend, to find someone for her since she was overage. This resulted in her marriage with a bank customer. She was thirty. Age is still a sensitive topic for this couple—it was revealed by the husband in an interview that she is four years his senior. I was surprised to learn that he did not know this until after they had married.

Urgency for matrimony because of the woman's age was compounded by her senior sib-rank. If the woman was the eldest of many siblings, she would practically be pushed out of the house to marry in order to vacate the seat of marital candidate for younger siblings, as convention prescribed the sequence of marriages according to sib-rank order. Pressure was also heavy, regardless of sib-rank, if an *atotori* (successor) brother was at a marriageable age, because an unmarried sister hanging around reduced his chances of attracting prospects. This was how Yumiko felt when her older brother received a marriage proposal, and she agreed to marry a man for whom she had no feeling.

Besides timing, there were other factors which made the women more agreeable to a mediated proposal. We have already mentioned the *structural constraint* which handicapped some women in the marriage market, namely, the status of successor daughter destined for *mukoyōshi* marriage. Two such women were involved in emotional affairs (too rudimentary to be called love affairs) with men, but were fully aware that marriage had nothing to do with likes and dislikes because theirs was not ordinary *yome-iri* (the bride's entry into the groom's house) but *muko-tori* (taking the groom into the bride's house). Neither was in any position to reject a mediated proposal in favor of her personal choice.

The *socioeconomic status* of the prospect is another basis for self-persuasion. A physician and graduate from the "highest" educational institution was accepted because of his obvious prestige. Also, a daughter from a poor family was agreeable because the groom was a candy wholesaler who owned a store right on a main street in Yokohama. Similarly, a schoolteacher was accepted because the woman had always wished to have a "salaryman"-type of a family (with the househead being employed with a secure monthly salary) instead of a commercial family like her own. Some cases indicated values affected by the war. Hiroe, who adored soldiers, had no objection to a proposal from an army officer and married in the midst of war. Escaping from Tokyo because of air raids to settle down in Shizumi, but still starving, *jogak-kō*-educated Hamako agreed to marry a primary school-educated country cousin "because in those days farmers were best off, with enough to eat." To be noted here is not just the desirability of the socioeconomic status but the proper balance between the two families concerned. A woman had to give up her love for a man because both families objected to the match on grounds of status imbalance: his family, being wealthy, wanted to take a bride from a more "honorable" family while her family foresaw that this match would make life hard for her.

All these examples suggest that the consent for marriage was given for an extrinsic reason—extrinsic to the person of the groom. Extraneousness went to its extreme in the case of Sonoko who "jumped" at the proposal from a commercial boat crewman. She did not want to marry a man like her father who would stay home all the time; she was determined, she said, to marry a sailor who would have to stay away from home for lengthy periods of time. After learning of the groom's occupation, she asked no other questions.

Some informants indicated a rationale which reflects the general view in Japan of marriage in association with human normality: a proposal was accepted by some at least partly because marriage was a necessary way to provide *proof of femininity*. This was particularly important for the *hinoeuma* woman who entered the culinary profession. The proposal was from her cousin's friend. Pressured by her brother, Sachi said: "You all make so much fuss about me, about my working among men, not being like a woman, and so forth. All right, I *will* marry."

Obviously, she was irritated by the family's overconcern, and in protest she complied—a strange but culturally understandable twist of behavior, namely, a masochistic compliance as a demonstration of recalcitrance. Underlying this behavior must have been the ambiguity of her sexual identity.

I could add a long list of other rationales as extraneous as the above, but it will suffice to mention just a few more. The *location of the domicile* was important in some cases: marrying a Shizumi man, for example, was desirable since it was a nice place to live. Also, a proposal was accepted as a *counteralternative* to enable one to avoid the other, less attractive but necessary alternative: a bus company clerk agreed to marry a fish broker because the only other alternative would have been to marry a bus driver who was less educated than she was. In one case no definite reply was given to a proposal for more than a year, and this passage of time caused a reluctant woman to owe a positive answer as a matter of *accumulated debt.*

Rarely did a rationale appear singly, but usually in some combination. Fuyuko received many proposals "because" she said, "I am a hard worker." They were rejected by her father and stepmother however. Finally a choice was made for the following reasons, which Fuyuko attributes to her parents but partially with her consent: the groom's house was located in the neighborhood so that she could visit her natal house every day to continue to work as a seamstress for the family shop; she was getting old, and the stepmother worried that people might criticize her for keeping the stepdaughter from marrying. The groom being a son of the father's friend, the father was convinced that his friend's son could not be a bad choice (judging a prospect by his or her parents was indeed a common pattern). Fuyuko also thought: "Once married, people will know I am not handicapped. If things go wrong, I'll come back, I decided in an easygoing manner. Since it's my parents' idea, I can come home easily too."

*Controlled choice.* While the rationalized consent referred to an exercise of autonomy on the part of the principal woman in agreeing with the mediator for some extrinsic reasons, the fourth type involved a stronger autonomy in choosing a prospect for an intrinsic reason, although a mediator still played a role. Two principals were introduced by a mediator(s), but in the course of subsequent interaction, they came to like each other. By the time of the wedding, the informants were not sure that it was a *miai* marriage. Whereas the first three types clearly exclude love, one finds here a mixture of *miai* and *ren'ai*, confounding to a survey researcher who has this dichotomy in mind.

It was when Sakiko was still a university freshman in Tokyo that a proposal was received through a chain of mediators—the landlady and her husband, the latter's brother, who is the prospect's father, and Sakiko's parents. Her father was not eager, but her mother was because "marriage makes women happy." Meanwhile, one of her schoolmates, an amateur palmist, had divined that her engagement would be imminent and would involve a wonderful man. Under the spell of suggestibility, she vacillated between yes and no every day until, finally, the prospect came to see her for the first time. Once they started to talk, he struck her as being "the type I like," sharing the same interests with her. They married within two months.

Controlled choice includes many of those women who came into contact with their future spouses directly and were even courted, and yet the choice was "controlled" in that commitment was made only after mediation by a third party, if only as a matter of formality, sanctioned the relationship. Yasu, then a schoolteacher, was courted face to face by her colleague, but "I was stubborn, and told him to come back through a proper channel [*suji*]." He did so by having a mediator visit her parents. A clerk at a stock firm was approached by her boss, the firm's manager, through a tea servant as an informal mediator. " 'My parents are very fussy,' I said, 'so please talk to them first.' " The wealthy suitor took the woman in his Packard to visit her parents and stunned the country folks who had never seen a foreign car. It was 1918.

Prewar courtship often involved "love letters" to avoid the embarrassment of direct confession. Ayano, the then nursery schoolteacher, received a love letter from a teacher at the school which housed the nursery. Sharing the same teachers' office—there being only one large room for all the staff in a Japanese school—she had been seeing him every day but did not have the courage to talk to a young man like him. Astonished, Ayano showed the love letter to her mother. Meanwhile, its author conveyed his wish to his parents, who, thereupon, went over to ask her parents to give their approval.

All the above cases met ready approval from the parents on both sides, but Tsuruko had to surmount her family's objections. She came to know a customer of her family's shop during his vacation from the university, and soon found herself in love. Paying no attention to countless proposals, she continued to exchange letters with the lover, but her father (a widower) and grandmother were determined to bless her with another man who already owned his own shop. Then came her lover's uncle as a formal matchmaker to entreat the objectors to relent. It was only after the uncle repeated his visit many times that the family gave its reluctant approval. The principals waited patiently, showing no sign of rebellion. Such patience may have stemmed from the conventional wisdom that unresolved resistance on the part of either family might prove detrimental to a truly successful marriage. A bank clerk was approached by a superior, and the latter's interest in her was simultaneously conveyed by the chairman of the bank's board to the suitor's family. The family, though unable to overrule the match openly because of the mediator's position, was actually opposed to it because of the status imbalance between the two families. The two married, but the fact that the marriage was not really blessed by his family was to continue to upset her.

As these cases suggest, mediation preceded, went hand in hand with, or followed courtship. Often it happened that, when a young man and woman appeared interested in each other or simply well matched, the people around them went into action as unsolicited mediators to "help" the couple. The group interview with schoolteachers revealed that colleagues would support such a couple by contriving an opportunity for them to be alone, and by teasing them with good wishes. The basic premise was that a young man and woman were too shy to communicate directly with each other.

This kind of supposedly "empathetic" mediation might go too far —so far that the affair could end up out of the principals' hands. A twenty-year-old secretary is a case in point. A man "one cycle" (twelve years in the Chinese zodiac system) older and employed in the same place organized a group of co-workers for the purpose of getting together regularly to read books—a common phenomenon reflecting the Japanese propensity for self-education under group support. As a member of that group, Shoko visited the organizer at home to "borrow a book." His elder sister, living there with her *mukoyōshi* husband, saw the young visitor and decided that she would be a good match for her thirty-two-year-old brother. Before Shoko gave a definite reply, the sister asked the section chief of the company where they both worked to arrange the proposed match. Many people became involved, and things were being arranged and decided on "around" the informant, but not "with" her. Despite her father's objection, it soon became clear that an irreversible commitment had been made "out of pressure from *mawari* [surrounding people]."

The surrounding people did not always mean well. "Nasty" interferences by women co-workers ended with the fixing up of another informant with her husband, also a co-worker. How this happened she refused to say, but it is clear that an affair developed as a result of such interference. At first she was unaware of what was going on, but was made conscious of the man as a possible marriage partner because of the "surrounding atmosphere."[3]

Controlled choice implies more autonomy and less compliance than the previous three types, and yet the last two cases show surrender of autonomy to collective pressures. The reason for including these under "controlled choice" is that both informants had direct exposure to their future husbands and soon became attracted to them. They are not sure in which category—*miai* or *ren'ai*—they should place their marriages. Incidentally, both look happily married.

### UNMEDIATED PROPOSALS: AUTONOMY AND COMPLIANCE

Only seven informants describe their marriage in a way that can be characterized as unmediated. Unmediated marriage might be equated with full exercise of autonomy by the marriage partners. This is not necessarily the case.

*Mutual involvement.* Let us start from autonomous cases which I put together typologically as mutual involvement of the principals. A man and woman meet accidentally, fall in love, and decide to marry, without bothering to have their relationship sanctioned, at least prior to marriage, by a third person's blessing. This may be regarded as the purest form of *ren'ai* marriage.

A university student in her freshman year and away from home, happened to meet a student from another university. Friendship gradually turned into acceptance of each other as marriage partners, and upon graduation they married. No third person was consulted. She did introduce her boyfriend to her family, not for consultation but to let them know the decision which she had already made. The family was opposed, "maybe because the father and mother had some plans for me." The parents had entertained the idea of bringing a *mukoyōshi* for her since she was the eldest daughter, the son still being too young, but the boyfriend was a successor son, unavailable as a *mukoyōshi* husband. The couple went ahead with their plan, ignoring her family's resistance.

Another woman was courted by a former junior high school classmate just at the time when she was heartbroken to learn that her love for another man was not reciprocated. The new suitor's voice sounded so sweet and tender to her at this vulnerable moment that she accepted his proposal without thinking. Again, her family was strongly opposed on the grounds that she would have to live with too many in-laws, but her decision prevailed.

The apprehension that nobody would bless her match drove a college freshman living in the dormitory to elope with her boyfriend, also a student. Not only were her adoptive parents against this union but she knew that the college would not tolerate a married student. "There was no such thing as a married student in those days." It was in the early 1950s. She denied that she did it out of love—she was at the mercy of some unknown urge, she said. Apparently, the husband-to-be was popular with the girls and she was afraid of losing him unless she married immediately.

Rin's family did not interfere with her because she had long been absent from home, moving from one job to another. While working as a barmaid, she became involved with a fisherman who was a customer. That it was a crude union of man and woman devoid of the ceremonial elegance of mediation was expressed by her use of the word *"kuttsuita"* (glued together). However irrational their actions were, these women exercised their autonomy in deciding on and consummating a marital relationship.

*Dyadic compliance.* Two women became involved in affairs that led to marriage against their better judgment. They succumbed to the proposal out of compliance, as in cases of coercive compliance, but here the compliance was not with a mediator but directly with the suitors.

"There was no love between us, but I was scared of him," said Ikuko. She became acquainted with her future husband when they were working at the same hotel, she as a live-in maid. Later, after they went to separate hotels, the former co-worker started to show up at her hotel, usually drunk. Ikuko had had no intention of marrying him, but his unruly manner of courtship frightened her into succumbing. Also, "pity may have turned into love for him."

Taeko was a live-in clerk and maid at a resort house when she encountered her future husband, a former classmate at an elementary school. Apparently, he tried to get her attention by sending her what looked like a letter. Discovering that it was a blank sheet of paper, the nineteen-year-old woman, instead of ignoring it, went to question him directly. It was then that something irreversible happened. Taeko blames this unexpected incident on her naiveté; the whole thing took place without her knowing what she was doing. It was not a case of rape. "No, not that bad. I was seduced." This one incident determined her future, she thought, and there would be no way of escaping marriage to this man whom she neither respected nor loved. Meanwhile, he demanded continuous interaction, threatening that, unless she complied, he would make scenes with her parents and neighbors, and at her work place. She had to respond to his telephone calls at her place of employment. Furthermore, it became clear that he had his eye on the money she was earning. In fact, he acted as if he were interested only in that, and he did take a lot from her purse to spend on gambling. The whole affair was kept secret from her parents for years, but eventually became known. With his blood pressure rising, her father declared that he would disown her unless she terminated the affair. This declaration did not shake resignation to the "fate" of marrying the man. Finally, they married formally, and even received the father's blessing because, after all, he was obviously very attached to this daughter, his eldest. She continued to work as a live-in maid, and it was not until sixteen years after the "incident" that the couple settled down in a house.

Both of these women were in a vulnerable state when approached by the men. One was stuck with a self-denigrating job which required her to wait on the drunken customers of the resort house whenever she was free of clerical work. The other woman had first had a love affair which had not worked out. Then a *miai* meeting was arranged, but it was followed by an embarrassing period of procrastination on the part of the groom's family until, in humiliation, she personally cancelled the proposal.

Dyadic compliance suggests a clue to a positive function of mediation, in that mediation by a third party would have protected the women from direct abuse by the men. In this connection it may be noted that in all but one case of unmediated marriage, the woman was living away from her natal family.

The foregoing analysis indicates that there is no strong correlation between mediation and compliance, or direct contact and autonomy. It is more likely that these two variables—compliance versus autonomy, and mediation versus non-mediation—combine in a curve. To schematize this likelihood in a graph, figure 1 shows four quadrants divided by the compliance-autonomy axis and the mediated-unmediated axis. The six types of decision making in reference to proposals are distributed over the four quadrants in a rough curve.

In frequency, however, as shown by the number for each type, the first two quadrants (both mediated) are the most crowded (the numbers total fifty-three known cases). This preponderance of mediated marriage points up the cultural importance of a triad in Japanese social relationships either in support of or in inhibition of an intimate dyad.

The figures in parentheses indicate the average age of the informants for each type as a possible clue to type change over time. Although some types are too low in frequency for the average age to be significant, nonetheless it is interesting to see age gradation along the curve from the first quadrant through the fourth, showing compliance types represented by the oldest and the youngest age groups.

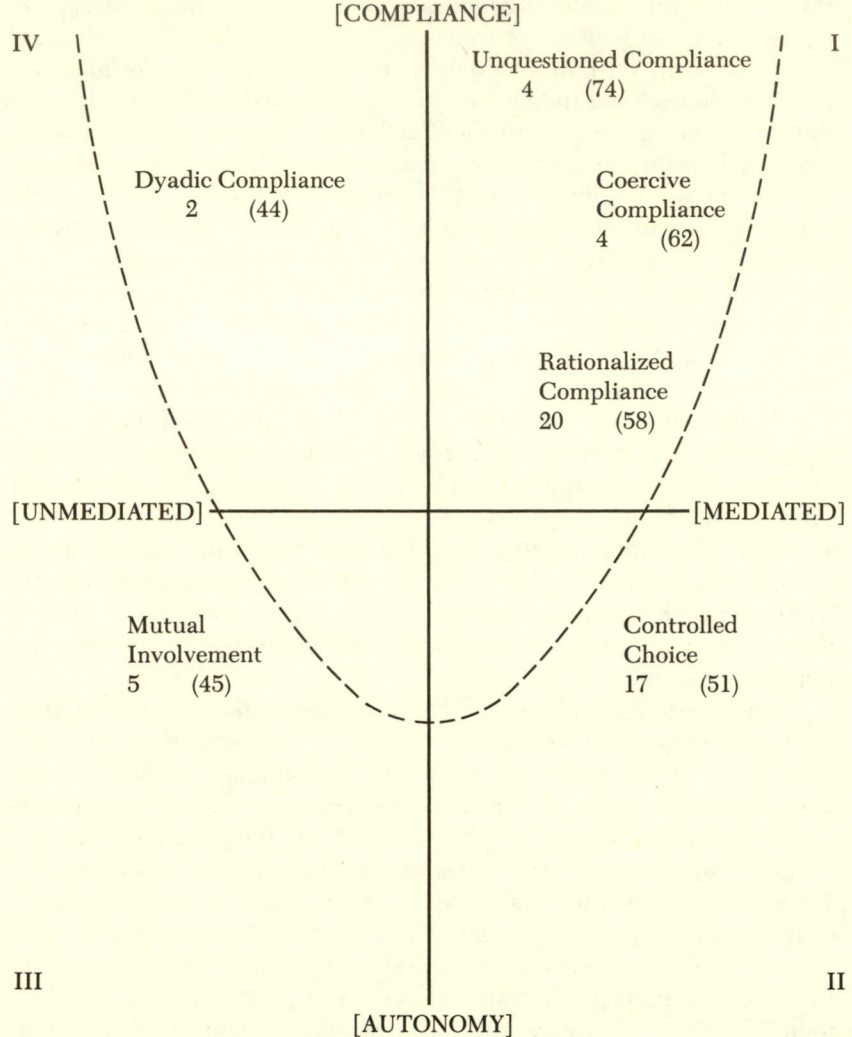

Note: The number in parentheses stands for the average age for each type.

FIGURE 1. Reactions to Marriage Proposals: Frequency by Types

REMARRIAGE

The local sample (n = 57) includes eight women who were either widowed or divorced at a relatively young age between twenty and thirty-eight, and five of these women were remarried. One of the striking characteristics of marital commitment on the part of women, as we have seen with regard to first marriages, is the general weakness of autonomy, or the subordination of the candidate's own desires or personal feelings to other factors, be they the wishes of parents, mediators, or diffuse "surrounding." It might be assumed that commitment to remarriage involves more autonomy once the candidate can claim more sophistication about marital affairs. In fact, these women turn out to have suppressed their wills as much as before or even more. Except for one case in which the widow married the late husband's cousin who had helped her with the litigation over property inheritance against the husband's brother, all marriages were mediated, and three women in particular accepted proposals despite themselves.

Emi, divorced and deeply remorseful, was devoting herself to the national war effort. Her active participation as a leader of a local chapter of the National Defense Women's Association, helping the recuperating soldiers, was as much a way of expiating her guilt as for the community to label her "soldiers' old lady" (hospitable to servicemen out of loyalty and without sexual involvement). The proposal for remarriage was brought over by an Association member from a family which had just lost a young man to the war. Driven by her zealous loyalty to the country, she married a fifty-four-year-old fisherman, eighteen years her senior, whose daughter had been left alone with a child by the death of her husband in the war.

A second woman was a widow, enjoying her secretarial job, with no special urge for remarriage, when an acquaintance came and pressed her to go through a *miai* "just to honor my face" as a mediator. After meeting the prospect, also widowed, whose impression was "not bad," Mieko visited his house with the mediator and was astonished at the miserable way the motherless family was living. She felt sorry that the father and two children were having wretched meals prepared in a filthy kitchen. Mieko decided to join them "as soon as possible to be useful to them."

Wakako, divorced under her mother's urge from her tuberculous husband, was operating her own bar to support her parents. Her second husband-to-be came to the bar as a customer. He fell in love and talked about it to everyone around whereas neither she nor her mother thought this fisherman deserved her. He urged his parents to make a formal proposal; the whole community was gossiping and he would have to leave town, he said, unless the marriage was consummated. She resisted the idea of having to treat another man "with deference"; she wanted to continue a free single life. But her father "loved" this *mukoyōshi*-to-be, and many others, kin and friends, put pressure on her to be "more sympathetic" toward the suitor. She gave in.

### Ultimate Self-Persuasion

However variable the processes of acceptance of marriage proposals may be, it is the woman herself who must make the ultimate decision at the innermost level of her selfhood. Even the woman who complied with her brother unquestioningly and trustingly was likely to have some fears, doubts, and uncertainty. This is where the culture provides a symbolic means of overcoming the existential uncertainty and ambivalence felt by a woman facing a radical transition in her life condition. Many informants referred to *"en,"* meaning predestined affinity, when speaking of their marriages. Indeed, the old term for marriage is *"engumi,"* *en* match. *En* is something to be accepted without a fuss, as something unavoidable. My informants seemed to frame their marriages in terms of *en* in order to reach the final self-persuasion. Some women were more inclined toward men other than their fiancés, but became resigned to the fact that those more desirable matches were not blessed with *en*. The absence of *en* was demonstrated in their minds through some unexpected event, such as the Tokyo air raids that separated a pair, or the disrupted postal service which delayed the delivery of a love letter. On the other hand, the unavoidability of the *en* bond was reaffirmed when a match about to break up became restored somehow or when a proposal came through more than one network. An informant described such a double or restored bond as *kusare-en*, literally "rotten bond," meaning an absolutely unbreakable relationship. In one case persuasion came from the prospect. Before he had a chance to meet Suzuko, he wrote several pages of a love letter expressing his conviction that the two were predestined to marry, "because he was born on August 1 [8/1] and I was born on January 8 [1/8]."

### Transition Rites

Rites for marriage vary from case to case in formality, number, and elaboration, nevertheless some patterns do emerge.[4]

## Ceremonial Mediators

If courtship or matchmaking is to progress from an informal, haphazard stage to a formal, stable stage, the families concerned must find ceremonial mediators. There are different, contradictory views of ceremonial versus actual mediators. Some informants said that formerly there was no distinction between these, the distinction being a recent phenomenon resulting from the increasing elaboration of marriage rites. Some others said there used to be a rigid rule to differentiate a *tanomare nakōdo* (the mediator solicited to preside over the ceremonies) from a *hashikake nakōdo* (the mediator who actually bridges the two principals) which is no longer followed so strictly. Three historical periods may be involved here: among common people there was no such distinction until early Meiji; thereafter the dual system became fashionable; in present-day Japan a new pattern is evolving which does away with such formalism. As far as the generation of my informants is concerned, the majority had ceremonial mediators who had nothing to do with matchmaking.

The reason given by Fusa for this distinction elucidates the relationship between the principals and the ceremonial mediators:

> The school principal was our *hashikake nakōdo,* he actually did take care of the matchmaking. Such a person does not mediate formally. . . . Why? Because once you become my formal mediator, you and I become bound by a permanent bond of parent and child.

A permanent bond entailed the obligation on the part of the "children" to make formal visits and offer gifts to the "parents" at least twice a year, midsummer and the end of the year.

Because of the heavy commitment involved, one was careful to choose the right kind of person, not just anybody who happens to be available (an actual matchmaker tends to be in the latter category). The "parent" should be someone who the "child" can respect more than his/her natural parent, "someone who had a good reputation and enough leisure, and could speak well" so that the "children" might be proud of their marriage and "people would talk about it as it was mediated by Mr. So-and-so." The mediator should also be able to elicit compliance from both parties in the marriage in case there was marital discord. The choice was thus made of the most prestigious person among one's relatives, the boss or president of the company employing the betrothed, a professor of one's alma mater, the father's most successful classmate, and the like. Tama, seventy-seven, referred to the formal mediator for her marriage as "One-hundred-yen bill," evidently a nickname given to him because he owned such a bill at a time when people had to work hard to earn five yen a month. Still today, careful attention is paid to the choice of a formal *nakōdo*. University professors are often asked to be *nakōdo* for their students.

Ceremonial mediation is not done by one individual but by a married couple. A man or woman, however renowned, is disqualified as a ceremonial *nakōdo* unless married. While formally the term *"nakōdo"* or *"baishakunin"* is assigned only to the male mediator—his wife being designated as "the wife of *baishakunin*"—the informants actually meant by these terms the couple together or sometimes the wife alone if she had a closer tie with the bride. The local custom further dictates that two such couples be selected, one for the bride and one for the groom although a major role may be played by only one couple, particularly the couple for the spouse-receiver. (There is regional variation in this, and the present trend in the local scene seems to be to settle for one pair only.) The male *nakōdo* for the groom used to be the same fictive "parent" who was selected for the young man who was a "child" at the time of his initiation, which corresponded to the time of joining a local youth group (*wakamonogumi*, see p. 17) and fire brigade or of taking an examination for conscription.

Such fictive parentage is no longer viable, and the relationship between the young couple and the mediator couples is becoming more superficial and temporary and, according to an informant, is often used politically. This change seems to correspond with the increasing tendency to make cash payment for the service of ceremonial mediation.

### Premarital Rites

*Miai introduction.* Conventionally, the meaning of *miai* is twofold: in a broader sense, it refers to arranged marriage in contrast to *ren'ai* (love marriage), and in a narrower sense, to the ceremony of introduction of the candidates to each other, *miai* meaning "mutual look." Here it is used in the latter sense. The *miai* introduction is dispensed with if the principals have gotten acquainted with each other directly before a mediator gets involved. As far as my informants are concerned, it was also omitted in some purely mediated cases where the bridal candidate had no voice at all in accepting a proposal—predominantly the cases of unquestioned or coercive compliance. For the rest, the *miai* was the first significant ceremony.

The *miai* was usually conducted at the bride's home, where the groom showed up with his mediator (at this stage the actual match-maker might still be responsible) and probably his parents as well. The bride-to-be would come into the room to serve tea. One can see the significance of femininity training here since the *miai* encounter thus exposed not only the woman's physical beauty but her ritual comportment and manners as well. But the future groom might also be looking for something totally unexpected. Right after the *miai*, Hiroe learned that groom liked her hands, which he had seen when she served the tea. Her hands had rough skin, indicative of a hard life, which in turn demonstrated her endurance in his mind. Convenience might dictate that the *miai* be held in a public place like a hotel lounge or a theater. Wherever it was held, the mediator was expected to play his/her role by tactfully helping both parties to relax.

The *miai* is a formal introduction, but its actual functions vary. For older and more compliant women, it was a transition rite in that once the candidates went through it they were considered to have made an irreversible commitment to each other as marriage mates. It was a *rite* to confirm that the proposal had been accepted.

Because of the irreversibility involved, the *miai* ceremony was preceded by a series of precautionary measures to minimize risk. Information was collected secretly regarding the family background, including the *koseki*, the house register, as well as the health and personal suitability of the prospective mate. The required secrecy and efficiency of this data collection might call for the expertise of a professional detective. Mieko chuckled, recalling that after her marriage she was surprised to discover how great a man her grandfather had been. She learned from her husband that before the *miai* was planned, her prospective father-in-law had investigated everything about her family through a detective.

While for many informants the *miai* was an irreversible transition rite, for others—younger or more autonomous—it allowed for exploration, options, and final decision making, including rejection. But degrees of freedom varied from case to case. In quite a number of cases casualness or coincidence was staged for a *miai* encounter. Harue, fifty-seven, said she had a five-minute *miai* without knowing it. All she did was serve tea to the guests in everyday dress; later she learned that she had been kept uninformed in case the match did not work out. But obviously the groom knew why he was there. This asymmetric *role blindness* on the part of the bride was experienced by many other women. What was the first introduction from the bride's point of view often turned out to be the second for the groom, for he had had a glimpse of her somewhere without her having had the same opportunity to evaluate him. A schoolteacher had her future husband in her classroom without knowing she was being inspected. The candidacy pictures, too, were often found to have been distributed asymmetrically: the groom saw her picture, but the bride did not see his.

The contrivance of such asymmetric role blindness might enable the groom, not the bride, to veto the proposal after the introduction, and therefore was likely to make the bride, not the groom, a victim of rejection. The general explanation given for this practice, however, was that it would protect a woman from being hurt should the matchmaking fail.

More updated forms of *miai* are casual, meant to provide an opportunity for both parties to consider each other, the matchmaker leaving the two to have further contact and reach a decision by themselves. Suzuko, newly wed at twenty-eight, had her first *miai* experience at twenty-three. Accompanied by her uncle, one of the actual mediators, she visited the twenty-seven-year-old candidate. No real conversation took place. Afterward, the two principals met again by themselves. "He is a nice guy, but the moment he came close to me I felt repulsed." Her rejection was conveyed through her uncle. An equivalent to the American "blind date" is now fashionable. A boy and girl are arranged by his/her friend, kin, or other matchmaker to meet in an impersonal place like a park or coffee shop. The matchmaker stays away from the *miai* scene and refrains from interfering with the principals about their post-*miai* decisions. The professional marriage brokers emphasize in their advertisements how easy it is to make a post-*miai* rejection of the prospect. All this change implies that the *miai* is no longer a transition rite, that it is more like a trial-and-error experience. Thus, older informants are shocked to find young people today going through *miai* introductions more than a dozen times. "They are not embarrassed about it; rather, they brag about how many *miai* they have had!" This lack of commitment may explain the persistence of *miai* practice in the contemporary marriage market where love is considered essential. A woman who has just passed marriageable age claimed that it is beyond her comprehension to find a marriage mate through *miai* as her parents did. She then confessed that she was in the midst of the *miai* process. "There are three kinds of marriage in Japan," said a twenty-five-year-old college graduate soon to become a bride, "*miai, ren'ai*, and interview marriage." In interview marriage, the two candidates meet through arrangement and try to impress one another instead of relying upon a third person's initiative. Hers was this type, she said.

*Engagement.* The *miai* ceremony, unless taken as a transition rite, may be followed by an immediate decision of acceptance or by a humiliating or embarrassing period of uncertainty. Needless to say, cancellation must be handled tactfully by the *nakōdo*. Once mutual agreement in favor of the proposal is reached, the *nakōdo* and the families decide on the date of the formal engagement, which should not be delayed too long. By this time the ceremonial *nakōdo* may come into the picture to play the primary role in the marriage transaction. On the engagement day, the groom's *nakōdo* carries the engagement message from the groom's family to the bride's family in the form of a gift called *yuinō*, the content of which has varied over time and regions from food to clothing to money (*Sōgō Nihon Minzoku Goi*, hereafter *SNMG* 1955–1956, 4:1666–67). Among my informants, the *yuinō* was primarily money. The older custom of giving clothing is symbolically retained by the designation of the money as *"obijiryō,"* the money to buy obi material for the bride. A farmer's daughter, married in 1918, remembers that the *yuinō* received was five yen and a pair of *geta;* a daughter of a government official received two thousand yen in 1948; and a butcher's daughter received one million yen plus a ring in 1977. The general consensus today is that the groom should pay the equivalent of three months' salary. The woman who married a schoolteacher in 1939 saw a one hundred-yen bill, received as *yuinō*, for the first time in her life. A schoolteacher's monthly salary at the time was thirty to forty yen. " 'Does this mean I am going to be bought with this much?' I said, and we all laughed." To accompany the money gift is a set of symbolically propitious dried seafoods including seaweed, squid, and bonito. The symbolic meaning derives from the sounds and Chinese ideographs of the name of each item.

Many of the older informants do not know what or how much was received, since the transaction was between the two families, not the two spouses-to-be, often involving the *nakōdo* and the parents only. As a formal indication of agreement to the engagement, the bride's family is supposed to make a return gift. The *yuinō-gaeshi*, the *yuinō*-return-gift, is ideally (by the local standard) half the amount initially received, but in actuality none of my informants followed the rule. Instead, only a token return was made with the tacit understanding between the two families that the initial gift would be spent toward the completion of *yomeiri-jitaku* (or simply *shitaku*), the dowry consisting of wardrobe, furniture, and an assortment of household utensils to be taken by the bride with her. Probably because the dowry usually costs more than the *yuinō* can buy, the *yuinō* is not associated with the idea of bride price. In the case of *mukoyōshi* marriage, the tables are turned, and it is the bride's family that makes the initial gift since "it is we who take a spouse."

MARITAL RITES

*Wedding.* The distinction between engagement and wedding is not always clear. As an informant in her seventies recalled, at the engagement ceremony "a sort of miniature wedding was held," which suggests the possibility that historically the *yuinō* ceremony was held for a tentative marriage (*SNMG*, ibid.). A similar ceremony was conducted for Fusa in 1921 which was called *ashiire* (the "stepping-in marriage"), meant to enable the engaged couple to make contact freely without provoking sanction from the sex-segregated community. A more recently married woman moved into the groom's house on the same day that she received a *yuinō* and made a token return gift; the wedding was held three months later when the bride was pregnant. This kind of pre-wedding cohabitation was prevalent among the commoners prior to their absorption of samurai values.[5] The premarital cohabitation, while frowned upon by many as a sign of Americanization, has this historical root, and as long as it is framed within the traditional *ashiire* custom it arouses no disapproval.

The wedding is a culmination of ceremonial elaboration in its setting, procedures, and invited guests. A propitious day, as defined in the Chinese calendrical lore, is set for this occasion. One important function of the wedding is to introduce two sets of kinsmen—the bride's side and the groom's side—to each other. Not only kinsmen but close associates of both families such as neighbors, colleagues, and friends may also be involved. Home used to be the place for the wedding, which entailed a clear differentiation between hosts and guests. Nowadays, the wedding has been drawn into the public domain—a wedding hall or hotel with its professional staff where both hosts and guests receive service. The main portion of a wedding is a series of introductory eulogies for the new couple, and a wedding dinner. This ceremony is called *hirōen*, the publicity banquet. Usually, seats are arranged so that the two groups of attendants face each other.

For my older informants, the wedding involved more than such an introduction. The ceremony was begun with the people on the groom's side, including the *nakōdo* couple and his family, forming a procession to visit the bride's house. A barrel of sake was carried along with the procession. When the company arrived at its destination, they were invited into the bride's house, where the bride-giving people were waiting to host a banquet for the bride-receiving group. The two groups were introduced to each other, the sake from the groom's house being served, and a gift (e.g., kimono fabric) presented by the visiting party. After this ceremony, another procession was formed, this time involving both parties including the principals, and bound for the groom's house. In the procession were not only the bearers of another barrel of sake supplied by the bride's family, but also the bearers of an oblong chest called *nagamochi* containing the bride's clothing. The rationale for the latter is not clear, but I speculate that it was symbolic of a dowry and derived its significance from its name, *nagamochi*, meaning durable. At the groom's house a final wedding ceremony was held, including the presentation of the sake and a gift from the bride's side.

What was implied in this double ceremony? My informants interpreted this in terms of the two aspects of marriage: the first part of the ceremony symbolized the groom's group coming to receive the bride, and the second part represented the bride moving into her new home with the groom's group as a guide. The wife-giving group and the wife-taking group were each to host a banquet accordingly. One informant, however, seemed to touch what was probably of a deeper historical root when she said: "The first was the ceremony for *mukoiri* [the groom's entry] and the second was for the *yomeiri* [the bride's entry]." The double ceremony is likely to have been an abbreviated, symbolic legacy of the old matrimonial custom among the commoners in which the *mukoiri* ceremony marked the end of the groom's clandestine sleep with the bride by legitimizing the match and allowing him to visit her as a husband until the *yomeiri* ceremony was held for the couple, who would finally settle down in virilocal coresidence.[6] The symbolic preservation of the old practice in this form appears to have contributed to an integration of the groom's kin into the bride's group and vice versa. Kazuko, sixty-one, added another sidelight when she said:

> On the wedding day, people came over from the groom's side carrying a barrel of sake, a gift of fabric, and a lantern. My family refused to present me. The visitors came back and tried again to fetch me. This way, the family pretended to be reluctant to let the daughter go, I suppose.

Here, the first part of the double ceremony seemed to dramatize the bride's value through a collusion between the reluctant bride-givers and the insistent bride-takers.[7]

These symbolic implications aside, it is obvious that such a ceremony would be impossible unless the two houses were located within walking distance of each other. It might be assumed, therefore, that this was a heritage from village endogamy. But one should remember that people did walk much longer distances than we do now. In 1918, Tama and her group walked in a procession several miles along the winding, rough mountain paths from her village to Shizumi.

Another function of the wedding is to consecrate the marital bond of the two partners. It was not customary but is now fashionable to give it a religious sanction by having a Shinto ceremony presided over by a priest. This part of the ceremony, attended by the principals, their primary kin, and the *nakōdo* couples, is held separately from and immediately before the banquet. The highlight of this ceremony is when the principals drink sake from the same cup—the traditional expression of taking an oath. One by one, three cups of sake are passed between the groom and the bride, each cup representing the taking of an oath three times by three sips. The ceremony is thus called *san-san-kudo* (three-three-nine times), meaning the taking of an oath nine times. Recently, oath taking has assumed other forms such as the bride and groom placing a wedding ring on each other's finger, or the making of an oral oath (the groom reading an oath ending with his full name and the bride adding her first name). The new forms of oath taking are an elaboration additional to, not substitutive for, the traditional *san-san-kudo*.

Shinto dominates the wedding as it does other felicitous occasions. This means not only hiring a Shinto priest together with a couple of *miko* (maiden serving a Shinto shrine) as assistants, but also the likelihood that the new couple belongs to the priest's shrine as its parishioners. Put more correctly, the choice of the priest is determined by the residence of the couple, since shrine affiliation is based upon the residential ward system (see p. 17). In actuality there are options. Christian and even Buddhist ceremonies are considered possible, if not common, alternatives. The motives for taking these alternatives turn out, however, to have little to do with religion itself. Suzuko wanted to have a Christian wedding in order to fulfill her long-cherished dream of wearing a Western-style wedding dress, but realized it had to be a Shinto wedding since her husband-to-be was determined to wear Japanese-style formal wear (kimono with the family crest and loose pantaloons). Then it so happened that the *miko* of the shrine where the husband's household belonged was a *demodori*, once-married-out-and-returned, meaning a divorcee (the word *demodori* shows that a woman, if divorced, has had no place to belong to but her natal house). The husband's parents rejected the idea of having the *miko*'s service as inauspicious. A variety of other alternatives were proposed and discussed by both parties until, finally, the bride's compromise idea was accepted by all—a Buddhist wedding. In a Buddhist wedding, according to this informant, rosaries instead of rings are exchanged, Shinto prayer is replaced by sutras, and an oath is taken to the family ancestors rather than to the gods.

Throughout, the *nakōdo*'s role is salient—much more so than the parents' role. The announcement of a wedding always includes the names of the *nakōdo*. At the wedding, the bride and groom are flanked by their respective *nakōdo* couples, the parents being seated next to the *nakōdo*, not the principals. In the old ceremony involving processions, there was a gesture symbolizing the fact that the ceremony was performed *through* the *nakōdo*: first, the groom's *nakōdo* led the procession to the house of the bride's *nakōdo;* the latter in turn led the procession to the bride's house. For the second part of the ceremony, the whole procession stopped at the house of the groom's *nakōdo* before it finally settled at the groom's house.

The center of attention in the whole drama, however, is the bride. Clad in a bridal costume, with a bridal hairdo called *shimada,* and professionally made-up, the bride is expected to draw breathless awe from spectators in the wedding hall, on the street, or at the entrance of the groom's house. At the banquet, she withdraws to change costumes (the custom called *ironaoshi* (color alteration) once, twice, or in one case, as often as seven times. The contemporary bride is likely to present herself first in a traditional costume and *shimada*-style wig, and then in a Western wedding dress and a permanent wave. The type of dress to be worn—Western or Japanese—could be an important decision symbolic of the future relationship between the bride and her in-laws. At her 1978 wedding, Suzuko wore four different dresses for *ironaoshi,* including two Western-style dresses which together cost one hundred twenty thousand yen (six hundred dollars). She also wore a kimono rented for two hundred thousand yen (one thousand dollars), which she considered foolish and wasteful but wore at her mother-in-law's insistence. *Ironaoshi* for the groom is also fashionable today.

In the Tokugawa era, the transition of the woman's status from daughter to wife (or from pre- to postpubescence) was marked by tooth blackening, as was the case with the mothers of my oldest informants. This old custom was simulated, according to seventy-seven-year-old Tama, at her wedding when her female *nakōdo* as *kanetsuke-oya* (tooth-blackening "parent") gave her a "substitute tooth blackener" consisting of face powder, lipstick, and toothpaste. Status transition was further indicated by a change of hairdo at the wedding: the bride first appeared in *shimada* style, and later reappeared in conjunction with *ironaoshi* in *marumage* style symbolic of the wifely status. The *shimada* hairdo is so associated with the bridal identity that, if worn by a single woman, it is locally called *saisoku-shimada* (*shimada* solicitous of a marriage proposal). In the days when the wedding was held at home, the last kimono in the series of *ironaoshi* was supposed to be an everyday dress in which the bride, no longer an outsider or guest, would go around to the invited guests to serve tea and see them off.

The wedding certainly represents what Turner (1969) calls "liminality." A close look makes us aware that a liminal phase can consist of a wide range of subphases. The banquet of a local wedding I observed, held in a large tatami-matted room of a hotel accommodating roughly one hundred attendants, demonstrated three subphases. First, after all the participants took seats at individual tables which were already set with full dinners, the master of ceremonies announced the opening of the banquet; this announcement was followed by a series of formal speeches. The speakers were "important" guests, well known to the local residents, including a prefectural assemblyman and the president of the company where the groom was employed. Reflecting the fact that the speakers were selected more on the basis of their prestige than their familiarity with the principals, their speeches were impersonal and flowery. The audience was quiet and attentive, not touching the dinner. This "sacred" stage was followed by an intermediary one where the attendants, upon toasting in unison, began to drink and eat. In the meantime a second set of speakers who were less important—such as the bride's schoolteacher, the groom's uncle—were giving more relaxed speeches commanding partial attention from the audience. The final subphase, by which time many people were drunk, was taken over by the intimate peers and friends of the newlyweds to perform their stunts before the guests. The stunts included singing lewd songs and telling obscene jokes. No longer was the audience sitting still, some were walking around the rows of attendants to pour sake for acquaintances personally; others were lying on the floor, half-asleep. I thus came to the conclusion that liminality can contain a whole cycle from the sacred to the profane, from ritually controlled to chaotic states.

While weddings are becoming increasingly extravagant, reflecting general affluence and invidious consumption, the opposite trend toward simplicity is also observable. The younger generation has invented an equivalent of the "no-host party" for a wedding. Such a party is attended primarily by the couple's friends who pay attendance fees. Junko had this sort of wedding in 1957, when there was a "new life movement" aiming at terminating wasteful, irrational mores; the wedding dinner consisted of sandwiches. Likewise, the principal couple these days often takes an active role at the banquet by making speeches or performing stunts, instead of sitting like a couple of dolls, silent and wooden faced, as in the past.

Change has also taken place in regard to the dowry. My informants mentioned *futon* bedding, *zabuton* cushions, wardrobes, a dressing table with a mirror, a shoe box, a sewing kit, a laundry tub, starching boards, dressmaking boards, and so on. In the case of *mukoyōshi* marriage, it is the groom's family that prepares these things, except those items which are inseparable from distinctly female roles, skills, or needs such as a sewing kit. The wedding thus involved a transfer of such furniture—a roomful at times—from one house (or group of furniture stores) to the other house. The older the informant, the more household tools and kitchen utensils she took. Today's brides have replaced these traditional items with electric appliances such as washing machines, refrigerators, vacuum cleaners, as well as luxury items such as stereo sets and color televisions. What has not changed is the "bridal set"; found in every furniture store, it is composed of a couple of wardrobes (containers), a mirror-dressing table, a shoe box, a cupboard, and so forth. It is great fun for a girl to browse around the bridal corners of furniture stores with her mother or fiancé. A college diploma is another form of dowry. "The best of my dowry," said Hanayo, "was my pharmacist's license." When a parent complains about the cost of a daughter's marriage—which can run as much as 5 million yen—he/she is counting this dowry plus the portion of the wedding cost to be paid by the bride's family.

There is some uncertainty as to who owns the dowry. As mentioned before, the *yuinō* usually contributes to this bridal expenditure, and the amount and quality of the dowry should be balanced with the *yuinō* to reflect its nature as *yuinō-gaeshi*. In this view, ownership is held by the groom or his family. And yet, more commonly the bride is regarded as the sole or ultimate owner. A fifty-nine-year-old informant remembers her family on the wedding day having handed a list to the groom's family of items brought over with her. Why? "To be sure that those things be returned [to the wife] in case of divorce, I suppose."

*Post-wedding rites.* The wedding is followed by a honeymoon trip, but this is only a recent phenomenon or was only done by "special," wealthy people in the prewar period, I was told. The wartime generation could not enjoy this luxury, although taking such trips had already become a common practice. Unimaginable to the old or deprived generations is the practice of the younger generation couples who go abroad for a honeymoon trip or to have a wedding there blessed by foreign Christian ministers.

Right after the wedding, unless the couple takes a trip, the bride is taken around the neighborhood of the new home by the groom's female *nakōdo* to make a courtesy call at every neighbor household. The house heads of neighbor families may have been at the wedding, but this time the main focus is on the domestic-level acquaintanceship between women. A small gift such as a bath towel, probably with the bride's name on it, is presented, and the mediator or a relative introduces her as a bride who "has come to such-and-such house" and solicits the neighbor's indulgence and help for the newcomer. This ritual of visitation underscores the existence of a boundary of residential community whereby insiders are differentiated from outsiders, and thus serves as an admission ritual for the new settler. It also foreshadows the importance of the role to be played by neighbors, especially neighbor housewives, in the bride's life space.

Where is the community boundary drawn? It may range from the smallest and closest unit called *mukō sangen ryōdonari* (three houses across the street and the two next door) to a whole block. From wartime on, "neighbors" became commensurate with a *tonarigumi* (neighborhood association, see p. 12) consisting of around ten to thirty households. A local woman who married during my stay distributed gift boxes of cake to ten *tonarigumi* member houses.

More post-wedding ritual visits may be made to the households of the husband's kin, employer, and superiors. Parties more informal than a wedding may be held by the newlyweds in their house where their friends are invited.

Formerly, the bride made the first *satogaeri* (return visit to the natal home) on the third day of married life. She was accompanied by the groom's female mediator again, and if the wedding did not include the double ceremony described above, she would be joined by her husband so that he would be introduced to her kin and neighbors—a transitional version of *mukoiri*. Asked if the bride or the couple could stay there overnight, my informants gave an emphatic no: "You *must* return to your new home on the same day."

Some of the food served during or after the wedding had a symbolic meaning. In some cases the soup contained the white onion root which looked like white hair and thus symbolized "a couple living together and becoming old enough to have white hair." Sweet rice cake —gluey rice balls covered with sugared red bean paste—was made at the new home right after the wedding or at the natal home on the *satogaeri* occasion. It had the special name of *ochitsuki-botamochi* (rice cake for settling down).

Most of what has been said about the bride holds for the groom in the case of *mukoyōshi* marriage.

Some informants, including those who had uxorilocal marriage, did not experience a sense of transition through marriage rites. Yukie, though married neolocally, feels that her wedding rite gave her no sense of a switchover because everything—the oath-taking ceremony as well as the banquet—was conducted in her natal home. She simulated entry into a new house by walking through the gate, but that did not help her gain a sense of change. Now when she sees others having a rite away from home, she regrets that hers was not the way it should have been. A proper rite is necessary, she thinks, for a woman to take a decisive step into a new life.

This chapter has described the women's experience of the life transition from marriage candidacy through the wedding rite. At all phases of this critical transition we have noted that marriage was not merely the concern of a man and woman but was structurally framed. It appears as if marriage, like other life transitions, called for a rekindling of a usually dormant social structure surrounding the principals. We have seen how marriage, at least in the past, was supposed to perform the function of sustaining and perpetuating the *ie*, and how, therefore, the successor or nonsuccessor status of a son or daughter was taken into serious consideration in proposing or accepting a marriage. The primacy of the role of the mediators, actual and ceremonial, was another indication of the structural significance of marriage.

The woman's personal emotions for or against a prospective husband were not always ignored, but older women in particular complied unquestioningly or were forced to comply with authoritative mediators. Even when a woman agreed to accept a proposal, her reasoning often turned out to be extrinsic to her emotions. More interesting is the fact that even the unmediated marriages where a man and woman met directly and married did not all involve a woman's autonomous choice. Some of them were products of a woman's forced compliance with her suitor's desire, and this was among young women.

Overall, we are struck with the lack of autonomy on the part of women in responding to marriage prosposals. They presented themselves as more or less helpless about their marital destiny, as pressured into a match by the "surrounding" situation, or as devoid of self-interest or conjugal love. And this tendency was even stronger when a woman, mature and experienced, was to remarry. This may have been to an extent a result of successful training in compliance; partly this may reflect the culturally preferred style of self-presentation. It should also be noted that the structural imperative of marriage was not always set, in the Japanese woman's mind, against her personal fulfillment. Indeed, marriage was and still is considered a mandatory condition for a person to attain full human status and to enjoy life. Guided by this belief, and pressured by the idea of the marriageable age, a woman would find herself under the internal urge as well as external coercion to meet a prospective spouse at the right time. This pressure was heavier upon women than men. Many women abandoned their professions temporarily or permanently as they reached the age for marital candidacy in order to restore a domestic identity. This choice between a professional and domestic career, needless to say, had to be faced exclusively by women.

The foregoing does not imply that the structural assignment of a prospective spouse upon the young woman happily matched her personal choice. We have seen several cases where the woman strongly protested the parental decision or where her own choice overruled anybody else's. It has also been observed that there were efforts to make a structural demand compatible with a personal feeling, as was well represented by the cases of "controlled choice." Related to this tendency is the difficulty of dichotomizing marriage into the "arranged" type and love type.

Still, change in the marriage pattern cannot be overlooked. The network through which a woman these days comes into contact with a prospect is more concentrated in employment and friendship and less in kinship and neighborhood. More conspicuously, young women today are much freer than the prewar and wartime generations to contact prospects directly, to have premarital union or cohabitation. (It should be noted, however, that this new trend among contemporary young people also harks back to their ancestors still uncontaminated by the samurai culture.) The result is a greater frequency of pure love marriages, and if mediation takes place it is accepted as just another option to meet a prospect rather than as an irreversible commitment as it was by older women. There is no doubt that young women today enjoy more options than those who were at marriage age two or three decades ago. These options are bought at the price of structural security however: fewer people, for example, may volunteer as matchmakers for a candidate.

As regards wedding rites, there are greater variations and innovations, and the bride has more voice in choosing an alternative. This change also must pay its price. The wedding is no longer a personal affair; it is conducted by a commercial agent in a public arena, calling for a complete programming of the procedure to which all participants, hosts and guests, principals and families, are subjected. This is another example showing that there are two sides of every coin, whether the coin is a traditional pattern or a modern innovation.

It is now time to look into what would be actually involved in the marriage which was so heavily invested or bought at such a high cost of the woman's autonomy.

# 4
## *Postmarital Involvement*

Although marriage for my informants was often followed immediately by pregnancy and childbearing, this chapter concentrates on a role cluster closely linked with marriage itself, leaving the discussion of motherhood for the next chapter. Here, motherhood will not appear unless necessary for the elucidation of marital roles. The postparental stage will be largely reserved for chapter 7, except where reference to it is necessary to characterize a marital relationship. Although recollections of the past do appear, this and following chapters will contain a great deal of the informants' present-day experiences.

## The Postmarital Household

The terms "family of orientation" and "family of procreation" may be useful for analyzing the American family, where these two tend to be mutually exclusive and, in combination, exhaustive, but they are difficult to apply to the Japanese family. A more appropriate distinction can be made with regard to the "household" than to the "family," and between the premarital and postmarital, than between the orientational and the procreative. Thus I am proposing the concept of "postmarital household."

### RESIDENTIAL FLUCTUATION AND AMBIGUITY

The postmarital household can be characterized, first, in terms of residential rearrangement. The three residential types—neolocal, virilocal, and uxorilocal—can be roughly applied, but a closer examination reveals many (about two-fifths of the total) ambiguous or complex instances for which a more elaborate classification is needed. First, there are cases of residential shift from neolocal to virilocal or uxorilocal, from virilocal to neolocal or uxorilocal, and from uxorilocal to neolocal, a few cases involving more than one move. The bride may move to the groom's natal household and stay there until a new house is built for the

couple; the newlyweds may be allowed to live alone with the understanding that they will eventually settle down with the husband's parents. Place of employment is another factor which either necessitates an
undesirable residential choice or permits a desirable move. While these
are more-or-less predictable occasions for residential transfer, unpredictable events can interfere with the residential plan. The destruction
of the neolocal dwelling by the Great Earthquake of 1923 forced two
women to move with their husbands to the latter's natal households;
Japan's defeat in World War II made a couple of repatriates from Manchuria seek shelter in the husband's parental house.

More commonly, residential shift has to do with unexpected conflict between in-laws: an initial virilocal arrangement is cancelled when
the bride finds coresidence with the mother-in-law or other in-laws
unbearable. Such conflict-related shifts in residence have happened decidedly more among younger informants. Harumi and her husband first
lived with his parents, but after realizing that the bride and her mother-
in-law were incompatible, the young couple left for Tokyo and stayed
there until they were called back to the mother-in-law's deathbed. (I
find four more similar cases resulting in neolocal residence, but will
reserve for a later section of this chapter the discussion of such postmarital conflict.)

There are more factors contributive to the ambiguity of residential
patterns in terms of the threefold typology. The term "virilocal" may
refer not only to the new couple's being totally integrated into the husband's household as its members but also to the establishment of a new
household near the husband's. But, then, how near? Furthermore,
however close the two households are, such an arrangement entails a
condition and style of life for members of both households that is quite
different from what would be the case if one were totally integrated
into the other.

For the sake of convenience, I have classified any household established in a separate dwelling as "neolocal" regardless of its distance from
either the husband's or the wife's household (a house attached to a main
house and within the same compound, commonly called *hanare*, will
not be considered as separate). Within this category we shall recognize a
qualified subcategory for those households located close enough to a
spouse's natal household to permit daily contact and thereby allow
members of the latter to exercise some control over or render support for
the newlyweds. The actual membership of a new household, apart from
its location, is another matter of consideration. Even though a new
house is established far away from either household and thus might be
classified as purely neolocal by the above definition, some kin of the

bride or groom may move in to join the young couple. This, too, must be treated as a subcategory of neolocal residence.

Furthermore, there are a few "duolocal" cases. At least for an earlier part of married life, husband and wife kept separate residences and had reunions once a week or less frequently for various reasons: economic constraint; the husband's employment imposing cycles of separation; the parents' refusal to let the daughter go; the wife's hesitation to live with the husband.

Taking all these ambiguous, variant instances into consideration, table 1 is presented to show the overall distribution of residential patterns. Residential shifts are counted only if the residence types are different. If one moves from Virilocal to Neolocal, two entries are marked with one score each; if another move is made back to Virilocal, this will not affect the score since Virilocal is already entered. Five cases of second marriage are also added. These categories are thus mutually exclusive only if taken simultaneously, but not so sequentially, and one woman can be placed in more than one category. "Neolocal with virilocal bias" and "Neolocal with uxorilocal bias" refer to those instances where the couple lives near the husband's or the wife's natal household or lives with his or her kin who have moved in. It might be noted that, although neolocal residence is of highest frequency, its pure type, which permits complete autonomy (or isolation) for the couple, is less frequent than virilocal residence.

TABLE 1 *Postmarital Residence*

|  | | | Frequency |
|---|---|---|---|
| Virilocal | | | 29 |
| | With Virilocal Bias | 9 | |
| Neolocal | Pure Type | 23 | 38 |
| | With Uxorilocal Bias | 6 | |
| Uxorilocal | | | 8 |
| Duolocal | | | 4 |
| Total | | | 79 |
| Subject Women Total | | | 54 |

CORESIDENTS

Who are coresidents? The number ranges from the smallest unit of a newlywed couple alone (if one excludes duolocals) in a neolocal residence to a large virilocal household containing a dozen coresidents. In the stem-family structure, a virilocally married woman can expect to live with her husband, his parents, his grandparents, and his unmarried siblings. It turns out that, while this expected pattern was followed in many cases, a number of women in the sample encountered more categories of coresidents than the above. The following are examples with the bride as ego (plurals are specified by numbers):

Bride A: husband, his mother, his father, his grandfather, his younger sisters (4), his younger brother, his father's brothers (2)
Total (including ego): 12.

Bride B: husband, his mother, his younger sisters (2), his younger sister's child, his cousin's children (3)
Total: 9.

Bride C: husband, his father, his stepmother, his divorced elder sister, his stepmother's daughter by a previous marriage, his father's and stepmother's son and daughter
Total: 8.

Bride A had not only five siblings-in-law but also two uncles-in-law. B had, in addition to unmarried sisters-in-law, a child of a married sister-in-law as well as a cousin-in-law's children. What overwhelmed C was not so much the size of the family as the complexity of its composition—both the husband's father and stepmother having had children by previous marriages as well as their own, and the divorced-and-returned *(demodori)* sister-in-law adding to the complexity.

A sister-in-law who was old enough to marry, had passed *tekireiki*, or had divorced and returned, was invariably considered by the bride as out of place, whereas the presence of the male counterpart was better tolerated. Such sisters-in-law were often designated "old miss" or, if divorced, *"demodori,"* indicating the prejudice of the designator. Even a married sister-in-law living in a separate household may happen to live nearby and continue to play the role of a coresident. Bride D had to prepare meals for fourteen people, including four members of another household across the street—the husband's sister, her husband, and two children. One bale of rice was consumed in a week. This woman had been brought into this household without even taking a look at the husband's picture and without knowing its membership.

For E, marriage brought many immature coresidents under her care, including two illegitimate children, one the father-in-law's and the other the sister-in-law's. Some women encountered non-kin coresidents, especially live-in employees of the house. Bride C, in addition to a complicated assemblage of "family members," lived with a shop manager and other employees. Yoshimi married into a house which owned and operated theaters, and found herself among "about twenty" coresidents, including film technicians, other theater-related workers and domestic servants.

For two women, although married to nonsuccessor husbands, the first residence was virilocal, which meant coresidence with the husband's elder brother (successor) and his wife as well as parents-in-law. Coresidence under such an arrangement often entailed the legal inclusion of the young couple and their children in the *koseki*, house register, of the successor brother's household, accompanied by the junior family's legal submission to the senior family's househead. To Tama's chagrin, her children had to go to school under the legal guardianship of her brother-in-law instead of the children's father (her husband). Here one finds a domestic unit deviating from the stem-family structure and approaching a joint family. This arrangement was considered far from the ideal pattern but was a temporary necessity prior to the establishment of a *bunke* by the junior couple separate from the *honke*. Temporarily, the junior couple was housed in a storage room.

## THE DOMESTIC STYLE

Each household has its history and may have developed its own cultural style or what the Japanese call *kafū*, the style of the *ie*. A virilocally married woman must learn a new *kafū*, which would require unlearning some of her natal *kafū*. Harue contrasted two households—natal and postmarital—in ideological terms. Her natal family was "liberal," and she had a hard time adjusting to the "conservatism" of her husband's family. This ideological disparity implied a more practical difference in everyday life: she, as a treasured daughter, had never lifted a single heavy thing, but as a daughter-in-law in the new home she found hard work a matter of routine; she had been a free consumer of whatever she needed before her marriage, but now had to face a frugally minded family. Her habit of wearing one new kimono after another was a source of worry for her mother-in-law in particular.

Some women were resocialized by a strikingly dissimilar *kafū*; the dissimilarity derived from the difference in household occupation and family size. Yukie was the daughter of a large commercial house which had over a dozen live-in employees to run a locally famous hot spring bathhouse. She married a schoolteacher in Tokyo and although the husband's younger brother lived with them for a while, this small postmarital household was "a totally different world" to her. It was not just that she found a difference between an always busy, commercial way of life and a salaried employee's quiet life style. Coming from a large family, she shook with fear whenever she was left alone at night. Resocialization in the reverse direction took place for Teiko, although her marriage was uxorilocal. As an only child she had lived with no one but her widowed mother all her life. Her husband, a son of a master carpenter running a huge household with more than twenty people, moved into this tiny household to find himself at a loss. She too was stunned when she visited his natal house to witness how they lived. "Over there, all year around, people come in and out so often that you can't tell whether it's your own house or somebody else's. One [worker] after another comes in, eats quickly with one knee up [ready to stand up], goes out to work. There is a long table where they sit. As soon as they finish eating, they take their own rice bowls to the sink. . . . In the kitchen there is a gigantic cooker like this." Under the encouragement of many female in-laws Teiko came to learn how to adjust to this totally different rhythm, to move around quickly instead of dragging her feet as she used to, to make herself useful to others instead of being a self-centered daughter under an indulgent, overprotective mother. She summarized her marriage as being a learning experience for which she is grateful.

When informants referred to a *kafū* the adjustment to which was difficult, they tended to attribute it to a special class origin of the postmarital household, particularly to the ancestral origin of the mother-in-law. One mother-in-law was identified as a daughter of the family which was founded by a warlord, "Taira Korekiyo or some such person," and has persisted for hundreds of years. "It is the *honke* of all *honke* surrounded by countless *bunke*." Another mother-in-law supposedly came from the family of the top administrator of a daimyo government under Tokugawa feudalism. It is interesting to note that the *kafū* of the husband's family is associated with the mother-in-law's rather than the father-in-law's ancestry. This suggests that a woman not only submits to the existing *kafū* but at the same time brings her natal *kafū* into the postmarital household, eventually to replace the latter's *kafū*, especially if she has married downward.

My reference to *kafū* in interviews drew laughter from some informants. "*Kafū?* Ha-ha-ha. Don't be ridiculous. If we had *kafū*, if ours were such a family, we wouldn't have been suffering so much poverty."

In the same breath, Fuyuko continued: "When I married into this house, my mother-in-law too was sewing for additional income. One night, while she was still at work, my husband said to me: 'Hey, let's go to bed.' I said: 'Oh, no. It would make me feel bad to go to bed while Mother is still working.' 'Don't be silly,' he said. 'A daughter-in-law cannot sleep while her mother-in-law is awake? You can say that only if you are wealthy.'" The husband was telling her with a mixture of cynicism and levity that his house lacked the dignity worthy of *kafū*—a point of view she shared.

Neolocal marriage permits a new *kafū* to grow out of the cohabitation of a young couple. Here women are creators of domestic styles. As Sayo admitted: "I had no in-laws, so I could build up the customs of my own house." This remark, however, meant an unhampered transplantation of the domestic style of the woman's natal house because, in Sayo's view, women are "completely" molded by their parents, as she was, according to the natal *kafū*. She brought her mother's perfectionism in manners and etiquette into the two-person household.

## Wife and Husband

Interpersonal relationship in the postmarital household is seldom confined to that of wife and husband alone, particularly in the presence of coresidents other than one's marriage mate. Nonetheless, for the moment, we shall focus on the marital dyad as the primary bond within a larger context, reserving other dyads and more complex triads for later sections. Naturally more cases of neolocal marriage will be cited here than of viri- or uxorilocal marriage. With the sex-role polarization as a point of departure, some salient aspects of the marital dyads will be analyzed.

### Intimacy and Distance

*Sex and love.* The first question is how our informants experienced intimacy unique to a married couple, or how they were bound by the segregation rule. I tried to obtain information on their sexual experience without directly referring to it in consideration of their embarrassment. (My initial attempts to ask direct questions on this matter alienated the interviewees.) The following is an inference drawn from the incomplete information thus gathered on this touchy subject. Some women had acquired knowledge about sex from girlfriends, female colleagues, or high school teachers, but the majority turned out to have been ignorant until the very moment they experienced it. Their mothers apparently did not give them any instruction. Many compliantly followed the strong leadership of their husbands without knowing what they were doing. I came to realize that their reluctance to talk about sex was due not only to embarrassment but to a sort of amnesia over the initial part of their sexual experience.

Despite such unpreparedness, nobody seemed to detest sex; rather, it took little time for most of the women to enjoy it. No sign of frigidity could be detected. While most informants were too prudish to talk about it, a *mukoyōshi* husband who volunteered to be interviewed was frank enough—to the embarrassment of his wife, who was present—to say: "Sex is something mysterious. The older we get, the more I appreciate that we are a fortunate couple because we have been successful in our sexual life."

Sexual compatibility seemed to have been achieved even in a marriage between total strangers or a marriage resulting from the woman's unquestioned or coercive compliance. Even in the case of dyadic compliance where the woman was bullied by the seducer into marrying him, she did not seem to mind intercourse at all. In fact, I learned that during their sexual contact this same man transformed himself into a loving husband. The wife became totally alienated from him and their sexual life only after witnessing too many times how he changed back to his usual self immediately after coitus.

The apparent success in sexual compatibility even between strangers may be partially explained by the culturally induced conviction that marriage is a naturally unfolding consequence of humanity, and of womanhood in particular. Asked if she had known what marriage meant, an informant said: "Absolutely nothing. But I knew all women must marry." Compliance training may be another contributing factor in view of the fact that many were blindly trusting of their husband's leadership. Contemporary adolescents appear quite different in this respect. A group interview revealed that premarital sex is taken for granted among young Japanese today. According to a 1972 survey of youth of eighteen to twenty-four years of age conducted by the national government, premarital sex was disapproved of by 27 percent and approved of by 72 percent of the Japanese respondents (Sōrifu Seishōnen Taisaku Honbu 1973:154).

Sexual compatibility is not always accompanied by love in the emotional sense; but both of these are independent of whether marriage was mediated or not, whether *miai* or *ren'ai*. Some informants are convinced that *miai* marriage is much more productive of love than *ren'ai* marriage. Asked if it is true that love grows out of cohabitation, a woman said: "Of course, it's only natural." In a few cases of mediated marriage, the bond of love developed and became so strong that the marriage was sustained despite efforts to terminate it on the part of the kin who were the very initiators and mediators for the couple. Harue who, after hesitating a long time, consented to marry under her father's forceful urging found the conditions of the postmarital household unbearable and became ill. While she was recuperating at her natal home, her father advised her to divorce. Meanwhile, all of her in-laws assembled to discuss the matter and reached the conclusion that since she was so fragile, she had better leave. Her husband declared that if they divorced he would never marry again and would leave home. Harue, telling her father that she had complied once but would not this time, ran away to Tokyo to be with her husband. Temporary or cyclical separation may stimulate love to grow in the otherwise loveless mediated marriage, or incite its periodic renewal. Two women, married through mediation to sailors, were alone at the time of interview and both sounded strongly attached to their absentee husbands.

*Suppressed intimacy.* A straightforward reference to love is atypical of my sample. Like sexual experience, any question on love tended to be either dismissed with a giggle or responded to with substitute expressions. Only one said "I love him." Another instead said: "My husband indulged me." Many others preferred the expression *"yasashii"* (tender) in describing their husbands, which sounds emotionally more neutral and distant than "love." Note the following communication:

Question: Did you come to love your husband?

Answer: I have never associated my husband with love or lack of love. I only felt I was blessed with this man. . . . People said he is like a god . . . he was a *yasashii* person . . . almost too good.

Question: Does love grow out of living together?

Answer: (Silence) . . . I had a baby soon, and my attention was drawn toward the baby. . . .

Question: Were you well matched as husband and wife?

Answer: I quietly followed him.

Rarely does the wife express her feeling toward her husband in terms of exclusive intimacy. The listener would have the impression that husband and wife do not belong exclusively to one another, that there is more aloofness than intimacy in their interaction, that communication between them is suppressed. In response to a question regarding the closeness of husband and wife, Kumiko remarked about her children:

"This may sound strange to you, but I have concentrated on the children. I am embarrassed to say so." "How about your husband?" I pressed. "That is another world [separate from me and the children]. In brief, I am sort of a kindergarten teacher." It is not that Kumiko is or has been an unhappy wife, but that the husband has never stepped into the intimate world of mother and children. Marital intimacy was not what she had expected.

While ignorant about marriage itself, some women were well prepared by their mothers for treating their husbands in a ritually proper manner, the maintenance of physical tidiness in front of the husband or the correct way to serve drinks upon his return from work being two examples. Far from mutual relaxation to be enjoyed in an intimate relationship, they were trained to present themselves in a disciplined way as if they were receiving guests.

Our oldest informant, eighty, joined her husband wherever he traveled on business or for fun. But this is an exception. Many women could not recall one thing they and their husbands had done alone together. Not even once had the couples traveled together or gone out to see a movie. "We did not even take a walk," said Sayo.

In several cases, the husband's occupation or the war took him away from the wife, leaving her alone with a group of in-laws soon after the wedding. Mutsuko complained that her fisherman husband left home the day after her *satogaeri*, on the third day of their marriage, to be on board the ship run by the *honke*, whose request he, a son of a *bunke* head, could not turn down. He did this without consulting her. By the time he returned, she had forgotten what he looked like.

The apparent distance between husband and wife turns out to be far from a simple phenomenon of segregation. It may be a matter of *social gesture* on the part of women in talking about their husbands to others rather than of faithful reflection of a real relationship. It may be that one is required by the norm of decency to refrain from displaying marital intimacy in front of others (including an interviewer); instead, the tendency is to exaggerate distance or even trouble between husband and wife. It is well known that Japanese women, in a group of close friends in particular, tend to compete with one another in tearing down their husbands. They do so, it turns out, with the understanding that nobody will take it too seriously, and that such talk is for nothing more than mutual entertainment. This behavior reflects the eagerness of the Japanese audience, particularly peers, to sympathize for a troubled marriage rather than envy a successful one. American women, too, may exaggerate about their relationships with their husbands, but my hunch is that their exaggeration would go in the reverse direction: they would display the success of their marriage probably over and beyond its real state. These contrasting patterns of behavior are likely to be more or less duplicated by the husbands in the respective societies.

The contrived aloofness may be a legacy of behavior patterns embedded in the structure of the stem family, where the dyadic bond of husband and wife cannot claim its autonomy, and to which the unrestrained display of exclusive intimacy of the dyad would be destructive. The gesture of sexual distance is further reinforced by same-sex solidarity whether in a play group or in a work group. A newlywed couple or a pair in love is a familiar target of teasing by peers.

Not necessarily discontinuous with the above is another interpretation. Because husband and wife are viewed as being *ittai* (fused into one body), it would be unnecessary to display love and intimacy between them. To praise rather than denigrate one's spouse would amount to praising oneself, which would be intolerably embarrassing. In this interpretation, aloofness is not a matter of deception but *a sign of* ittai *feeling*, or an extreme form of intimacy. Many Japanese seem to convey this view when they wonder how American spouses can express their love for each other without embarrassment. The feeling of fusion develops in the course of cohabitation, culturally aided, to begin with, by the weakness of individuality as well as by the identification of household members as *uchi* (inside) in clear distinction from *soto* (outside).

All of these explanations make sense. What I want to add here is that I have come across many women—women in my primary sample as well as others—for whom marital aloofness is not at all a matter of social gesture or a sign of intimacy itself but is really indicative of *estrangement*. Harumi described her marital relationship only in negative terms: "We are not really husband and wife, nor lovers, in no such relationship at all. . . . No word can describe it. Nor are our characters well matched. It's really strange that we had children." The husband goes out all the time and neighbors warn her about his destination (hinting that he is seeing another woman), but she never bothers to ask where he goes, and never feels jealous. Her life-style is not affected by his presence or absence, nor is his; it sounds as if they are completely autonomous of each other. She is thirty-six years old, and her marriage was by her choice and against her family. Contrived aloofness seems in her case to have turned into real aloofness—a point where a cultural design meets personal affect.

Aloofness is most often associated with the lack of conversation. It is more often the husband than the wife who says "nothing." Sayo stressed that there has been nothing wrong with her marriage, that her husband has never failed to provide for her and the children, that he has never complained about her being a poor housekeeper, and that there has not been a single quarrel between them. And yet she admitted that her life has been lonely because there has been no conversation between husband and wife. As I observed the couple, the husband occasionally talked to me, but ignored his wife's solicitous questions, and if he had to respond, he did so only reluctantly and in monosyllables:

Wife:       Would you like to have rice cake, Grandpa?

Husband: . . .

Wife:       Wouldn't you like some?

Husband: Tea only.

Surprisingly, he turned out to be talkative on topics of special interest to him, like botany, but then it was a monologue rather than a conversation. While talking he never looked directly at either me or his wife but stared into space. "Silence is a masculine quality," remarked the wife with a tone of resignation when we were alone. Some women referred to their own reticence, but then only as indicative of their endurance or compliance.

The husband thus tends to be more aloof while the wife is solicitous than the other way around. However, the situation was reversed with two couples. Fuyuko described her husband as being fond of enjoying "moods," taking a walk and having tea with her or some such thing. "But I was reared in a poor family, preoccupied with nothing but work, work, work. I just couldn't relax and play. Taking a walk—that was preposterous for me." She tried to comply with him once in a while but was unable to enjoy it. Hamako's husband was basically *yasashii*, and would nurse her with extreme care and tenderness whenever she became ill (she often faked illness). He really loved her. But Hamako could not bring herself to reciprocate even though she tried. She just did not feel true love for him until a few years before her husband died.

To be added is the idea of women's *pollution*, as conveyed by a few older informants. The utmost denigration of masculinity is often symbolized, as in popular comedies, by a man laundering his wife's underwear. Implicit in this symbolism is the deep-rooted asymmetry with respect to body pollution: a woman's body is believed to be dirtier than a man's, and so is her underclothing as an extension of her body. Not only physical but ritual pollution used to be associated with the female sex and demonstrated by a variety of taboos that were imposed upon women in both Shinto and Buddhism. Some of the all-male occupations have defended themselves from women's ritual pollution. Emi was separated from her husband, employed at a sake brewer's, for six months every year. During the sake brewing season, the husband, like all other co-workers, stayed with the master in order to avoid contact with a woman, "because women are polluting, they say, and will spoil sake."

*Addressing and referring to the spouse.* My question on the terms of address for the husband embarrassed many informants. The immediate response to "What did you call your husband?" was *"Otō-san"* (Dad) or the English, "Papa." But when I pressed them with, "But before you had a child?" some said *"Anata"* (You), or mentioned such attention-calling utterances as *"Chotto"* or *"Moshi"* (Look here). Many could not think of any term and concluded that there was no need for calling their husbands, which confirms Fischer's (1964) "zero form" proposition. Two younger women, both in their thirties, started to call their husbands *"Otō-san"* before they became parents. An intriguing case of teknonymy was presented by the woman married into a household where the husband's sister's child was reared. Following the existing custom of that household, the bride addressed her husband as "Uncle." A kin term was often replaced by an occupational designation if there was one: the doctor's wife in addressing her husband sometimes used the term *"Sensei,"* and the wife running a bar with her husband called him "Master" (meaning a bartender) in English, as well as "Otō-san."

The husband had more options in addressing the wife in that he could use her personal name without offending her simply because he was her senior in terms of sex status as well as age, whereas the wife's use of the addressee's personal name would have been either offensive or embarrassing. Nonetheless, many husbands reciprocated the wives' termlessness by using an impolite version of attention-invoking expressions like *"Oi"* (Hey), and after the first child was born, used *"Okā-san"* (Mom).

What does all this imply? Terminological identity is difficult to establish for husband and wife in relation to each other, and thus it is uncertain until they become parents. This reinforces some of the points made with regard to marital aloofness. Cultural pressure creates a tendency to resort to a term shared by all (or most) members of the household in avoidance of a term indicative of a unique and exclusive relationship between the addressor and addressee. In other words, the Japanese are inclined to prefer sociocentric terms to egocentric terms. For family members, sociocentricity boils down to *ie*-centricity. The trouble is that husband and wife prior to parenthood lack *ie*-centric terms by which they can be addressed. An occupational status designation for the husband is one solution since it is used and reinforced by customers. If a kin term is to be used, the general inclination is to take the youngest child as the central focus (ego) of reference.

This child-centered term may serve as an *ie*-centric term. Hence, the wife's calling her husband "Uncle" makes sense, since others in the household will be as likely to call him by that term as the husband's nephew will. By this logic, it should not surprise us to hear a woman calling her husband "Elder Brother" in certain situations if he has a younger sibling as the youngest coresident. Once a child is born, the address terms for spouses stabilize comfortably as dad and mom, and other members of the household may follow suit. The mother-in-law, then, may address the daughter-in-law as "Mom," while allowing herself to be addressed "Grandma" by everybody. The old couple will address each other as "Grandpa" and "Grandma." One variable which may distort this system is the status consciousness on the part of the speaker. It may be too self-belittling for a man to address his wife as "Mom" unless the child is present, and he would rather continue to use her personal name or the attention-invoking *"Oi."*

The *ie*-centricity of address terms for spouses permeates reference terms as well, even though reference terms are more sensitive to the ego-centric point of view. The wife may refer to the husband as "Dad" or "Grandpa," the same as the address term, or the more formal *"Shujin"* (Master), depending upon whom she is speaking to. Usually these terms are preceded by *uchi no*, an equivalent of "my" but literally meaning "the house's," *uchi* and *ie* being used as synonymous. Some women identify their husbands as *uchi no hito* (the person of the house) or simply as *"uchi."* Husbands, too, are likely to speak about their wives as *uchi no nyōbō* or *uchi no kanai* (*nyōbō* and *kanai* are the most prevalently used conversational terms for wife).[1] To be sure, this is a cultural convention which defies a logical analysis of its literal meaning, but to me this convention symbolizes a diffuseness of the husband-wife relationship. If "my" indicates the exclusive, direct relationship, *"uchi no"* gives the impression that husband and wife belong to the house or to all the members of the household before they belong to each other.

The emphasis upon the collective sharing of a spouse does not necessarily imply a feeling of separation between spouses. When both spouses were present in an interview, there was embarrassment in referring to each other in talking to me. In one case the terms for "my wife" and "my husband" were replaced by "this one"—an example of "directional indicators" (Passin 1965a:106)—while an index finger was pointed to the spouse. The same sort of embarrassment, I feel, underlies the derogatory or frivolous terms often used to refer to a spouse, such as *yadoroku* (literally, inn keeper) or *oyaji* (old man) for the husband and *gusai* (foolish wife) for the wife. Embarrassment expressed by terminological muteness or derogation is consistent with the claimed "oneness" of a marital dyad. It is embarrassing to address or refer to one's spouse, as it would be to address or refer to oneself. There seems to be no clear demarcation between husband and wife as separate individuals, as subject and object. The marital dyad, then, is doubly diffuse: first in terms of collective sharing of spouses, and, second, in the lack of a boundary between the two individuals. The term *uchi* is illustrative of these two aspects of diffuseness.

Among women in their twenties or early thirties we find a sign of change in spouse terminology. Both husband and wife may use each other's personal name or nickname for both address and reference. The youngest informant referred to her husband as *"Ichiro-san"* throughout, the only such case in my sample. Usually there remains sex asymmetry in that the wife respectfully adds *"-san"* to the husband's name whereas the husband speaks down in the *yobisute* form (without *"-san"*). Suzuko protested when she heard her husband call her "Suzuko". He settled for the more intimate "Suzu-chan" instead of "Suzuko-san."

## POWER DISTRIBUTION

Informants are least inhibited when talk about their marriage centers on the distribution of power and authority, but this too is more complicated than it appears.

*Husband, the ruler.* Many characterized their husbands as *"teishu kanpaku"* (husband, the ruler) or "one man," meaning a despot. The husband's alleged autocracy turns out to have a variety of facets which are not necessarily mutually consistent. First, in some cases *teishu kanpaku* indeed referred to the husband's (1) *tyranny.* Sakiko, a thirty-one-year-old university graduate, allowed me to visit her only in secret because her husband would disapprove of her outside contact. As I was told, she waits on him like a lord, puts his socks on for him, and takes a waitress's role when she serves meals for him, never joining him as a co-diner. She had not experienced the pleasure of a honeymoon, since her husband displayed his displeasure from the very beginning with the way she did housework. He orders her to redo ironing, cooking, and whatnot. What displeases the husband is not simply her inadequacy in domestic skills; he also disapproves of the way she eats, talks, and looks. "Try to practice smiling wherever you are, in a bus or train," he will say. Not until she was told so by her husband had it ever occurred to her that her face was expressionless and repulsive. (She certainly did not strike me as such.) In short, she is constantly subject to impatient socialization by the disgruntled husband.

A few other women appeared frightened in the presence of their husbands, too frightened to respond articulately or meaningfully even to the most innocuous questions, whereas there was no such sign of tension when they were interviewed alone. Rather than volunteer to respond, they conceded the role of speaker to their husbands.

Tyranny overlaps in part with (2) *violence*. Sakiko's husband occasionally throws things at her, but recently Sakiko has learned how to turn her body to avoid being hit. The husband's physical assault comes as the climax of a heated argument; instead of giving another thrust of verbal aggression, the husband silences the wife, as has often happened to another informant, by beating her, stepping on her, or dragging her down the stairway by her hair. For some husbands, proclivities for violence become activated only when they are drunk—this is what the Japanese call *shuran*, drunken violence. Ikuko, forty-one, was beaten up, her eyes struck, and her teeth broken by her *shuran* husband. Many times she threatened to divorce him but would relent after having him write an oath never to take another sip. The oath was violated over and over again, each time resulting in abuse, until some years ago in his late thirties when he was suddenly converted into a sober, considerate husband.

Physical abuse is coupled with social abuse for another husband. He is irritable and easily provoked to violence. What scares Taeko even more is his threat to go wild, make scenes, and yell at her, in the neighborhood, at her work place, or even with her kin. To avoid this embarrassing eventuality, Taeko takes great pains not to irritate him, and once his yelling does start the first thing she does is to shut all the windows. Her shame is painfully shared by her mother, who lives nearby.

Wife abuse is not necessarily an expression of male dominance or superiority, but is often a cover for the husband's inferiority feelings. Faster with his fists than with his mouth, a farmer would beat up his wife, Hamako, who had been reared in Tokyo, was better educated than he, and was esteemed by neighbors as a smart, sophisticated, and hardworking wife. Despite this, Hamako did not doubt that he was basically *yasashii* (tender, considerate, thoughtful) and loved her.

There are two contrasting situations where wife abuse is committed: in the exclusive privacy of the marital dyad, where the husband feels unrestrained, and in public, as will be seen below, where the husband displays his power to a third party.

The claim to the *teishu kanpaku* status may be limited to (3) *onstage dominance*. To the amusement of women, many a husband is concerned with maintaining his authority over his wife and being treated as dominant only in front of others. Salamon (1975:27) refers to a man who made his fiancée promise to permit him to behave as a *teishu kanpaku* outside the house while giving her total freedom to act any way she wanted at home. She cites another man who pretends to be a ruler when he and his wife visit his parents. The apparent aloofness, like that described above, on the part of a husband may well be a derivative of onstage dominance. The above-mentioned farmer's wife revealed that her husband was *yasashii* only when the couple was alone. When guests were around, he was harsh and abusive, "probably to show that he is not a henpecked husband." In these examples, it looks as if there was no alternative but to appear dominant in order to avoid appearing dominated. Even a child may make an effective audience for the onstage behavior. Burdened with a sense of inferiority in education and literacy, Tomiko's husband sometimes humbles himself to ask his wife how to read Chinese characters but becomes infuriated once his ignorance is revealed in front of the children. A clever wife, finding herself in this situation, might exchange her onstage subservience for backstage matriarchy.

Paradoxical as it may sound, the concept of *teishu kanpaku* is often associated with the husband's (4) *dependency* (Lebra 1978). This derives from a compulsion for role polarization which assigns a clearly bounded role territory to the wife on which the husband refuses to intrude. The idea that "no male should step into the kitchen" is extended to all domestic work; some men refuse to share any work relating to the house maintenance, including fixing kitchen shelves or even trimming trees in the yard, as if helping their wives with these chores would endanger their masculinity. The result is the husband's ineptitude and total dependence on female labor and skill in housework. Dependency goes still further to encompass the husband's personal daily routine. It is not just that the husband depends on the wife's cooking, laundering, housecleaning, and whatnot, but that he comes to rely on her service "around his body" *(mi no mawari)*. In the morning he needs his wife's help in finding a complete set of clothing to wear that day. "Every morning, I put out one thing after another, saying, 'Here are your socks, here's your shirt, here's your handkerchief and so forth.' " The wife may help him put on a tie and coat, and place his shoes, which she has polished, where he can put them on easily. Morning is the busiest time for a wife burdened with such around-the-body care. Many Japanese women take this duty for granted. I am reminded of a Japanese woman who was married to an American and found herself at a loss when her mother, during a visit with them, told her to leave all the kitchen work to her in the morning so that she, the daughter, could "take care" of her husband. "What is there to take care of?" she wondered and then realized what most Japanese wives are subjected to every morning. "My husband would hate to be taken care of in such a servile manner."

The around-the-body care resumes upon the husband's return from work and continues as long as he is around. The wife is called upon to help him change clothes, to serve him at the table, and to bring him whatever he wants—cigarettes, an ashtray, a glass of water, or a newspaper. When he relaxes to watch television, all he has to do is to call out: "Channel eight!" whereupon she rushes in from the next room where she is working to turn the dial. The wife may be expected to accommodate a variety of the husband's needs without being told so verbally. "While at the table, my husband may stretch out his hand, and I must sense what he wants. His eyes turn this way, and then I should know what those eyes are demanding. Accordingly, I must move fast." When the husband travels, it is the wife's job to put everything necessary into his suitcase. The idea of the husband's dependence on such attendance is so ingrained in the wife's mind that special note is taken by the woman whose husband is more self-reliant. "My husband, even when he comes home drunk, hangs his clothes by himself."

Not all the women informants were prepared for the around-the-body care of the husband. Mieko was astonished when she married for the second time. Unlike her father and first husband, this former naval doctor would do absolutely nothing for himself:

> When he gets out of a bath and finds no *fundoshi* [G-string] placed there, he walks out nude. . . . When he goes out, he does not know which shoes to wear, so he stands there waiting. Nor does he have any idea what to wear, what drawers contain what. He has deaf ears if I try to instruct him. "It's not my job to remember those things," he dares to say. . . . He drinks tea at ten and three every day, and if I bring it a few minutes too late he blows up. [During the interview, we heard the husband clap his hands at three o'clock to signal for the tea service.]

When the wife leaves home on a short trip, she must prepare every meal in advance so that all the husband need do is reheat it. Even coffee is made, and she leaves a note for him so that he can locate cream for it. Without all these things having been prepared, "my husband will eat nothing for days."

A cross-national survey[2] shows that Japanese housewives spend more time in doing housework on Sundays than those of many other countries, and that housework time actually increases on Sundays in Japan as far as childless housewives are concerned whereas it decreases in all other surveyed countries. It may be that the Japanese full-time housewives without children feel more strongly compelled, as interpreted by the survey analysts, to demonstrate the value of housework to their husbands. I would like to advance another interpretation: Sundays are when the around-the-body care is in constant, day-long demand. Small wonder that many women I know do not like Sundays, and that many prefer that their husbands make extended business trips. Housewives would complain, "As long as Papa is around the house, my chores don't come to an end."

In this sense the husband is a nuisance to a certain extent. Nonetheless, wives do not necessarily mind responding to their demanding spouses. In fact the husband's dependency turns out in some instances to be contrived to create one of the few opportunities for intimate contact and communication between the marriage mates. Intimacy, then, is closely associated with the husband's childlike helplessness and the wife's motherlike nurturance. Some informants described their husbands in this context as *amae*. Mieko's husband is sixteen years older, and yet people tell her that, despite his seniority, he behaves more like a baby in *amae*. Salamon (1975) insightfully saw a link between *teishu kanpaku* and love through *amae* dependency and concluded that male chauvinism is a manifestation of love for Japanese couples.

For Toshiko, the husband was not merely a child but a spoiled child (*dadakko*) who deliberately gave her trouble (*dada o koneru*). With jealous frustration that she did not always sit around him as he wanted her to, he would declare his intention to divorce her, but by the next day he would have forgotten it. Her marriage was a failure, she said, but admitted that, "looking back, I don't feel like hating him; I must have loved him."

The husband who was reared in a family with more females— mother, grandmother, sisters—than males tends to be more dependent. By contrast, men who were deprived of female caretakers are autonomous and skilled with housechores. Thus, not only the female-scarce family but the exclusively male group occupation such as fishing tends to give rise to self-sufficient men. The only exception is that the hierarchy within the all-male occupational structure allows a superior to depend upon a subordinate for femalelike care. The above-mentioned naval doctor was accustomed to being waited upon by his subordinates for the around-the-body care.

The idea of *teishu kanpaku*, as well as the husband's aloofness, is often associated with either the era or the place of his birth. The husband's dependency, for instance, is explained as "because he is Meiji-born" or "Taisho-born" even if it was in the last year of the Meiji or Taisho era. Likewise, a Kyushu man is said to typify "the husband, the ruler."

*Domestic matriarchy.* The husband's childlike dependency is an attribute of patriarchy, yes. But it also gives the wife leverage to wield power by making her services indispensable. Further, the husband's onstage dominance may be bought with a blank check for the wife's off-stage manipulation. Patriarchy and matriarchy, far from being mutually exclusive, can be reciprocals of one another. Some of the women who described their husbands as *teishu kanpaku* admitted that they, the wives, throw their weight around in the house. The husband who is autonomous or indifferent to onstage dominance is in fact less manipulable from the wife's point of view. This may explain why the labels *teishu kanpaku* or "one-man" are sometimes attached to a husband who does everything by himself. A woman described her husband as a despot because he cooks and does laundry for and by himself; his domesticity deprives her of domestic matriarchy.

Central to domestic matriarchy are the household purse strings. The widespread assumption is that the wife controls the household finances while the husband earns the money. Most informants, unless their in-laws were still active financiers, have had this privilege (or obligation) as part of their domestic chores. If the household business where both husband and wife participate is the source of income, the husband may have no idea how much they are earning.

> In our house, my husband has nothing to do with taxes either. He does not know how much we have, how much debt we have. Sixteen years ago we built an additional house across the street, and I did everything from the bank loan to the completion of payment. He takes a monthly allowance from me.

Fuyuko learned at a primary school alumni reunion that almost all of her female classmates hold the household purse strings as she does.

Paradoxically, it is the salaryman's wife who has complete control over the financial management of the household. The husband's authority is felt at the moment when he hands the sealed monthly salary envelope to his wife. This is one of the main reasons, I was told, why many Japanese employees still welcome cash salary and are opposed to the system of direct bank deposit now coming into practice. This fleeting moment is captured by Yumiko's salaryman husband in a sort of ceremony: he places his salary envelope upon the *kamidana* (household god shelf) instead of dropping it into profane wifely hands; after a time, the wife solemnly takes it.

The wife, in turn, gives the husband a portion of the salary—10 to 20 percent among my informants—as an allowance (to buy cigarettes, to have a haircut, to have a few drinks). Inflation over the last few decades has promoted the "hundred-yen-per-diem husband" to the "one-thousand-yen husband." The husband who needs more allowance has either to beg the wife or to depend upon a secret saving of extra income.

There are a few cases where the husband takes the bookkeeping responsibility. The husband's wifelike role in this respect is coupled, I find, with role reversal in other respects as well. The husband stays home, doing some work there for a supplementary income rather than working full time in an occupation, whereas the wife has a full-time, professional occupation. Two such husbands happen to be victims of poliomyelitis, which is the reason why they are homebound.

The cultural pattern is clear: two financial responsibilities—earning and managing—clearly divided, and the latter is assigned to the one who stays at home, male or female. This division is easier to make for the salaryman family than for the husband-wife-team business family.

Since the wife's power over the household finances is so culturally patterned, the husband's refusal to conform to the rule is most frustrating. Two women have experienced extreme frustration due to their husbands' monopoly of the household finances. Not to be trusted with the purse strings but, instead, to have to ask her stingy husband for a little cash each time she went grocery shopping drove one of the women to divorce, leaving the children with him. "If I bought one fish, my husband would say, 'Half would have been enough.' " The other husband inflicted hardship on his wife by spending money solely according to his whims, including affairs with women. Widowed now, she still will not forgive him: "Low, low intellect. He just could not recognize the wife's human right."

The opposite type of deviation was also observed. The wife's exclusive responsibility for financial management may make the husband irresponsible. The husband's lack of responsibility amounted to exploitation in three cases. The husband, jobless or having no occupational identity, came to rely on the wife's earnings for his indulgence in hobbies, gambling, drinking, or even women.

> I was tricked into marrying [my husband]. He was a bum. He would spend the last penny on women instead of paying the wholesale dealer. He had affairs with one woman after another. Furthermore, he drank all the time. It was me who had to make money to pay his debts.

After "eight or nine years" of cohabitation, Rin finally succeeded in talking him into signing the divorce application; she then left him, and settled down in Shizumi. After the divorce, the husband still tried to approach her "in order to trick money out of me." But she kicked him out, yelling: "Damn you, you are no longer my husband. Get the hell out!" The other two women, seeing no alternative, are still persevering with their parasitic husbands.

Domestic matriarchy is further based upon the wife's control of household property. The house furniture is usually regarded as under the wife's jurisdiction mainly because the significant portion of it originated in the dowry. The house itself is usually the husband's (or the husband's parents'), but what is inside belongs to the wife. The husband, then, refrains from using the wardrobe, for example, and this is one of the geneses of his dependency upon his wife for getting a set of clothing ready every morning. The husband's dependency extends to his indifference to household matters in general. It was exclusively her decision, said Sayo, to build a new house in the present location and to move there. "My husband? He would never think of that unless I propose it." He only followed her decision without resistance.

The wife does not necessarily enjoy this power but often takes it as a burden. Nonetheless it seems safe to assume that the dowry provides the initial building blocks for the wife's domestic castle or *shufu-ken*, housewife's privilege. The significance of furniture for the wife's autonomy was well perceived by Perry (1976). Teruko Mizushima, a public educator, said that the furniture is an important factor to consider in the course of divorce procedure. The problem of moving out a large amount of furniture becomes detrimental to easy divorce, which makes the couple think it over (personal conversation 1978). If divorce involves the husband wishing to stay in "his" house and to get rid of both his reluctant wife and "her" furniture, the immobility of furniture will protect her right to resist.

Spatial occupancy in the house is another point of consideration. The husband, as house head, is symbolically situated in a reception room *(zashiki)* with an alcove which defines seating hierarchy for receiving guests. Domestic architecture has changed its focus from the reception room to the livingroom (Hirai 1974), and the latter is taking on the American model in which the livingroom is connected with the "dining room and kitchen." (Note the Japanese designation of apartments as "2LDK"—two bedrooms, livingroom, dining room, and kitchen.) This change implies the loss of the spatial basis for patriarchy. The wife and children occupy the whole space, while the husband tends to feel an intrusive outsider.

Finally, the wife's domestic power is affected by the husband's regular absence. A nautical engineer and his wife, subject to cyclical separation, present an interesting case. When the husband is at sea, the wife is supposed to assume all responsibilities and to make all decisions to run the house. "So, seamen's wives are all strong they say. They *become* tough as there are many times women must be like men. In the company's newsletters I find seamen complaining that their wives are no longer lovable." As if to complement the wife's masculine role, the husband was found to be helpless when on land. Suzuko was surprised to learn that her husband, with such a manly occupation, did not know what to do once he was on shore, and that all he could do was to follow her wherever she went. Newly wed, she wants to remain feminine whenever she is with him, to become tough only when alone. She wrote him so.

## GENDER-PROPER PERSONALITY

In describing one's own or someone else's husband, our informants often use the term *yasashii* (tender, considerate, thoughtful) obviously as one of the key attributes required for an ideal husband. This attribute is also desirable for wives, and thus transcends sex difference. Along with this sex-neutral quality, wife and husband tend to look to each other for gender-proper personality, often undefined, regardless of power distribution. No woman has turned out to like an unmanly husband even in a matriarchical household. Yumiko, fifty, confessed that she and her husband fight "365 days per year," and she accused him of not being broadminded like a real man but fidgety like a woman. "My husband complains about trivial matters," said another woman. "I would rather be married to a manly man who might even slap my face." It may be noted that this husband has been tormenting the wife with his "incurable" promiscuity. A dressmaker and breadwinner has not divorced her jobless, weak husband, only because she feels nobody else would rescue the abandoned man. "But if I were to marry again, I would choose a real masculine, dependable man who would lead me with irrestible power." The informant does not seem to realize that such a strong man would not tolerate the full-fledged career occupation and power she is admittedly enjoying.

The husbands also tended to emphasize the desirability of femininity for wives. A forty-two-year-old husband commented that he had not looked for a beautiful woman to marry but for a pliable, womanlike type. The implication was that he did find such a woman—the wife sitting there smiling. He does not approve of "women's libbers," mainly because they are unfeminine. "I don't mind a woman air pilot, but cannot stand an unfeminine one." Another husband is violent with his wife for the express reason that she is not feminine enough.

Whether women regard femininity as desirable for themselves is another matter. A number of women characterized themselves as masculine and sounded proud of it. One of these believes that her marital friction is partly due to her lack of femininity; she feels sorry for her husband, who would have been happier with a womanly wife. Her tone betrayed a scornful pity more than guilt. Another is amused that her daughters keep saying they have no mother but two fathers. The relationship between these women and their husbands tends to be a cool or estranged one.

## PROMISCUITY

It is predominantly the husband who gets involved with extramarital affairs. Such has been the case at least in the past, reflecting the culturally institutionalized tolerance of or even support for male promiscuity in contrast to the sanction against female infidelity. Five women disclosed that their husbands have had mistresses.

*Structured versus unstructured promiscuity.* The triangular relationship that results from the husband's extramarital involvement takes different forms along the structured-unstructured scale. In the structured relationship, the status of the two women is kept apart, the wife claiming the sole legitimacy and privilege. The wife will be admired if she keeps her composure, confident of her superior status, and even inclined to be generous toward her rival. For the mistress it is imperative not to step out of her limited, inferior status. This clear distinction between the two women must be kept in mind by the husband also. Some of the unfaithful husbands, I learned, were not only religious in maintaining this distinction but strongly attached to their wives as well as their mistresses. One such husband was jealous and would not let the wife go out to see a movie alone; he always escorted her.

The tragedy of one informant, in her fifties, is that her husband has failed to draw a clear line between the two women. He started his *uwaki* (fickle, or extramarital involvement) as early as six months after the wedding and his *uwaki* still persists. He used to have several different women, but for the last twenty years has settled down with one woman. Apparently he is most concerned with the feelings of this mistress. For example:

> Let's suppose he is walking with me. People will see us together, and among them may be the woman's friends, who then will report to her that my husband was walking with his wife. When he meets her the next time, he will get a lot of nagging. To avoid this, he tries to slow down so that he and I don't have to walk abreast.

It sounds, in this instance, as if the mistress has assumed the wife's status. The informant contrasted her husband, who is thus confused between the two women, to a typical old-fashioned Japanese man who would reserve a wife's status for the wife alone while having a mistress as a mistress. The latter type would, if the mistress began to complain about his wife, slap her in the face. "I admire such a man."

A well-structured relationship usually involves as a mistress a geisha, bar hostess, or other professional in the hospitality business, because such a woman knows her place, and, as the above informant said, makes an effort to please the wife. The former geisha informant confirmed this point by saying that the geisha mistresses delivered gifts to the wives twice a year to maintain a congenial relationship with them. A thoughtful husband, then, would choose a geisha, not a "lay" woman as the above unhappy informant's husband has done.

Structured promiscuity in its traditional form further involves housing the mistress as a full-fledged concubine, *mekake*. The man must be wealthy enough to provide a house and all the living expenses for the mistress—here is the reason why promiscuity has been regarded as symbolic more of a man's social status than of virility. Under this setup, the husband becomes a bilocal resident. Some of my informants' husbands alternated between the two residences.

A mistress, under an unstructured arrangement, which is more common in contemporary Japan, is more autonomous, more likely to demand a wifely status, or to be available to more than one man. The old-fashioned terms for a mistress like *mekake* and *nigō* (the second woman) are felt inappropriate to such an autonomous mistress.

*The wife's strategies.* Even a perfectly structured triad is not without strain. The wives resorted to one or another strategy to overcome the strain. One such strategy was the *pauperization* of the husband by refusing an allowance to him. "Once I held money tight, I stopped worrying about him." Fuyuko was confident that a penniless man is romantically incapacitated. The husband continued to play around, but "couldn't do much."

Yone also retaliated by tightening the purse strings, but the husband had occasional income from his side job of stock brokerage, which he could spend on women. She turned her strategy on the mistresses, and tried to form a *coalition* with each of them through propitiation. The wife befriended one mistress after another with her generosity, always buying two sets of kimono—one for the mistress.

I manipulated the women like this [Yone stroked her hand to show how gently she molded someone into a shape at her will as if she were dealing with a piece of clay], so that [the mistress] would become absolutely unable to do any harm to me.

The wife of a dry food wholesaler resorted to *disengagement* from the triadic conflict. "If it were now, I wouldn't have remained married," she said. "But it was wartime, and we were supposed to put up with any hardship." Having suffered from the husband half residing with his *nigō-san*, she finally became determined to gain autonomy, economic and emotional. Moving to Shizumi, she tried out a series of trades from operating a restaurant to keeping a brothel and a hotel. Successful as a businesswoman, she became confident, autonomous, and even wealthy. No longer upset by the husband's infidelity, she even felt grateful to the mistress for looking after that fussy man. Nonetheless, her gratitude was not unlimited. When one of the mistresses (the husband had "three or four" women serially) decided to leave the husband and came to her for the payment of "alimony," she was enraged. " 'Take as much money as you want from my husband,' I said. 'It was not me who asked you to be a mistress. Why the hell should I pay?' "

Of all the things that can happen in one's marriage, the husband's promiscuity is said to be the worst. The wives thought of suicide and of divorce many times, only to be dissuaded by kin or by their own thoughts on the price they would have to pay if they killed themselves or divorced. The final strategy, then, is to attain mental emancipation through *resignation*. My informants tended to do so by concluding that *uwaki* is a man's disease. Thus, women talk about *uwaki no mushi* (bugs causing *uwaki*) and try to persuade one another to wait patiently until the bugs cease to be active. The bugs are expected to lull by the time the man is in his forties. Some bugs, however, remain active, as with the husbands of two informants, until the death of their hosts.

*The wife's promiscuity.* Promiscuity has been a male monopoly, but apparently change is taking place. According to a 1968 government survey showing a distribution of reasons presented by couples filing divorce by consent, 21 percent of the wives accused their husbands of extramarital affairs and only 3 percent admitted the same of themselves, whereas 20 percent of the husbands claimed their wives to be promiscuous, with 6 percent admitting having had women (Sōrifu 1978:121). In one issue after another, women's magazines reveal through confessional articles that more and more wives are taking extramarital adventures. A Shizumi government worker, in charge of the Citizen Counseling Office, said: "Now men come over to get help from us to have their wives stop playing and return to themselves." When he described these men, he could not help expressing his irritation at their unmanliness. Despite the alleged change, there is still a sex bias: the wife's patience with the husband's promiscuity is regarded as admirable or necessary while the husband's in a reverse case is improper or contemptible.

In the future-autobiographies, one girl referred to her own *uwaki* activity resulting in divorce, one wrote about her *uwaki* in retaliation against her husband's promiscuity, and another female writer described constant fighting with her husband because of his *uwaki* which is to be terminated by his death. No male autobiographer mentioned his own promiscuity or that of a spouse.

None of the primary-sample women admitted an extramarital involvement except for a widow who had a series of men in her thirties—the age she considers a woman's worst in terms of her bodily dependence upon a male. Instead, some women substitute fantasies for actualities. A woman who wants to but is unable to take the risk to divorce her unfaithful husband concluded that "all Japanese males are equally hopeless," and wondered what it would be like to be married to a foreigner. "If I were to be reborn, I would certainly marry a foreigner, even a Korean."

## In-Law Relationships

Virilocal marriage involves a bride in an in-law relationship as much as or even more than in a husband-wife relationship. Even in neolocal marriage, one is unlikely to be totally free from the role of daughter-in-law or sister-in-law. As girls, the informants were instructed by their mothers, and sometimes by their fathers as well, primarily to be good daughters-in-law, and only secondarily to be good wives. To be accepted as a daughter-in-law was regarded as a major step toward *inchinin-mae*—full adulthood—for a woman. Implied here is what is called *yome-ibiri*, bride hazing. It is no wonder that a mother-in-law's presence or personality was a decisive criterion for acceptance of a marriage proposal. One of my informants consented to marry her husband, hoping—and her family assured her—that his mother would die soon. Alas, after twenty-five years of marriage, her eighty-year-old mother-in-law is still alive and kicking. The general obsession with the in-law relationship is further indicated by the spontaneous responses to a vague question like "How was your marriage?" The respondents tended to call my attention immediately to how much they suffered under severe mothers-in-law or, conversely, how lucky they were to have nice in-laws.[3]

### Role-Demands on the Daughter-in-Law

Older informants who were virilocally married recall how they were immediately subjected as brides to the role-demands by their mothers-in-law who might or might not be joined by other in-laws.

First, the bride was expected to supply labor. A good *yome* was supposed to be a hard worker. Many mothers-in-law took an exemplary role by being compulsive workers themselves and by demanding that the daughters-in-law work with them. "Our grandma [mother-in-law] was an extraordinarily hard worker," said Ayano. While hanging the laundry, for example, if any part of an article of clothing was found to be worn, she never failed to patch it right away while it was still wet and then she hung it again. Every night before going to bed, she took pains to sweep the rooms, clean the fireplace, and put everything in perfect order so that there would be no problem in an emergency, such as an earthquake. She was never found sitting around doing nothing; as soon as she sat down after doing the dishes to listen to the radio, she started sewing. Everything in the chests of drawers was spotless and ironed. This mother-in-law Ayano admires as *rippa*, outstanding, but also admitted that it was painful to live up to her expectations as a daughter-in-law since the same standard of diligence was applied to her. When she and her husband were about to relax after a day's work, the mother-in-law was standing with a needle and thread signaling that the two women were to sew together. "For my mother-in-law, playing, joking, or eating cake was all wasteful nonsense."

Harue was also subjected to nightly sewing (*yonabe*) with her mother-in-law and sister-in-law. At ten o'clock she wished to retire but the in-laws hinted that it was still too early. The mother-in-law instructed her that, in order to get ahead of other people, one should get up one hour earlier and go to bed one hour later than others. When carrying firewood too the mother-in-law used to say, some would carry a few pieces, but some would load themselves with as much as possible. The difference would show up soon. This mother-in-law was also described as *rippa*, and once again the admirer felt as if she were strangled.

The exemplary mother-in-law, having died, is recalled with admiration and sometimes with appreciation for having trained the daughter-in-law, her successor. But a mother-in-law who extracted hard labor from the daughter-in-law while she herself sat around doing nothing is resented even in recollection. This type may be labeled "exploitative" as juxtaposed with "exemplary." Some brides were treated like live-in maids. A dressmaking school graduate had to sew all the dresses for her mother-in-law and sisters-in-law as part of her bridal assignment. A fisherman's wife was the sole domestic worker and sewed all the kimonos and *futon* bedding for everybody in the ten-member household, her mother-in-law being a disgruntled but lazy recipient of her services. When she visited her natal home after six months of marriage, her mother stroked her cheeks, saying in tears: "Your face has changed, you look like a man."

The demand for hard work was often accompanied by pressures for frugality. Many a woman recalled having been excoriated or subtly condemned for not being tight enough, for carelessly discarding useful things like a piece of used paper or string, extravagantly replacing old things with new. Some mothers-in-law, and sometimes fathers-in-law controlled the household budget for a long time, much longer than generally expected, refusing to hand it over to the junior couple. Hamako had to submit to her father-in-law the income from a tea factory which was in her charge, and to ask him for a little cash whenever she went to buy things like cigarettes for her husband and school supplies for her children. Food consumption was basically limited to what was produced by the farming household, except that the father-in-law's father, and he alone, was served a dish of fish.

Having been used to a spendthrift way of life as a daughter of a stockbroker family, Yone had insufferable experiences with her mother-in-law, who held the purse tightly. Once she ventured to cook something at her own discretion. The senior woman was infuriated; "When did I turn the house property over to you?" she demanded.

What was most unbearable even to a patient daughter-in-law was the overt or covert restriction on the amount of food she could have.

> I don't know if I should tell all this. I was always the last to eat a meal. When I was going to have a second bowl of rice, my husband's sister asked her mother [pointing to the rice container]: "Grandma,[4] is this enough for lunch?" Grandma said: "Men go out to work, therefore they must eat a lot. Children, too, need to eat a lot because they are growing up. But women are just playing in the house, they don't have to eat."

The daughter-in-law withdrew her rice bowl. Apparently all this was not witnessed by her husband—in an interview he stressed how harmonious the relationship between his mother and wife had been.

A similar deprivation was experienced by Hiroe. When she distributed the fish onto individual plates, her mother-in-law complained that Hiroe served herself more than others. As a young nursing mother right after childbirth, she was hungry all the time. Awake and unable to wait longer, she got up before dawn to eat the leftovers from the previous supper, which enraged her mother-in-law.

Some in-laws were fastidious in demanding perfection in performance. A daughter-in-law in charge of cooking had to be alert to the mother-in-law's fussing over her seasoning. The method of cleaning the house or doing the laundry was also under the scrutiny of a compulsive in-law. More important than these instrumental skills was the expressive aspect of performance such as manners, speech style, and facial expression. In the fishing community the language was rough, but a mother-in-law demanded that the bride speak politely while she herself was an unrefined talker. "Nothing but an old woman's meanness" was the now seventy-three-year-old bride's comment. Even highly educated postwar-generation brides were not totally free from such demands of in-laws. Harumi, who as a university student had long lived freely away from home, suddenly faced a fastidious mother-in-law who carped about her manners as well as her cooking. Her criticism ended in the young couple's departure. "My mother-in-law was displeased with every single thing I did," began a working wife. "She dared to tell me she wished I were a traditional daughter-in-law even for one day." She did not like the way the daughter-in-law signaled her return from work. The junior wife was supposed to say face to face to the senior wife in a polite form: "Mother, I am home." Her humming songs and eye expression—just about everything invited criticism. She recalled that she did not go a day without crying under this "nasty mother-in-law."

Underlying all these demands was the imperative of compliance with the senior supervisor. Though generally compliant, young women wished to enjoy role release for a few hours a day, once a week, or so; they wished to be alone. But privacy was most scarce. Visiting the natal home would be one way of getting role release, but this was exactly what the mother-in-law did not like. An eighty-two-year-old told me that since her mother-in-law never gave permission for her home visits, she had to catch a moment when the mother-in-law was not alert to sneak out; she was, needless to say, prepared to face scoldings upon her return.

The above examples are typical of bride hazing among old-timers in particular. I have a few more, not so typical instances of role-demands. A widowed father-in-law may expect the bride to wait on him as a wife substitute. This is what happened to Yoshimi. "Typically Meiji-born and selfish," the father-in-law refused to call on anybody else but the daughter-in-law as an attendant despite the fact that several live-in servants were present. He would be displeased unless she rushed to him in response to his call, and would get mad if she came home a little late. At night, if sleepless, he would come to wake her and have her read a magazine aloud to him. When sick, it was her job to nurse him around the clock. "I don't know whom I married," she complained to her husband. Within a few years, Yoshimi was widowed. Still very young, she wanted to be alone and to start all over again, but succumbed to the demanding father-in-law's urge to stay with him. There was nothing sexual in this relationship, but as a typical male he was dependent on the services of a trustworthy female.

Another case involves what the informant called "religious war." Her family belonged to Risshō Kōseikai whereas her husband's family was converted to Sōkagakkai, both sects being known for their militant missionary activities. Sonoko herself had no particular religion but refused to join Sōkagakkai, and this was understood, she thought, at the *miai* meeting. But as soon as she moved in, the sister-in-law who ruled the household accused her of being influenced by an "evil religion" and undertook to convert her. She was taken to the district leader of Sōkagakkai to undergo indoctrination. When no one was around the house, she sneaked out to run away from all this pressure. The husband, torn between religion and love, decided to chase after the runaway, while the sister-in-law and mother-in-law tried to separate them. " 'Aren't we like Romeo and Juliet?' I said to my husband."

Clever daughters-in-law contrived various strategies to propitiate in-laws. A forty-seven-year-old housewife, after having suffered like everybody else under a now ninety-three-year-old domineering mother-in-law, came to realize that "in-law problems disappear once you catch your in-laws' weaknesses." Learning from experiences that her mother-in-law loved flattery more than anything else, she began to praise everything she did and soon succeeded in becoming a favorite. She also found that the eldest sister-in-law, even more nasty than the mother-in-law, expected her to *amaeru* (solicit indulgence), and so started to ask her advice and instructions on whatever question occurred to her. Help was eagerly rendered. The informant feels she hit two birds with one stone: the sister-in-law's meanness was turned into love and at the same time, she, the informant, learned a lot from the "erudite" sister-in-law about such matters as how much should be paid for *nakōdo* service at the wedding.

## Harmonious Relationships

Just as the husband's dominance was found to be multifaceted, so were the in-law's demands. The stereotype of an onery mother-in-law is certainly not a myth, as was confirmed by certain instances cited above. But we have also come across more innocent or well-meaning mothers-in-law who made superficially similar demands. Most notable are those who made severe demands in order to train the daughters-in-law.

I should also mention several other in-laws who made no particular demands, or who kindly taught how to run the household, how to fulfill domestic obligations toward the *shinseki* and neighbors, or how to conduct ancestral rites, and so on. Not a few women take pride in being a repository of information on the kinship network and the household customs information that has been handed down from their mothers-in-law, bypassing their husbands. "My husband knows nothing; he must ask *me* how *his* family relates to such-and-such families." Some women attribute their overall ignorance regarding life to having had no mother-in-law. The daughter-in-law's confidence of this kind intensifies over the years, and therefore I shall take up this topic again in chapter 7.

Some of the respondents' in-laws are considerate of their daughter-in-law's privacy. One way of insuring privacy is to draw a clear demarcation line of jurisdiction between the two women. "My mother-in-law," said Yukie, describing her as "manlike," "does not like feminine work such as cooking and cleaning, but does like farming and brings me crops. So our jurisdictions are well divided." The two women complement and appreciate each other with their respective specialties. Equally, they do not intrude upon each other's spatial territory: when one has visitors, the other serves tea and withdraws. In some cases intimacy has developed between in-laws: "My mother-in-law and I were often mistaken for real mother and daughter." Intimacy or mutual trust is greater where the two women have some ties other than those of in-laws: examples are aunt and niece in the case of cousin marriage, and *senpai* (senior graduate) and *kōhai* (junior graduate) from the same *jogakkō*.

Harmony or intimacy between in-laws, however, is more characteristic of neolocal than virilocal marriage. This will be detailed below in conjunction with the triadic relationship.

## TRIADS

In-law relationships can be analyzed more realistically in light of a triad (or quadrad) than a dyad.

*Wife/husband/in-law triads.* A triad may or may not include the husband. The triad with a husband in it, as recalled by older informants, typically manifested itself in *rivalry* between in-laws over the son/brother/husband. A widowed mother-in-law was most likely to become locked into such a triad, but even prior to her widowhood there may have developed a strong dyadic tie between mother and son which the bride would try hard to loosen. One mother-in-law told the bride: "I loved my son Takao more than I loved my husband." A typical wife-husband pattern as manifested in the caretaker wife and the dependent *teishu kanpaku* obtained between mother and son, to Ayano's frustration. In her house it was the "grandma" (mother-in-law) who was in charge of the around-the-body care for the husband.

> Upon coming home from work, my husband changes into kimono. Grandma felt sorry that he had to put on the first underwear, the second underwear, kimono, and *haori* coat one by one—it would be too much for a man who comes home after using so much of his brain. So she had the whole thing sewed together so that he would have no trouble in wearing it all at once. When a new pair of *geta* was bought for him, grandma wore them for a few days to make the straps loose and comfortable for him. She would be sorry if they were too tight for him. She also saw to it every night that the clothing my husband was going to wear the next morning was properly prepared with a handkerchief and cigarettes in the pockets.

In the morning, when a wife was expected to be busy with such care for a husband, Ayano had to be standing around, stupidly watching the mother-son drama. In this case the mother-in-law was still married.

The jealousy of an in-law, coupled with the space limitation of the dwelling, inhibited the sexual intimacy of the young couple. Mutsuko, who felt she had had no honeymoon, was subject to the jealousy of her widowed father-in-law. The house had two sleeping rooms divided by a *fusuma* sliding door, and one of the rooms was occupied by the jealous father-in-law and a brother-in-law. When the newlyweds were going to a public bathhouse to bathe together in a family compartment, the father-in-law forced them to take a ten-year-old neighbor child with them. "He never got cured of jealousy to his last day."

Most crucial to this triad was the reaction of the husband. Some husbands took it for granted that they belonged foremost to their own kin. Table arrangements in one case symbolized the inaccessibility of the husband to the wife; the husband ate at a separate table with his father; the rest, including both the senior and junior wives and the children, sat at another table. In a conflict, such husbands sided with their parents, which then meant a *coalition* between the husband and in-law, leaving the wife in insecure isolation. Other husbands leaned more toward their wives but would not risk offending their mothers, to whom they owed filial piety. "My husband was *oyakōkō* [a devoted child]" usually alluded to the husband's reluctance to support his wife against his parents. Harue's husband was in love with his wife, and he tried to instruct her to behave in the way acceptable to his mother and sister: "Pretend to be a fool, or else you cannot be accepted in this house." The best the husband could do was to take the role of *mediator*. Any sign of a husband's protection in the situation of triadic rivalry would be repelled or jeered at, as happened to Yuri's fisherman husband. His mother ridiculed him, yelling: "When did you become so stretched underneath your nose?"[5]

Most husbands found themselves in *conflict* and eventually escaped from the scene of rivalry. "The home situation being so inhospitable, my husband started to stay away under one excuse or another" was often heard. Some men became exclusively involved with their work (or pretended to do so), but others found an outlet in bars, which strained the household economy. The total upshot of triadic rivalry tended to cause marital estrangement as well.

Some of the in-law's demands are no longer tolerated by a young daughter-in-law and will fail in securing support from his/her son. Suzuko, after she moved to live with her parents-in-law, learned that her husband's monthly salary was to be taken by the mother-in-law as had always been the case, and that she was to receive an allowance only. She thought this outrageous, and through negotiations between the two pairs of *nakōdo* it was decided, against strong resistance from the in-laws, that the young couple should live apart from the old couple. "Ichiro-san had to choose between his parents and me, and decided in my favor." A coalition was thus formed by wife and husband. The conjugal bond, thus, seems to be superseding the vertical bond or obligation between mother and son or between in-laws. As will be shown in chapter 7, this change tends to involve a reversed hierarchy between generations rather than equalization: the daughter-in-law is now coming, it seems, to dominate the mother-in-law. At least, this is the way the older women today tend to feel.

The wife could be in the pivotal position of the triad. Hamako found that there was some estrangement between her husband and his adoptive parents, that little communication took place between them. Instead of the husband standing in the middle as a mediator between the wife and her in-laws, as would be expected, it was the wife who came to assume that role. When the in-laws had something to say to their son, they chose to talk to the daughter-in-law, who then transmitted the message to her husband. The wife tried to harmonize the two parties, but her efforts only intensified the husband's sense of isolation and humiliation which hurt the marital relationship as well. Mediation thus ended in further conflict.

Likewise, the in-law may play the central role in mediation, as in the case of the wife-husband estrangement triggered by the husband's promiscuity during a household economic crisis. The wife alone was trying to overcome this crisis by doing dressmaking day and night, but running out of patience, Fuyuko made up her mind to divorce and leave the children with her husband and in-laws. The husband, eager to save face, did not resist. A few days before the couple was going to announce their decision to the parents, the latter, probably sensing the marital crisis, suddenly proposed that the junior couple take over the responsibility of financial management. Fuyuko told them of her resolution and dumped all of her frustrations with her husband, accumulated for years, on them. The father-in-law took this opportunity to tell her: "You are a perfect daughter-in-law. You work hard and wait on us faithfully. But as a wife you are not so good, as Tadaichi's wife. Please be a little more tender toward him." At the same time the in-laws begged her to stay, and the husband apologized and promised to reform. Fuyuko realized from the in-law's admonishment how blind she had been to her own errors and relented, cancelling the divorce plan. Mediation, in this case by the in-laws, was successful in harmonizing the husband and wife. (He did not live up to his promise, but then the wife as the financier could keep him impoverished in retaliation.)

*The bride/in-law/in-law.* Two or more in-laws may form a triad with the wife which the husband may or may not join. A mother-in-law alone is not a menace for some daughters-in-law. What is insufferable is a coalition of two or more in-laws, and this is where sisters-in-law are most detested. A mother-in-law's power often depends on her access to her daughters to form such a coalition.[6] The coalition may be further strengthened by other personnel. Hiroe encountered a mother-in-law–sister-in-law alliance from which her army officer husband was unable to shield her. But even worse was the housemaid, who was the real power wielder. Having worked there for ten years before the bride's arrival, the maid felt that her status was being stolen by this newcomer and would not allow her to invade her role territory. The in-laws, whose dependency on this employee had led to their loss of control over domestic affairs, allied with the maid against the bride.

An in-law coalition when combined with husband-wife discord can develop into something quite formidable. A bride realized that her stepmother-in-law, in an effort to spoil the marriage, not only tattled to her stepson against the stepdaughter-in-law but collaborated in his promiscuous venture. Worst of all, the senior woman incited her daughter, according to the informant, to flirt with the stepson, the informant's husband. One day, warned by a neighbor, the wife changed her plans to be away overnight and returned home unexpectedly, and there to her astonishment she saw her husband bathing with his stepsister.

A woman need not be a victim only. She may also be a party to an in-law coalition which inflicts suffering upon her brother's wife. Some informants have had enough insight to reverse the in-law roles in this manner, and admitted with a suggestion of embarrassment that they were *kojūto* (the bride's husband's sibling, more often applied to a sister than a brother), quoting the saying that "one *kojūto* matches for one thousand devils." But such informants usually emphasized how considerate they were toward the brides, how they tried to shield them from their own mothers. Most others, however, tend to be oblivious of their role as *kojūto,* instead remembering their plight as brides as if it had happened yesterday.

Two in-laws are not always united, and should they be split, a situation evolves which either softens the otherwise insufferable strain for the bride or promotes her to the status of *tertius gaudens,* the third who enjoys (to borrow Simmel's idea in Wolff 1950:154). The predominant pattern is that, while female in-laws are allied against the newcomer, a male in-law gives support to her behind their backs. Many a victim of bride hazing recalls her father-in-law as having "sympathized" with her, "protected" her, or "begged" her to stay and persevere. While this relationship remained a covert and subtle alliance in most cases, one father-in-law turned out to be an open rebel against his wife and demanded the wifely around-the-body care from his daughter-in-law. Feeling that both son and husband had been stolen, the mother-in-law could not forgive the bride. "I am embarrassed to say this, but my mother-in-law was jealous of me because I married her son, and she also became jealous every time I talked with my father-in-law." If the parents-in-law are no longer able to communicate with each other as a result of habitually established aloofness, the bride may be welcomed as a newly supplied communication channel. In one instance, the father-in-law began to send messages to his wife by talking to the daughter-in-law, and the mother-in-law, realizing that her old man was willing to listen to the daughter-in-law, started to chastise him through her daughter-in-law's mouth.

So far we have equated "sister-in-law" with the husband's sister. But one may have a more symmetrically related sister-in-law, namely, one's husband's brother's wife. Both being outsiders, these co-sisters-in-law may well form a coalition against the common enemy, be it the mother-in-law or the husband's sister. Indeed this has happened in some cases, but more often the triad of the mother-in-law and two co-sisters-in-law leads either to rivalry between the junior wives which the senior wife as *tertius gaudens* can manipulate, or to the conflict between the mother-in-law and one daughter-in-law which can be taken advantage of by the other daughter-in-law. Usually, the mother-in-law finds her eldest son's wife, a coresident, incompatible with her, and, to get *compensation*, tries to ally herself with a younger son's wife, a non-coresident. Indeed, several of my neolocally married informants were or are on extremely congenial terms with their mothers-in-law; some regard their mothers-in-law as mother surrogates and wish to live with them. Such congeniality in one in-law relationship tends to be a triadic reaction to animosity in the other in-law relationship: "My mother-in-law is warm and kind to me, but [my husband's] elder brother's wife tells me she is very fussy." An exclusive intimacy may develop in this sort of coalition, as Tsuruko told of her mother-in-law: "She was a nice grandma. She loved me, and I looked after her. She would not take a bath with anybody but me. I cut her hair and shaved her face." A similar alliance was formed while, temporarily, Tama and her husband lived in the *honke* house with her mother-in-law, the husband's elder brother, and his wife, and remained viable after they moved to a new house of their own. From Tama's ambiguous remarks I gathered that her mother-in-law rejected the other daughter-in-law and favored the younger son's bride, Tama, exclusively. A few mothers-in-law, unable to get along with their eldest son's wife, did move to live with other daughters-in-law.

## The Role of the Natal Family

As the house into which a woman marries becomes her own *uchi*, her natal household is now referred to as *jikka* (natural house). She identifies her mother as *jikka no haha* in distinction from her mother-in-law who is now her *haha* (mother). This identity change, however, is not accompanied by a complete severance of ties between the young woman and her natal family. Rather, the latter usually plays a significant role in the daughter's postmarital life. In other words, a bride is not only a wife and daughter/sister-in-law but to a certain extent continues to be a daughter/sister.

### Buffer and Intervention

An indulgent family may try to mitigate the shock that transition might inflict on a daughter by offering a buffer. It was a common practice among upper-class families in prewar Japan to protect the daughter by sending maids with her to facilitate communication between the old residents and the newcomer as well as to help the latter with housework. In my local sample I find two such women, both being from relatively wealthy families. This was a temporary measure: as a new routine became established, the human buffer was to depart.

Proximate residence allows the daughter and her family to visit one another on a regular basis, insofar as in-laws tolerate such interchange. A bride of a *musume bunke* (daughter branch house) used to visit her natal and *honke* house every day, while her brother, head of the *honke*, came around to "peek" at how his "kid" sister and her husband were doing.

Through a retained bond, the bride's kin can intervene in her marital state. If marriage brings a woman unexpected suffering, whether caused by her husband or in-law, her natal family, in most instances, will exert its influence to save the marriage rather than to encourage a breakup. Kuniko, determined to divorce her womanizing husband, visited her natal house for consultation and was told by her father that she must persevere "because a man has only to get aged to be cured of *uwaki*," and that if her husband gave her no money, he, the father and his son (Kuniko's elder brother) would work harder to aid her. She was advised not to complain.

A filial daughter does not need such admonishment from a parent. When she thinks of divorce or suicide to put an end to her hardship, she faces the question: What will happen to her *jikka* if she commits such an act? It will be her natal family more than anybody else, she reasons, that will suffer from the disgrace thus caused. If she happens to be the eldest child, her divorce will cost all her younger siblings marriage opportunities, and her suicide will spoil her brother's promising career. Three informants stressed that they persevered out of a sense of obligation as the eldest sister in this context. I learned that many sufferers avoided saying a word about their experiences to their kin simply "not to cause any worry [*shinpai*] for them."

Intervention is not always to restore marital stability. Some *jikka* continued to, or in crisis came to, rely on the married daughters' service and labor, which naturally did not please the husbands or in-laws. Kumiko was called upon, when her mother fell ill, to come every day and nurse her. The only reason her husband acquiesced was that he, as a propertyless second son, found himself in no position to claim a monopoly on his wife. Another husband did complain "like a spoiled child" that the wife, working to support her mother and bedridden younger brother, did not belong exclusively to him. The continued influence of the father or brother upon the daughter/sister humiliates the husband; for example, Sakiko's husband was offended by the letters that her father kept writing to her. He told Sakiko: "From now on I will be in charge of educating you."

Some kin tried to intervene to terminate a marriage. Yone's brother did so twice, once when her husband went bankrupt and as a last resort opened a brothel with her as its main operator, and once when the husband's extramarital affairs became known to the brother. The brother tried to take the sister and her children away from this good-for-nothing husband forcibly, but each time the sister stuck with her husband. The brother punished her by a declaration of *kandō* (disowning her).

## TRIADS IN UXORILOCAL MARRIAGE

The natal family fully participates in the daughter's married life in the case of uxorilocal marriage. Interestingly, informants who lived as wives under this residential arrangement indicated that they have been generally contented with their husbands. If there was any tension, it involved a triad including the wife's parents. A mild version of rivalry seemed to be felt by a mother toward the daughter over the marital love the latter was enjoying: "Mother was sort of hysterical." Similarly, another mother continued to play the role of housewife, refusing to concede it to the daughter. The husband tended to play the part of a generous third, trying to be nice to both women and obviously enjoying the best position in the triad. These cases suggest that an uxorilocally married husband is not necessarily a mirror image of a virilocally married wife. Rather, in both types of residential arrangement it is the women who are placed under strain.

I have come across complaints made by mothers and daughters living together under this condition: both parties tended to attribute the trouble to the selfishness of the other due to the *amae* inherent in blood relationship. "In-law relationship is smoother because both sides would be more reserved and considerate." It is not that the husband was not involved at all. In some cases there was conflict between the husband and his in-law, male or female, but then it was the wife who suffered even more by being caught in the middle. If the parent-in-law tried to dominate and undercut the son-in-law to reduce him to a typical *mukoyōshi*, the wife stood up to resist in support of her husband. The stereotypic image of a henpecked *mukoyōshi* that appears in folklore is likely, therefore, to be a product of cross-generational dominance by the wife's parents and less likely to reflect the wife's dominance. Nor is the daughter-parent coalition against the husband/son-in-law likely. By and large, uxorilocality seems to create a better-balanced relationship than does virilocality among coresidents; the former at least lacks, as far as my sample goes, the formidable nature of strain associated with the extreme imbalance of power which often arises from the virilocal arrangement.

*Mukoyōshi* marriage is thus evaluated differently by a child and a wife. It might be recalled that *daughters* of *mukoyōshi* marriages were critical of their mothers as being "spoiled." On the other hand, *wives* in such marriages are contented. The reasons for this discrepancy will be further explored in the next two chapters.

To conclude this and the previous sections, it might be noted that, as far as human relations within a household are concerned, cross-sexual alliance is more common than same-sex alliance, that the household members of the same sex tend more toward rivalry and jealousy. Similarly, solidarity is harder to come by between age peers (e.g., sisters-in-law) than cross-generationally. Cross-sexual *and* cross-generational relations appear most prone to alliance. This generalization, needless to say, is not meant to overlook the unpredictability of an actual situation which encompasses a wide variety of permutations and combinations of four or more adult household members, each with a distinct personality. Nor does it preclude the prevalence of solidarity by sameness *outside* the household. Relatively speaking, however, Durkheim's (1960) "organic solidarity" seems to hold for the household membership.

## The Management of Household Reputation

The *ie* as a corporate body assigns every member with the duty of maintaining its honor, reputation, and status vis-à-vis the outside world. The wife in particular as a generalized caretaker assumes a major responsibility for the day-to-day tasks of honor preservation, although it is the husband who formally represents the household. In other words, the substantive burden of *sekentei* (the honorable appearance as viewed by the surrounding world) maintenance falls upon the wife. The *seken* (surrounding world) in whose eyes the *ie* reputation is to be preserved consists of *shinseki, nakōdo,* neighbors, employers, employees, bosses, subordinates, colleagues, customers, or a more vaguely defined "community." The husband's untidy appearance, as much as the children's, will be blamed on the wife's negligence.

The most important for reputation preservation is the fulfillment of *giri* (social obligation). Among the primary obligations are hosting the *seken* people by proper feasting and visiting them with proper gifts. A physician appreciates his wife's culinary expertise as a key to maintaining his reputation as a host with his colleagues who often come over to play *go:* "I don't have to feel ashamed." Feasting and/or gift-giving is called for on ritual occasions involving life transitions (birth, marriage, funeral, and many other interval rites between these primary ones); postmortem transitions (death anniversaries); nationwide festivals (midsummer, year-end, New Year's); annual or semi-annual local festivals. Emergencies like illness and disaster or special occasions like a shop opening also warrant *giri* fulfillment. (More on such rites will appear in chapters 5 and 7.)

As a ritual host, one must exercise good judgment as to who should be invited and who should not without offending anybody. As a gift giver, one must be wise enough not to be too stingy or too extravagant. It should be noted that Japanese gift-giving is often in cash, and the more important the occasion, the more that is likely to be the case. It may not be only an expression of the giver's good will or general gratitude, but an actual payment for some service such as *nakōdo* role in a wedding.

The wife, as a reputation manager, must be well informed of to whom the family owes what kind of *giri*. Specially important is her knowledge of the network of her husband's kin together with the history of what has transpired between her postmarital household and each of these affinal households. Some husbands are compulsive about ritual obligations toward *shinseki*, whether on his side or hers, but do not bother even to learn who are involved in the network, considering such to be under the wife's jurisdiction. As an outsider, the wife takes it as her absolute duty to maintain the acceptability of her household in the eyes of affinal kin. This explains why the information on kinship network and mutual rights and obligations among kinfolk is transmitted from mother-in-law to daughter-in-law—outsider to outsider. If the house happens to be the *honke* of a large *dōzoku*, such compulsion on the part of the wife is overwhelming.

Women need one another's help to sustain their house reputation. A ritual feast, for example, requires a group of kitchen helpers and waitresses who are familiar with the hosting household. Until around 1960 it was primarily neighbor women who helped one another as joint performers of *giri* obligation. Not only labor and service but instructions were exchanged on such occasions with regard to proper codes of obligatory conduct. A woman who had moved from a distance to marry a local man under a neolocal arrangement and thus had no kin around "was well taken care of by grandmas and mothers" in the neighborhood. While she was helping a neighbor household with kitchen work, they taught her local customs and mores: "For example, you should not come to help on a wedding unless you are asked to, but you should volunteer to help without being asked if it is a mortuary rite." When she moved there in 1945, "neighbors were tightly organized, everything was conducted by *tonarigumi*."

In an extended household it is usually a senior woman's concern to maintain the household reputation. This subject, therefore, will be taken up again in chapter 7.

In summary, one can say that marriage imposed a more or less drastic resocialization upon the woman through an exposure to the new life-style of the postmarital household and coresidence with her husband and in-laws. Even sexual union was not prepared for by many brides, although the premarital sexual experience is one of the most conspicuous changes recognized among the contemporary adolescents.

The resocialization often involved interpersonal strain in the household. Some strain stemmed from the husband's extramarital affairs, abuse or exploitation of the wife, or indulgence of other personal whims. In many instances, we have also seen poignant conflicts between the daughter-in-law and mother-in-law and/or sister-in-law, so stereotypic as to remind one of the "home drama" series shown on Japanese TV. The genesis of marital strain, then, might be twofold: structured and unstructured. Structured strain was built into the domestic institution as when two adult women, senior and junior, co-living as in-laws, competed for the control of a man or of domestic power. Many older informants were subjected to this type of strain, bound by the notion of the *ie*. Unstructured strain stemmed, conversely, from the individual's unpredictability or deviation from a structural norm, as exemplified by a husband who was an economic parasite upon the working wife.

The above interpretation suggests the possibility that the traditional structure of the domestic institution also played a positive role in stabilizing marriage and restoring harmony in the household. Our sample does include the cases where a daughter-in-law became strongly bonded with her mother-in-law or where the presence of the in-laws saved the marriage from a breakup. Whether a trouble-ridden marriage was really worth saving is, of course, another matter, and will be taken up in a later chapter.

Aloofness, contrived or actually felt, between husband and wife seems to indicate that sexual intimacy, or more correctly, an open display of sexual intimacy had no place in the structure. This further relates to the probational status of a purely sexual couple, as illustrated by the terminological mutism of husband and wife for each other prior to their parenthood.

Many women described their husbands as tyrannical or despotic, but it turns out that male dominance in Japan takes various forms including the husband's patriarchical "show" onstage as well as his total dependency on the wife for the around-the-body care. These aspects of the Japanese patriarchy coexist with the wife's monopoly of domestic rights and duties including the household treasury. Patriarchy is not incompatible but rather interlocked with domestic matriarchy. The existence of matriarchy, in other words, does not preclude that of patriarchy.

The *mukoyōshi*-married woman has turned out to regard herself as lucky, whereas such a woman was not favored as a mother from a daughter's point of view. The wife, we have learned, tries to bolster the autonomy of her *muko* husband against her parents' attempted domination. Even though the wife and the daughter evaluate such a marriage differently, they seem to agree that the father/husband should not be henpecked but unequivocally manly.

Again, the present-day change is remarkable in some respects, especially in in-law relationships. A domineering mother-in-law such as is described in this chapter appears strikingly outmoded. We have noted how in one case the conjugal bond took precedence over the mother-son bond. This change, supported economically and ideologically, tends to be taken by the older generation as tantamount to a reversal of the old order, the daughter-in-law now dominating the mother-in-law. We also know from government surveys and media reports of rises in divorce rates and the increasing incidence of women's promiscuity.

Such changes should not blind us to the continuous aspects of marriage. From the previous chapter we know that almost all women in their late twenties continue to be eager to marry. Further, a couple of college-educated women in their mid-twenties, one newly wed and the other about to marry, said in interview they were eager to serve their husbands as around-the-body caretakers. With regard to abuse, young neolocally married women, while totally free from the in-law's abuse, are no less likely to be prey to their husbands' whims or abuse. But, above all, marriage still ties in with motherhood for most women: that is, the wife's role is inseparable from the mother's role. A woman as a mother may revaluate her identity as a daughter-in-law and wife in a more conservative perspective. We shall now turn to motherhood.

# 5
# *Motherhood*

Role specialization by sex maximizes in a woman's motherhood. Most local informants make no distinction between womanhood and motherhood, or marriage and parenthood. Our young future-autobiographers, too, immediately associate marriage with having children.

## The Cultural Significance of Motherhood

Again, we shall look into the twofold implication of motherhood—structural and personal.

### STRUCTURAL MOTHERHOOD

From the standpoint of the *ie* structure, motherhood is regarded as essential to the perpetuation of the stem family. The bride and daughter-in-law is expected, foremost, to mother an heir to the *ie*.

*Incorporation and status maturation.* Marriage, insofar as it is regarded as instrumental to this structural imperative of producing an heir, can remain, as it did in prewar Japan, subject to cancellation. To avoid legal complication, or as the Japanese would say, to prevent the house register from being smeared, it used to be a common practice to postpone the legal registration of marriage until the bride's fertility was evidenced. Harue was a victim of this practice: she was a *naien* (privately married, or common-law)[1] wife until one week before her parturition. The full incorporation—legal or psychological—of the incoming wife into the postmarital household was thus contingent upon her reproductivity.

The prolonged sterility of a bride, then, was and to a lesser degree still is a source of worry for everyone involved, including the bride's parents. An alternative to divorce would be child adoption. Childless for many years, Yukie was pestered by her parents-in-law to adopt a child, which, though apprehensive of disobeying them, she refused to do. Fortunately for her, she did mother a first child and heir in the thirteenth year of marriage, which, needless to say, brought joy to everyone, and most of all to the father-in-law. When he saw his first grandson in the maternity hospital, he shed tears of happiness and expressed his joy by hosting a large celebration banquet to which all the kinfolk and neighbors were invited. The bride's probational status thus finally matured into a fully tenured status. The terminological mutism or ambiguity in addressing a wife was also replaced by the use of a full-fledged kin term, "Mom."

There is a structural bias for a male child, and this bias is strongly articulated in those households which have lacked male offspring for generations.

> This house of Suzuki has had no sons and has adopted sons [including *mukoyōshi*] for four generations. When I gave birth to the first son, since this was the first male child born into this house, Grandpa and Grandma [father-in-law and mother-in-law] rejoiced, wondered if he came from heaven or earth, and took good care of him. Joyously and jokingly, Grandpa said to me: "If you don't want to stay in this house, you may leave, since we have our heir now."

The father-in-law's remark was a joke, but it unwittingly epitomized the view that the essential worth of a bride lies in her fertility, especially in producing a male child.

As underscored by the above example, childbearing may involve more than the parents. My informants referred to their in-laws or parents more than to themselves or their husbands as the most expressive of delight at childbirth. The child was a gift, so to speak, presented by the bride to the *ie* as a whole or to its representative, her parent-in-law. If the mother-in-law was young enough, the first baby might well come under her care, bypassing its mother.

Status maturation through childbearing may also result in binding the bride to the *ie* to an extraordinary degree. Yoshimi, then twenty and facing the inevitability of her husband's death from tuberculosis, wanted to terminate her pregnancy in order to avoid being bound to the fatherless child. But the father-in-law was strongly opposed, insisting that she give birth to his "direct descendant," the eldest son's child and heir to the house. The idea of replacing the dying eldest son by a younger son as successor did not occur to him. Yoshimi knew that once she mothered a child there would be no freedom for her, no freedom to leave this house, to start a career, or to remarry. The father-in-law suggested that she marry a *mukoyōshi*—a thought that horrified her. In agony, she often thought of killing herself together with the child in her womb, but changed her mind each time, fearing that such an act would spoil her brother's future and strain the relationship between this house and her natal house, which were *shinseki* (hers was a cousin marriage). She gave birth to a boy one month after her husband passed away, and has stayed in the house as a widowed mother for nearly thirty years. She feels her life has been cruelly wasted and blames it on the old system of *ie* and the long-deceased father-in-law who embodied it.

Viewed in a positive light, a woman through motherhood becomes the most indispensable person in the household: an informant regarded the mother as the pivot of a fan, as she saw a large household *(honke)* torn into pieces since its mother's demise.

*Woman, the womb loaner.* The foregoing suggests the culturally biased view of fertility in that it was the wife who was blamed for sterility and appreciated for her fertility. That is not to suggest that the Japanese are like the Trobrianders, who were unaware of the paternal contribution to conception. In fact, in the Japanese ethnoembryology, it was the male "seed" that generated the life of a fetus, "borrowing a *hara* (belly or womb)" as the environment in which the seed was planted and nourished. This androcentric view went hand in hand with the belief that the hospitality of the womb as a receptor and custodian of the seed was crucial to childbirth. Only recently did the male begin to concede to sharing responsibility for sterility and to present himself for medical diagnosis.

The theme of loaning or borrowing the womb is no longer taken literally; or at most it is more like folklore to be occasionally retrieved in conversation. Wakako had married her niece to a son of the *honke*, Wakako's husband being the head of its *bunke*, and brought her back by force every time, she, the niece, ran away. At the fourth retrieval,

> I gave the ultimatum, "If you want to leave so much, all right, go. But the children all belong to Ōya [*honke*]. The *hara* is only borrowed, they say. It doesn't matter how much your *hara* hurt in your childbearing. We borrowed your *hara*, but the seed came from our side.

Note Wakako identified herself with the affinally related *dōzoku* more than with her blood kin. Incidentally, the same folklore was found to be perpetuated by Japanese Americans when I interviewed a *nisei* (second-generation Japanese abroad) man in Hawaii under an extraordinary circumstance. He had been converted to the Tensho Kotai Jingu Kyō, a sect transplanted from Japan, against the wishes of his old mother, who, also intensely religious, expected him to follow her steps in her religion. The mother died, refusing to talk to her son. Obviously guilt ridden, the son tried to propitiate his conscience by saying, "Well, after all, the *hara* is only borrowed." He meant that he was a son of God, the father, not of the womb loaner.

The idea of a woman being a womb loaner was well developed among the aristocrats, to whom perpetuation of the (ideally patrilineal) *ie* was more crucial than to commoners. My *kazoku* informants referred to the polygynous marriage of their grandfathers or fathers-in-law. The women, other than the legitimate wife, who bore children under polygynous arrangement were identified as *"Ohara-san"* (Womb Lady). *Ohara-san*'s children were removed away from their mother and brought up by servants to belong properly to their father's household, and trained to call his legal wife *"Otā-sama"* (an aristocratic term for mother). The legal wife, coming from another aristocratic family, tended to be sterile probably as a result of inbreeding and poor health, and for this reason, the higher the status of the family, the larger the number of womb loaners waiting upon the master, the seed carrier. The natural mothers, whose status ranked even below the head maidservant, were addressed by their children and others by their personal names, indicative of their servile status. An eighty-eight-year-old informant whose memory is vanishing recalled having called her grandmothers—both paternal and maternal—by their first names as distinct from her legal grandmothers. What promoted an *ohara-san* into the household membership was her giving birth to an heir, and yet incorporation was not quite complete. A woman of the Tokugawa family in her childhood saw a number of such mothers of heirs, widowed by then, on their occasional visits to their former masters' household. They came in, but stayed away from the main parlor, unlike a guest; and yet neither would they enter the adjacent room reserved for servants in attendance. "They belonged somewhere between, so they were not sure where to sit. They were around the hallways."

The androcentric bias of this ethnoembryology seems to underlie the exaggerated appreciation of male contribution to pregnancy particularly when made by a *mukoyōshi* husband. Fusa's house had been "matrilineal" in that for two generations in a row the daughter brought in a *mukoyōshi* husband. When Fusa, the successor daughter gave birth to a son, the grandpa (in this case her own father) was jubilant, praising and thanking the *muko* for bringing in new blood. Fusa acknowledged her debt to her husband's ancestors for this genetic transformation.

## PERSONAL FULFILLMENT: FILIOCENTRIC IDENTITY

The personal implication of motherhood refers to the subjective meaning penetrating the core of a woman's self-identity in an existential sense. I found most of my informants intensely filiocentric, so much so that oftentimes my questions were taken as referring to their children instead of themselves. For example, when I asked an informant's birth year, she tended to give her child's birth year—confusion likely to occur partly due to the absence of the subject from a Japanese sentence. Also, when a personal event was recalled, the child's growth stage (age, school year), instead of her own, was referred to for dating: "That was when my older child was six." This kind of filiocentric dating never occurred with male informants.

Ikigai *(life's worth)*. The innermost meaning of motherhood is often referred to as the child being one's *ikigai*. According to a 1972 governmental survey (NSKK 1973:52–54), 70 percent of the thirty- to thirty-four-year-old women found their *ikigai* in the children rather than eight other alternatives. Men in the same age bracket found *ikigai* more in their occupations (47 percent) than in the children (35 percent). A young mother who is in the midst of caring for an infant told me that a woman, while rearing her children, does not need a husband except as a supplier of money. The husband's worth, if not reduced to this money-making function, might be attributed to his paternity. Fuyuko, who is otherwise indifferent to her husband, said, "Well, after all, I must be grateful to my husband because he gave me two such nice daughters."

The first priority thus goes to the child. Whatever suffering a woman has in her marriage—with either her in-laws or her husband—becomes surmountable if it contributes to the welfare of her child. A neglected wife or an abused daughter-in-law would thus become determined to endure silently, putting aside all the temptations for divorce or suicide which had haunted her.

> People in this town knew all about [my husband's *uwaki*]. "How admirably you persevered!" they say. All this was because of my children. If I divorced out of anger, wouldn't the children left behind be pitiable? . . . When I saw my children sleeping next to me, I wondered how I could possibly leave them under a stepmother's care. The thought of my children calmed me down every time.

Another woman, Emi, did divorce, although she knew that under the prewar civil code she would have to leave the five children behind with her husband. The penalty for this "selfish" action was overwhelming however. She felt so painfully guilty toward her children that she became intensely religious. "Single-mindedly to apologize and seek pardon from my children, I sat under a waterfall to be beaten and went through *ohyakudo* [walking up to a shrine a hundred times as a form of religious discipline] while chanting sutras." She no longer submits to such "rough" discipline, practicing a milder form of religious devotion instead; and yet, at seventy-one, widowed by her second husband, Emi is still deeply repentant. Her divorced husband does not enter this guilt complex.

If immediate divorce is deemed harmful to a child, a mother will wait until her child grows up and becomes self-reliant. When I asked about her plans for her old age, forty-year-old Tomiko, after a moment of hesitation, confided that she intends to divorce her husband as soon as the children have grown up. Until then the children should be protected, she feels, from the stigma of being fatherless.

A concern for the child thus takes precedence over everything else, including the mother's welfare and autonomy. No wonder, then, that a widowed mother must first ask her child's permission for her remarriage—a point which Americans would take as a sign of filiarchy. A child can and sometimes does veto the mother's decision.

The extent of maternal preoccupation can be shown by a childless wife's remark regarding her close friend. The two women in their mid-fifties usually enjoy mutual visiting and talking like two little schoolgirls. "But whenever her children return from Tokyo on vacation, we find nothing in common. She becomes nothing but a mother—so boring to me. Even her face color [*kaoiro*] changes."

The woman's filiocentric *ikigai* is further manifested by the strong sense of inseparability she has about her child. We might look at the instances of divorce avoidance not only from the standpoint of the child's welfare but also from the view of the child as *bunshin* (split part) of the mother's body, in light of the mother's feeling of inseparability.

The child's death is the most unforgettable experience of separation. Kuniko, having lost a son in an accident—falling in a pool— would not forgive herself and was long tempted to commit suicide although she had two other children.

> The only way I could redeem my guilt, I thought, would be to go through the pain of drowning myself exactly as my son did. I kept thinking that . . . it was so hard to bear. The death of your parent or husband is nothing by comparison. Your child's death, that's the worst.

Eight years ago Kuniko's husband passed away, but her mind is still preoccupied with her son who died twenty-seven years ago. Bereavement was a turning point in life style for Yoko. Preoccupied thus far with this-worldly and external success, she became introspective and came to find a way to pacify her agitated soul in *shakyō*, the brush copying of sutras. There were other women for whom the loss of a child was the catalyst to become religious and learn Buddhist sutras for the first time in their lives.

The child's death is thus extremely tragic, and yet this does not prevent a mother from taking a child's life just before she kills herself. This combination of infanticide and suicide, known as *shinjū* or more specifically *boshi-shinjū* (mother-child *shinjū*), has been a common topic in newspaper reports, and continues to occur despite the growing public outcry against it. To outsiders such a practice might appear to be nothing but cruel, but I suspect that the mother involved in *shinjū* views her act not so much in light of infanticide as in light of an unbreakable bond between mother and child. Far from being cruel, she would be unable to stand the horror of leaving the child behind to be neglected by the world. In my sample, I find that all the women who, in despair for one reason or another, decided to leave the house and went out with possible suicide in mind were carrying their children. A woman might be suspected of being suicidal more if she was with her child than if alone. Kuniko, determined to leave her promiscuous husband, visited her parents for consultation. Persuaded by her father to endure the situation, she started toward the train station pulling her daughter by the hand and carrying her son on her back—a scene ominous enough to cause concern. Her mother followed this suspiciously *shinjū*-prone group to be sure nothing would happen.

Such mother-child inseparability contradicts the structurally defined status of a child. A child, as pointed out earlier, belongs to the *ie*, and through its *ie* membership, belongs to the community; in wartime, children belonged foremost to the country. The traditional mother thus embodied the conflict between the structural prescription for impersonal, collective sharing of a child on the one hand, and the more "natural" and yet equally culturally reinforced tie between mother and child, on the other, which forms the core of the mother's personal identity. The same contradiction may have contributed to the maintenance of an equilibrium, preventing the excesses of either one of the two forces. The abolition of the legal status of the *ie*, together with the general decline of communal solidarity in postwar Japan, seems to have given rise to the increasingly exclusive nature of the mother-child bond. This change may further explain why family *shinjū* has occurred with such high frequency in the postwar era (Takiuchi 1972).

*Attainment of adulthood.* A woman's filiocentric self-identity is further associated with her attainment of full adulthood through motherhood. If marriage is a major step toward *ichinimae*, motherhood fulfills it. Maturity comes with confidence based on a newly acquired sense of power, strength, or bravery. Kumiko, mother of a victim of quadriceps muscle contracture caused by intramuscular injections (over twelve thousand children in Japan had been affected as of 1976 [*Japan Times* 11/3/76]) had no time to reflect on her own life; she tried all possible measures to cure her daughter of this tragic disease, taking her to the very best hospitals in the nation. Through this she came to realize the strength of a mother. While her husband avoided confronting the tragedy, she, the mother, did not hesitate to try everything possible. "Motherhood strengthens a woman," said another informant. As a bride she cried all the time, but when she became a mother she realized that crying would get her nowhere, that from now on she must assert herself (toward her in-laws). A sense of power may also be structurally supported in that a mother is not only a mother for a child but for the whole household. She becomes *uchi no okā-san,* mother of the house, and may be addressed as "Mom" by her mother-in-law as well as by her child.

It may be that the mother's power derives from the child's growth. The woman who intends to divorce her husband when her children have grown up expects her elder son to have become physically strong enough by then to surpass her husband and to protect her from the abusive spouse during the divorce procedures.

Mentioned along with strength as a sign of maturity is human warmth. Not until one bears a child, I was told, can one truly understand the essence of human love or empathize with other human beings. A mother-in-law (the husband's adoptive mother) who had never had her own child was described as being basically "cold," even though she happened to be nice to the daughter-in-law. "A childless woman is somehow lacking with respect to love. Not that I am treated badly, but there is something cold about her."

Human warmth associated with motherhood derives from the mother's capacity for empathizing with the child, which further stems from her tendency to see a mirror image of herself in the child. The mother, in caring for the child, realizes how easily she can influence him, and comes to take the child's behavior as a reflection of her own. When she finds faults in her child, she blames herself—as did my informants who found their children spoiled, too easygoing, lacking in perserverance, dependent, timid, egocentric, and so on. As the child grows older, he will articulate what is wrong with his mother and how she should behave as a mother, to which she tends to respond most sensitively. "Double socialization" takes place here in a vivid form. By accepting and reflecting upon the child's acts as a mirror image of her own, the mother learns to objectify herself and acquires insight into her character and deficiencies.

The ability to put oneself in another's shoes is an important sign of maturity by Japanese standards. Once a woman becomes a mother, I was told, every decision she makes becomes contingent upon its effect upon her child; she can no longer afford to be self-centered, but must carry a double identity—self plus child. Her empathy for her child then tends to be generalized to other children so that a tragedy that happens to a stranger's child now strikes her heart. "I previously did not pay particular attention to newspaper reports on things like a child being killed in a traffic accident. But now, with my own child, I get emotionally involved whenever I read such news."

It might be recalled that some of the sampled women have an unflattering view of their mothers. And yet the woman's preoccupation with her own child turns out to be almost universal. Even when she leaves the childrearing responsibility to someone else, as in the case of a full-time working woman, she proves filiocentric all the same. It might be speculated that a woman, once she herself becomes a mother, accepts the cultural stereotype of Japanese motherhood without question and presents herself as such, whereas quite another view of her may be held by her daughter. I do not mean that a mother's filiocentric self-image always involves a culturally aided self-deception, but that it may also be a consequence of long years of role investment in motherhood—a topic to be dealt with in what follows.

## Becoming a Mother

Becoming a mother is a cumulative process involving an incessant coordination between physiological unfolding and psychosocial learning, or natural givens and cultural designs.

### CONCEPTION, PREGNANCY, AND PARTURITION

In contrast to the cultural embellishment of motherhood with all its aura, the process of becoming a mother at this earliest stage is devoid of drama and poetry and often dismissed into amnesia.

*Destiny/nature or choice/artifice.* Postmarital conception is taken as a matter of woman's destiny, and the majority of my sample did become pregnant within a year of marriage. This physiological "naturalism" may contribute to the prosaic nature of this phase. Few informants planned parenthood, and no birth control was exercised until after the war. "Birth control? How could we have done such a thing? You would have been condemned as disloyal to the country." It was not just a national policy that accounted for unplanned parenthood; to war-

Table 2  *Change in the Number of Children*

| Mother's Age | Average Number of Children |
|:---:|:---:|
| 70 – 80 | 4.0 |
| 60 – 69 | 3.6 |
| 50 – 59 | 2.6 |
| 40 – 49 | 1.8 |
| 30 – 39 | 2.2 |
| 28 – 29 | 1.0 |

timers in particular, the idea of birth control never occurred. Radical change has taken place. The postwar legitimation of voluntary sterility, including the government-sponsored campaign for birth control, the dissemination of information and facilities of contraception, surgical sterilization, and legalized abortion, has made it possible to plan on the desirable number and spacing of children, and has led to a lower rate of pregnancies and childbirths. The number of births per married couple has declined nationwide from 5.1 in 1940, to 3.6 in 1952, to 2.3 in 1962, to 2.1 in 1972 (Sōrifu 1978:110). My sample shows a similar trend, as inferred from the age of the mothers. Table 2 indicates a striking drop from the average number of children among the mothers in their sixties to that among those in their fifties and forties, and this is likely to be due to the fact that the latter were at the most fertile age when Japan entered the postwar era. The average for the total is 2.8, ranging from 0 to 10. The general tendency now is to have the first child as a matter of "natural" course, and then to plan whether and when to have a second and third child. Two children, preferably a girl and a boy, seem to have stabilized as an ideal number. This generally was confirmed by our future-autobiographers as well.

As far as involuntary sterility is concerned, the rate is higher among the older women, and therefore the highest age bracket (seventy to eighty) shows a maximal range in the number of children—from 0 to 10—whereas the lowest age group (twenty-eight to thirty-nine) ranges only between 1 and 3.

All this points up a radical change in a relatively short period of time from motherhood as destiny to motherhood by choice. Involved in this change is woman's passive acceptance of "nature" being replaced by her use of technology to control her body. But this is not without ambivalence and hesitation. With regard to surgical abortion, every informant regarded it as undesirable for health reasons, although several admitted having undergone it and many more, I suspect, did so without admitting it.[2] Even a stronger resistance is expressed to surgical operation for sterilization. Two women had the ligation of the fallopian tubes (described as "tying") after having six and four children respectively, while in no case was vasectomy administered to the husband. The idea of reversing this asymmetry occurred to Suzuko, about to give birth: she told her husband to "cut the pipe" because she was having her share of pain and discomfort, to which he agreed.

When the question was raised regarding delivery itself, favor for "natural parturition" *(shizen bunben)* was overwhelming against "artifical parturition" *(jinkō bunben)*. For old-timers there was no choice but natural delivery, but, if they were to choose now, they still would reject *jinkō bunben* without reservation. Even postwar women have turned out to prefer *shizen bunben*, and have practiced their preference.

According to an obstetrician, the so-called artifical parturition can mean different forms of intervention such as the inducement, acceleration, or postponement of labor, various kinds of anesthetization, caeserean section, the use of forceps, and the like. But to my informants it tends to be synonymous with *mutsū bunben* (painless delivery by means of some form of anesthetization). The reasons behind their preference for painful over painless delivery subtly varied:

Woman A, seventy-three, mother of three: "The old-fashioned way is more worthy. Think, you are bringing one whole human being to this world! Better to be hard than easy. I, too, was born that way, so I should go through equal pain, shouldn't I?"
"Do you mean you wanted to pay back?"
"Yes, indeed. That's exactly why we bring up our children. You cannot possibly understand how much you owe to your mother until you bear your own child."[3]

Woman B, forty-nine, mother of two: "I favor natural delivery. Only by tasting [*ajiwau*] it you come to understand the truth. You will understand precisely how *you* were born and what your mother was up to. Painless delivery is certainly easier, but lacks that much of value."
"So you want to understand your mother?"
"Yes, I do. The first person who appears before you is your parent, and it is she who influences you most. That's why I want to know. Your parent is absolute to you."
"Some say the experienced pain deepens love for your child, do you agree?"
"Yes, I think so. You will love your child more because you have suffered so. Anything you obtain easily will be abandoned as easily."

Woman C, twenty-eight, mother of a one-year-old: "Since I was born female, I wanted to taste that pain just once. You might call it curiosity."
"The mother-child bond intensifies through labor pain they say. What do you think?"
"I don't think it has much to do with that."

All these women stressed learning and understanding through bodily experience, particularly suffering—very typical of Japanese thinking. They differed in that A and B saw labor pain as what links self to mother and/or child whereas C was more self-oriented.

The above-cited obstetrician said he had few clients who wanted painless parturition, although he occasionally applied local anesthesia at the final moment. In this sense he too favors natural delivery. But as regards the manipulation of labor time, he resorts to artificial intervention more often, sometimes at the request of the clients and sometimes at the clinic's convenience—the availability of hospital staff, supply of blood from the blood bank, and so forth.

The preference for natural delivery is often accompanied by the woman's show of stoicism during her labor. Several women proudly stated that they had endured the pain quietly:

Mother of two children, age thirty-eight: "I am tough. I bit my teeth [*ha o kuishibaru*] to keep quiet."

Mother of three, age seventy-one: "I made no utterance. My grandma used to say, 'You can make any noise any time except when giving birth.' "

Such stoicism exhibited at the time of parturition was traditionally regarded as the ultimate test of feminine discipline. Not every woman was a conformist to this traditional ideal however. Mari, when hospitalized, witnessed women on a row of beds screaming and shrieking, and was determined to be different. Her quiet patience in fact led to the misjudgment of the delivery time by the nursing staff, nearly causing a disaster. The pain was admitted to be "indescribable," or as old-timers would say, "as much as the shoji doorframe becomes invisible." Each woman may come up with her own mental armament for this crisis. An eighty-one-year-old woman said, "I just kept thinking this is endured by every woman, low-class and high-class, even by the empress."

The most unreserved confidence in the "wisdom of nature" was expressed by a public health nurse. She is strongly opposed to the inclination of most doctors to use machinery and drugs, and claims that hospital delivery is synonymous with artificial delivery.

> Nature is such that a baby comes out by itself, rolling around. It comes clean along the birth canal after it is disinfected by forewaters. Nature is so well made. . . . So I keep telling them [mothers-to-be], "Do have natural delivery, please, and after birth, feed your baby with *your* milk" and so forth. . . . They completely agree with me, but upon seeing a doctor they get persuaded by him to disclose what I said, which creates a mess for me.

This woman goes as far as to disapprove of a woman being well read about childbirth and childrearing because such knowledge will stand in the way of the "reason" of nature.

The parturient experiences of some women indeed verify the above informant's confidence in nature. One such woman worked outdoors until evening on the day the midwife came over to deliver her first child. While they sat around a hearth, the midwife looked at her face and decided it was time. As soon as they went upstairs and she lay down, the baby was delivered. The same mother had a second baby without a midwife's help. All four of her deliveries were so easy that she would like, if possible, to bear more children for other women who are frightened.

Nonetheless, the wisdom of the body more often turns out to be less than perfect. My sample includes cases of miscarriage, stillbirth, death by premature birthing, neonate's death, ectopic pregnancy, umbilical cord blocking the fetal passage, abnormal presentation, placenta praevia. To this list may be added such hazards as continual *tsuwari* (morning sickness) throughout pregnancy, premature loss of amniotic fluid, "four-day-long" labor, excessive bleeding, fainting or falling asleep during labor. Nor is the exact time of delivery predictable even under labor-inducing and accelerating drugs. Mari was hospitalized at 8:00 P.M. soon after losing amniotic fluid, and was given labor inducements. At midnight labor pains started and became intensified while she took drugs every thirty minutes. "At first, it felt like a severe case of menstrual pain, but then every two hours overwhelming pain attacked you, so painful that you felt the lower part of your body torn and fallen." She tossed about, braced her legs, drowsed off, and was awakened by her aunt, who was nursing her together with her mother, and yelled, "Don't sleep." After the doctor's diagnosis, all decisions were left to a staff nurse, who predicted it would be about 6:00 A.M. The "patient" felt it imminent and sent for the nurse; this was repeated twice. At 4:00 A.M., sensing the fetus going down fast, she exclaimed, "It's coming out!" The aunt told her to persevere a little more, but then went to the nurse's room only to find its occupant asleep. Reluctant to bother her with another possible misjudgment, the aunt returned just as the patient heard a baby's cry. When the nurse came, the baby's head was out. The criticalness of the situation was thus realized when it was almost too late, and the patient's mother was petrified.

*Symbolic insurance.* The improved medical technology, facilities, and personnel would certainly reduce these hazards, and this is why older women, deprived of the technological aid to compensate for the deficiency of the body's wisdom, suffered more miscarriages and greater involuntary sterility. Nonetheless, safety from such life-and-death hazards will never reach perfection. As a way of meeting the apprehension of possible hazards which lie somewhere between nature and medical technology, the mother-to-be resorts to symbolic intervention.

The first to be mentioned is *obiiwai* (the bellyband ceremony). The period of pregnancy, uneventful except for morning sickness and the craving for sour food which some women have, is marked by this ceremony, which is held on a day of the dog,[4] believed to be propitious for a mother-to-be, in the fifth month of pregnancy. A cotton sash is delivered, usually by the marriage mediator, particularly the female *nakōdo* on the husband's side, as a gift for the five-month-pregnant woman, together with other gifts such as cooked red bean rice (symbolic of festivity). With the help of a midwife or female kin, the woman has her belly wrapped in the sash. A feast may be prepared for kinfolk and neighbors who are invited over to celebrate the occasion. The significance of this ceremony was variously stated by my informants. Some emphasized the "medical" significance of binding the belly with a sash: it is "to prevent the excessive growth of the baby"; "to stabilize the fetus in the womb"; "to keep the woman's body warm." Others attached more symbolic meanings to this ceremony: "to publicize [one's pregnancy]"; "to feel the love of your kin and neighbors [who present gifts] around you and to feel you have really become *ichininmae*"; "to pray for safe delivery." A young informant summarized this dual function by saying that the sash was just for the ceremony and replaced by a more manageable elastic band for actual use. Like all other rites of passage, the ceremony tends to be most extravagant for the first child, and to become abbreviated for later pregnancies. Sometimes, this "first-child" syndrome is carried over into a second generation. Kumiko had a simplified *obiiwai* even though it was her first pregnancy "because *my husband* is not first-born."

While following the doctor's dietary instructions, some women also mentioned complying with folk-medical advice on food taboos given by their mothers or mothers-in-law. The food which was most frequently mentioned as taboo was "boneless seafood" such as squid and octopus. Such food is believed to produce a boneless child. "I knew it was a superstition, but I did not want to take any risk."

Another example of symbolic insurance is found in amulets for safe delivery *(anzan no omamori)* which are obtained at Shinto shrines. Friends and relatives may visit the pregnant woman to present her with such amulets.

*Assistance in childbirth.* Parturition is carried out at home, a midwife clinic, or a maternity hospital. The trend has been toward "patienthood" at a hospital under an obstetricians's "treatment," and a midwife informant admitted that her occupation is doomed. My observation does not necessarily support this prediction. Relatively young informants, particularly from the second delivery on, tend to use a midwife clinic primarily because it provides complete, around-the-clock care *(kanzen kango)* whereas a hospital, short of nursing staff, requires —and this was confirmed by the interviewed obstetrician—the patient to supply her own caretaker, namely, *tsukisoi* (personal nurse staying with the patient at the hospital).[5]

Older informants had home delivery with the help of hired local midwives. The "home" refers either to the postmarital or the premarital house, and by and large, women opted for the latter, that is, their *jikka*, if there was a choice. Especially the neolocally married women returned to their *jikka* for parturition and subsequent recuperation. Even some virilocal women did so or else had their mothers or other kin of the *jikka* over to help them. The importance of the role played by the *jikka* in the daughter's childbearing was explained as a custom which permits the birthing woman maximal relaxation and uninhibited dependency. I might add that this is not an obsolete but a still viable custom, although the new version is likely to be that the natal mother takes on the *tsukisoi* role at a hospital.

The above suggests that parturition is not a private matter of a individual woman. In those instances where the midwife assumed the major responsibility, assistance was rendered by others—kin and sometimes neighbors and female *nakōdo*. Parturition thus gives rise to a temporary little "community" confined in a delivery room. The *tsukisoi* system permits a perpetuation of such a joint venture into a modern hospital setting, as we have seen in the case of a hospitalized informant being helped by her aunt and mother.

At one time the community consisted exclusively of experienced mothers, whether one's own mother, mother-in-law, grandmother, elder sister, or middle-aged neighbor women. No males, including the father-to-be, were allowed to step in unless exigencies demanded their participation as helpers. My older informants emphasized that there was no place for their husbands. Some husbands were totally indifferent to what was going on to begin with, but some concerned husbands impatiently waited elsewhere. Even a gynecologist husband stayed away, leaving everythi⟩g to a midwife and his mother. Obviously, acceptance of male obstetricians meant an end to this segregation. Furthermore, young husbands today are beginning to challenge the old taboo by insisting on watching how their children are born. Even the Lamaze method, which involves the husband as a helper during child delivery, is no longer alien to the Japanese. Such a "revolution" in the parturient culture is rather remote for most of my informants, however, and my informant obstetrician said he is inclined toward discouraging such husbands.

As experienced childbearers, these senior women—*senpai*—not only perform whatever job assigned by the midwife but provide guidance and assurance for the junior woman *(kōhai)*, saying, "Strain yourself a bit more," "It's almost over," or stroking her belly. When the drama of delivery is completed, these women comprise the first audience to applaud for the main actress. Furthermore, while the new mother is recuperating after delivery, it is they who look after her and her baby. According to older informants, the postpartum rest should last for twenty-one days, "a period necessary for the womb to settle back to the original position," during which time one should not touch a broom or bathe or wash one's hair. Although many of them could not afford such a "luxurious" period of recuperation, some followed this ethnomedical prescription religiously. This meant that those senior women also took over the housewifely chores for the new childbearer.

### INFANCY MANAGEMENT

Bearing a child does not make a mother. To become a mother, a woman must have the postpartum experience of infant management. The mammalian "symbiosis" of mother and infant turns out, as revealed in interviews, to be more than an outcome of a "natural" unfolding; it has to be "created" through deliberate efforts. At the same time, the newborn is far from a blank sheet upon which the mother can stamp anything of her choice; she must adjust herself to the demands of the new organism. The two, through continous interaction, must come to an optimal state of interorganismic coordination, involving trials and errors as well as learning from *senpai*. The phase of infancy management, then, seems to offer a testimony against both genetic determinism and environmentalism.

*Feeding*. All women in the local sample believe the mother's "natural" milk *(bonyū)* to be more desirable than *"jinkō eiyō"* (artifical nutrition referring to animal milk and all baby foods other than *bonyū*). Note the natural-artificial dichotomy again. The informants agreed that *bonyū* is not only nutritionally superior but that breast-feeding affects the child's personality favorably. The majority did suckle their babies, but the rest either partially or totally relied upon cow's milk not by choice but because their deficiency in lactation or their work demands prevented breast-feeding. Generally, the younger-generation mothers have had the problem of lactational insufficiency or incapacity, despite their richer diet. The use of tight bras is blamed by some, but then older women used to press their breasts with a heavy obi. "They don't make enough efforts" is a more common accusation made by older women who are proud of having suckled all "six" or even "ten" of their children. Indeed, the older women themselves "worked hard" at suckling, they claimed.

Usually a professional masseur is hired to give daily breast massage, the pain of which has to be borne. Some local maternity hospitals are said to have their own staff masseurs to provide massage as a matter of necessary routine "to prevent mastitis." Some babies must be "trained" to suck the nipple, while others prove to have excessive sucking power, more than the mother's mammary glands can tolerate. The coordination between the mouth and nipple must thus be learned by both parties with perseverance. The midwife and other senior women present during the postpartum rest period are eager teachers on this matter. "Grandma used to tell me how difficult it is to have your baby begin to suck your nipple. So I knew it. I developed shoulder ache trying so hard to nurse my child." A younger informant, Mari, experienced two extremes of coordination difficulty. First, her baby refused to suck after being bottle-fed at the hospital. As a compromise she squeezed her milk out and bottled it, "because I wanted to give *my* milk by all means." Then, the baby girl began to suck so strongly that the mother's nipple was torn, with the result that the milk got mixed with blood. Finally she gave up.

*Circadian coordination.* The mother's diurnal rhythm must be coordinated with the infant's shorter cycles of sleeping and waking as well as feeding and diapering. For those mothers who had to work hard all day long in or out of the home, it was particularly hard to feed or diaper during the night. The advantage of breast-feeding was especially mentioned in conjunction with mid-night nursing; Sayo regretted having bottle-fed her first child, which required her to get up several times a night to heat cow's milk in the kitchen. Furthermore, this need of nocturnal coordination was often given as an explanation for why the mother sleeps next to the baby. The baby is located close to the mother's breast, either in a separate bed or in the same bed. The majority of the local women had *soine* (by-sleeping) beginning at least several months after birth when they felt more confident of not stifling the baby with the pressure of their bodies while asleep. Thus, circadian coordination is interlocked with a buildup of mother-infant intimacy—a point to be taken up below.

*Body manipulation.* Controlling and manipulating the infant's "fragile" body is no easy task for a new mother, particularly before the head "settles" *(suwaru).* Changing clothing was the most difficult for one informant, but for all the others bathing was the most challenging. Small-tub bathing was given by the midwife or another experienced caretaker during the period of postpartum recuperation, and the new mother attentively observed the way the *senpai* cleaned the baby's limbs and trunk with one hand while pressing the baby's earlobes with the other. Thereafter, the baby was taken to a large, deep bath *(furo)*—private or public—where the mother herself bathed while giving a bath to the baby. This "double" bathing was usually beyond a new mother's capacity so that she still had to have her mother, mother-in-law, or another experienced woman help her at this stage. In other words, infant bathing normally meant "triple" bathing. Even with her mother's help, Midori "profusely sweated" during this daily adventure.

For knowledge about infant management younger women read books, but all the women, young and old, stressed the importance of learning through experience and the relative insignificance of book learning.

## Bringing up the Children

Once a child is born, the bulk of the mother's energy is committed to its rearing unless some other female caretaker substitutes for her. Let us examine how women bring up their children in and around the home, leaving the child's school phase to the next section.

### THE MOTHER-CHILD DYAD

*Intimacy.* In the course of infancy management, mother and child begin to form an exclusive, most intimate dyad. Breast-feeding among respondents usually lasted until a second pregnancy—for six months at shortest but longer for most of the women. Shoko, thirty-eight, said that breast-feeding for her first son lasted two-and-a-half years. Weaning him was much easier, she believes, because of the birth of her second son, although "he looked jealously at my nursing the younger one as if he wanted to touch my breast." Her comment implies that the nursing period for the second (last) son lasted much longer—indeed "he would come over to hang onto my breast until he was a first grader [six years old]." Obviously the relationship was no longer between a giver and receiver of milk, but for tactile intimacy. A sixty-year-old dressmaker recalled how painful it was to wean her daughter. Instructed by her mother not to relent for a week, she desisted from succumbing to the child's demand. "My child cried, and I cried."

Among older informants co-sleeping followed a similar pattern—the first child slept with the mother until the birth of a second child. In the first winter after the child's birth, the mother would move the child from its separate bed into hers "to give warmth," which is understandable in view of the inadequacy of heat preservation in old-style houses. Not only *soine* (by-sleeping) but *dakine* (co-sleeping with the child embraced) was mentioned as a way of maximizing warmth. The instrumental reasons for co-sleeping, such as the convenience of nightly feeding and the use of bodily warmth to compensate for housing inadequacy, were then replaced by the enjoyment of physical contact itself on the part of the child and/or the mother. After the first birthday, it was the child itself, said a forty-six-year-old mother, who took the initiative: sometime during the night after being placed into a separate bed, the child would move into the mother's bed. "In my days," declared a seventy-three-year-old grandmother, "no children slept alone."

Co-bathing is more common across generations, and lasts even longer, since the *furo* bathing permits co-bathing of more than a dyad. Even when a child is mature enough to be able to bathe by itself, it may continue to bathe with its mother (or some other adult). The only problem to be faced sooner or later, particularly around puberty, is that of sex. Mothers were amused to recall how and when their sons began to refuse to bathe with them. Busy with making money, a mother, now sixty-two, left all childrearing work to a maid except bathing. It was when her son was attending junior high school (at the age of twelve to fifteen) that he stopped taking a bath with her, that he began to lock the bathroom from inside. The use of a public bathhouse which is sexually segregated forces separation between mother and son at a certain growth stage: a mother of one son recalled how the son, soon after they moved to a house without a private bath, suddenly announced at the public bathhouse entrance, "I am going into the male compartment." He was about twelve.

There are many other opportunities to reinforce mother-child intimacy. Generally speaking, the physical intimacy of this dyad, as described by Caudill and Weinstein (1974) with regard to the Japanese mother and infant in contrast to the American counterpart, was acted out by most informants without questioning, and continued through the post-infancy period regardless of the child's sex. The desirability of "skin-to-skin contact" *(hada to hada no fureai)* in a literal sense was shared by most of the women. One informant used to carry her son on her back, skin to skin, with a single kimono wrapping both mother and child.

*Infantile tyranny and distance training.* The above physical intimacy, while gratifying to many mothers, may get out of the mother's control. During interview I often witnessed the child's tyranny in demanding the mother's exclusive attention, apparently to the latter's annoyance. One interview was totally disrupted and suspended by two unruly children who demanded to be held by their thirty-six-year-old mother, assaulted her, and on discovering that I was competing for her attention, tried to destroy the tape recorder. The mother's efforts to control them were in vain. She admitted her ineptitude as their caretaker: "My husband says I am being enslaved by the children." Another mother, at thirty-one, picked up her nine-month-old infant to nurse or rock it each and every time it cried. These familiar strategies soon stopped appealing to the child, who then continued to cry, leaving the mother at a loss. These observations suggest that the mother can lose her autonomy, finding herself pushed around by the little tyrant precisely because of the latter's helplessness. Some mothers were frank enough to admit that being tied down to a child like this around the clock was unbearable.

> Whenever my son cried, I used to hold him up in my arms or on my back. My son refused to be left alone on the tatami floor. He never felt assured unless he was in touch with my skin. Always he was either in my arms or upon my back. How insufferable it is to rear a child, I said to myself.

No wonder that the religious cult called Gedatsu (see p. 19) recognizes in its theology the supernatural poignancy of an infant as a source of misfortune: the spirit of a deceased infant can afflict illness or other misery upon its mother through its possession of her.

In order to forestall the insatiable dependency of the child and the mutual entrapment of mother and child which it entails, three mothers took measures to train themselves and their children in distance maintenance. Mieko, fifty-one, never had *soine* with her son because she felt *soine* was a bad habit—she herself did not recall having slept with her mother. As soon as she finished nursing, she would "throw" her child into a basket used as a bed substitute. In this context, she mentioned the possible influence of her father, who had been exposed to foreign culture. University-educated Harumi had her daughters sleep in another room from birth on and stopped co-bathing as soon as they became able to stand in the bathtub. Her mother does not approve of such "heartless" treatment of the children, and her neighbors, she claimed, regard her "separatism" as odd. Mari, twenty-eight, proudly told that she had trained her one-year-old daughter to be self-sufficient, to play by herself, to drink milk from a glass unassisted. Again "public opinion" tends to be opposed to such autonomy training at this early stage—nurses told Mari she should hold the child in her arms while nursing. In retrospect, evaluations of intimacy versus distance vary: a woman in her early sixties expressed regret at having brought up her son to be independent, not having indulged his *amae*, and deplores his "coldness" toward her, which she attributes to her "cold" way of rearing him; another woman in her forties, now a grandmother, praised her daughter-in-law for the "smart" way she manages to leave the child alone, in contrast to the way the senior woman was helplessly dominated by her intimacy-seeking child.[6]

## CO-SOCIALIZATION

The mother-child dyad can exist only under certain conditions such as the neolocal arrangement of residence, or at a certain stage of the mother's life or child's growth such as the period between the first and second childbirth. Actual circumstances abound with cases of shared socialization or co-socialization either with respect to caretakers or children.

*Co-caretakers.* In a virilocal or uxorilocal residential pattern, it is most likely that the mother's mother-in-law or own mother participates in childrearing. Most of the women with career occupations were helped with childrearing by their mothers or mothers-in-law, a fact they acknowledge with gratitude. "I could leave my children under my mother-in-law's care without worry. She was a skilled caretaker." "My daughter was reared by my mother, so she always cried for 'Granny,' not for 'Mama.' " Understandably, one's own mother was preferred to one's mother-in-law as a substitute caretaker. The easy availability of the most desirable surrogate baby-sitter may partially explain why the uxorilocally married women in the sample appeared more contented than either virilocal or neolocal women. The same factor is also likely to account for why mothers married to *mukoyōshi* fathers were disapproved of by their daughters (as seen in chapter 2): such mothers were not exclusive caretakers for the children.

It was not always in accord with the mother's wish that her mother-in-law shared socialization of the children. Sometimes the young mother was deprived of "the right" to rear her child either because she was needed for tougher labor, farming or assistance for fishing for example, or because the grandmother practically usurped the child as her own. Harue, mother of three daughters, confessed that it was her mother-in-law who read books on childrearing in preparation for the birth of the first child. Except while nursing, the daughter came under the granny's exclusive care, shared a bed with her, and when she reached school age, had her grandmother come to the PTA meetings. She attended a college in Tokyo, and the grandmother accompanied her to live in a rental house together with a maid. "People did not know *I* was her mother." Harue was often asked by her friends if she did not feel lonely, to which she would respond, "I stole the most treasured person [son/husband] from my mother-in-law, so I gave away my endeared child to her."

It would be wrong to assume that a grandmother smoothly transfers her maternal love for her child to a love for her grandchild.

> My husband was an only child, and when a dish was served for all the family to share, he used to eat it up without consideration for others. He would take quick bites, regardless of whether the children or I too were sharing it. Grandma encouraged him, saying, "Eat more." She would even take a dish away from the children's mouths, and insist Papa alone would eat it. So much she loved her son.

These are two extremes which deviate from a daughter-in-law's expectation; instead of a jealous attachment to a grandchild or the failure to extend maternal love to grandmaternal affection, she would expect something in between.

The husband's participation in bringing up the children shows a clear-cut bipolarity: he either participates intensely or not at all. There is a general tendency for the husband to participate only if there is no other surrogate caretaker; if his or her mother is available as a willing participant, on the other hand, he tends to withdraw. By and large, the husband has less resistance to child caring than to other house chores, and the maritally estranged husband often turns out to be *kobonnō*, a blindly indulgent father. A 1968 survey of Tokyo residents reveals that husbands are more cooperative in "looking after children" than in any other activities including "carpentry" (Fujin ni Kansuru Shomondai Chōsakaigi 1974:224–25).

Again, physical intimacy is a major channel through which the husband becomes a co-socializer. Some husbands were eager co-sleepers with the children, while for others father-child co-sleeping was unthinkable or even repulsive.

When I conceived a second child and time came for me to sleep alone, the first child was moved from my bed to Papa's. Papa did *dakine*. This was repeated for the third, fourth . . . child [six children in all], one by one. He slept with each for about a year.

If the child had a separate bed of its own, that bed was usually placed between father and mother. As the child developed physical control over its mobility, it would creep into either the mother's or father's bed during the night. In the case of a couple with one son only, this sleeping arrangement lasted until the son was in the sixth grade (twelve years). A mother of two sons, thirteen and eight, described how her husband still continues to sleep between the two sons so that they move closer to him from both sides. The husband, a schoolteacher, believes such skin-to-skin contact necessary for healthy child development.[7]

Similarly, child bathing may involve the husband's willing cooperation. In a few cases, the husband took sole responsibility for "double bathing." As the child grew older, the husband often became a playmate in rough contact play such as wrestling or playing a horse for the child to ride upon.

An overattachment of a daughter to her father is a cause of disturbance for thirty-five-year-old Tsukiko. The husband admitted he has gone too far in looking after their eldest daughter, though it was originally intended to lift a burden from the wife who was having a second daughter:

Husband: "I took the older one with me everywhere I went. . . . So she continues to seek my *amae* indulgence, even though she is a fifth grader now. . . . Because I looked after her so well, this one [pointing to the wife] became less inclined to do so. That way it has become worse and worse."

Wife: "Upon the younger one's birth, Papa slept with the older one, holding her in his arms. I thought it was bad. So, the older one likes Papa more than me."

When the younger daughter started to attend a kindergarten, both daughters were put together into an upstairs room to sleep by themselves. And yet the father-daughter intimacy has not come to an end. The wife predicted that "the older one will never be able to part with her male parent."

The husband's co-socializing role becomes indispensable as the child passes puberty, when he/she enters junior high school at twelve, or at the latest by the time of his/her high school entry. By then, the husband is expected to transform himself from an indulgent, physically oriented playmate or an aloof nonparticipant into a disciplinarian and educator. "You can handle your children up to the end of elementary school, but from junior high school on they are unmanageable for a female parent. They start to talk with reason [*rikutsu*], and ask questions you cannot answer. Only the father can keep them down."[8] The husband's educational role is thus reappraised, but not without ambivalence on the wife's part as will be seen shortly.

How the husband comes to influence the children is a mystery to some women. Several wartime women agreed in casual conversation that their postpubescent children, reared in the postwar era, have their own ideas and convictions and are not ready to be pushed around. This makes them feel inferior and inadequate as parents they said. But for some reasons unrevealed to them, the same children are almost frightened of their fathers, will never talk back, and volunteer to comply with their authority, even when the father is absent from home. These women cannot get over this phenomenon. One of the mothers told of her son subjecting himself without resistance to the father's punishment with the pain of moxacautery (see p. 188). Mother may well be an object of emotional attachment and guilt, but it is still father who is respected and feared. This is another reminder of the fact that the question of whether Japan is patriarchical or not should take into account this triad —husband, wife, and child—not just the male-female relationship. It may be the postpubescent child as much or even more than the wife who buttresses "male dominance." After all, do the children themselves want a strong, authoritative father or does this only reflect the parental value—paternal and/or maternal—instilled through socialization?

Widows expressed surprise at how the children turned out to "love" their late fathers. Although Kuniko was sure that all the children shared her feeling of estrangement from the absent father/husband (who had been living with a concubine), they threw her off by displaying their love and deference for him in front of the house altar *(butsudan)* where he was enshrined.

Despite the increasingly significant role the husband was to play at a later stage of childrearing, in no case was he the primary caretaker, and in some cases he even continued to stay away from the paternal role. "As for my husband, his profession has consumed him," says Sayo. "He had nothing to say about the children. How to rear and educate them was entirely my responsibility throughout." Conversely, even if the wife was not always a primary agent, she was in no case totally free from childrearing.

*Multiple children: birth rank and sex.* Co-socialization also refers to the situation where more than one child is reared at once. It is often the number of children that is associated with the mother's heaviest hardship. The most difficult period for a mother of ten was when she had to take the first three children, all at preschool age, to a public bathhouse every day. The burden lightened thereafter because the younger children were looked after by older ones. Another woman had four children all attending school at the same time. This involved her busy preoccupation every morning with grooming them, feeding them, and preparing lunch boxes. For New Year's and annual community festivals, mothers stayed up late at night to sew new kimonos for all the children. "While I was rearing all these children," said a fifty-six-year-old mother, "I never stepped out of the house."

One child is referred to in distinction from another child not by its personal name but primarily by sib-rank ("the older" and "the younger") or sex ("male child" and "female child"). If three or more children are involved these two variables are combined, such as "first son, second son, first daughter, third son, and second daughter." This practice reflects the legal identity of a child in terms of such combination as recorded in the house register. Even twins must be registered as the "first" and "second" (son or daughter); a set of male triplets, who had become "celebrities" in the local community through mass media exposure, were introduced to me by their mother as "oldest, middle, and youngest."

Mothers of two or three children stressed differences and contrasts rather than similarities between the children. "I brought them up exactly in the same way and yet they are so remarkably different." Differences are well patterned nonetheless. An older child is appraised as timid, nervous, delicate, sickly, sensitive, cautious, circumspect, tidy, subdued, and so forth, whereas a younger child is contrasted as bold, daring, open, and abrasive. Another contrast is between "disciplined" (older child) and "spoiled" or "unruly" (younger child). Further, an older child is described as having been "difficult" to handle, whereas a younger child "was easy" or "grew up by himself" rather than was brought up.

One explanation may be found in the different ways in which the caretaker treats the two children. In dealing with the first child, the inexperienced mother's double socialization (of the child and herself) must be exploratory and cautious, involving her overreaction to the child's behavior. Thus, a slight sign of disturbance in the child made one woman rush to take the child to a pediatrician. In contrast, the same mother, now well experienced and confident, leaves the second child alone. In other words, the childrearing experience (success and failure) gained from the first child is "recycled" into the second-child socialization. The recycling of experience may end up molding two children into two polar types:

> I reared the *chōjo* [first daughter] very carefully and *shinkeishitsu ni* [nervously]. That was a mistake. She grew up to be extremely sensitive to others' feelings, prone to do things in accordance with others' wishes. I realized she always tried to figure out what they wanted from her by watching their faces [*kaoiro o ukagau*]. I made up my mind to leave the younger children [a son and another daughter] as free as possible. They have turned out to be too free and self-directed.

The child's personality thus faithfully mirrored the mother's attitude: "My younger child is bold, because I brought him up boldly."

Coupled with the difference in the mother's experiential background is the cultural emphasis upon the birth-order identity of each child, which further accounts for a differentiation between the children of the same parents. The above-cited triplets, two years old, are a case in point. During a casual observation, I noticed the "oldest" child being most socially responsive, most expressive of attachment toward his mother, always closest to her, most compliant and supportive of her. Whenever a question was asked of the boys, it was this boy who answered—he spoke best also. I observed special attention being paid to this child by neighbors and other visitors, which obviously further encouraged him to be socially adept. The "second" son looked "inward oriented" and cerebral. According to the mother, he was the first to learn the Japanese alphabet and numbers, and most of the time I saw him absorbed in "reading" the children's books without much attention to other people around. The "third" happened to be athletic, of the outdoor type, tough, fearless of outsiders. This one was joined by the first in rough-and-tumble games, the second one sat alone, arranging alphabetical letter pieces. It appeared as if once the "first" child established himself as a typically first one the others "chose" to be as contrastive as possible to the immediately preceding sibling, even in the case of triplets.

Differences seem further exaggerated and reinforced through the typical maternal proclivities to display the child's "unique" strength and ability to outside audiences. The mother of the triplets told the second son to read aloud a passage in a book for me, which he did. Meanwhile, she was describing each child to me with emphasis upon contrasts, which of course the children overheard.

The special status of the first child, often without regard to sex, may be reinforced by the immaturity of motherhood calling for specially careful socialization. It is further confirmed by the fact that other caretakers get more involved with the first child than with the younger children. The mother-in-law in particular tends to monopolize the first child, and no other children, as her own. Favoritism may become a domestic issue. Asked what aspect of childrearing confounded her most, Ayano pointed out that her parents-in-law's "educational plan" had superseded hers. The parents-in-law, she elaborated, discriminated against the younger son simply because *they* had brought up all the children except this one. They would praise the oldest son and compare him with this "no good" younger son. "Since Papa was not around, I could not interfere. I wished they would leave the children to me. . . . Grandma gave the thickest portion of *yōkan* to the first son." This sort of conflict involving three generations within a family was referred to in chapter 2 in the context of ego as a child.

The privileged status of the eldest child is sometimes compensated by an overindulgence of the youngest child. This ties in with the difficulty of weaning—physically and mentally—the youngest. A mother of a daughter (older) and a son admitted she is often "scolded" by the daughter for overindulging *(amayakasu)* the son.

The mother's interest in the child's sex is first expressed with regard to the detection of the sex of a fetus. Some local women claimed that the maleness of a fetus can be identified with its sharp, violent movements, with the pain it causes in the mother's hips instead of belly, with the mother's angular rather than rounded countenance. It was also contended, half jokingly, that if the male partner to coitus comes to orgasm first its product will be male.

Sex difference in dispositions among the same-parent children is not as clearly recognized as difference by birth order, or the former is always contaminated by the latter. Nonetheless we have enough data to draw upon for a generalization. If the child is female and younger, childrearing is the easiest, whereas an older male child makes the most difficult case. If one has an older female and a younger male child, the question of difficulty is not quite predictable—chances are fifty-fifty— while the reversed combination is free from such uncertainty. Other things being equal, then, we can say that girls are perceived to be easier than boys to handle.

Informants tend to impute this difference to the sex identity of mother and daughter, which enables the caretaker to "understand" the child fully and thus to train her with unequivocal confidence.

> I am female, so when my daughter does not do a job well I can push her around and tell her, "Do it again." But male children cannot be handled this way. If my son says, "Cut it short, Mom," I can say nothing more. Boys are mute, hard to understand.

In this case, the daughter is older than the son. It is under the same assumption of mother-daughter continuity or similarity that Shoko feels happy about having two sons and no daughter: "It would be too much to bear if I find faults with my daughter—the same faults that I have." The idea of a child as a mirror image of its mother seems to apply more to a daughter.

The difficulty of rearing a son is further rooted in the cultural standard of "manhood."

> This child, my son, is a headache. Somehow he is unsteady. You don't worry about girls. All she has to do is to find a nice man and become homebound. But boys are different. They must have steady occupation. Today particularly, women are so strong that men are easily henpecked. Males must be tough and strong all the more.

Here it is not so much the mother-son sex discontinuity but the higher standard of attainment culturally imposed upon a male offspring that accounts for difficulty. Also implied in the above remark is the likelihood that mothers of boys are strong supporters of male dominance. To be noted here is the fact that the same informant is discontented with her husband being despotic.

By and large, local mothers tend to recycle their childhood experiences as daughters and sisters into rearing their own daughters and sons in such a way that the culturally standardized sex polarization perpetuates itself over generations although the standard is less rigid. Some try to "counter-recycle" the sex discrimination experienced as daughters. Kuniko, reared in a family where one son was treated like a prince in contrast to the six underprivileged daughters, was determined to be fair to her daughter and son. Intended fairness resulted in reversed favoritism: for example, she gave the daughter a better, southeast-facing room and the son a poor one. Now she regrets what she has done, convinced that it accounts for the son's underachievement. Yumiko, also disapproving of the way she was brought up "to be like a girl," never demands her daughter to be such. The daughter, when in high school, would come home late after extracurricular activities and caused the grandma (mother-in-law) to worry, but the mother firmly backed her up. Then Yumiko went on to say that she was worried only about her son not being masculine enough.

## The General Goals of Socialization

What kind of personality did these mothers want to develop in their children? Cutting across the sex lines and birth ranks there emerge some patterned goals of socialization. First, an emphasis was laid upon a free, unhampered development of the child's potentials as shown in the comment, "Children should go any direction they want." One might get the impression that the mothers have abandoned their right or duty to guide the children. Behind this laissez-faire attitude are several factors: the mother's filiocentrism in that she subordinates her own wish to that of her child; her sense of inadequacy and obsolescence as a guide for her better-educated child; counter-recycling of the overly severe discipline she received from her parents; the culturally patterned "naturalism" favoring the child's natural "unfolding." "I wanted my children to grow naturally and unrestrained [*shizen ni, nobinobi to*]" was a common remark.

The above goal, which sounds like Carl Rogers' ideal, turns out to be qualified or tamed by other goals. Juxtaposed with this emphasis upon the child's freedom is the mother's expectation that the child be of common type, like everybody else, not unusual, as variously expressed (*futsū, tsukinami, ōkata*). The child's freedom or spontaneity, therefore, should not go beyond normative limits. There seems to be a general belief that a child, if developed naturally and fully, will become a conventionally acceptable type instead of turning into an eccentric.

To add another qualification, the child is strongly cautioned against being a social burden. Specifically, informants mentioned the avoidance of causing *meiwaku* (trouble) for others. "I say to my son, 'You can do anything you please, even wild things, only if you don't cause *meiwaku* to others. *Meiwaku* is absolutely forbidden. Don't ever do anything that displeases other people. Must be careful even with the way you talk.' "

The positive counterpart of *meiwaku* avoidance is the exhortation for the child to be *yasashii* (tender) and to have *omoiyari* (empathetic kindness) toward others. "I don't mind if my children have undistinguished careers, but do insist they will be *yasashii* and have *omoiyari* at heart and render help for those on the side of justice." These social virtues join hands with the desirability of "being liked" by others or at least "not being mean" to others, which were also mentioned by informants. Implied here is the admonition against the child's selfishness. The above emphasis on the child's self-orientation does not include a tolerance of its egotism. The child's egotism must be reprimanded whether it goes against other people or the mother herself.

As an extension of *meiwaku* avoidance, informants stressed self-reliance as something the child should develop. "My goal was to bring up my son into one who can do everything by himself, who doesn't have to be helped by others." This self-reliance training goes against *amae* indulgence. While many mothers admitted that they had indulged their children with *amae* at an early stage, they said so with embarrassment; they regard self-reliance, though difficult to inculcate, as an ultimate goal. Akiyo, a career midwife, claimed to have brought up her son in exactly the same way as she was raised by her mother—to be able to handle everything that concerns him. She did not even bother to go to his school for PTA meetings. "I told him to educate himself, find a job by himself, not to depend upon his parents."

Akiyo added that her goal was to have the son "liked" by people. This suggests that self-reliance is not necessarily contrastive with "other-directedness." Indeed, for the Japanese, self-reliance or "self-orienta-tion" closely dovetails with social congeniality and acceptability. If not, it is devalued as egotism. For my informants, these are aspects of one and the same goal. The inculcation of *omoiyari* in the child does not necessarily entail an endorsement of self-renunciation or unprincipled compromise.

Also stressed was the value of perseverance which was differently labeled as *shinbō*, *gaman*, or *konki*. "I say only one thing to my chil-dren, 'Once you start something, don't quit until you complete it. Don't start anything you can't finish.' " A mother sends her two sons out for piano lessons after school, although music training is usually for girls only, in order to "train them in *konki*."

No informant mentioned compliance as a socialization goal despite that this was a main value most of these women were trained in. In-stead, the term *sunao* was used. This term refers to a wide range of attributes, from "straightforward," "frank," "honest," to "pliant" and "docile." Thus, it could imply a self-assertion on the one hand, and com-pliance on the other. When a mother says, "All I want from my child is *sunao*," she is likely to mean a mixture of both.

Most of these goals sound familiar to us from the accounts of the informants' premarital experiences. They may represent some of the most basic and persistent cultural values transmitted from mother to child. Some change may be noted also. Granted that self-focus inter-locks with other-focus as argued above, the local women tend to be more biased for the former with regard to their children than was the case when their parents trained them.

## HEALTH CARE

To the question whether it was difficult to rear the children, many informants immediately referred to the children's health: "Fortunately my children were all very healthy." "The hardest was when a child got sick." "All I cared about was for the children to be in good health." An older child more than a younger one, a male more than a female tended to be vulnerable. Tuberculosis, pneumonia, and dysentery were mentioned as having caused near death. According to a local pediatrician, dyspepsia used to be the most common disorder, and now eruptive fever is most frequent. Another change he sees is in the medical knowledge of mothers: mothers used to take a doctor's prescription literally without bothering to know why, but today's young mothers, college educated, know about virus and ask "sharp" questions.

Informants recall the days when, in treating the child's recurrent disorders like fever, diarrhea, stomachache, and cold, they or their mothers were a combination of physician, pharmacist, and nurse. Such a "home therapist" would select one from among their home supply of Chinese herbal medicines which were obtainable from itinerant drug peddlers from Toyama. She would often combine medication with tactile stimulation like massage and with "psychotherapy" in such forms as sutra recitation and supplication by the patient's bedside. Rice gruel was given as the "best" medicinal diet. Due to nationalized medicare and the overall improvement of medical facilities, young mothers now take their children directly to a hospital or clinic at the first sign of a disorder. A mother with a sickly child, then, associates childrearing with nothing but "visiting hospitals all the time." This overconcern on the part of a "modern" mother was often reproached by doctors, as informants recalled.

One of the folk therapies widely used and still regarded as a viable panacea is moxacautery. Along with chronic physical diseases, temper tantrum attributed to the activation of *mushi* (bugs) was often treated by this "shock" method with some punitive intent. If the mother alone was unable to control a recalcitrant child, well-experienced women in the neighborhood were called upon to insure its immobility so that a burning moxa (grain-sized dried grass) would stay put on the child's body until it extinguished itself. The same remedy was also applied for what is called *hikitsuke*, convulsion, which was also very common among preschool children.[9]

Hospitalization of a child does not necessarily free its mother from nursing. A local pediatrician said he demands that the mother stay with the child as a *tsukisoi* throughout. Not only is she supposed to perform most of a nurse's duties, but should cook meals for her patient-child at the hospital kitchen as well. "A hospital could make money if it prepares meals, but then the unique condition of each child will have to be disregarded."

The child's disability is of greatest concern to the mother. Two women in the local sample each have a polio-stricken child, and their lives have centered around this misfortune. One of them, with a husband who was busier with other women than with earning money, had to work hard as a seamstress late at night to meet medical expenses while her daytime hours were devoted to nursing her patient-daughter. The combined striving of mother and daughter resulted in the latter's successful graduation from a high school and achievement of the status of a licensed koto teacher. With fees from several students and the government's pension for the handicapped, this girl is now economically independent. Having witnessed the mother's dedication to her, the daugther, at the time of interview, was writing a fictionalized biography of the mother, which was being published serially in a local magazine. Her admiration for the mother was expressed in every line. For the other woman, when she discovered her son's right leg paralysis incurable, she felt dizzy and lost, "unable to tell which way the sun is coming, which way it is setting." Most heartbreaking for her was the son telling his parents how his playmates at kindergarten imitated his walk. Like her husband, she became a Sōkagakkai member. The first woman also became a frequent visitor to shaman-diviners.

The most tragic of all are the other two cases, each involving a daughter destined to live a vegetablelike existence—one suffering from cerebral infantile paralysis, the other from meningitis. Within less than a month after birth, said Mutsuko, her daughter got pneumonia, which then turned into "meningitis or some such things." For twenty-seven years since then the daughter has not stepped out of the house even once. A fisherman's wife, Mutsuko could not afford to stay home; she went to work instead as a hired fish processor in the neighborhood so that she could come home many times each day to care for the homebound patient. She accepts it as her "fate."

The other woman experienced a double tragedy. During postpartum recuperation at her natal house under her mother's care, Junko learned of the accidental death of her husband, a helicopter engineer. Meanwhile, the baby delivered with forceps remained with her head unsettled (*suwaranai*). She carried her child from one hospital to another, to not only local but national hospitals including Tokyo University Hospital. This only led to the final verdict—cerebral paralysis. Now nineteen, the victim has been bedridden all these years. Fortunately for Junko, she shared caretaking with her mother. "Every day we change her diapers, give an enema to her, feed her, and so on, do everything for her. . . . Unequipped with intelligence, she is unable to identify me as

her mother." It is not that there is no institutional care available, but no
nursing home is willing to accept such hopeless cases according to
Junko; either that, or acceptance means virtual imprisonment, only
waiting for the patient's death. The double tragedy, instead of ruining
her life, put her into gear toward a career commitment as a koto
teacher, whereas she had thus far been playing koto as a hobby. The
development of Junko's career will be detailed in chapter 6. Many religious sects including Risshō-kōseikai and Sōkagakkai have tried to convert her, but she has evaded their attempts. While admitting to her dis-
interest in religion, she is convinced that her husband, dead for nineteen
years and enshrined in the house altar, has been protecting her and their
daughter.

## ADOPTION AND STEPMOTHERHOOD

*Child-taking.* The childless couple may choose to adopt a child. Two
distinct types of adoption emerge out of my sample. One is the adoption
of kin—nephew or niece—in which it is no secret to the adopted child
or the public. The child retains the filial identity in relation to his/her
natural parents. Three out of the four child adopters in my sample
belong to this type. None of the three children were adopted in infancy
but rather at school age or in adulthood. Kayo's baby died at birth, and
becoming widowed, she adopted her brother's daughter, who by then
had left her husband because he fathered a child by his concubine. The
parent-child tie in this type of adoption does not seem strong. Toshiko,
married at forty-three, also adopted a brother's daughter, but the latter
did not stay with her as expected but married out.

Stronger commitment is found in the other type of adoption where
the child is made to believe that the adoptive parent is his/her natural
parent. Wakako, convinced that she was sterile after having been in *mi-
zushobai* (hospitality business), adopted a son born out of wedlock and
managed to enter his name on her house register as her real child. The
illegitimacy of the child in such adoption seems typical. Special efforts
may be made to deceive the public. In one case of which I was told the
childless woman accompanied the woman about to give birth into the
maternity hospital, and convinced the public of having had her own
child. Such commitment to secrecy has its price. Wakako and her *mukoyōshi* husband had emotionally and economically invested in two sons
adopted from the same mother when she discovered her own fertility.
At thirty-six years of age Wakako gave birth to a son. The whole family—the couple and Wakako's parents—tried hard not to discriminate
against the adoptees. A greater challenge had to be faced when the se-

cret was uncovered. One of the adopted sons, eighteen at the time, was informed by a Shizumi resident that he was a *moraikko* (although he was reared as a true son, not as a servant). Upset, he ran away, drifted, and lived like a bum until he "became awakened" (for the exception to the generalization, see p. 39). Efforts to conceal the truth thus tend ultimately to prove futile, particularly in a community like Shizumi.

*Child-giving.* The reciprocal of child-taking is child-giving. Three women in my sample have given away their children to be adopted, and the adopters were their husbands' kin in all cases. No one was a willing giver, but the affinal *giri* demanded compliance with the childless kin's request. Again, all these cases belong to the first type of adoption defined above, and thus no complete severance has occurred. Tsuruko was strongly opposed to giving one of her six sons, who had already graduated from the university, to her husband's mother's brother. But the husband wanted to comply with his uncle's wish, and the son himself did not mind being adopted since the adoption was combined with marriage, arranged by the adoptive parents, with a girl whom he happened to like—a case of *fūfu yōshi* (adoption of a married couple). It has turned out that the son thus adopted out remained closest to the natural parents because he was locally bound as successor to the adoptive household whereas all the other sons left the hometown for city jobs. Tsuruko was inhibited so long as the adoptive parents were alive from displaying affection for the son's children, who called her "Granny" and would hang around her. But now there exists nothing in the way of intimacy among the three blood-related generations.

The above account of adoption suggests that blood ties are hard to break, and yet adoption is practiced frequently and quite successfully.

*Stepmothering.* Because of the general belief that the child beyond a certain age will never relinquish his exclusive attachment to his real mother, together with the association in folklore of stepmothers *(mama-haha)* with heartlessness, women would rather avoid marrying a man with a child. Some stepmothers do have a hard time. A local woman married a man with three children (eight, five, and three years old) when she was thirty-three. She was a target of gossip among the husband's kin and neighbors: "If I scolded the children, they felt sorry for the children. If I treated them kindly, they said I was a monster in my heart." She remained a stranger for a long time to the two older children in particular.

The motherless child, while he is detrimental to remarriage for the above reason, is what necessitates remarriage. My sample includes one such case. Mieko, after seven years of widowhood, made up her mind to accept a proposal from a widower doctor primarily because his children

needed a nurturant mother. The children warmly welcomed the stepmother and collaborated with her to extricate their father from a continuing affair with a nurse. She also succeeded in having her own son
accepted by his stepsiblings. All this happened when they lived in Tokyo. The absence of close neighbors and kin around may be a partial
explanation for successful stepmotherhood.

## School Education and Motherhood

SCHOOL-FOCUSED FILIOCENTRICITY

Modern Japan has seen an increasing engagement of its children in
school education, so much so that their lives are entirely embraced by
schools. The child's identity is based upon the school and class he attends, and his age upon his school year. Indeed, media, reporting on a
child, identify him in these terms.[10] Accordingly, the mother's orientation has been increasingly school focused. Woman's filiocentricity, in
other words, has become primarily or exclusively school-bound, and
this is much more so today than when the present-day mothers were
schoolgirls. Most informants, asked about childrearing, elaborated on
school problems. Even those women who resumed working outside the
home upon the child's school entry tend to be mentally preoccupied
with his school performance. Their life histories are dated and punc-
tuated by the childrens' school years or school events such as "When my
first daughter was about to enter junior high school, . . ." The previously cited local obstetrician has observed that there are more births
in March and April than in other months because women coordinate
their parturition in accordance with the desired year for the child's
school entry. An academic year in Japan is from April 1 to March 31.
The child's enrollment in a particular school may be so important that
many a father today must live alone when he is transferred by his company or by his choice to a place out of commuting distance from
"home." For a university professor, to live by himself for the same
reason is nothing unusual. "In my childhood," said a Tokyo woman,
"mother and children used to follow father wherever he moved either within Japan or overseas." She deplores the present educational
system which virtually prohibits the child's school-to-school mobility
within the same academic level. For Shizumi residents, however, this
kind of husband-wife split for educational purposes is not a typical
problem.

   The mother's resolution to minimize domestic inconvenience for
the child's school life and, instead, to facilitate his/her school conformity and performance typifies the local sample as well. While the child
studies at home, all television sets are turned off and mother too may

engage in study to be a good example. The husband may go along with the child-centered schedule; if not, the wife may work some device to insulate the schoolchild's life space from the husband's interference. This entails a protection of the wife's vicarious participation in the child's school life. An informant told me of several of her classmates who have started to divide the couple's bedroom with a heavy curtain so that their sleep will not be disturbed by their husbands coming home late, and so that in the morning they will be able to wake up early enough, without bothering the now sound-asleep husbands, to get the children ready for school. While the husband's availability during the child's preschool period was appreciated, Kumiko gave the following qualification:

> You would like to have your husband around when your child is still small. You need his help. Your responsibility for taking care of the crying baby at night is shared by him. You don't want him to be out until the child is about three. As the child gets to school age, things become hard to handle. Your husband's presence disrupts the child's life. You are all too glad to know in advance that he will come home late. You can then schedule the child's bathing, the time for his school preparation, and his bed time. . . . The child too is more straightened out when your husband is not around.

This statement contradicts what was said previously about the indispensability of the father in socializing an older child. A possible explanation is that some women are strongly ambivalent toward their husbands' participation in educating their children. It is also likely that there are three stages of child development—preschool, primary school, and high school—the first and last of which require the husband's involvement.

The mother of a schoolchild is no longer just a mother, but an agent or delegate of a school. She seems to have renounced her privilege of being a home educator juxtaposed with schoolteachers. The content of the mother's vicarious or auxiliary participation in the child's school education is detailed below.

## COLLABORATION FOR SOCIAL TRAINING

Mothers are generally preoccupied with the academic achievement of the children, but at the same time they are aware of the indispensability of nonacademic training, especially social and moral training of the children through school education, and this is truer with the mothers of young children.

*Separation and incorporation.* First, the child's school entry entails training in the child's separation from the mother and the familiar scene of the domestic sphere. The mother, while indulging a preschool child, often warns him of his first day of school when everything will suddenly change and no more indulgence will be granted. To mitigate the trauma of separation, mothers are most likely to send their children to kindergarten (starting at four) and nursery school (even earlier).

Separation is completed by incorporation of the child into the "public" world of peers and schoolteachers. The four city-operated nursery schools, which originally were provided primarily for broken families whose economic plight deprived the children of full-time maternal caretakers, are now being used by better-off families for getting the children used to "group life" as early as possible. As if to respond to the expectations of mothers, teachers of nursery schools, kindergartens, and first-year classes of primary schools try hard to incorporate the freshman pupils into classes. I witnessed a boy who stayed with his mother in the kindergarten playground being teased by his peers, "You are a baby, Yot-chan." To dramatize such a transition, the mother tends to feel that they should wear formal kimono with solemn black *haori* coats for the school admission ceremony.

*Regimentation*. The main cultural method of incorporation is regimentation of appearance and action. The mother will see to it that the child wears a proper uniform, cap, shoes, socks, and carries the right kind of bag and stationeries which usually are on sale at school. Some schools, local junior high schools for example, require that hair be closely cropped for boys and straight down to the shoulder for girls. All this standardization is familiar to the mother's generation, the only difference being that the children today look much more colorful, however regimented. It appears that the teachers are trying to adhere to this rule of physical uniformity as the last means to control the children. Certainly, this may hasten the child's separation from home and incorporation into school.

Physical regimentation is accompanied by the group synchronization of action. At nurseries and kindergartens I witnessed how the children's activities were rhythmically synchronized by formalized greetings, songs, utterances of slogans, hand clapping, dancing, and marching, in which all joined at the teacher's signal, as when class began or when they started to eat lunch or when they finished eating. Not only teachers but peers also supervised one another's actions. In the class of five-year-olds at nursery school, a boy who was staring into space during lunchtime was reminded by another boy, "Do eat, Takashi-kun." Recalcitrant, noisy ones were also reprimanded by peers to "be quiet."

Entailed in regimentation is a sense of order. The children learn to line up for their turns, uttering *"junjo, junjo"* (one by one). After lunch, the nursery children lined up to get toothpaste on their brushes and then to brush at the classroom sink "one by one." The same lining up took place when the children were leaving class "one by one" through the door, and all this in tune with the teacher's piano.

*Support.* Hand in hand with regimented control is the emphasis upon support as observed in classrooms. There is a deliberate effort on the part of teachers to avoid embarrassing the children. The child is reminded of his error with a full understanding of the circumstances which account for the error. A two-year-old, when failing in toilet control, was told by the teacher, "You just did not have enough time did you?" *Omoiyari*, again, is a dominant recurrent theme to be instilled in a subtle way. If a child assaults another child to snatch away the latter's possession, the victim will be told, I was informed, to cause the same physical pain in the assailant so that the aggressor may understand the victim's feeling.

In a nursery class of about twenty, the children were assigned to draw their own portraits. Those who finished the task would stand up in front of the whole class, again one by one, and show the picture to the class. Asked by the teacher if the picture resembled its producer, the class gave approving utterances to every child and not a single vote was negative.

A high premium is placed upon cooperation and friendship cultivated through mutual support. In a class of forty-five second-year primary schoolers, a question raised by the teacher was answered by a boy, and then a girl stood up to say, "I agree with Tsukuda-san, and I also think this way." When another student was unable to answer a question, a boy raised his hand, saying, "I want to help Yamada-kun." I noticed this form of communication was standardized across classes.

Mothers collaborate with schools in sensitizing the children to obey their teachers but encourage them to develop and care for friendship with peers or to differentiate "good" friends from "bad" friends. The children's group activities are watched, supported, and sometimes participated in by the mothers on occasions like the annual athletic day, the extracurricular exhibits, excursions, or camping.

COLLABORATION FOR ACADEMIC PERFORMANCE

However important social training may be, it is the child's academic achievement that obsesses the mother, and it is here that the mothers are labeled *"kyōiku mama"* (education mother) justifiably or unjustifiably.

The mother's preoccupation with academic education is often rationalized in terms of her child-centered wish to actualize the child's potential
to the fullest extent. While social training is more or less left to teachers
and schoolmates of the child, the mother plays an active role in academic collaboration.

   *From conventionalism to elitism.* There is variation within the
*kyōiku mama* type. One kind of mother is concerned with keeping the
child up at least within the average level of performance. Aware of the
child's limited ability, the mother does not aim at a top level, but tries
hard to maintain the child above *ochikobore* (the dropped debris). A
performance level may refer to: the child's rank within a class which
may be told by the *ukemochi*, the Japanese version of a "homeroom"
teacher in full charge of a single class all year around; the level of school
completion (e.g., high school graduate versus university graduate); or
the reputation of the school the child is admitted to through the "infernal examination." What exasperates the average-seeking mother is the
fact that the expected average fluctuates over the years. A woman in her
late seventies brags about having all the children graduated from high
school, and another in the same age bracket is embarrassed about her
eldest son having dropped out of high school because of her husband's
illness. For a fifty-year-old woman, on the other hand, the eldest son's
high school graduate status is quite embarrasssing, and many women in
the late forties have "all the children"—both sons and daughters—
enrolled in universities or junior colleges, as if such higher education is
taken for granted as an average level.[11]

   As for the level of school reputation, the average-seeker is likely to
enroll her child in local schools up to high school without inquiring into
other alternatives. For the same mother, it would be an intolerable disgrace to have a child who cannot make even the local high school. The
*ochikobore* student out of this average course may opt to attend the
vocational high school regardless of his interest, or another high school
out of the city rated as still lower. The city's vocational high school has
been plagued with the problems of low morale and delinquency due to
its stigma.

   After the local high school (academic course), the student may go
on to a higher institution, but this time away from home, most likely to
an average college in Tokyo. Sayo recalled how difficult it was for her to
make a decision on her son's educational career. She had long wondered
what career would best suit the son, what school would accept him
without overburdening him "because mother knows the child's ability
best." A dental school, preferably, to succeed the occupation of his den-
tist father, but then the burden of examination might torment him and

drive him crazy. She finally chose a pharmacological school for her son. But how about the son's own wish? The type of son who had a strong will of his own would not have caused so much worry in her, she said. In any event, he would go anywhere she suggested. Thanks to the mother's determination and collaboration, the son passed the examination to the pharmacological school in Nippon University. Meanwhile, the husband refused to participate in this important decision making. To the mother's great joy and satisfaction, the son is a pharmacist employed by the prefectural government.

Ambitious mothers with enough income opt for an "elite course" for their children. Elitism entails alienation from local schools at the high school level or earlier for the obvious reason that local school graduates would be hopelessly and irreversibly disadvantaged for admission to a top-rated university. An elite-course school out of town must be chosen; this is likely to be the mother's decision in consultation with local teachers. Elitist mothers frankly admit they were or are *kyōiku mama*, whereas conventionalist mothers, however strenuously they tried to keep their children out of the *ochikobore* basket, emphatically deny they were.

One alternative elite course is to send the child to the junior or senior high school of a top-ranking private university with a built-in "escalator" from primary school on. At the suggestion of the class teacher *(ukemochi)* of a local junior high school, Kuniko chose precisely this course, that is, to send her daughter and son to the high school attached to Keio University, and as expected, she eventually produced two Keio University graduates.

Another, and more common elite course for locals is to aim at a high school—either a prefectural high school or a private school in Tokyo—which is known for its reputable record in the number of entrants into Tokyo University, other former "imperial" universities, lesser national universities, first-rate private universities such as Keio or Waseda, or medical schools in general. Two mothers sent their children to the six-year system (junior and senior high) of Azabu, a well-known private school in Tokyo regarded as a solid stairway to Tokyo University. Several other mothers chose one of the two best prefectural schools, which is cheaper than the above alternative and also allows commuting.

For an elitist parent, the choice of a high school is more important than that of a university, and yet success in high school admission does not insure university entrance—the ultimate goal. Even the "escalator" is not necessarily a smooth one. A local physician wished his first son to succeed him in the medical profession—the profession inherited from his grandfather on—but realized there was little hope for the son to be accepted by the medical school of Keio even though he was a Keio High School graduate. Even its own number "must win the one-to-thirty-seven competition for the medical." Instead of putting up with studying for two or three more years as a *rōnin*, the son opted for Keio's School of Science and Engineering. The second son, also at Keio High, does not stir up the father's hope either. The above mentioned Azabu High enrollees did make good universities, including Keio, but not Tokyo University as might have been expected. Mothers, and sometimes fathers too, thus cannot relax until their children successfully enter universities.

My sample includes a mother whose son entered Tokyo University, a mother of a Tokyo Institute of Technology entrant, and three mothers of private medical school students. All these high achievers except one have turned out to be first or only sons. To be recalled in this connection is the fact that the oldest child was more difficult to rear than younger children. It may be that the mother (and/or father) had run out of steam by the time of the second son, or that a small initial difference in academic achievement between the first and second was progressively magnified as the second developed an inferiority complex at the parental or grandparental teasing for his underachievement in comparison with the first. As for daughters, mothers are obviously and understandably much more relaxed, and yet some daughters, particularly older daughters, did better than younger sons. A number of mothers who have one son and one daughter said that the daughter studied voluntarily and scored high in class ranking while the son would reject the mother's encouragement and did poorly at school; they wished the children's sexes were reversed.

Mothers display their children's academic achievement to its maximal degree through a symbolic maneuver. If the university or high school to which the child is admitted is truly first-rate, the mother will give the proper name of the institution, such as Azabu, Keio, or Tokyo University. Former imperial universities other than Tokyo may be identified by proper names or as "former imperial," and other national universities as just *"kokuritsu"* (national). Third-rate institutions, whether a university or a junior college, are referred to simply as *"daigaku"* (university or college) without a name. In this respect, most mothers are elitist, or more correctly, vicariously elitist. Here is a situation of reversed attribution of status: while status usually flows from father to child, mother (or father) derives her status from the child's performance. The depth of academic elitism is revealed by the enthusiasm with which women talk not only about their own children but the children of their kin or friends as well as their children's classmates who are distinguished achievers.

*Educational investment.* The mother's identification with a successful child reflects her energy investment in his/her education, particularly in those families which can afford it. Mother-child communication at the preschool stage gives the first clue. I have often come across a mother asking questions of a small child on a street or in a train. Questions may concern the names of colors ("What is that color, Haruchan?"), computation ("How much change do you get if you buy six tangerines of one hundred yen each with a one thousand-yen bill?"), reading ("How do you read that ad?"), and so on. It looks as if the mother's mind is already set on the future examinations that the child will be subjected to. Once in school, a full-time mother is in charge of the child's homework and preparation for the next day's classwork. A busier mother would just say, "Study before you watch TV." While I was interviewing Harumi, her two daughters joined us. After some conversation, they were dimissed by the mother with "You bathe now, study for one hour, and then go to bed. You understand?" She is the opposite of the *kyōiku mama* type, she said. Another mother confessed that since she was more enthusiastic about her daughter's home study than the daughter herself, the latter developed no initiative. This was confirmed by the daughter when she said, "I used to ask, 'What shall I study today, Mother?' "

In the meantime, the mother attends the child's classes on the parents' Class Observation Day, which may occur once a month or less often, depending on the grade level. On one such day I joined the mothers in a third grade class of a local school. In order to encourage fathers' participation, that particular day was named Fathers' Class Observation Day, but more mothers than fathers showed up nonetheless. In the class of forty students, thirty-one parents including twenty-three mothers (as "deputies of fathers") were present. While the children were "practicing" a math test and grading their own answer sheets following the teacher's instruction, the mothers stepped forward to look into their children's performance whereas fathers all stood behind and looked bored. After the class observation, the teacher and parents stayed on to exchange ideas. Again I noticed a clear difference between male and female parents in the kinds of questions they asked. Fathers brought general problems into question like: "What is the standard level of sexual development for the third grader?" or "What can be done to develop the child's individuality?" Mothers were more concerned with specific problems regarding homework: "What would happen if one does not finish the study scheduled on a certain day?" It was obvious which of the parents was in charge of the child's day-to-day study progress.

Informants agreed that the main function of class observation is to see "where my child stands in comparison with other children." The mother would be blind, I was told, about her child unless she saw other children in the classroom. Another function is to "meet fellow-mothers, talk with them about the problems of children, and find how mothers share the same problems." Two mothers in the same class may happen to be former classmates and will possibly revive friendship through the class tie of their children. Indeed the strongest classmate bond among women is found under this condition of double-generational class-mating.

From class teachers too mothers learn about their children. At a teacher-parent conference such as described above, the teacher may suggest how to guide, reward, or punish one's child. In the above class, the teacher pointed out, among other things, that the children, when they deserve it, should be praised but not flattered since they can see through empty flattery. He also advised the parents to be aware of the importance of physical, nonverbal communication. The teacher himself, during the class, had gone around the room and stroked the heads of some pupils to indicate his approval and pleasure with their test performance. In individual-consultation hours, each mother learns her child's performance level as well as emotional problems. Sometimes the teacher reveals what the mother had never suspected about the family condition to which the child's low performance is attributed. A mother of two sons was told by the teacher of one son that the family discriminated against this son and favored the other. She then realized that her mother-in-law always praised one and scolded the other, and she herself joined the granny. She changed her strategy and supported the disfavored one every time the granny complained about him. This new strategy was effective in reforming the son in discipline and academic performance. Class teachers obtain such clues not only by observing the children's behavior but by reading their compositions and assigned diaries.

Mothers are aware of the decisiveness of the class teacher's influence upon the children particularly at the primary school level and therefore are keen in discriminating good teachers from poor ones. Although none directly challenge a poor teacher, indirect disapproval is expressed by singling out "the best teacher" in school or gossiping among concerned mothers. Popular teachers are usually male. A young mother complained to me about her son's teacher being a housewife: "After all, teaching is secondary for her. While teaching, she must be thinking about her children at home. She just cannot concentrate." The greatest excitement that ripples throughout the gossip network of mothers on the first day of a school year is over the allocation of teachers to classes. "Winners" of popular male teachers congratulate themselves, I heard.[12]

With regard to a very popular teacher, Yukie, a mother of two sons, said:

> All the mothers of his class will stay on at a teacher-parent conference until it adjourns. We never fail to gain some insight from what this teacher says. Sometimes, we mothers initiate to hold *"haha no kai"* [mother's meeting] and invite him. Most mothers participate. From what he tells us, we can get a clear idea of what our children are doing. We also raise questions. We don't understand "set theory," we say, and the teacher will agree to give a special class on it. . . . He creates opportunities for the children, mothers, and teacher to be united into one.

Open criticism was heard of high school teachers who are "busier with striking than with teaching." Over the years, the local high school has acquired the reputation of having one of the most radical teachers' union chapters in the prefecture. This partly accounts, said a nonunion teacher, for the school dropping out of competition for entrance examination training, and for parents' gravitation to nonlocal schools.

Rank order among mothers, which used to be based more upon family occupation and wealth, tends to be determined by the child's class ranking. The mother whose child is top in the class feels her "nose risen," or her "shoulders broadened" vis-à-vis other mothers, and is more privileged to have intimate access to the class teacher. Moreover, such a mother is more likely than other mothers to be appointed officer of the class or the PTA as a whole, which necessitates her further involvement with school and in turn is reflected in the child's greater achievement.

Apparently, some classes develop intimate interaction between the teacher and mothers over and beyond the degree necessary for educational purposes. A local bar hostess said that a group of mothers and a teacher drop in after PTA meetings, that they are her "regular customers."

As the child advances in grade, the mother faces the inadequacy or obsolescence of her stored knowledge in guiding his/her homework. Even the Chinese characters she is most confident of have been changed and standardized into more precise forms than what she is familiar with. Along with her child, she too must study to catch up. One of the prewar *kyōiku mama* joined her son and sat in the classroom like one of the children, much to the embarrassment of the teacher and son. Contemporary mothers have more alternatives: watching the NHK Educational TV programs, many of which are addressed to different levels of students, including serial courses of history, chemistry, physics, math, English, Japanese, social studies, and the like; attending classes for educating mothers which are sponsored by schools or the local government. "Mothers' Class," "Mazā Sukūru" (Mother School), and "Home Education University" are among such classes. Some class teachers are eager to teach mothers on the same course topic as given to the children, as mentioned earlier in connection with "set theory."

Mother's tutorial role, nonetheless, comes to an end as the child enters junior high school, or as some mothers become too busy to bother with their children's schoolwork. In a few families, the college-educated father takes over the tutorial job. The woman who has had a miserable marital life depicted her husband as more concerned with the son's schoolwork:

> When son came home from school, he faced homework assigned by his father, mainly mathematical questions. At suppertime, he was supposed to show his answers to father. If he could not perform the assignment, father banged son's forehead against the table. I felt sorry for son, but refrained from interfering. . . . This lasted until son was in his second year of junior high school.

An increasing number of mothers have come to rely upon external resources, partly due to affluence. They may hire tutors, or send their children to a private-home class run by a local schoolteacher or college graduate. Particularly prewar *kyōiku mama*, deprived of auxiliary educational facilities, scouted around for a possible tutor. One such mother invited home the locally available college students and schoolteachers to play with her children, and while playing, to teach them chemistry, painting, and whatnot. She paid no attention to the neighbors' gossip about her being a "lover" of college students. But the most common pattern today is to send the children to *juku* after regular schoolwork. *Juku* training may be categorized into three types. One is to aid "the elitists" strictly for entrance examination to a nonlocal "elite-course" high school or university. Locally, there is one such *juku*, which enjoys more prestige than does the regular high school, and mothers are proud to call attention to their children's attendance at this *juku*. English is the main subject taught there. Most other, smaller *juku* are for conventionalists, namely, for the children to keep up with regular school lessons. The third type has little to do with schoolwork but teaches nonacademic skills including vocational (e.g., abacus), artistic (calligraphy, painting, ballet and other dance styles, piano, violin), and martial-athletic (karate, jūdō, kendō) techniques.

More ambitious mothers dismiss the local *juku* as inadequate and send the children to more competitive *juku* or *yobikō* in Tokyo. Yoshimi had her only son commute to an examination-specialized *juku* in Tokyo in his sixth year of primary school with the intent that he eventually enter the junior high school of Azabu. In addition to the six-day-a-week regular work at a local school, the son took the four-hour round trip to Tokyo every Sunday. On top of that, the mother invited a nonlocal schoolteacher to tutor the son in math each day from two o'clock in the afternoon on into the night. This meant that the son was unable to perform the after-school duty of classroom cleaning which every pupil was assigned. Compromise was made by his cleaning a part of the room during lunch break all by himself while all his peers were playing. His classmates jeered at him, the parents of the class complained and protested, and a teacher, at a teacher-parent group conference, shamed Yoshimi by exposing what she was doing to the whole assembly. He said, "Among you people there is a foolish, insane mother who sends her kid to a Tokyo *juku* to practice multiple choice tests." Mother and son together endured this humiliation, and he made Azabu, "the school which had as many as one hundred students yearly pass Tokyo U examinations."

Even after the child is admitted to a Tokyo school of first choice, the mother may have to worry about his/her daily life, unless the school provides a secure dormitory. Some mothers put their children in an expensive boardinghouse run and controlled by an authoritarian father figure imposing strict discipline upon its boarders. Kuniko rented a house in Tokyo for her Keio-admitted daughter and son, and spent three days a week with them, while active locally the rest of the week as a businesswoman.

*Examination crises.* Mother's investment of energy, time, and money in the child's education is primarily oriented toward examinations, as is clear from the foregoing. The series of examinations that a child goes through is, indeed, a prolonged period of crisis after crisis for the child and family, not unlike a lengthened version of initiation rites in preliterate societies as observed by Kiefer (1974). Throughout the school years from junior high school on, the parent and child must worry about his/her class performance since his/her grade points count in terms of options to apply to a higher school of his/her choice at the "suggestion" of the class teacher. But in the very year of examination, tension heightens to its peak, and the whole household is caught up in "examination tornadoes." Parents may stop enjoying routine activities which are considered disruptive to the candidate's concentration. Competition is such that the last year of high school may not be taken so seriously under the parent-child agreement that it would be too much to expect him to pass the exam "straight" from high school. If an elite university or a medical school is aimed at, one or two years of concentrated preparation as a *rōnin* is taken for granted by some parents. But as the candidate keeps failing year after year and continues to be a *rōnin*, tension naturally builds up. A local father admitted that when his eldest son, after the exam, received a telegram from the medical school he had applied to saying "Cherry has fallen" (a euphemism for "fail"), he and his wife were shaken up. This was the son's third *rōnin* year. For another try the next year, father and mother intensely cooperated to maximize the son's study efficiency. The couple talked about nothing but his study and examination, but not to disturb him, they went out to discuss the matter. "There was absolutely no time for *fūfu-genka* [husband-wife quarrel]," said the wife. The son made it finally. Both parents regard the son's examination crisis as the peak of their own life crisis.

Sayo, who chose a Tokyo pharmacological college for her son, had to struggle with the examination crisis by herself because of her husband's aloofness from the matter. When notified of the son's failure, mother and son cried and went to bed as if they were sick. While crying in bed, she was called by a friend telling her of another pharmacological college still accepting applications, whereupon the application was made. The mother accompanied the son to take the examination in Tokyo. While waiting anxiously in the room reserved for them, parents received copies of the questions the children were answering in the next room. Sayo also got hold of a "correct answer" sheet. How anxious she was to throw it to the son whose head she could see. The son passed this time, and the mother cried again. She too recalls this experience as the climax of her life crisis.

Supernatural assistance is invoked. Mother, alone or together with the candidate, visits shrines to pray, do *ohyakudo*, buy talismans. At least she will pray at the *butsudan* (household altar) to invoke the ancestors' support, and at the *kamidana* (god shelf) for the blessing of gods. At times examinations involve a critical decision which can be made only at supernatural instruction. Yoshimi had her son take examinations to a small private engineering college at the suggestion of an Azabu teacher instead of a better institution like Tokyo Institute of Technology as she and her son personally wished. The son passed the examination, but she was still ambivalent, wondering if he should not study as a *rōnin* to take exams the next year for a national university. She procrastinated in paying the admission fee until the deadline. Unable to decide, she told the son to join her in asking her deceased husband. Mother and son together sat in front of the *butsudan* and recited sutras until "my husband appeared to say, 'Go, go' [to pay the fee]." The decision proved to be a fortunate one because that year the campus unrest was such that even Tokyo University was prevented from giving entrance examinations. The college the son chose was familylike, free from student rebellion.

Deeply involved in the examination crisis, parents come to learn of an easier alternative to get the children admitted, namely, outright bribery. Agents of some universities did approach the anxious parents for "donations" in exchange for "back-door admission," and a few of my informants admitted this option was exceedingly enticing although none confided to having succumbed to the temptation.[13]

The above description of crisis is not necessarily typical of local residents. Many mothers have compromised their aspirations with a more easily attainable level of performance; some cannot afford *juku* expenses or sending the children to Tokyo. Even the most ambitious group of local mothers seem weak aspirants compared with typical middle-class families in Tokyo and other large cities where educational facilities are abundant.

## Educational Dilemma

The reason why most mothers denied they were or are *kyōiku mama* is that there have been floods of criticism of such mothers in all quarters of society, particularly from education specialists and social critics through mass media. Critics stress how harmful the examination-geared education is to the healthy development of the child's potentials and blame mothers for taking a major part in this destructive enterprise.

Under the operation of competitive exclusion in terms of directions of a child's development, "the hypertrophy of examinations" (Vogel 1971:64) entails the atrophy of other experiences in the child. First, the examination-centered training creates a child only responsive to questions or tests given by somebody else, and thereby inhibits the development of his/her spontaneous interest, creativity, initiative, and imagination. Study is then reduced to what one must do as a duty passively accepted rather than what one is genuinely motivated to do. No interest is stimulated unless the subject directly relates to examinations, as shown by a student who can translate a passage from an English book very competently while totally disinterested in the content of the passage (Ito 1977).

Secondly, it is argued that the examination system curtails the development of a well-rounded personality and hurts the mental and physical health of the child by neglecting all activities irrelevant to examinations: study takes precedence over play, intellectual learning over emotional experience, mental over physical exercise, symbol manipulation over social interaction, head over spirit, and so on and so forth. In this connection the media have exposed incidences of mental aberration among schoolchildren, such as a growing rate of child suicide as well as instances of school phobia or what is called "school refusal" by Japanese psychiatrists. (It is interesting to note, with regard to the symptom of school refusal, that psychiatrists tend to attribute it to the power reversal of parents, namely, the combination of a domineering mother and a weak or absent father. A local schoolteacher, when he lectured at a "Home Education University" class, parroted this cliché word for word to my amusement. Obviously these predominantly male critics impute this problem to the single-minded *kyōiku mama*.) Not only the mental but physical vulnerability has been pointed up. Despite the remarkable growth in stature, today's children lack bone strength and muscle power, report the media, as demonstrated by their propensity to injury. Also, health specialists point out that schoolchildren have begun to exhibit symptoms typical of diseases among adults and the elderly, such as stomach ulcers, chronic fatigue, articular pain, and the like (*Asahi* 7/10/76; *Hawaii Hochi* 9/29/77).

The third concern is that schools are so rank ordered that the choice of a school or field has very little to do with the speciality of the child's interest but much more with his level of confidence in examination performance as revealed through a series of mock exams at regular schools or *juku*. A high achieving candidate, then, is likely to opt for a medical or natural science division of a university even though his real interest may lie in the humanities. The rank-order system thus can stifle the individual's unique interest or commitment. Furthermore, the same rank order is unambiguous in the manner in which it creates losers and failures as well as winners and successes. The high morale of a winner thus dovetails with the low morale of a loser. This monolithic hierarchy based upon school entrance records has inevitable implications for the handicapped, particularly the mentally retarded children. While these children are trained in special classes and the public is taught to discard its prejudice, their stigmatized status is built into the whole academic rank system.

Finally, while the value of social training, as described above, is unquestioned, the examination system tends to cancel out solidarity training in that one's peers are one's potential rivals. A junior high school student, I was told, pretends to be lazy about his schoolwork in front of his peers, while in fact working hard day and night. He will have his parent watch a popular television series and summarize it to him so that he can repeat it to his friends the next day as proof that he had watched television instead of studying. This episode illustrates an examination-festered situation inviting mutual deception and mistrust.

Local mothers are aware of these problems but, at the same time, they know the hard fact that an elite-course school record is the surest, or perhaps the only, way to a promising career for their children. *Kyōiku mama* never doubt their filiocentric motives: what they are doing is for the benefit of their children, no more or no less. This confidence is particularly unequivocal with regard to sons, especially first or only sons. Sayo, a mother of three children said that her two daughters went to whatever colleges they chose, and she does not even remember the name of one daughter's college. For the son, however, school education is "a life-or-death matter." This mother equated a success in examination with a necessary step toward manhood: "Unless you pass the exam, the road to manhood [*otoko no michi*] will be closed to you." Attending the son's commencement, Sayo cried with joy and gratitude, saying to herself, "Son has become a man at last."

As if to challenge the examination-centered educational system, one of the Shizumi primary schools, as I saw, was making a special effort to encourage spontaneous expressions and activities among the children. The teachers appeared to be following John Dewey's educational philosophy faithfully. This school went as far as to abolish report cards in order to develop each pupil's unique potentials fully without being hampered by grades. This decision was not popular among the mothers, and the principal was obliged repeatedly to explain this policy to the frustrated parents. Such idealism tends to weaken in the higher grades, being replaced by the examination syndrome in the junior high schools, and definitely so in the high school.

The mother's claim that her educational investment is only to benefit the children is indeed verified by the latter's appreciation. While some children do reject maternal encouragement as interference, some others complain about their mothers not being *kyōiku mama*. Many a mother observed that *juku* attendance was her child's idea and that she only gave permission. A mother confided her awareness of her daughter's mediocrity, but said that she, the daughter, insists on going to a difficult college. As a mother, the informant feels that she cannot prevent her daughter from trying. Furthermore, as we noted, fathers are as intensely involved in sons' education in some families, and some informants described their husbands as *kyōiku papa*.

The accusation of mothers as *kyōiku mama* is thus somewhat unjustified. Nonetheless, it is mother much more than father who is

trapped in the education dilemma described above. She is caught between educational ideals and the facts of life, between what the public
advocates and what the child (and therefore she) wants. Such entrapment may be experienced within a family. A fisherman's wife, a prewar
*kyōiku mama*, encouraged her eldest son to go to a boys' middle school
out of town. This flabbergasted her mother-in-law, to whom education
beyond primary school for a fisherman was wasteful nonsense. "She
told everybody, 'Our *yome* has lost her mind.' " The submissive daughter-in-law was adamant this time, convinced that the fishing industry
promised no career for her son. It may be the husband who represents
the critical public. Kumiko, a postwar *kyōiku mama*, recalled how she
encouraged the children to study day and night against her husband's
demand for help with his wholesale business. " 'No, no,' I would say to
him, 'they are studying now.' " Mothers are also trapped in a dilemma
between what regular schoolteachers endorse, often reflective of John
Dewey's educational goals, on the one hand, and what *juku* teachers
offer. Teiko, a housewife who was once a schoolteacher, expressed this
dilemma by complaining about schoolteachers' opposition to *juku*.
"Teachers, including my husband, don't understand what most children
do need. School education is not enough to get one into a first-rate
higher school."

Torn between *tatemae* (the declared principle) and *honne* (the undeclared actual feeling) in educational goals,[14] Harumi is experimenting
with both. She transferred two daughters from a local public school to
an out-of-town private school known for its liberal, individualistic
education. In contrast to the examination-centered rote learning, this
school trains children by "doing" rather than by reading and, at least
initially, did away with textbooks and timetables. While attending this
"unusual" school as a regular enrollee, the elder daughter was sent to a
strictly examination-oriented *juku* in Tokyo during a summer vacation.
It seems that the ambivalent mother is having the daughter pursue two
diametrically opposed goals. This may be one way of converting a
dilemma into options. Another, more common strategy is to send a child
to two types of *juku*—academic and nonacademic *(okeiko-juku)*—to
supplement each other. These strategies, however, tend to apply only to
daughters, sons being more exclusively bound to an academic course.

Maternal responsibility continues to bind women after the children
enter universities, graduate, take jobs, marry, and so on, probably as
long as they live. In this sense, there may be no such stage as "postparental." Chapter 7 will resume the discussion of motherhood in its
later stage.

## Community and Motherhood

Motherhood marks the peak of woman's domestic career, and yet it is as a mother that a woman also becomes more involved with an extradomestic life or community in a broad sense.

### MATERNAL PEER-GROUPING

As children become friends or classmates, their mothers are also drawn into peer-grouping as co-parents. This may begin in the neighborhood where the children play together. I often observed several children playing in an alley where traffic was not too heavy while their mothers were talking. Young mothers of about the same age—with no grandmother involved—were obviously enjoying this daily peer interaction while watching their children, which for some meant a temporary relief from a mother-in-law's surveillance. Some may have been friends before they became mothers, but my informants, local and nonlocal, including apartment dwellers, stressed how they became "neighborly" as an unavoidable consequence of mothering. Friendship with neighbor women was mentioned as a benefit of being a mother, and a childless woman deplored her isolation from neighbors.

Partially overlapping the neighborhood peering is the co-motherhood of schoolchildren. The strongest peer-grouping through children is found among mothers of kindergarteners. According to Yukie:

> Most of us were sending our first kids to the kindergarten. Every day, we mothers took kids there, and returned there to bring them home. While waiting for them to come out, we discussed our experiences. We talked about our children, and this exchange was extremely helpful. Everyone was sort of groping in the dark. . . . Friendship of this mother group is still surviving. We were together [as mothers of classmates] throughout until our children completed primary school. Now we meet every three months to talk about our children and dine together. In summer we have an overnight trip together with children. There is a membership list, and announcements are sent to everybody including the [former kindergarten] teacher. Around fifteen out of the total nineteen usually show up. We have a network of communication. . . . The association is called the Violet Club.

This peer association is through Yukie's first son, and another such grouping involves her through her second son.

It was found that this sort of secondary alumni grouping is widespread and not just among mothers of kindergarten children. School PTA activities may give rise to a permanent tie of secondary alumni. Tsuruko, mother of six children, remarked:

> I used to stay home, withdrawn, blind to what was going on outside. But because of my children I became involved with school, was elected PTA vice-president, and became active with Mothers' Classes. This way a new world was opened up for me. As for Mothers' Classes, I joined the Music Club and Dance Club, and made intimate friends with their members. This friendship is still unchanged. We meet three times a year, twelve of us. Not just locals, but some come from Tokyo and other places. Formerly, we talked about the children's examinations, next about their marriages, and now about the grandchildren.

Mothers whose children were involved in some unforgettable events tend to form a strong bond. Yoko, sixty-three, more than twenty years ago lost a son when the boat he was on sank during a school excursion on a lake. She still regularly meets the mothers of the twenty-two other victims. They hold memorial services together, go on group tours, and have dinner parties.

As was mentioned already, a previous, primary tie of two or more women such as that of class mates becomes intensified by secondary ties through children. Former classmates thus go through a microevolution of realignments from a group of single women, to married women, and then to mothers. These women find one another a main source of instruction and support regarding how to rear children—a source more trusted than any other.

The child-centered sociability may result in a change in the lifestyle of the household. An informant told of the next-door household having had a birthday party for its eldest son. There used to be no such thing, she said, but recently every household in this neighborhood began to hold one for the eldest son—eldest son only. The reason for this sudden change is that once household A invites its son's friends to his party this "new culture" spreads to B, C, D . . . through a chain of reciprocity. Thus a child's birthday party has snowballed into a huge, time-money consuming event. Furthermore, continued the informant, almost every household has remodeled the house and added a second floor in order to be able to invite the child's friends without embarrassment. The child who has been invited to a nice house demands the house reconstruction so that he can save face.

## COMMUNAL NURTURANCE

Outside school, the family takes primary responsibility for its children. However, the community also participates in socializing children, and again through or for them, socializing mothers. A local supermarket, for example, publishes newsletters called "Oku-sama Shinbun" (News for housewives) for its customers to pick up free of charge. One issue had information on recipes on one side, and on the other a set of instructions on "Childrearing and Discipline," including the following items: how to sensitize children to musical sounds; how to make them fond of animals and plants; how to train them to take care of themselves; how to develop in children the right habit of using chopsticks; how to discipline them to put away the things they have used; the normal state of intellectual development for four- to five-year-olds; how to have them greet properly; how to deal with them when they lie; how to make them cognizant of the distinction between their own and somebody else's possessions; how to train them to report whatever has happened to them; how to discover their fatigue early enough.

A more systematic set of programs is offered by the local government, as an agent of the national and prefectural governments, to guide mothers in the proper care of their children. Health care begins with pregnancy. At around the fifth month of pregnancy, the mother-to-be delivers the "pregnancy certificate" received from her obstetrician to the city government, which in turn issues her a "mother-child booklet" which not only gives guidance but is to be filled out with diagnostic records by the doctor. In the meantime, the government's public health section provides "pregnancy schooling" which consists of public health nurses' guidance for pregnant women on such matters as proper diet, physical exercise, the method of infant bathing, or infant clothes sewing, followed by obstetricians' lectures. After birth, the government again intervenes through a series of health care measures for the infant—periodic checkups, innoculations, medical consultations, and so forth. The health checkup for three-year-olds, conducted by the Child Welfare Office every month in rotation, involves not only physical but mental examinations with simple "tests." I observed over one hundred mothers and their children milling around and being processed from examiner to examiner in an office. Most children answered without difficulty the questions about their age, name, and the like and performed tasks like matching erector pieces; the mothers, meanwhile, sat by watching nervously. A few children resisted with shyness or hostility. Upset, the mother of one such child tried hard to make her son respond, and told the examiner that the child knew the answer, that in fact he was way ahead of most children but only being too shy in front of strangers. The examiner's advice was as follows:

> Your child is intelligent and capable of doing anything alone, but you, Mother, *amayakasu* him too much because he is the youngest. Try to let him do things by himself, don't help him.

The mother blushed, agreed with him nodding many times, and promised to do as advised. Another example of advice:

> Does your child have playmates in the neighborhood? It is very important to have friends of the same age. With older children or adults the child is too inhibited, loses the ability to express himself freely. You understand?

The examiner is not a psychologist but a dedicated civil servant with whom mothers comply willingly. The reason for their nervousness about this "mental test" is that children marked as disturbed or retarded are potential candidates for a special city nursery devoted to "problem" children.

As exemplified by the above examiner's advice, the government has many projects to educate mothers. Its newsletters, which are distributed to every household in the city through the neighborhood organization (see p. 12), are theoretically addressed to every citizen, male or female, but their contents often reveal that the writers have housewives in mind as their readers. The following is a quote from one article in an issue with the headline, "Every third Sunday is a family day: Greetings cheer up your family":

> In the morning, your family gets up, sees one another, your husband goes off to his company, and your children go to school. Ask yourself if all this does not transpire without greetings like "Good morning," or "See you later" [*itte rasshai*—"go and return"].

A variety of classes for mothers is held or sponsored by the social education section of the government, organized primarily by age levels of children. Classes include "Class for Mothers of Three-year-olds," "Home Education Class for Mothers of Kindergarten Children," "Home Education University for Mothers of Elementary School Children," and so on. Schoolteachers, local or nonlocal, are mobilized as lecturers, and NHK Educational TV programs are often shown and discussed in such classes. Most classes are held once a month for a year, involving the mothers' formal enrollment and the calling of roll. In one of the classes for mothers of three-year-olds I saw about thirty mothers and their children participate. For the first thirty minutes they were in a tatami room where they danced in a circle, mother and child paired, at the instruction of government workers. Thereafter, the mothers went upstairs to listen to a schoolteacher's lecture on *"Hitomishiri"* (Stranger anxiety) and *"Hankōki"* (Rebellious stage). The children, left behind and thereby being trained to overcome separation anxiety, were given paper and crayon. But only a few held these, while the rest just moved around in a disorderly manner. Finally the leading government worker began to lead the bunch of children in activities—racing, falling down on the floor, lying on top of one another. There was constant running, fighting, and crying. Some children were trying hard to climb upstairs to mother only to be stopped. The government worker (male) and a few mothers on duty were also taking care of the children's toilet problems. At the end, the mothers joined the children and danced together again.

What had been accomplished in this class is not too apparent. The mothers in the lecture room looked more bored than interested, and the children were left undisciplined. Yet, one is impressed with the sense of communal nurturance pervading the feeling that being mother and child is not a private matter but involves the community's responsibility and guidance.

Government-sponsored classes are indications that Japanese mothers expect to benefit from the government's programs, and that they tend to comply with its intervention in their mothering. "Educators" of mothers are predominantly male, whether a schoolteacher or a civil servant. The only exception is the public health nurses, who are all female, and yet, even they are administratively headed by a male section chief. No mother I have talked with questioned this sex asymmetry. Even the *mama-san* volleyball tournaments, participated in by snappily uniformed mothers from Shizumi and several other adjacent cities, were organized by males, and such key roles as coaches and umpires were all taken by males. Mothers are, in other words, willing and trustful clients of male-initiated, male-organized programs and services.

The woman, as we have seen, acquires a fully tenured status in the stem-family structure only after giving birth to a child, particularly to a male heir. More importantly, a new identity unfolds in the woman as she finds her *ikigai* in mothering and develops self-confidence as a competent mother. Her single-minded maternal commitment begins with prenatal care and intensifies with painful "natural" birthing, her struggle with infant management, health care, and socialization. The child's school entry, far from lifting the maternal burden, turns the mother into an intense educational collaborator and a vicarious achiever. Many local mothers (and sometimes fathers also) have gone through the very climax of life crisis at the time of the children's entrance examinations. The *kyōiku mama*, whether or not so designated by the woman herself, is convinced that her educational concern is entirely to benefit the child or to help him do whatever he wants to do with his life. Only to an outsider does she appear more self-centered than child-centered. The truth of the matter may lie in her double identity, where the two centers are united.

Motherhood is the peak of a woman's domestic career, demanding full-time concentration and keeping her homebound. And yet, paradoxically, it is motherhood that releases a woman into the public domain. As a mother she becomes a fully participating neighbor and member of the community. As a mother of a schoolchild, she participates in PTA meetings and other school-related activities. A devoted *kyōiku mama* may aggressively explore the entire educational institution and *juku* industry. Mothers organize peer groups among themselves and exchange information. No wonder that women say they have come to learn what goes on outside the home since they have become mothers. The government and community on their part pay special attention to mothers as molders of the coming generation and offer help and guidance. It seems that a woman, through motherhood, acquires not only her domestic but public tenure. The structural significance of motherhood thus extends to the public sphere.

Despite the changes taking place in childrearing practices, one can detect some repetitive aspects. Sex polarity is one of these, though to a lesser degree than a generation ago. According to our informants, the first child is difficult to rear, and that is more so if the child is male. Other things being equal, sons are harder than daughters to bring up. This is partly explained by the fact that the mother as a female cannot be a model for the son nor can she understand the son's inner world as much as the daughter's. But more importantly, the difficulty stems from the higher expectation placed on the son, especially the eldest son, for achievement, whereas all the daughter has to do is to find "a nice man" to marry. Educational investment is thus quite asymmetric. The above-mentioned life crisis concerned sons' examinations only, no daughter was involved in such family tensions. In terms of personality development too, the mothers are concerned about their sons being weak, not self-assertive enough. The mother of a boy thus tends to repeat and reinforce the sex-biased training that she herself received as a daughter a generation ago.

This conservatism may reflect the persistence of the mother's greater reliance upon her male offspring for her future security or vicarious self-fulfillment. Again, inseparable from this self-centered attitude is the mother's child-centered concern that the son be well adapted in the existing social order. The educational preoccupation is indicative of the awareness on the part of the mother of how society at large is rank ordered so that an examination winner will be a lifetime winner and a loser will remain a loser. This awareness of the societal stricture explains some uncertainty regarding the goals of socialization. While insisting that the child's potentials should be developed fully and freely toward his own self-fulfillment, the mother usually adds other criteria for bringing up the child such as "to be normal," "to avoid causing trouble for others." The mixture of the self-oriented and other-oriented expectations seems to be symbolized by the diffuse word *sunao*, connoting an ideal personality type.

The potentially exclusive bonding of mother and child is loosened by the presence of other caretakers. The mother appreciates or even solicits her own mother's help in childrearing. This suggests another reason why the *mukoyōshi* marriage is evaluated positively by the wife but negatively by the child: the wife has the most desirable helper at hand, her own mother, whereas her child will then be left deprived of access to his own mother. The mother-in-law as a substitute caretaker is not always appreciated, but often considered disruptive of mother-child bonding or of an educational plan. This adds another dimension of mother-in-law—daughter-in-law conflict.

The husband's role is variable. An unfaithful husband intensifies the mother-child bond, which may drive the mother to attempt *shinjū*, suicide together with her child, or persuade her to desist from divorcing in order to avoid creating a fatherless child. The husband's absence is not always a source of frustration however. The absent father, instead, is regarded as desirable at one phase or another of childrearing: at an early phase when the child still does not need paternal discipline or at a later phase when the child has to be strictly disciplined by the mother alone without disruptions by a third person. This reasoning implies that there are phases when the husband's participation is desired. Many a husband did or does participate. Some patterns emerge: the husband either totally stays away from the world of children or becomes deeply involved in it; when he gets involved, his role tends to be specialized either as an intimate, indulgent father (co-sleeping, co-bathing), or as an authoritarian trainer. His participation, evidently, is not always visible to the wife, as some women admitted that the children's willing submission to their father was a mystery. The commonly shared image of the Japanese family as matrifocal or fatherless, therefore, captures only half of the whole truth.

Motherhood captures the depth of complexity inherent in a woman's self-fulfillment. On the one hand, it is mothering itself that constitutes *ikigai* for her; it is the child's growth and achievement that fulfills her life goal. On the other hand, it is as a mother that she loses her autonomy, enslaved by the tyranny of her child, who seeks her attention and care insatiably; motherhood is thus identical to sacrifice and selflessness. Japanese women today have begun to question whether motherhood is the surest road to a woman's self-fulfillment, whether or not they should look for other alternatives.

Being a daughter-in-law, wife, and mother does not, in actuality, exhaust a woman's energy or potentials. She becomes involved, as an obligation or an option, in an occupation(s), and thereby participates in the public domain not only as a client but as a worker or professional. Her involvement in an occupational career(s) will be the topic of the next chapter.

# 6
## *Occupational Careers*

In categorizing women's occupations, we shall ask whether the occupation under consideration is contingent upon woman's domestic roles or independent from them, whether it is an extension of domestic responsibilities or not; whether, in other words, it is a secondary or a primary occupation.[1] We shall start from the extreme of the secondary type, proceed to the more-or-less intermediary, and end with the extreme of the primary type. Within each class there is variation from the more secondary to the more primary. To be noted also is the fact that the occupational career of a woman may fluctuate over her life cycle from one type to another in contingency upon the evolution of her family as well as her personal commitment.

### Postmarital Household Occupations

A woman gets involved, as an extension of her domestic assignment, with the occupation of the household into which she has married. By "household occupation" I mean a private enterprise which, although represented by one individual, such as the head of the household, is identified as *kagyō*, household business, due to its location within or near the residential compound and/or its mobilization of household members as team workers or auxiliary staff. Unless married to a salaryman, a "housewife" is expected to undertake a portion of such a collective enterprise. Even as a wife of a salaryman or wage earner, if the postmarital household has a *kagyō* run by in-laws, the bride will be required to participate.

Furthermore, one household may have two *kagyō*. Ai had to divide her time between two household industries: a woodwork shop established by her husband, and a laundry run by the widowed mother-in-law. The bride was in charge of retailing small wooden utensils manufactured by her husband while being subjected to the hard labor of carrying water from a well for laundry. Fumie and her husband, after taking over from her father-in-law the business of running a hot spring bathhouse, decided to start a camera shop, this being more up-to-date than the bathhouse, which was doomed to fail eventually. Until the new shop became firmly established, two *kagyō* were run simultaneously. Fumie was in charge of the old business and sat on a raised platform— the position that commands a view of both male and female bathers—to collect fees and cater to the customers' needs. It was found that seventeen women in my sample have in one way or another participated in postmarital household enterprises which either existed before their marriage or became established after marriage under their husbands' initiative.


ROLE COORDINATION

*Duality and priority.* These women were (or are) "housewives," like a salaryman's wife to the extent that they were not pursuing their own occupations but merely accepted the household occupations as part of their domestic tasks. None was, furthermore, totally free from more typical housework. They thus represent a dual involvement in the occupational and domestic spheres without a demarcation line between the two. Nonetheless, there is variation from case to case in terms of the priority of one sphere over the other. Those occupations which require strenuous and regular work, particularly those of primary industries, tend to find in a woman, first, a work partner, and only secondarily a housewife. This was clear for a farmer's wife, Hamako, from the very beginning of her married life. The question of whether farming was compatible with domestic chores did not occur to anybody. The *kagyō* of agriculture claimed absolute priority. The wife, husband, and father-in-law worked all day in the family-owned fields, planting, growing, and harvesting rice, wheat, vegetables, and tea all year around. Harvesting was followed by processing and marketing. In particular, everything related to tea, including the tea factory operation, was in the wife's sole charge. During the agriculturally slow seasons, Hamako, together with others, engaged in sericulture, wove straw mats, made ropes, and sewed work clothes. There was no time to sit around. The hardest thing was that there was not enough time for sleep. Now in her fifties, Hamako still works at the same pace. I had to start to interview her around seven o'clock in the evening while her hands were still busy sifting tender tea leaves from coarse stems. One wonders whether this extent of work involvement can be labeled "secondary occupation."

How did she manage to do housework? She came home from work a little earlier than the others to prepare supper, but the primary responsibility for housework rested with the mother-in-law, who was too old to work as a full-time farmer. This indicates that the availability of an additional female houseworker is necessary for the wife to devote herself to the household occupation. Fuyuko worked day and night as a seamstress for the family's upholstery store. This was made possible by her mother-in-law, first, and then her daughter, who discharged the domestic chores. Full-time partnership for the household occupation is not too common however. Most of these women alternated between the domestic and occupational roles, balancing one against the other.

*Role specialization by sex.* For my informants, role splitting on the woman's part was accompanied by a more-or-less clear differentiation of occupational responsibilities by sex. The husband took the technically specialized and "pivotal" (Nadel 1957) role, and the wife performed diffuse, multiple, and/or "peripheral" tasks. In the lumber business it was the husband's responsibility to make decisions on the purchase of timber and to saw the timber into lumber, while the wife received customers, answered the phone, kept books, and managed employees. At night Kazuko sewed work coats for the employees. The contrast was not a matter of hard versus easy. Just to serve tea to a customer was hard labor during the wartime when there was no gas; it was necessary each time to make a charcoal fire to boil water. And all these tasks had to be carried out while she was carrying her baby on her back or preparing a meal.

The paradox is that the more specialized the occupation is by sex lines, that is to say, the more masculine in terms of either muscular effort or skill required, the more demanding are the tasks imposed on the female partner as an all-around support person. A good example is a fisherman's wife, particularly the wife or daughter-in-law of a master fisherman (*oyakata*) who leads a crew as his followers (*funakata*). As early as two o'clock in the morning when the boats were departing to take her father-in-law and husband out to sea, Emi got up to make rounds to all the *funakata* to make sure that they would be ready on time. It was a woman's job to do so, as confirmed by another fisherman's wife. Unless a woman from the boss's household, Emi explained, took this trouble to request their cooperation each morning, no crewman would have shown up at the harbor. "Nowadays it is a matter of rule for every crewman to show up without being asked in this manner. But when I married no one would unless I made rounds like this." And all of this was done by the woman alone. Emi was frightened of her lonely walk in the dark along a rough road. When the boats were returning to the shore, the boss's woman (wife or daughter-in-law) was expected to rally the crewmen's wives to meet the men at the shore, to help them unload the catch, to classify it, and carry it to the central fish market. To buy and prepare bait was also a woman's task. Furthermore, Emi burdened herself with the job of recruiting new crewmen, a difficult task during the war. One might wonder who was the mainstay of the fishing business. A pediatrician's wife, after learning that nurses did not like to have her around the "office" as a female boss, tried to help her husband "on the back stage" by bookkeeping (primarily for tax purposes), and cooking and doing laundry for the live-in nurses. Her responsibility also included the recruitment of nurses.

The multiplicity, diffuseness, or generality of the female partnership for a household occupation, as suggested by the above examples, involves the female's specialization in human relations. The management of employees often falls under the wife's jurisdiction. Whether the employer can keep up work morale among the workers largely depends, I heard, upon the wife's expertise in treating them personally. Customer management is another aspect of specialization in human relations. A wife who retails ready-made dresses in the household's shop gets "a kick out of spotting a dress which pleases a customer," while the husband specializes in stocking the goods.

## SOCIALIZATION

*The pecking order.* As the newest recruit, the bride may have to start at the bottom of the pecking order. The wife of a fish dealer was expected, as part of wifely chores, to process the fish fresh from the central market. Splitting fish open for drying is a skilled job. A beginner unable to participate in a circle of women doing this job, Yorie was designated *"hachirobē"* ("eight-man Jack," meaning the person, usually a young man, assigned to do the work of eight people). The *hachirobē*'s job was to keep an eye on the progress of the fish processing, to replace a basket with an empty one as soon as it was filled with layers of split-open fish, and to cleanse and salt the basketful. She was supposed to be a perceptive and quick helper to aid the whole group of accomplished processors in keeping the work going smoothly—the least skilled but the hardest job.

Another new recruit was a licensed pharmacist. Married into a house owning an unlicensed drugstore, Hanayo was expected to take it over eventually. Meanwhile, she was regarded as a newcomer subordinate to the established hierarchy, which included her father-in-law, sister-in-law, and the employees. She was a mere "shop girl."

*Training.* Full-fledged participation in the household occupation must be preceded by some training. Some women were trained by their husbands. Yoshimi, the daughter-in-law of a theater operator, first had to learn how to treat the theater employees and their families, many of whom were living with the employer family. Her husband, nine years older than she, was a single-minded trainer, intent on seeing his nineteen-year-old bride mature as quickly as possible into a wise manager of this enormous household. She was corrected in her speech in addressing the employees. "Instead of saying: 'Go and buy this and that for me,' I was told to say: 'Sorry to bother you, but will you kindly go and buy such and such?' " Whenever there was anything nice to eat, particularly right after the war when people were starving, her husband reminded her to distribute it to the staff. Her resistance drove him to lose his temper and slap her in the face. Thanks to such training, she now appreciates having become a considerate employer. When she takes a trip, she never forgets to bring home souvenirs for the employees and their families.

Not only social tact but highly technical skill may have to be learned by the newcomer. The *jogakkō* graduate wife of a physician was expected to work as a substitute nurse, and eventually to be a substitute pharmacist. "But my wife," said the husband with pride, "remembers those difficult names of new drugs much better than I." He could not say enough how much he depended upon his wife, and how helpless he was as a physician as well as a husband without her.

In-laws were major trainers for some other women. But lesser and covert agents for socialization were ubiquitous in and out of the house. It was employee women who socialized Midori, the wife of a dried fish wholesaler.

> I felt as if I were surrounded by so many mothers-in-law—they were much older than I was, you see. If I was lying around, for example, to recover from *tsuwari* [morning sickness], they would say: "*Tsuwari* is not a sickness. You will forget it if you get busy working."

A customer can be as effective a trainer. When she was an inexperienced telephone receptionist, Midori's husband reported back to her a customer's criticism: "Your wife is not cut out for business. She says [when answering the phone] there is none left in stock. That's not good for business. If there is none she should tell when the new stock is coming in, and that as soon as it's in the customer will be notified." This was indeed an eye-opening experience, which still sticks in her mind. People in the same trade, particularly the female counterpart, turned out to be helpful consultants also, instead of being competitive and antagonistic, so long as the learner presented herself as uninitiated and solicitous.

FEMALE PROMINENCE IN HOUSEHOLD OCCUPATIONS

Even though household occupations usually are headed by male representatives with females as auxiliary staff, certain circumstances call for a wife to take leadership or to play a predominant role.

*Hospitality businesses.* Hospitality industries are notable in this respect. A bankrupt husband was advised by a friend to go into a quick-buck business, and prevailed on the reluctant wife to rent a house to be opened as a brothel. It was the madam who would be the actual operator and manager. Seeing no choice, Yone undertook the job of running a *"panpanya"* (house of whores) with "the determination of a dead person," a Japanese expression which connotes a strong commitment in face of a hopeless situation. The first and main thing was to recruit women. She went to Tokyo, put out newspaper ads, interviewed applicants, and brought the selected women with her. It was hard for her to overcome her self-revulsion. While taking such entrepreneurial leadership, she also substituted as a maid. Unable to hire one, she prepared the meals and made *futon* beds and kimonos for the live-in prostitutes. What challenged her more was to keep the business out of racketeers' control. Her strategy was to "tame" and win over the gangsters' hearts by offering motherly care. As a result not even once did they dare to disrupt the business, she said proudly. What did her husband do? Well, it might appear that this kind of business did not need a man. "But actually you cannot get around too well without a man. An all-woman household will not be taken seriously. It doesn't matter if he cannot do a thing. Just by sitting around, a man is useful for show." Such window dressing was particularly necessary in Yone's view to protect the business from the underworld extortionists.

The idea of operating a bar, another hospitality business, occurred to Tomiko's husband when they went into debt. The wife, who came from a family involved in a similar business, became a *"mama-san,"* or hostess, backed up by a number of young barmaids. The husband, the nominal operator, occasionally comes around and is addressed as "Master," but takes no responsibility. He even gets jealous, suspecting that the *mama-san* is having affairs with customers.

A few of the uxorilocally married women involved their husbands in their natal household businesses. One husband became thus converted from a bank employee into a hotel staff person to help his in-laws, another from a government employee into a cabaret operator. Both being hospitality businesses, the wives or their mothers have taken a leading role.

*Succession by the widow.* When the husband dies before a son is ready to take over the business, the widow is likely to nominate herself successor even when the business is of a masculine type. Under a widow's presidency, a company has continued to operate a lumberyard with thirty employees. Another widow is in charge of a food processing factory and wholesaler as successor to her husband. While these women became widowed in their fifties, Yoshimi encountered her husband's death shortly before she, at age twenty, was to give birth to a child. At her father-in-law's insistence, the widow stayed on as the mother of the future house head, her son. Eventually she came to assume the responsibility of the house business of running several theaters. As television came to replace movie theaters, she was confronted with enormous debts and bankruptcy and had to solicit help from *shinseki* and negotiate with banks. She wished to put an end to the theater business, but felt it did not belong to her alone but to the whole group of *dōzoku* and *shinseki* and therefore had somehow to be perpetuated for their sake. But something needed to be done to survive financially. As a compromise she took steps to reduce the theater business to a symbolic minimum and opened restaurants.

House-business succession by a widow is nothing unusual by Japanese standards since the business belongs to the *ie*, not to the husband personally. I recall one event which illuminates this point. I was invited to a monthly social gathering of a group of tough construction workers including those in carpentry, masonry, plumbing, gardening, tatami making, and electrical engineering. They had formed this group because they often worked together as contractors and subcontractors. I was suprised to find a woman among them who turned out to be the widow of a member. Not only had she succeeded to the husband's business but she participated in such a male peer gathering as the present incumbent of house-business headship. She was fully accepted by the "peers" and entertained by geisha as if she were one of the guys. A widow, under this circumstance, assumes a sex-neutral or male role.

*The wife as virtual successor.* Even when the husband is alive, it may be the wife who actually takes over the house business, either because her husband chooses another occupation or is occupationally delinquent. A retired school principal said, "In my days eldest sons of farming families became schoolteachers," as he himself did. I asked if it meant they did not succeed to the house occupation of farming. "Yes, they did. But it means their *wives* worked on farms." While commenting so, he acknowledged what an imposition it must have been upon the wives, and added, "I feel sorry for them." Another case involves a hardware wholesaling business. Every time I passed by the shop, I saw the wife at work but seldom saw the husband around. She herself did not confide, but another informant reminded me that Yoshiko-chan's husband is so engrossed in "archaeology or some such thing" that the wife is totally in charge of the business. The husband who is neglectful of his "real occupation" is gossiped about like this, even though this particular husband apparently is struggling to make a profession out of his hobby. Again, it is not the eldest son but the eldest son's wife who virtually has succeeded to a supposedly patrilineally held occupation.

## Intermediary Jobs

The "intermediary" type is negatively defined in that it includes a wide variety of jobs which are neither household occupations nor the women's full-fledged, independent career professions.

### Supplementary Income

While the husband works as a main breadwinner, the wife may have another job to supplement the family income. Supplementary income is needed, according to local informants, because of the uncertainty of the husband's income; medical expenses for sick family members, especially children; educational expenses for children; gift-giving obligations; financial aid for the wife's natal family; the wife's personal allowance.

*Cryptic work.* Many of the so-called housewives engage from time to time in the kind of job which is cryptic and usually unreported. This is called *naishoku* (private job) or *arubaito* (derived from the German *arbeit*). *Naishoku* is normally carried on at the home site so that its compatibility with domestic tasks, as well as its public invisibility, is ensured. The most common home-site *naishoku* is sewing. Mari, mother of a twelve-month-old, has resumed Western-style dressmaking, taking personal orders from her friends, but is adamant about this *naishoku* not interfering with her childrearing responsibility. She does hand sewing only once the child is asleep and leaves machine sewing (which would wake up the child) to the time when her mother baby-sits in her own house. Mari is critical of those mothers who insist on working "out of their selfishness [*wagamama*] or just for diversion." "For me the children come first. . . . Nowadays there are many people [women] who think children and mothers are separate beings. That worries me." Ikuko also does sewing whenever she is asked to, but is careful to stop the work before her husband comes home, "otherwise, he will get mad at me."

The income from *naishoku* is usually low and supplementary at best. But the shortage of skilled labor like sewing, particularly hand sewing of kimono, has made it a source of unprecedented remuneration for some housewives. One wife earns more sewing kimono than her husband does as a city-government employee.

*"Part-time" jobs.* If the family needs more money or the wife has no special skill, she must go out to be employed as a part-timer. When the youngest child enters school or later, the mother may step out of domestic confinement to work as a store clerk, restaurant kitchen worker, and the like. In Shizumi, the labor market dominated by part-time female workers is represented by hotels (whose labor demand fluctuates seasonally), the bicycle stadium (which is in operation for a week a month), and fish processing industry (subjected to seasons and chance). Mutsuko, a fisherman's wife, used to, and still occasionally does, work as one of the fish processors hired by an *oyakata* (boss). (I have observed a circle of women squatting and handling horse mackerel on a concrete floor of one of many such shops.) Later on, Mutsuko found a better-paying and more secure job at the stadium, where women constitute an overwhelming majority of over one thousand employees. The stadium work includes ticket selling, reimbursement, computation of sales, accuracy checking. In the meantime Mutsuko also began to work as a part-time hotel maid (a job she had prior to marriage) when her husband became a victim of hemiplegia.

Mutsuko's case makes us wonder what part-time jobs can involve. Although she never doubts that she is a part-timer, hers is a double job which demands as much, if not more, time as a single full-time job. Moreover, she seems to fulfill a breadwinner's role rather than to earn supplementary income. It is hard to imagine how she also manages to look after a bedridden daughter.

What was initially a "part-time" job may develop into a virtually full-time job as a matter of course beyond the worker's control. Yumiko, anticipating increasing educational expenditures as the older child entered junior high school, obtained a half-day job as an insurance saleswoman—another typical job available to women in Shizumi, although this is not unique to the local labor market. As a local *jimoto* resident, she had a solid network of potential clientele—kin, neighbors, and friends. Also her "layman" approach was taken as a sign of trustworthiness, and thus she began to make more money than expected. The initial contract of half-day work was then disregarded. Meanwhile Yumiko was involuntarily incorporated into the labor union, and elected to be a local officer. Whenever there was an officers' meeting, she was unable to get home before 8:00 P.M. Sometime after, the company appointed her a local chief of business affairs, involving her participation in monthly meetings of chiefs which again kept her late at night. The husband was furious, but has since become resigned.

Unlike *naishoku*, these jobs, despite the label of "part-time," lack flexibility and thus tend to interfere with the woman's domestic roles. It is usually these part-timer women who are blamed for the neglected children, for the phenomenon called *"kagikko"* ("key children" who carry house keys to let themselves into their empty houses after school). Schoolteachers, male and female, tend to be critical of these mothers. A local principal deplored that no PTA meeting could be held during the stadium week or tour seasons. The women workers respond to these pressures by emphasizing the economic necessity and denying their personal enjoyment of the work.

## Lone Women in Business

Single, widowed (except successors to the husbands' legacy), separated, or divorced women may have to support themselves as full-time workers. If they have no professional career, they are either hired for unskilled jobs or set up their own businesses. The local-sample women in this category tended to choose the latter. Furthermore, all the businesses are service oriented: food shops, restaurants, hotels, a brothel, and an amusement shooting gallery. It is interesting to note that these women, generally considered anomalous, have settled into "female" businesses, handling food, or running hospitality enterprises catering primarily to male customers. Even a woman, like Akemi, who hates male drunks, runs a sake serving restaurant which forces her to wait upon such men. This suggests that the options for female entrepreneurship are narrowly limited, whereas, paradoxically, the successors to late husbands can operate a wide variety of "male" businesses in the name of *kagyō*. The above businesses, therefore, were taken up probably out of necessity, not by choice. This may also reflect the limitation of the local labor market. I should add, however, that I have encountered many women, local and nonlocal, ranging from housewives to elite professionals, who cherish a dream of "opening a cozy coffee shop" or restaurant.

Crucial to success is the support of local residents, particularly those in the same business. Kayo congratulates herself for having been blessed with "helpful people" every time she was in trouble. When she launched the hotel business, the lady of a locally well-established hotel in the neighborhood assured her of her help. This *senpai* loaned the *kōhai* necessary things like bedding and kimono for customers, sent one of her cooks as a helper, gave instructions regarding hotel management. Fukiko, a single woman, was not so fortunate. She opened a tiny shop near a school with the schoolchildren in mind as customers. Her idea of selling hot dogs and "American sandwiches," which she had learned to make as a maid for American families on a military base, turned out to be a smashing success. There was more demand than supply every day.

The owner of a similar food shop in the neighborhood, upset by the sudden emergence of this upstart rival, stopped greeting *(aisatsu)* her and began to mobilize neighborhood organizations, the district *fujinkai* (women's association) and *kodomokai* (children's association) to patronize his shop and boycott hers. Fukiko claims that her recipes were stolen. At the time of interview, the two shops were still at war. Neighbors are caught in the middle, Fukiko told me, often exposed to embarrassing confrontations of the two rivals in neighborhood association meetings. A lone woman is handicapped here too. As noted in the preceding chapter, women get involved in public affairs and neighborhood interaction primarily through their children. Fukiko's rival could rally the neighborhood organization more effectively through his wife and his children.

Fukiko, as a *jimoto* woman, has had support from her natal kin at least, but Rin, an outsider and divorcee, has been all alone and is convinced that everybody—including her father and ex-husband—has taken advantage of her: at the shooting gallery she ran, the maids she hired pocketed her earnings and the customers too came only to "trick" her.

## Career Professions

The career profession is another extreme type in that it is theoretically independent of the domestic roles. By "professional career" is meant a career which involves: lifetime commitment instead of transient engagement; reliance on it as the major source of livelihood rather than its enjoyment as a hobby; identification with it over and beyond economic necessity; and long-range training, development, and accumulation in expertise. These are ideal-typical criteria which are not all necessarily applicable to actual cases. For women in particular the distinction between a professional career and other types of work career is often difficult to draw; even those women who satisfy all the above criteria may have started their careers as nonprofessionals. This section will be concerned, therefore, not only with established professional women but with the gray area where the professional and nonprofessional careers intermesh in the hope that the latter will provide a clue to understanding women's professional career patterns. What's more, a wide range of occupations will be regarded as professional—from university professor to kindergarten teacher, from national government official to nurse, from "pink-collar" to "male" occupations, from manual (e.g., hairdresser) to cerebral professions. Both the local women and the external sample of "career women" will be considered. To differentiate the latter from the local women, fictitious full names (e.g., Yoko Jinbo) or initials (Y. J.) will be used.

CAREER UNFOLDING

The recollections of career experience turn out primarily to refer to the exploratory or precarious process of career unfolding. Chapter 2 has foreshadowed some aspects of this process with reference to premarital education and employment. Let us begin with career dropouts.

*Career revocation.* Of the nineteen potential professionals in the local sample—those who had higher education, professional training, and/or had started to work as a professional—eight have revoked or suspended their careers. Harumi, an English major, married into a dress shop and has been a partner to her husband in this house business. She admitted that she was not strongly career oriented to begin with, and that she does like trading. Yet, her frustrations surface as she reflects on her postmarital life. She could have had a totally different life if she had not married the eldest son of this house, she said. She regrets her educational investment has been wasted in this way, particularly when she recalls how much sacrifice, economic and emotional, she and her parents made to get her admitted to the university.

Sakiko struggled in the first years of her marriage; she had married prematurely, in her freshman year, with the understanding that the husband would allow her to attend class and graduate. Settling down in Shizumi where the husband had been transferred by his company to head a branch shop, she had to commute by train to Tokyo and stay a few days a week in the school dormitory. The husband, who would have preferred that she quit the university, demanded that she pay the price by being the devoted wife on Sundays and holidays, which she did willingly. Dismayed as she was by her husband's grumbling, she did not vacillate in her determination to get a degree in music, and she finally graduated. But what did she hope to do after graduation? The husband had looked forward to the day when the wife would leave all her career dreams behind and assume a full-time housewife role to compensate for his long deprivation and endurance. Guilt ridden over her "selfish" negligence of housewifely duties for the previous three years, the wife was trapped into complying. Graduation from an elite national university of music and arts thus turned out to be the end instead of the beginning of a career. Or, more accurately, her career climaxed several months after her graduation when she held a recital in her hometown and starred as a singer. Her kin, in-laws, and friends were all proud of her, but her husband did not bother to come. It was an elating, exciting event, which she would never forget, but which also marked the beginning of full-time domestic drudgery, soon to be compounded by motherhood.

Because both women are in their thirties, it may be too early to conclude that they have forsaken their careers for good. In fact they claim that they are waiting for their children to grow up so that they can start or resume career-related activities. Nonetheless, it seems that the "revocability," as Epstein (1970:27) phrases it, of a woman's career is built into her own expectation as well as the social structure.

Four women quit their jobs in coordination with marriage or motherhood after three to seventeen years of employment. All happen to have been schoolteachers. Three of them admitted they had never been devoted to teaching as a career, while one, though devoted, finally made up her mind to be a full-time mother when she was about to give birth to a sixth child.

In some instances, quitting was at the urge of the husband or family, as in the case of Sakiko. A husband, while verbally encouraging his wife to pursue her career, may block it by his actual conduct. Yoshimi wanted to be a painter and agreed to marry a cousin under the condition that she pursue that interest. For a while, she attended a class run by a now "nationally famous painter," but it became increasingly difficult and finally impossible to continue in the face of her husband's displeasure at her absence. It is not always against her wish, however, that a woman gives up a career. All four of the above schoolteachers dropped out as a matter of their own choice, and two of them did so against the protest of their economically minded husbands.

Revocation is not unusual among the most highly educated. Doctoral candidates, particularly those who have finished all but their dissertations—what the Japanese call "over-doctor"—tend to show a high rate of atrophy, especially if they do not find a professional job by the time of completion of course work. Once out of campus or drawn into a home, it is extremely difficult to resume a career in Japan. Yoko Jinbo, a university assistant and doctoral candidate, told of her peers, most of whom have quit and become full-time housewives. At first, such dropouts tried to encourage Y. J. to do the same and enjoy the domestic life, but now, after several years of domesticity, they regret their choice. Another woman, a Tokyo University Ph.D. candidate, abandoned lectureship at a private university upon becoming a mother. When her daughter reached kindergarten age, she hoped to resume her career and also wanted to complete her degree. Every time she saw her advisor, however, she was discouraged from continuing: "He says, 'Being a wife and mother is the best thing for a woman.' " Still she wanted to be "free." It was when she was contemplating how to become free that a car hit and injured her daughter right before her eyes. Shaken up by this accident, and convinced that it was a punishment for her self-centered desire, she became even more firmly tied to the house. All she can do now is go out occasionally to see kabuki plays or some such things in order to escape from the routine drudgery.

*Circumstantial pressure.* Some women—eleven out of the nineteen in the local sample—continued or resumed their careers. It might be assumed that, given a sociocultural handicap for professional women, these were exceptionally motivated and single-mindedly committed to their career goals. However, interview revealed that a career had unfolded more often in a haphazard manner than in a self-directed, goal-minded fashion. Put another way, career commitment is a complicated process, involving different themes. Circumstantial pressure is one of the typical themes.

Some women stressed how they were compelled under certain circumstances to start, continue, or resume their careers. It was environmental factors, not a subjective preoccupation, that committed them to a career. Sachi, trained in the culinary profession, devoted herself for seven years to her mother-in-law, husband, and children, discharging housework and taking part in her husband's occupation (tatami making) as a caretaker for the apprentice-employees. She then began to avail herself of jobs as a free-lance cook for banquets on occasions like funerals, weddings, childbirth, the *shichigosan* (third-, fifth-, and seventh-year celebrations of children), passing the examination for conscription (which corresponded to male initiation), fishing boat launching ceremonies. It was not only the persistence of her commitment but the historical accident of war that made her return to her profession. The wartime shortage of male labor called for a full-time resumption of her career, which eventually resulted in her salaried appointment as head cook at a corporation and then at a school. Yaeko wanted to continue to work as a beautician but was dissuaded by her husband, who decided that permanents would not suit the fishing town women. But again, accidental events such as the husband's bankruptcy and the disastrous ending of the war triggered her to reactivate her profession. With a one thousand-yen down payment, she bought a permanent machine, opened a shop, hired trainee-employees, and has been the "master" beautician, teacher, and shopkeeper ever since. Likewise, Kaoru, a temporary schoolteacher, quit her job when she became pregnant and remained a wife and mother for five years, during which time her father and *mukoyōshi* husband, together running a charcoal broker business, went bankrupt. Just to get out of "the most miserable poverty imaginable" she grabbed a timely job offer and thus started a long career as a kindergarten teacher.

A Kyoto businesswoman, Mie Baba, also attributed her career to the war and subsistence need. Her husband was drafted and later killed in the Philippines, and she was left with her mother, son, the five children of her war-dead brother, plus three more children, kin and non-kin. It was her responsibility to feed this large "family." Because her husband had been an employee of his *honke*, a candy maker, she tried to make *yōkan* and other sweets though she had no skill. Fortunately for her, it was right after the war when people were more eager to buy anything sweet than critical of confectionary mediocrity. Under the ration system at that time, there was no legal way of obtaining sugar, flour, red beans, and other materials, but the black market—which she claims was run by Koreans—kept her in business. She and her helpers worked at night to run this illegal business. As the ration system was lifted, the business expanded, and the customer's palate became more discriminatory, she trained herself and employees as professional confectioners, holding classes under invited instructors. Over thirty years after that beginning, she is president of a reputable confectionary company in command of 230 employees and three dozen shops.

Sometimes it is social pressure that commits a woman even against her own wish. Ayano was ready to quit teaching at a nursery school to become a housewife as soon as she married, but was urged by the local government to take a recently vacated position in the city's kindergarten. She could not turn down the request and eventually converted herself into a career teacher.

Circumstantial commitment is found more or less in every professional I have come across. In fact, the desirability of higher education for daughters is generally contingent upon an anticipated emergency such as widowhood, in which case they must support themselves. Utako Higuchi characterized her parents as devoted to the daughters' education so that they would be able to live alone "just in case anything happens."

*Cumulative commitment.* Chapter 2 has observed how educational and occupational exposure and investment committed the initially unmotivated women gradually and cumulatively to a career. This theme is also found among elite professionals. Kyoko Aoi, a judge in her sixties, admitted that even though she and her father decided in favor of her studying law, neither had a clear notion of her future occupation. Studying at a law school still did not irreversibly commit her to a legal profession. When she was about to graduate, her father suggested that she take the national law examination "just to test how much you know after studying law for six years." That advice drove her to study with fierce intensity and renewed her commitment to law. In the meantime, her mother, initially opposed to a professional career, began to make repeated visits *(ohyakudo)* to a shrine to pray for her success. Happily, she passed the exam, which then committed her to become a licensed lawyer, one of the first three female lawyers in Japanese history. This process of career crystalization was described by K. A. as *"zuruzuru,"* which means one step of commitment slipping to another step. *Zuru-zuru* commitment may be both positive and negative. Positively, it connotes a natural unfolding of a career, and negatively, a sense of inability to stop or steer the process of career crystalization. It refers to cumulative investment and also to a sense of being "trapped" or a feeling of "irreversibility." Energy investment in passing a national licensing examination appears to be a significant turning point, as was seen among pharmacists in chapter 2.

The aforementioned confectioner, Mie Baba, did not plan to make a career out of this business, considering it a temporary measure to feed many mouths. The time had come, she realized, when an untrained candy maker could no longer survive, and she decided therefore, she should quit. By then, however, she had around forty employees. "What are they going to do if I quit? I thought about an employer's responsibility and decided to make it into my lifetime work."

Procrastination in career commitment eventually faces a deadline. After spending her undergraduate years at a women's university, alienated from classmates who considered college education a dowry and from the institution's concern with students' personality development more than with academic training, Yoko Jinbo went on to graduate study at a former "imperial" university. Being, as she was, the first woman admitted to the department, this challenge did not lead to commitment to a career goal. Her father was only willing to go along with her wish to continue her education because it was a lesser evil than having a job. For a long time she felt like an outsider, excluded from a tightly organized club of men. Then she joined with all the other students in the campus struggle of the late 1960s and this involvement provided a breakthrough for her to develop intimacy with her peers. The newly acquired camaraderie motivated her to go on from the M.A. to the Ph.D. program. Nevertheless, she still was far from setting her mind on a career profession. In fact, while attending graduate school, she went to a cooking school, "ready to quit graduate work any time." Without a career anticipation, she accepted the invitation from her advisor to be his assistant and moved to another national university where he had taken a new professorial position. It was not until her marriage at twenty-nine with a fellow graduate student without the blessing of her parents that she finally made up her mind to pursue a scholarly career. Had she married a conventional type of guy instead of her husband, who expected her to have a career, she would not have minded dropping out. For her, marriage was the deadline for choosing between a professional and a domestic course.

Both themes of circumstantial pressure and cumulative commitment apply to most women in varying degrees, including the cases to appear in the following categories.

*Professional retrieval of bridal training.* This theme refers to a conversion of a trainee in a bridal art into a trainer for bridal candidates, of a client into a professional. Perry (1976:204–8) took special note of this kind of "professionalism," where there is no clear distinction between amateur and professional, student and teacher, hobby and work. Probably under some circumstantial pressures, in consequence of cumulative commitment, or just to put an end to boredom a woman may begin informally to teach a small group of young women in whatever she has learned and possibly acquired a teaching license for, be it tea ceremony, flower arrangement, calligraphy, piano, Japanese dance, koto, sewing, or cooking. This start then may develop into a career commitment.

The foremost example in my local sample is Junko, the koto teacher. While at grade school, Junko "happened" to visit a koto teacher in the neighborhood, and began to learn koto "for no particular reason." After the wartime interruption, she resumed attendance at a koto class, again nearby, taught by a *sensei* who was to be nominated a National Cultural Treasure. When Shizumi High School created a koto club as an extracurricular program she joined it and was trained by the school-appointed teacher. Meanwhile, as the eldest daughter she felt responsible for helping the war-impoverished family, and she switched to the Vocational High School with an intent to work as a clerk or some such thing immediately upon graduation, "So I had no dream about becoming a koto teacher at all." At her father's insistence, she went to live with a company president's family ostensibly for *gyōgi minarai*, but actually "to work just as a maid." Back home, while helping her father with his wholesale business, she resumed koto study again, "just because I liked it." She was then asked to assist her teacher at the high school, and began to teach students as a substitute whenever the teacher was not available. The teacher moved to Tokyo to marry, which led to Junko commuting to study under the same teacher, to her taking over the koto club teaching at the high school, and starting to gather her own *deshi* (disciples) and hold classes at her home. By then she had been promoted to assume the formal status of *shihan* (licensed teacher) and to receive a professional name *(natori)* derived from her *sensei*'s name. Even with all this accumulation of training, qualification, and teaching experience, the koto was largely play and hobby for her. It was the postmarital double tragedy—the husband's accidental death and the daughter's cerebral paralysis—that converted a dilettante into a serious professional. Her *deshi*, numbering around sixty at interview time, are organized into a club named after the paralyzed daughter. Two large rooms of her natal house have been transformed into a classroom large enough for a concert. Her success can be inferred from frequent references to her name and club in the local newspapers.

The above case suggests that bridal training generally tends to remain no more than a matter of a trainee's own consumption. The art learned in childhood or in bridal candidacy is retrieved and converted into a teaching profession usually under circumstantial pressures, especially economic need. Indeed it is a widow, divorcee, or single woman more often than a married woman who teaches Japanese dance, music, tea, and so forth, as a full-time professional. Sayo, a former student at a Japanese sewing school after *jogakkō* graduation, began in her thirties to hold a sewing class at home for young women in the neighborhood. Married and wealthy, she did so for fun and never considered it a profession although she continued to teach for thirty years. In her mid-sixties, she closed down the class with reluctance. "It may have been a matter of *sekentei* [honor to be upheld in the eyes of the public]. If I continued any further, people would have talked about me as a fiendish old bitch [*onibaba*]. I had no reason to work." She felt guilty about pursuing her own pleasure through teaching.

Again, impoverishment due to the war triggered bridal art trainees to emerge as professionals. A Tokyo informant, daughter of one of the former top five court aristocrats and wife of a priest of a national shrine, had learned several arts since childhood. The war and postwar social change condemned her and her family to near starvation, and she took up whatever job was available, including cigarette sales. When her children grew up, she retrieved her long-invested training in tea ceremony and flower arrangement and began to teach. In this case, she emerged as an independent *iemoto*, herself heading a new school of tea and flower art.

The causal relationship between circumstantial pressure and the professionalization of hobbies might be reversed. It might be argued that if one is sufficiently trained in one of such arts to be a professional, endowed with a professional name and teaching license, one tends to be more independent, less likely to be stuck with an undesirable marriage. Probably it is with this reasoning that some parents do not encourage their daughters to go too far even in bridal art learning. A fifty-two-year-old local woman has been studying Japanese dance since her childhood with no intention to acquire a diploma of any sort, despite her teachers urging her to apply for one, "because my father was absolutely opposed to a woman having an occupation."

*Anticipatory commitment.* In contrast to all the above themes, this involves a goal-oriented commitment in anticipation of a career. A candidate finds herself placed on a career track prior to her entry into a higher or vocational education institution or at least by the time of her graduation therefrom. While this theme may be more typical of males, we do find cases in point among our women, particularly among elite professionals.

Fundamental to this type of commitment is *anticipatory socialization*. The most influential of all in this respect is the family, as may well be expected, in that a parent or other kin has strongly encouraged or even demanded a daughter to pursue a career, and that a family member has offered a model to emulate or identify with. Particularly crucial is the role of the father.[2]

Education at an elite university directly linked to a professional career was taken for granted by most of the elite career women partly because their fathers (and in some cases mothers also) supported that idea, and partly because the fathers themselves often were university graduates and served as career models. For Kyoko Aoi there was a father-daughter conspiracy, while the mother was away, for the daughter to choose the particular college which was the only channel available then to women aspiring to become lawyers. The mother cried, convinced that such professional education would ruin the daughter's bridal qualification, thus far acquired as a graduate from a prominent *jogakkō*. The father, a bank executive who had lived in the United States, insisted that women, like men, should be well educated and economically independent. Naoko Chitose overcame her mother's persistent objection by hanging onto the confidence which her already deceased father had had that she was different from ordinary girls. She passed the examination to Todai (the University of Tokyo). Utako Higuchi, another Todai entrant, attributed her career aspirations partly to her father, also a Todai graduate, who "may have wanted one of the two daughters to follow his steps." In the case of Shizuko Fukuda, the grandfather, as surrogate father, instilled in the granddaughter the resolution to go to medical school and to succeed him as a physician. This woman somehow knew her talent lay elsewhere, but could not resist the grandparental expectation. She pushed herself hard to go along until she took an exam and ultimately proved unfit for a medical career. For Reiko Egawa, whose father died early, the mother played the fatherly, career-inspiring role, but it turned out that R. E. had been imbued with an ambitious image of the mother's own father as a model to follow.

There are a few cases where the mother was more influential than the father or other male relatives. Such a mother was college educated with some career experience, or "matriarchal," or frustrated with her status as an economically dependent housewife. In no case among the elite professionals, however, was the father an opponent to the daughter's career aspirations.

There is one theme cutting across the local and external samples, and that is what might be called "succession syndrome." The daughter, when regarded as a successor, was pushed toward higher education by the father or some other incumbent of the main household role. The succession syndrome alone explains why sons more than daughters are expected to go on to higher educational institutions. Sometimes a daughter becomes a substitute successor, as when a family has no sons, when a daughter is the eldest child with an age distance from younger siblings, or when an elder son has died.

This pattern is a "syndrome" in that such expectations for a successor are psychologically generalized over and beyond the actual incumbency of a successor role. Particularly in the case of a daughter it is quite unlikely that she is really to succeed her father in a literal sense; rather, succession tends to mean a replication of a career achievement, no matter what kind of career it may be. It may be that the imperative of cross-generational perpetuation of household occupation, built into the traditional social structure of Japan, has overflowed the structural boundary and become generalized into a succession syndrome as a culturally pervasive obsession.

Alongside the family is the influence of a school at the primary through high school level, and this is truer with the postwar generation under the coeducational system, and with students of elite schools. After a severely competitive exam, Utako Higuchi enrolled in the junior and senior high schools attached to Tokyo National University of Education, and hardly questioned her candidacy for Todai as a next step toward a career. Her peers, male and female, were all from "good" families, bright, and motivated; the teaching staff was first-rate. In this school atmosphere a career anticipation was taken for granted, regardless of sex. U. H. did pass the examination to Todai, majored in international relations, took the upper-level national civil service exam upon graduation, and was admitted to the Ministry of International Trade and Industry as the third woman who had ever served that ministry. She represents the smoothest career track laid out in advance.

By contrast, anticipatory socialization in some cases consists of a period of trials and errors including pre-career work experience. Though reared by professional parents, the father being a lawyer, the mother a mathematics teacher, Orie Date found herself a zealous patriot during the war and chose to work at a navy research institute right after *jogakkō* graduation instead of going on to a women's college as her parents wished. Through this exposure to adult society, she came to realize the importance of higher education as a key to promotion, witnessing graduates from colleges and universities climbing the ladder and leaving the rest behind. Partly resentful of this injustice, she also had to admit there was some correspondence between educational level and ability. After the war she learned typing, both English and Japanese, with a view to supporting herself through university education, which she did. With a university diploma, she became a producer of radio and later television programs at NHK.

Naoko Chitose had an interval of about eight years between *jogakkō* graduation and university entry partly due to exigencies like the war, illness, subsistence need, and partly in consequence of her search for her career identity. She first entered a pharmacological college but soon quit, totally bored and also fallen ill. She then worked as a clerk at a naval hospital and, after the war, as an overseas telephone operator for the servicemen of the Occupation. She too realized the absolute necessity of a university diploma for a promising career. Meanwhile, at her mother's urging she submitted herself to *miai* meetings with a few men, none of whom looked worthwhile. "Marrying for an economic reason is like prostituting, I thought. I must be economically independent, and to be independent I must have a university diploma." While supporting herself as a telephone operator, she studied for and passed the government's examination to qualify herself to take university entrance examinations under the postwar system—a procedure necessary for *jogakkō* graduates under the old system. She then took the exam for Todai, and to her surprise passed it. To take full advantage of being a Todai student, she majored in law. Anticipating the difficulty for a woman to get a good job, she studied hard for high grades so that no employer would find any excuse for not hiring her. Like other Todai graduates, she too chose the national civil service as her career, passed its upper-level exam, and was accepted by the Ministry of Home Affairs.

For Taeko it took over twenty years after *jogakkō* graduation before she finally found her career identity in nursing. At forty, she quit being a clerk and maid and began to work as an unskilled helper at a Shizumi hospital. At forty-six, she made up her mind to become a registered nurse, attended a city-sponsored nursing class while working at a hospital, studied hard to graduate as one of the top four in the national licensing examination performance. She thus became a licensed nurse, with several more years to study to become a registered nurse. At forty-eight she looks youthful, firmly committed to a long-range career.

Those women who had their adolescence during or right after the

war, as did the above two women, tended to be ideologically committed
to women's independence and sex equality as a reaction to the wartime
or prewar oppression. Further to be noted is the role of models. While a
positive model was not totally lacking, more women underwent anticipatory countersocialization in which a career candidate steers her life
away from a countermodel. For several informants, the mother or another female kin happened to be a countermodel: "My mother was a
counterteacher [*hanmen kyōshi*] for me. All I wanted was not to be like
her. . . . Father and mother married by arrangement, had nothing in
common. With low intelligence, she was disdained by father. In her
view, woman is privileged to lead a peaceful life just by marrying and
having a family. Why abandon this privilege? She kept saying I am stupid and crazy to choose a painful course of life." War widows, totally
unequipped for self-support, also offered a lesson as a countermodel for
younger generations.

Anticipatory commitment is either conflict-free or conflict-ridden.
By the former I mean those cases where commitment is made with no
discrepancy between ego and others, where the candidate's own motivation is matched with the expectations of her family and others. Most
of the elite career women belong to this type. The conflict-ridden type
refers to a discrepancy between ego's motivation and others' expectations. As might be recalled from chapter 2, one of the pharmacists long
resisted her father, who practically forced her to specialize in that voca-
tion. The reverse form of conflict also happened. A woman, aspiring to
a nursing career, fought her parents, whose pride in family ancestry
would not tolerate such a "base" occupation for their daughter, and
risked being disowned when she entered a nursing school. Finally the
parents gave in. What sustained her motivation were model nurses—
"Nightingale" and the Japan Red Cross nurses, whom she adored. She
obtained licenses for nursing, midwifery, and public health practice,
worked first as a school nurse and then as a government health nurse.
She thus has persisted in her initial resolution.

Anticipatory commitment, therefore, is not absent, but, by and
large, women's careers unfold gradually and haphazardly, or crystallize
retrospectively. This is natural in view of the special risk that women
must take in launching a career.

## CAREER MATURATION: LOCAL PROFESSIONALS

In the course of career pursuit, one matures professionally and comes to
enjoy the fruit of one's energy investment.

*Expertise.* Professional expertise develops, first, through repeated experiences, and this is particularly true with the professions like midwifery which require body contact with clients. The number of deliveries, for example, was mentioned as a measure of expertise: starting from scratch, Maki has "performed nearly ten thousand births." Experiential learning involves trials and errors. Motoko, a pharmacist, honestly admitted that she has learned what medicine does or does not suit a certain *taishitsu* (physical constitution) or what medicines should or should not be taken together *(nomiawase)* from her customers' complaints about the drugs she had chosen for them. The expertise developed through such experiences is usually called *kan*, intuitive judgment. Shizuyo, a clinical dietician, stressed how the dietary prescription by a medical doctor has to be supplemented by her *kan* to arrive at a specific recipe fitting the unique state of a patient. Veteran kindergarten teachers are proud of their *kan* ability to grasp what has happened to a child at home merely by looking at his face or holding his hand.

Along with experiential learning, every professional has gone through systematic, planned training either by reading professional publications or by attending classes. Most professions change in their technologies, vocabularies, or values, and old-timers have to reeducate themselves to keep up. Professional associations hold classes to disseminate the latest information. The postwar Americanization of education compelled schoolteachers and kindergarten teachers to learn a whole new vocabulary: "We were at a loss with so many English words to learn, like *karikyuramu* [curriculum]." Even the midwives had to attend local and national study meetings to catch up with the increasing trend toward "artificial parturition." Attendance at a series of intensive and regular classes and examinations awarded an unlicensed worker with a full license or promoted a low-ranking professional to a higher rank. Some went further than usually expected. Ayano has turned down no opportunity to present "a paper" at a kindergarten teacher association meeting, "because this is the only way you get exposed to outsiders' relentless criticism." Hanayo, when she foresaw the saturation point for the use of Western drugs, made up her mind to study *kanpō* (Chinese herb medicine) and attended a monthly "seminar" in Yokohama where "first-rate" specialists gathered as lecturers. Then came the *kanpō* boom, promising prosperity for her store.

Expertise is not only technical but is social as well. *Social expertise* refers to the skill for establishing rapport with one's clients, employees, or colleagues. The pharmacists must be able to recall the health history of each regular customer and, according to Hanayo, to recommend a drug which is not beyond his solvency. Yaeko, the beautician, used to give a morning class every day for her employees to improve their attitude toward customers. They prayed and read the shop mottos like "Take good care of your customers." Her shop enjoys a high reputation for being "kind and polite," she said proudly. To educate little children, Ayano realized that she had to develop a good rapport with their mothers, mostly fishermen's wives. Through participation in all kinds of women's activities, she succeeded in convincing these mothers of the importance of kindergarten education. Kaoru, another kindergarten teacher, thinks that it is most important to memorize the children's names. She takes pride in being the first among her colleagues to memorize all the names of new entrants each year.

*Promotion, achievement, and reward.* Career maturation corresponds to promotion for some professionals. Ayano started as a nursery schoolteacher, moved to a kindergarten, was promoted to supervisor of another kindergarten, and after a number of transfers, was appointed vice-principal of the city's main kindergarten—the highest position a woman could attain in this field. The principal was a male who, at the same time, was a primary school principal. This long tradition of male supremacy was broken when Ayano was further promoted to principal. She held this position for several years despite her illness, so that "no one would say a woman principal is no good after all."

A variety of achievements or rewards were mentioned by those who are not incorporated into a promotion system. The pharmacists cited their successes in "curing" their clients. Sachi, having been a chef at school for twenty years, is proud that she has never caused one single accident (e.g., food poisoning). Her achievement was cited in a local newspaper. A common token of accomplishment is found in an award of honor given by a local government or some other organization, consisting of a sheet of paper which states the awardee's performance. The ultimate award—the imperial or national government one—was received by Maki and Ayano for their long service in their respective fields.

What appears the most gratifying reward is again a social one. As one's career matures, one's *human network* expands and consolidates. The beautician has trained about one hundred apprentice-employees, many of whom have established their own shops. The *sensei-deshi* (master-disciple) bond is reactivated through reunions. Yaeko feels she has one hundred "daughters." Even Sayo, once a *naishoku* teacher in sewing, gets invited to reunion parties of her former "students," who still appreciate her discipline and regard her as a role model. Needless to say, schoolteachers and kindergarten teachers have built up a vast multigenerational network. The midwives and their clients feel a special bond of intimacy, and this feeling is extended to the children delivered.

The human network thus built up sustains the woman's remaining years of life and serves her as social capital.

## WOMEN IN MALE-DOMINANT CAREERS

The local professionals, who are almost all in feminine fields, do not have much to do with sex discrimination. It is the woman in a male-dominant, elite profession who has to confront the problem and spend enormous energy to surmount it. Interview, however, revealed more than just the andocentric nature of career structure.[3]

*Unprecedented entry.* A career candidate may face a rigid structure of bureaucracy which has never opened its doors to women. Reiko Egawa, having specialized in economics at Todai and passed the civil service examination, applied to the Ministry of Finance, where Todai graduates preponderate, but received only an evasive answer. She then tried the Ministry of Health and Welfare, hoping that her sex would be no barrier to welfare administration, but was told she would be acceptable for a middle-level position (corresponding with junior college education) but not for an upper-level one. A third choice was the Ministry of Education, which she knew housed officials who had planned and implemented the postwar coeducational system. One such official admitted that he was certainly responsible for initiating coeducation but had never anticipated a woman applicant for an administrative position at the Education Ministry. Finally, the candidate conceded to accept a less desirable alternative—a position at a public corporation which had never hired a woman at the upper level.

Similar bureaucratic rejections were met by Naoko Chitose, the only woman graduate from Todai's law school to pass the civil service examination that year: "It's incredible. The Health and Welfare Ministry, for example, would not hire a woman except for janitorial work." As of 1954, there was no upper-level woman in the whole government except in the Bureau of Women and Minors, the Ministry of Labor. N. C. accepted the offer from the Ministry of Home Affairs because there was nothing else available. Academic positions, particularly those at national universities, still remain decidedly male dominated. Utako Higuchi entertained the idea of an academic career but saw no hope of being accepted into the academic bureaucracy based upon the *kōzasei* system (a system in which a discipline has one position for each rank—one full professor-chairman and one assistant professor). Yoko Jinbo was fortunate enough to be invited as a tenured assistant under her professor's patronage, even though her duties to help the professor, assistant professor, and graduate students leave little time for her own research.

Having been an assistant for five years, she feels pressed to find an instructor's position somewhere, though she knows most universities rule out women for faculty appointments.

Alongside of such structural rejection of women, one also hears about the sex blindness of the Japanese bureaucracy. All one has to do, I was told, is pass the universal examinations for civil service, for instance. This de-sexualizing function of the examination also applies to the entrance examination for top universities. Those women who have passed the examination for Todai can thereby remove the gender stigma they have carried as women. In this sense, universal examinations for entering male-dominant elite universities or employment may be regarded as "transition rites" for women to become sexually neutral or masculine.

*Seniority rule.* This structural duality—sex-biased and sex-neutral —holds true for seniority rule. Both N. C. and R. E. witnessed their male peers (*dōki*, same year entrants) promoted to the *kachō* (section chief) status, leaving them behind. Their protests did not prevail over their superiors; instead they were placed in "research departments" which are out of the promotion track. Nor did the courts of justice, which were opened up for women in the postwar era, follow the seniority rule automatically. Every time a woman was to be promoted there was resistance for a period of time before the promotion took place. Women were believed to belong in family courts only, considered inept for criminal cases, ruled out as presiding judges or court directors. Each time, women had to deliver protests and demands.

At the same time, I was told, often by the same informants, that within a bureaucracy, especially that of the national civil service, there prevails a seniority-based universalism cutting across sex boundaries. "It is hard to get in, but once in, you are equal to men." Theoretically a woman can expect to be promoted to the same rank exactly at the same time as any male colleague who had entered service with her. Whether this is actually so remains to be seen.

*Administrative role.* Bureaucratic universalism does not apply to women especially when an administrative position is in question. It is presumed that no male is willing to serve a female superior. This is why women are blocked from promotion to the *kachō* status—the first primary administrative position in a typical bureaucracy. The same reason underlies the fact that women are promoted without much difficulty to administrative positions within a female-staffed bureaucracy.

The truthfulness of the above presumption about a male subordinate's resistance to a female boss must be verified. My informants refuted it on the basis of their personal experiences. While she was head of the corporation's local branch, R. E. became convinced that in Japan, although there are many obstacles for a woman to become an organizational leader, she will have no trouble once she becomes one. I observed an unwitting demonstration of the above claim while interviewing N. C., director of a government research center supervising ten research staff, all male university graduates. The interview was occasionally interrupted by her subordinates stepping into her office for consultation. Their speech was polite and formal and their posture was low (some squatted to coordinate with the director's sitting position), while N. C., relaxed, expressed her views and decisions in a non-polite, informal style of speech. The Japanese usage of rank terms like *shochō* (director) or *kachō* for address facilitates stabilizing a sex-blind hierarchy. It might be speculated that in Japan the hierarchical orientation insulates men and women from their sexual identities whereas, in the United States, sex identity is inseparable from each individual, male or female, precisely due to its equalitarianism and individualism, which does away with a structural insulator.

*Patronage.* My informants concurred in stressing the importance of informal social networks as a springboard for success and in recognizing the female disadvantage in this respect. The typical social network supportive of one's career tends to have a vertical relationship involving guidance or patronage. Such a relationship is often paired as *oyabun-kobun* (boss-henchman), *sensei-deshi* (teacher-disciple), or *senpai-kōhai* (senior-junior), though equals like former classmates may also form an alliance. A patron-client bond like this may emerge between a chief and his subordinate within a ministry, a professor and his student in a seminar, an older and younger graduate from the same university, a senior and a junior member of the same department of a company, and the like. Patronage, as a basic component of a clique, exists side by side with a bureaucracy's formal structure to supplement or interfere with the latter's function. Patronage thereby plays a large part in determining the individual's career prospect. Beyond a certain level, the seniority rule is replaced with patronage.

> When a new class of university graduates enters a ministry, they do not join a clique immediately. Rather, they spend ten years or so in one or another post learning the work of the ministry. During this period they establish working relationships with their seniors. Seniors want able juniors. By the time a junior becomes a section chief, he will probably have established particularly good relationships with one or two senior officials. When the senior official becomes a bureau chief or vice-minister, he may recommend those juniors who are close to him for key positions. And after

the senior official has retired, if he should enter the Diet or the cabinet, or join a government commission, these relationships may become even more important. (Craig 1975:11–12)

Women are disadvantaged because patronage does not cross sex boundaries: Rohlen (1974:123) noted the *senpai-kōhai* relationship at a bank to be clearly sex-segregated. Women could form such a bond among themselves, but the career advantage to be derived from it is decidedly limited since most desirable positions are monopolized by male patrons.

Woman is precluded from a higher position not only because she cannot have a male patron but also because she is considered unfit to be a patron for male followers. When N. C. confronted the chief secretary of the ministry with a demand for the same promotion to *kachō* status as her peers,

> He said, "If you become *kachō*, your subordinates will suffer pitiably. Let's take my own experience. I am most grateful to my superior for his speedy rise, thanks to his ability, in the hierarchy. From rank to rank he moved up quickly and became vice minister [the apex of the civil service hierarchy]. With his power, he pulled me up. You are not possibly hoping to become a vice minister, are you?" If the *kachō* is going to be stuck at a rank not much higher, he said, the subordinates will not be rewarded for their loyal service. They would be happier to work under a promising boss, he said.

While the bureaucracy is off limits to a woman applicant simply because there is no precedent, its doors may be slightly opened by the arbitrary decision of a powerful top administrator at his personal risk. So, I was often told that whether a woman gets into a ministry or not entirely depends upon what kind of men the ministry happens to have at its top. Being a risky investment as a career employee, a woman needs a special "guarantor" responsible for her. Women are more likely to be admitted or promoted to an unprecedented position when and where an influential man in or behind the bureaucracy happens to be self-confident, courageous, and sympathetic to women. In developing their professional expertise, a number of informants also mentioned specific male mentors as indispensable to their careers.

Academic patronage spills over the sex lines more freely. A woman who has graduated from a first-rate coeducational university may be able to elicit support from her academic ties (with professors and alumni holding key positions in society at large). A Todai graduate is advantaged by her easy access to her *senpai, dōki,* and *kōhai* who predominate in government, industries, or wherever. A free-lance career may have to rest even more heavily upon academic patronage. In launching a career as a free-lance journalist, Shizuko Fukuda relied upon academic ties built at her high school as well as university thanks to the elite status of both institutions. One of her high school classmates, working at a radio station, invited her to one of his regular programs, providing her the first chance to publicize her essays. More importantly, her career as an organizer—be it a founder of adult education classes or of an international cultural exchange program—drew support from her alumni, professors, and distinguished members of PTAs.

Tomoe Goto, unlike most others, regards her career as an unusually "smooth" one. To begin with, she was free from the entrance examination hell thanks to her enrollment in an "escalator" school system containing all levels from kindergarten up. An honor student, she was allowed to stay on at her alma mater, a women's university, after graduation, as an assistant while studying for a doctorate in biology. Several years later, she received her degree and was promoted to an instructorship and then to the rank of assistant professor, and at forty made full professor. No doubt, T. G. owes her academic career to her ability and strenuous work, but in addition she has benefited from academic patronage. Her professor-advisor recognized her ability, provided supportive guidance, and even took her to the United States with him to do graduate work. It is apparent that the professor-student bond has sustained T. G. throughout. Furthermore, it is probable that she found her career within her alma mater without competing with male outsiders simply because Japanese universities tend to protect their own graduates by hiring them for a substantial portion of faculty positions (Shimbori 1965). T. G. benefited from academic patronage more fully than Y. J. whose alma mater is a coeducational—and hence male-dominated —national university.

*Clients.* Women may encounter a more blunt expression of sex discrimination from their clients, whereas there tends to be some communal solidarity within their work places. Orie Date, producer and "chief director" for a television network, does not feel her sex to be detrimental to her work and position, "because what counts after all is your ability." It is outsiders like the audience who are openly prejudiced against women. When there was a telephone call from a viewer protesting about the program of which O. D. was in charge, she tried to answer. The caller stopped her by saying, "Why! You woman! Let me talk to someone responsible," and refused to accept her self-identification as officially responsible. This caller happened to be a minority-status person (former outcast) who would take being handled by a woman precisely as a sign of discrimination against him.

*Role ambiguity and female advantage.* Career women, thus handicapped as outsiders in the world of men, find some compensatory opportunities or advantages by virtue of their outsider status and role
ambiguity. First and foremost, most of my career women have converted their career frustrations into creative energy. R. E., having been
exposed to the prejudice of male colleagues and superiors (e.g., disapproval of the assignment of important tasks to her as inappropriate to
her sex), lost self-confidence and decided to go to the United States in
search of a breakthrough. Under a Fulbright grant she studied industrial and labor relations at Cornell University and enjoyed "an American life" for a year. This American exposure opened up her perspective
and was to influence her career after she returned to her employment.
Her employer remained resistant to putting her onto the promotion
track for administrative positions. She finally gave up the hope of moving up within the corporation, and decided to reeducate the Japanese
people, particularly employers and managers. Without renouncing her
employee status, she started to write books, make frequent appearances
in the mass media, give public lectures, and so on, primarily to promote
a utilization of women's capabilities and resources. In line with "Student Power" or "Black Power," in vogue in America at that time, she
took the lead in spreading the catch phrase "Woman Power," and con-
vening a woman-power meeting, the novel program of which attracted
the mass media. She has attained national fame as a public educator,
which her employer does not mind because her fame serves as an advertisement. In other words, she created a new role for herself or converted
her peripheral status within the corporation into a central one outside of
it. This would have been inconceivable, according to her, if she were
a man.

While men can rely on the operation of the bureaucratic system for
their career maturation, women as outsiders must be alert to any opportunity as it presents itself, primarily depending upon their individual
talent and insight. This is particularly true with self-employed career
women. Wakako Ishii has been involved in creating commercially feasible information (useful for city planning, construction projects, advertisement, etc.) as an employee or member of research teams. She now
heads her own research corporation, which employs several women.
For her, opportunities for information production are ubiquitous but
only if one's eyes are open enough to see linkages between various things
which most people are blind to. Inexhaustible curiosity, sensitivity, and
imagination seem to be the woman's main capital; there is no predetermined course for navigation.

A research position, open to a woman kept out of the regular promotion track, may turn out to be beneficial. The promotion track requires one to be a generalist with a variety of experiences, according to my informants, with no expertise developed in a single field. For such a person the bureaucratic status is all he carries with him, whereas a specialist with research experience will be called upon even after his/her retirement. This is an important consideration in view of the Japanese system of early retirement—the informants in their forties contemplate retirement to be realized soon—and that necessitates that the retiree take up a post-retirement job for which specialized expertise may well be taken into account.

There are other compensatory benefits inherent in the outsider status. Women may have easy access to men at the top of the bureaucracy because they are less constrained by "proper channels" whereas their male colleagues are not permitted to bypass their immediate superiors. This freedom allowed R. E. to participate in top-level decision making in the national government—a privilege unimaginable to her male peers. Easy access may be because women do not threaten men or are not taken seriously by men, as was W. I.'s experience. "Men are not on guard against women and so tend to divulge the information we look for more readily than they would with men." She counsels her employees to take advantage of that. "Be a telephone beauty," she tells them, so that they can more easily get appointments for interviews.

The male-biased career structure thus functions both for and against women.

## COMPATIBILITY OF CAREER AND DOMESTICITY

The woman's career occupation, by virtue of its independence from her domestic role, raises the question of the compatibility of the two roles, occupational and domestic. The question is a critical one in view of the Japanese "work ethic," which dictates that the public/occupational sphere remain aloof from the private/domestic sphere (except in the case of self-employment). This rule of sphere segregation is asymmetric in that the occupational demand can be fulfilled at the expense of the autonomy of the domestic sphere whereas the reverse is strictly forbidden.

*Surrogate housewife.* Under the rule of sphere segregation, an employed career woman must work like a male peer, that is, as if she had no domestic burdens. Unless she chooses to stay unmarried and childless, she needs a substitute housewife to assume domestic responsibilities, and this is what most of my informants resort to. Fortunate women have had their own mothers living with or near them—this explains why *mukoyōshi* marriage is overrepresented among professional women. "Without mother, I could not have possibly continued to work like this." A sister or brother's wife was available to some others. The mother-in-law, while a menace to a daughter-in-law, nonetheless has often proved to be an indispensable houseworker and baby-sitter. It may be safely assumed that professional women tend to live with extended kin more than do nonprofessional women. A live-in maid is a common solution for those who have no kin helper available. Orie Date put her infant child in a "baby home" providing custodial care around the clock, which allowed her to continue to work. Ten months later, the child was taken back home to be placed under the care of a resident maid. This was repeated for her second child.

Some husbands, particularly in "dual-career families" (Rapoport and Rapoport 1976), share housework and turn out to excel the wives in cooking, child caretaking, or home management in general. U. H.'s husband, also a government official, shares more housework than she expected—preparing breakfast, giving the infant child a bath, housecleaning, trash collection, grocery shopping, dishwashing, and so on. Nonetheless, he warns his wife not to reveal this to his colleagues. Not that his male ego is vulnerable, but his domesticity could be taken as a sign of a lack of occupational dedication. The rule of sphere segregation is in operation psychologically.

By comparison, the husbands of nonelite professionals tend to be more resistant to domestic participation.

*Duolocal residence.* The asymmetric rule of sphere segregation demands sacrifice in the domestic life, sometimes imposing a residential separation of husband and wife. The usual pattern is that the nonworking wife stays home with the children while the husband lives alone in a place where he has been transferred. With the professional wife who is also subjected to a transfer, there is more likelihood of separation or duolocal residence. Many professional women I have met, including the two in my elite professional sample, were separated from their husbands, having reunions only weekly or monthly. Instead of complaining about this conjugal strain, they accept it as a price of equality and some even take it as an opportunity to concentrate upon their own work.

Transfers are built into the promotion scheme of some bureaucracies, and women's immobility would be detrimental to their career advancement. Women thus may have to choose either mobility-and-promotion or immobility-and-womanhood (being wife and mother)—either career or domestic fulfillment, not both. Shinobu is a case in point. After graduation from a nursing school, Shinobu returned home to take over the housework, being the oldest female (the mother was dead and the older sister married out). At the same time, she started to work at a private clinic to which she could commute. After getting up at 5:00 A.M., she prepared breakfast and box lunches for younger siblings, and after a day's work at the clinic, did the laundry at night. With frustration she waited until her younger sister grew old enough to take over the housework, and then she applied for a hospital job and was accepted. A graduate of a national nursing school, Shinobu became a government appointee with a promising career before her, tied into the promotion system of the national civil service. She was transferred from one job to another, from place to place, so as to have well-rounded experiences, and each move meant a promotion. After starting as a hospital-attached nurse, she became a ward head nurse, an instructor at a nursing school, and a faculty dean at a hospital. At the time of the interview, she was the general head nurse for a whole hospital—the national hospital located in Shizumi—in charge of administration and education for the nursing staff.

Shinobu has not always been firm in her professional commitment however. She thought about marriage many times. Her kin worried and urged her to marry, and she received many proposals, including one from a surgeon. In the meantime, challenged by her work and its demand for increasing expertise, she became more and more preoccupied with her profession. Every time she faced the choice between marriage and career, she found the latter having more weight on the scale. It was not until after the age of thirty that the matter was settled in her mind. She never once thought of having both a career and a married life. To her these are incompatible, as demonstrated by her married colleagues who, if they continue to work, can do so only as noncareer peripheral workers. Above all, marriage ties a woman down to the house site geographically and thus puts her out of circulation for promotion since geographical mobility is a key to promotion in the national hospital system. Incompatibility may further involve a woman's unwitting withdrawal from the marriage market in that the more involved she is with her career, the less available she would appear to be as a marriage candidate. It may be that age thirty represents a turning point not only in overcoming ambivalence but in realizing that proposals are tapering off.

*Conflict: overloads and guilt.* Even under the best conditions of role compatibility, the career woman must carry her share of conflict. The availability of a substitute houseworker does not insure total equality of a career woman and man. Helped by her mother-in-law as a baby-sitter, Y. J. still finds her mind drawn toward her child even while she is attending an academic convention away from home. At night when she should be concentrating on the subject under study, the child's cry interrupts her. Like all others, she feels exhausted with the role over-loads.

If the woman enjoys her mother's help, she should also be aware that her husband is constrained by the wife's kin's constant presence. Also there tends to be disagreement between herself or her husband and the substitute child caretaker. The granny is likely to spoil the kid. The real test comes when the child grows up to face an entrance examination. R. E. regrets having neglected her son: spoiled by his grandmother (R. E.'s mother), he was not well prepared for entrance examinations and could not make Todai as his mother did. Convinced that being a government bureaucrat is the best conceivable career (and for that goal a Todai diploma is absolutely essential), she does not see a bright future for the son. She believes in equality and in careers for women, but still seems to feel guilty with regard to her son's education. Almost all other women working outside, professional or nonprofessional, local or non-local, also tend to exhibit guilt, sometimes toward their husbands or mothers (who are surrogate housewives), but primarily toward their children.[4] Local women show it more intensely. Their guilt is, in a few cases, expressed in the form of exaggerated domesticity, femininity, or conviction of male superiority. "Most working women neglect house-work but I am different. As a woman I cook everything by myself, sew everything by myself." "Men excel women in every field, though I shouldn't say so as a woman. [A male hairdresser apprentice] learns it and passes the exams by far more quickly than a woman who has started at the same time." For Ayano, guilt and ambivalence is not something to overcome but what all working women should adhere to. She herself was ambivalent about her dual role throughout her career. In the evening when she had to prepare supper after work she wondered why she was teaching, and next morning she was eager to go out to work and could forget all the hardships while she was with the kindergarten children. She could survive, she said, thanks to this persistent ambivalence. She added that she would recommend a career only for a woman who likes housework and motherhood, but not for one who does not.

Women's occupational careers were classified into three types in terms of whether they are part of or independent of their housewifely role: household occupation, intermediary job, and career occupation. Even though a woman may present herself as a "mere housewife," it turns out that she has been indispensable for the postmarital household occupation as teamworker or in some cases as the primary worker and manager. When there is sex-based role specialization in the occupation, the general tendency is for the husband's role to be single and narrowly specialized and for the wife's role to be multiple and generalized. Women's speciality, if any, lies in handling human relationships. There is nothing that suggests that the wife is less active than the husband in the household occupation.

A woman in an intermediary job, typically a "part-time" job, tends to be burdened with a dilemma: the job often demands a virtually full-time commitment and yet is not elevated to the status of "career," so that the worker's basic identity remains that of a housewife. It is women in this type of job who are blamed for the neglected children.

A "career woman" turns out not to be as different from other women as expected, at least at the outset of the career. Typically, a career for women unfolds gradually and haphazardly under circumstantial pressures and through a step-by-step commitment. A career woman is identified as such only retrospectively. But through such unfolding, the woman does develop an expertise, matures into an accomplished professional, and is promoted or otherwise rewarded to her great satisfaction. In those exceptional cases where a career was anticipated and committed to at an early stage of life, it was discovered that the daughter was so socialized within her family often under the influence of her father. Such career socialization was further attributed to the "succession syndrome" of the Japanese domestic institution.

Women, in pursuit of male-dominant careers, have met rejection and resistance, if only because there was no precedent. Embedded in the same social structure that blocks the female career seekers, we also found accommodations for them. Success in the entrance examination for Tokyo University and subsequently in the national civil service examination, for example, served as a transition rite for a woman to remove gender stigma. The seniority rule of the Japanese bureaucracy, too, functioned as an equalizer for men and women, though only to a limited degree. Sometimes, the discriminatory system itself was found to enhance career opportunities for women. But, of course, it would call for special perseverance and creativity to take advantage of the structurally built-in female disadvantage.

What concerns a working woman most is the problem of double workload, unless she has renounced a family life. A career woman tends to resolve this problem by having a surrogate housewife to help her, again her own mother being the most desirable baby-sitter and housekeeper. Since it is impossible to be perfect both as a housewife and an occupational worker, even with a domestic helper, no one is completely free of guilt. Hence, paradoxically, compulsive domesticity is adhered to, or at least so expressed, by working women more than by housewives. Two extreme types—the women in the household occupations and those in male-dominant careers—are relatively free from such guilt compared with those in intermediary jobs or ordinary, nonelite career professions.

Despite the guilt and dilemmas, no woman regrets having had a career. Beginning with a timid or even reluctant commitment, she ends up with the conviction that she has *chosen* the best possible life course. She would not, I was told repeatedly, trade her career, however trouble-ridden, for just a domestic life, however full it might be. The conviction intensifies as she enters into later years. This is in marked contrast to those women who are regretful of having relinquished their careers to become full-time homemakers. The media report an increasing number of career women specializing in the traditionally male professions. This trend forecasts one future alternative for women's self-realization.

# 7
# Later Years

"Later years" refers to the last life stage beginning with the mid-age when one's children have attained adulthood and relative independence and ending with old age and death. This period poses a challenge because of its prolongation at an unprecedented pace: Japanese men and women had a life expectancy of 59.5 and 62.9 respectively in 1952, and extended it by 1978 to 72.9 and 78.3 (Sōrifu 1980:92). It is also the most paradoxical period characterized by its dual nature. On the one hand, this is a stage when a woman, freed from the burden of childrearing, can enjoy autonomy, obtain power and leadership in and out of the household, begin to have her past hardship and energy investment repaid, taste a sense of accomplishment and *ikigai*, and develop a retrospective insight and wisdom on life. On the other hand, she must confront her role atrophy and eventually the inevitable tragedy of aging, possible invalidism, and death. As far as sex polarity is concerned, this may be the period when women come to transcend their gender or assume male prerogatives.[1]

## The Remaining Domestic Roles

### THE LATE AFFINAL BOND

Within the domestic domain, let us first return to where we left off in chapter 4 regarding the woman's postmarital life.

*Change in the daughter-in-law's role.* At this stage, a woman may still be playing the role of a daughter-in-law in an extended household, but its contents are likely to have changed radically. The locus of power has shifted from the senior generation to the junior one. The power shift primarily refers to a transfer of the control of household finances but may include other changes such as a transfer of the household *jitsuin* registered seal) as a symbol of authority, and of important household records as well as room redistribution (exchange of rooms between the two generations or the moving of the old generation to a newly built annex). The old couple thus become *inkyo* (retirees), though this "old-fashioned" word was seldom used by my informants. For most informants such a shift was gradual and recognized as such only retrospectively, but for some it was sudden and triggered by a specific crisis event. According to Ayano:

> In our *ie*, Grandpa and Grandma tightly held sovereignty for a long time. My husband, their only child, knew too well what hardship they had gone through in raising him to resist their authority. Then, Grandma got injured and was forced to stay in bed. A strange thing [happened]. I wonder if words have a force of a living thing. Until that time Grandma called me Aya-chan and I called her Mother. When bedridden, she began to call me *Okā-chan* [Mommy] and I naturally felt like calling her Granny. It was then, I believe, that I became a true mistress of the house [*shufu*].

This happened when the daughter-in-law was forty-one.

The above case exemplified the interlocking of power and dependency to the extent that the power shift is accompanied by the responsibility of taking care of the aged, helpless in-laws. The former compliant "trainee" transforms herself into a nurturant "caretaker." As the junior wife nurses the sick senior wife, there may develop the kind of intimate, exclusive bond which had never existed before between them. Ayano, who had had a hard time as a younger daughter-in-law, now became attached to the granny as if she were "a baby to be fondled," or even felt something akin to *"dōseiai"* (literally, "homosexual love," but meant here as sisterly love). For the granny's part, too, the daughter-in-law became *the* indispensable caretaker and "mother," for whom no one, including the patient's blood daughter, could substitute. The daughter-in-law, for example, knew exactly what part of the patient's body felt itchy and needed to be scratched. Toward the end of her ninety-one years of life, the mother-in-law, now senile, recognized no one except Ayano.

The responsibility of nursing a mother-in-law has lasted even longer for Ai. At seventy-six, she is still looking after her hundred-year-old bedridden mother-in-law, preparing soft meals for the toothless patient, and taking care of her incontinence. Ai herself is a mother-in-law who has her own grandchildren and great-grandchildren. Her own daughter-in-law, therefore, could have substituted for her as a nurse, but the old mother-in-law does not want anybody but Ai partly "because young people talk loudly about her bed-wetting" whereas she will change the diapers quietly. Hot tempered, incorrigible, and somewhat senile, the mother-in-law "obeys" no one but this senior daughter-in-law.

Not all in-law relationships are like this. Some informants frankly admitted that until the in-law's death they had had no emotional relief, neither had they enjoyed any generational turnover in power and mastery. With death, the once "nasty" mother-in-law (or father-in-law) seems to be converted into the image of a harmless, even wise, person as if death had purified her.

Conflict itself changes its form. No longer does the parent-in-law take the role of an active party to the conflict but may instead by relegated to a passive role or an object of negotiation. Kumiko's husband's eldest brother, the head of the *honke*, died leaving his wife, children, and his old father behind. The widow could not get along with her father-in-law. Deciding to return to her natal house, she tried to negotiate for the aged father-in-law to be moved to Kumiko's house, the *bunke*. Kumiko was in a rage and had her husband reject the proposal firmly, which resulted in all the *shinseki* ganging up on Kumiko to condemn her. The widowed wife of the *honke* head apparently thought that the father-in-law should now come under the care of Kumiko's husband (and therefore his wife), who was his last surviving "blood son." Kumiko reasoned that the father belonged to the *honke*, and, besides, her family should have no responsibility because her husband, the younger son, had inherited no property, received no aid, from the *honke*. The conflict thus involved the principle of consanguineal obligation as against that of jural integrity of the *ie* and of economic reciprocity. Meanwhile, the old father-in-law seemed to have no say about where he should live.

Even when a senior in-law is a party to a conflict, the two generations tend to reverse their roles. The senior in-law now endures quietly as the junior in-law used to do, or removes him/herself from the conflict scene. Thus, my informants complained about their mothers-in-law rejecting their help, spending too many nights with their other children, or confining themselves in the *inkyo* annex to avoid seeing and depending on their daughters-in-law in coresidence. Being overburdened with a helpless in-law is not desirable, of course, but equally intolerable is his/her overindependence.

*The wife-husband dyad.* The married couple also undergoes its evolution over the years. One pattern is the development of a warm intimacy in the course of co-living which gradually replaces the earlier aloofness. This is especially true with mediated marriage. "Only after living together for twenty or thirty years, you come to realize what husband and wife are for one another." This is contingent upon the loss of other intimate bonds. An aloof husband may be converted into an affectionate one, as happened to some informants, when his mother dies. For the wife it is the children's departure that reminds her of the need to rebuild conjugal solidarity. When her eldest son confided his plan to marry a girl friend, Hamako realized that "from now on we, as husband and wife, must look after each other tenderly."

A promiscuous husband may begin to have his "bugs" calm down, and an alcoholic, violent husband may become reformed. A "workaholic" husband may reach a turning point and reflect upon his personal life, and a wife, thus far preoccupied with her children or occupation, may feel guilty toward the neglected husband. On a TV life-counseling program (8/24/78), a counselor advised the client, who wanted but hesitated to divorce her promiscuous husband, to the effect that a husband and wife are unable, throughout their marital career, to reach real harmony until they start to "walk down toward the grave," full of repentance and guilt vis-à-vis one another. "That's what marriage is all about," he concluded. Guilt and reappreciation may be released, again, in a crisis situation. When Ayano was hospitalized with pancreatitis, her husband, who had always been a receiver, never a giver, of caretaking, came to the hospital every day to nurse her. She, too, realized that it was her husband whom she loved most. Looking back with hindsight on their marital careers, many women are glad that they did not carry out what they had intended time and again—to divorce.

Again, there are marriages which do not fit this pattern. Hanayo at fifty-four still suffers because of her womanizing husband and yet feels hooked with him. The only hope is to outlive him and then enjoy the freedom of being alone. The main reason she does not divorce him is her fear of starvation. Although she has her own store to run and admittedly is self-supporting, she fears that her customers will be alienated from a divorcee. Taeko, childless, unable to extract a divorce agreement from her husband, alternated between the temptation to commit suicide and the temptation to kill him. Now she is resigned to postpone her salvation to the postmortem period: she does not intend to share the same grave with him. To make sure of this, she has taken an oath to "dedicate" her body to a medical research group. This-worldly divorce is thus to be substituted by other-worldly divorce.

While a peaceful, passion-free co-living is regarded by many as an ideal of a durable marital life, some women in their seventies bring their uneventful marriages into question. "Husband and wife should have something to burn [*moeru*] for each other," said Sayo, "but my life has not been burned yet." To end a life without knowing love at all is "abnormal." Her frustrated emotions must find expression, but "if I play *shamisen*, my husband will say I am like a geisha, and if I play koto he worries it will be mistaken for *naishoku* [teaching]." Both possibilities would damage the honor of the house. As a "soundless" outlet, she has settled on haiku composition whereby she can "recapture" her "adolescence" in the world of fantasy. Indeed, in the countless haiku she has composed are many on romantic love. She laughed, saying it is all a joke, but also referred to a young man whose face appears before her every time she closes her eyes. Is it only a fantasy or a recollection of a rudimentary love affair that she actually experienced in adolescence? Her answer was evasive. What is evident is that she is trying intensely to retrieve the sexual passion which has been buried unburnt. Similarly, Fusa, at seventy-six, widowed by a "godlike" *mukoyōshi* husband, confessed having never "tasted love." She went on to give a lengthy account of a man who secretly loved her without hoping to marry her because both he and she were *atotori* (successor). He is dead now, but her unspent sexual emotion seems to keep this experience of "being loved" alive although she had never had a chance to talk to him.

Discrepancy in marital satisfaction is reflected in widowhood experiences. Depression, loneliness, emptiness, and disorientation were experienced by some widows. Businessmen's widows tend to live up to their husbands' wills and goals by succeeding to the businesses, as described in chapter 6. Kazuko holds not only the presidency of a lumber company her late husband built, but also followed him in his religious faith as a local branch leader of the Sōkagakkai. Religious identification with a late husband is more direct for Yoshimi: she prays at the household *butsudan* to "listen to his voice" and has been guided by his supernatural messages. "My husband is incorporated into my personality." When she comes across a male companion, she thanks her husband for bringing the man to her as his "substitute."

Other widows are more ambivalent or frankly "liberated." "I felt empty. But I can now play around [see friends, pursue hobbies, or otherwise enjoy leisure] without being bound by anybody. . . . Coming home after having a good time, I apologize to the *bustudan*." "When my husband died, I said to myself, 'Being alone is nice too.' " "If I were to be reborn, I would never marry. To be so constrained again? Hell no! I am sorry to say this, but my life has improved since my husband's death." No widow, even one who has had a good marriage, entertains the idea of remarrying, not so much because of her devotion to her late husband as because of her aversion to be tied down as a caretaker again. Some elderly women, still married, envy their widowed peers.

*The domestic rites for ancestors.* A woman's responsibility as a domestic caretaker extends to the deceased members of the *ie* as identified as *senzo* (ancestors). A secular-minded housewife may become interested in the cult of the dead or obligated to assume the role of a domestic priestess when her old mother-in-law hands this duty over to her together with financial and other domestic power, when death occurs in the household, or when she finds herself getting old. Whether or not they actually conduct rites, my informants concurred in recognizing the importance of "worshipping" or "serving" the ancestors. They learned how to conduct the rites in their childhood by watching their mothers perform.

The domestic rites center upon the household altar *(butsudan)* where the ancestral spirits are enshrined. The rites vary somewhat by sect, but generally involve: candle lighting, incense burning, offering cooked rice and tea, placing fresh flowers, bell ringing, and prayers. This is done every morning, and at night a thanksgiving service may be given. A devotee will further elaborate the rites and chant sutras, whereas a "Western-style breakfast eater" is embarrassed to say that she cannot even offer rice.

The ancestors are symbolized by *ihai* (mortuary tablets). As recognized by Plath (1964), there are two kinds of *ihai*—communal and individual. The communal *ihai* is a single tablet representing all the "generations" of the dead of the *ie* whose individual identities have been lost from the memory of the living generation. The individual *ihai* stands for a recently deceased member who is still remembered, and has his/her *kaimyō* (posthumous name) inscribed on it. Among my local informants, the *ihai* of the latter type usually represent parents-in-law, husband, and/or children. Some *butsudan* contain what Smith (1966) calls "unusual *ihai*," particularly the *ihai* of the wife's parents and other natal kin. Such apparent deviation from the patrilineal principle occurs more among neolocal households (in the case of uxorilocal, *mukoyōshi* marriage this is not a deviation), devout members of nontraditional sects, as well as among divorcees. The most unusual collection of *ihai* is in Akiyo's custody: her first husband, his mother, his father's two previous wives (Akiyo lives with her second husband and her ninety-year-old father-in-law by her first marriage). When my informants talked about *senzo*, they meant all or some of these or the recently departed only, without clear discrimination. But if asked whether their *senzo* are of their husbands' side or whether their natal ancestors are also included, their answer was unequivocal in pointing to the husbands' ancestors, thus revealing their conviction in the patrilineal principle. Indeed, their sense of responsibility as a custodian of the *ihai* is intensified by their self-identity as outsiders. Yukie, for example, takes the responsibility of "protecting" the ancestors seriously and is eager to learn, before it's too late, everything necessary to be done for them (e.g., the burning of the individual *ihai* on the thirty-third or fiftieth death anniversary so as to incorporate it into the communal one). Her teacher is her mother-in-law, another outsider. The insiders like her father-in-law and husband are bypassed in this transmission of the domestic culture.

Occasionally, family conflicts surface over the placement of *ihai* as a symbolic target. Mieko, married to a widower, had custody of the *ihai* of his first wife. When this couple moved to join his mother, the latter would not accept that *ihai*. The same trouble was repeated when Mieko's stepson, also widowed, remarried, leaving his first wife's *ihai* in the stepmother's charge. Her mother-in-law insisted that this *ihai* go to the postmarital household of the son's (her grandson) "blood" daughter. This was an outrageous alternative for Mieko, who believes in the *ie* system whereby the daughter, virilocally married, is not permitted to bring her own mother's *ihai* into her husband's household. What really upset Mieko was the old woman's reasoning: "Because they [son's first wife, and grandson's first wife] are strangers." If so, "I am a stranger too," exclaimed Mieko. In this case, there was conflict between Mieko and her mother-in-law, ending with the latter's departure. The *ihai* issue was only a symbolic manifestation of this conflict, but it does suggest the psychological weight that an *ihai* tablet carried for the Japanese, particularly for its female custodians.

As an extension of the domestic priestly responsibility, women also inherit the obligation to fulfill the duty of *danka* (parishioner) of a Buddhist temple such as dues payment, making donations, inviting the professional priests to important household rites, arranging memorial rites to be held at the temple. In the course of interaction with temple priests, some women become personally involved, taking them as counselors.

Bound by her roles as a custodian of the *butsudan* and household religion (one of the Buddhist sects) and as a liaison between the household and the temple, a woman tends to be conservative in her religious attitudes. Now and then, she is drawn to another sect or even Christianity, but becoming a member is another matter. Sayo attended Seichō-no-ie meetings for a while and was impressed by its teachings but never thought of joining it as a member "because I would feel guilty toward the ancestors." Those who do join other religions or sects try to be sure that these are compatible with the household religions, as most Japanese religions are. Another alternative seems to be a conversion of the whole family as in the case of Kazuko, a Sōkagakkai convert. More on religion later.

## LATE MOTHERHOOD

A mother, or rather a Japanese mother, however old, seems never to graduate from the maternal role, and this is why I avoid the term "postparental." The prolongation of motherhood may be a strategy to meet the empty-nest crisis (Sekiguchi 1975:52). This section is, then, a continuation of chapter 5.

*Vicarious achievements and disappointments.* Educational investments for children, sons in particular, may be well recompensed by their occupational success, which mothers share as their own. Tsuruko's cautious modesty relaxed a little whenever she talked about her eldest son, who graduated from Todai and is a career staff member of a gigantic industrial corporation. As pleased are the mothers of engineers employed at nationally or internationally prominent companies specializing in construction, automobile industries, and the like, of M.D.'s in residency at university hospitals. More mothers, however, while proud of the college education of their children, disclosed some disappointments and regrets with their professional underachievements. Exorbitant costs for sending sons to elite private universities like Keio have been wasted. The mother's disappointment leads to her regrets and even guilt for having been an inconsiderate *kyōiku mama*. Kuniko, discontented with her Keio-graduated son, who seems uncommitted to a career, now has hindsight as to how her educational preoccupation was compensation for her frustration with her unfaithful husband. What should have been instilled in the son, she regrets, is the spirit for work. She believes that more important than academic training is the development of a moral character. Fortunately, the son joined a sports club which taught him the values of human relationships such as rank order. "That was the best thing that he learned at the university."

*Children's marriage.* Another challenge that a mother encounters is the child's attainment of marriageable age and embarkation on a marital career. She may be reluctant to forgo the child whom she has raised with such care *(teshio ni kaketa)*, but would be more upset if a daughter of twenty-six or older received no proposal or refused to marry, and would consider it her own failure. Indeed, it is the mother's responsibility to marry off the children and it is *her* accomplishment to have discharged that responsibility. Women in their sixties and seventies proudly told of their "success" in marrying off all the "six" or "nine" children or "letting them have their own households [*shotai o motaseru*]." One smug mother boasted of the promising career of her daughter's husband and the smartness of her son's wife who is a graduate of a four-year college. Conversely, desperate mothers asked me to introduce marriage candidates for overaged daughters: "even an American would do"—although Fumie, whose daughter did marry an American, seems still unable to recover from the shock. The daughter's university education does not help in the marriage market. This explains why Teiko, while impressed with her twenty-seven-year-old daughter for her self-reliance and career commitment, is intensely worried.

Most mothers are aware that their children, exposed to nonsegregated classes and offices, might choose their mates by themselves, and yet they still try to influence their children's decisions. When the mother herself married she was ignorant, but by the time her child is about to marry she considers herself a marriage expert. Why should she not, she reflects, utilize her experientially gained wisdom for her child's marriage?

In choosing or approving the daughter's future husband, this *senpai* in marriage tries to make her daughter avoid repeating the mistakes she has made. If, for example, she had been a victim of an oppressive mother-in-law, she is likely to preclude an eldest son as her daughter's spouse. Harue, mother of three daughters, went as far as to refuse to "give" any of them as a bride, but instead insisted on "taking" bridegrooms. She took the trouble to explore "everywhere" in the marriage market until she found a man who was both well matched for her eldest daughter and who did not mind coming over as *mukoyōshi*; her second daughter met a boyfriend on campus, and Harue agreed to their marriage only under the uxorilocal condition, though without *mukoyōshi* agreement; she hopes her third daughter, a medical student, will find a doctor so that together they will open a hospital in Shizumi. The women who regret their loveless marriages tend to endorse a love marriage for their daughters.

Quite another criterion is drawn upon in considering a son's spouse. An alleged sex-equalitarian, a wife who has resented her husband's male chauvinism, turns around to expect her son to assert his male authority over his wife. What worries Yumiko most is that her eldest son is not "firm" enough. "Nowadays, women are so strong. He will be easily henpecked [*shiri ni shikareru*, "mounted on"]. Man must be invincible, man is different from woman." What is implied here is not just the son's male authority but Yumiko's own power as a mother-in-law. Thus, the whole role cycle seems destined to be repeated despite her acknowledged unhappiness as a daughter-in-law and wife.

Even as they spoke in this way, some women came to realize their inconsistency and double standard. Particularly those who have both sons and daughters showed embarrassment about their egocentricity. Ai, who has married out all but one of her eight daughters to "houses without mothers-in-law," admitted that all women, regardless, eventually become mothers-in-law. To be good mothers-in-law, Ai wonders, her daughters probably should have served as daughters-in-law. Yumiko was embarrassed to confess that she does not care what she does to her husband but cannot stand her son being pushed around by his wife. I am not sure whether this awareness of the inconsistency or the discrepancy between *tatemae* and *honne*, in recycling itself, contributes to cultural resiliency or change. But the ability to put oneself in a daughter-in-law's shoes is not lacking. Every informant presented herself as a considerate, patient mother-in-law, and some said they have instructed their sons to be faithful to their wives so that the latter would not have the same suffering as they had.

The mother's responsibility includes a successful execution of matrimonial ceremonies. Some women came to learn what exactly is contained in a *yuinō* box only through their children's engagement. What preoccupies her mind is the wedding ceremony. For her eldest daughter's wedding, Harue took sole responsibility including the selection of one hundred guests, their seating arrangements (which indicate the degrees of intimacy or esteem that the host attaches to the guests), decisions on the banquet and take-home gifts, and even writing speeches to be delivered by the master of ceremony. Not long afterward she fell ill, obviously owing to overexhaustion from this enterprise. "It was a magnificent wedding," said Hanayo, still excited about her son's matrimony held at a locally prominent hotel. More than one hundred guests were invited at a cost of twelve thousand yen (sixty dollars) each. Again it was she who had decided single-handedly on the feast, cake, gifts, and so on. Instead of following the traditional pattern, she interjected her own innovative idea about the take-home gifts for the guests: silver spoons. "I may sound boastful, but since my son's wedding, no wedding has appealed to me as gorgeous enough."

*Residential arrangement.* The children's postmarital residence pattern indicates some change from that of the mothers. No longer is it taken for granted that the successor son and his wife come to live with his parents upon marriage. The parents tend to allow the young couple to enjoy their "honeymoon" by themselves. But such parental indulgence only partially accounts for neolocalism. More important is the location of the son's work, usually Tokyo or another urban center, which precludes intergenerational coresidence. Furthermore, the parents, with a prospect of many more years to live, do not necessarily welcome the in-law co-living, which would restrain their autonomy as well as the young couple's.

Neolocalism, however, is a temporary arrangement. As the parents become aged and the mother is widowed, the two generations tend to draw together. Among the thirty-two applicable cases of my sample (where the successor son or daughter has married), seventeen were co-residential at the time of the last interview and these concentrate in the oldest age bracket (the mother's age being sixty or over). If we exclude from the remaining fifteen those who anticipate co-living some time in the future and those whose children live nearby, only three cases are left. Prolonged life expectancy gives rise to a new pattern of timing for coresidence: a son with a career job away from the hometown looks forward to making a "U-turn" upon his retirement to settle down with his family at his parental home. Naturally the mothers prefer to have their children move back, but some face the choice between their own move to their children's house and living alone. The above three cases chose the latter option.

Compared with the informant's own time, there is a greater flexibility over the choice of viri- or uxorilocalism, which may result in inequity in the allocation of coresidential children. Sayo lives with her son and his wife. She also has her daughter and her family living across the street, which makes her feel guilty toward the daughter's parents-in-law, who thus have "lost" their eldest son. Conversely, Yuri could not help complaining to me that not only all her sons have married out but the eldest son is married to a successor daughter and lives with her parents.

*Grandmotherhood.* The children's marriage is soon followed by the mother's exercise of her expertise as a mother for the pregnant daughter or daughter-in-law. She once "became" a mother, and now she "makes" a mother out of a junior woman. This project begins with giving guidance on pregnancy care and conducting the belly-binding ceremony, and climaxes in parturition and postpartum nursing. Through parturient cooperation, mother-daughter ties are simply reinforced, but the heretofore distant relationship between mother-in-law and daughter-in-law is elevated to a new plane of intimacy. "By helping my daughter-in-law in childbirth, we became 'real' mother and daughter." The physical care given to the daughter-in-law seems to be a crucial human investment for one's old age: the daughter-in-law thus cared for will not mind nursing the aged mother-in-law's incapacitated body.

As a grandmother, the senior mother further exercises her experiential knowledge either by instructing the junior mother or by, herself, looking after the grandchild. Again, she tries to counter-recycle her experience, that is, to guide the younger woman to avoid the errors she herself has made. A career woman who neglected her children tends to guide her daughter-in-law to spend enough time with her child; the grandmother who regrets having brought up her son to be too independent and therefore "cold" in human relationships deliberately indulges her grandchild's *amae.*

The grandchildren are viewed in two contrastive ways. Freed from maternal responsibility, the granny-grandchild relationship can be purely emotional: "Grandchildren are nothing more than lovable." "As a mother I was too busy but now I can enjoy fondling my granddaughter." Hence, the stereotypic tendency to spoil the grandchildren is repeated. Husband and wife, or two adjacent generations, incapable of mutual conversation, may communicate *through* a grandchild as the focus of affection. While interviewing an old couple, I was introduced to their daughter-in-law and grandson. The couple proceeded to pay exclusive attention to the grandson, talking to him only, and I came to realize that this is their way of conversing with their daughter-in-law. Likewise, Wakako found the whole house frighteningly quiet when her grandson and his parents were away on a trip, leaving the old couple alone. She realized that without the grandchild around, she and her husband had nobody to talk to.

On the other hand, there is "role distance" in grandparent-grandchild interaction. In referring to her two granddaughters who occasionally visit her, an informant quoted a proverbial saying, "It's all right for grandchildren to come over, and all right to leave." Such mild interest or even indifference is expressed more by those grandmothers who still have things to preoccupy them. For some women, grandchildren are nuisances, and baby-sitting for them is far from a pleasure. Fumie reluctantly accepts the baby-sitting obligation, which disrupts her haiku study, as a bargain with her daughter-in-law in the expected exchange for care in her old age.

As the grandchild grows up, a new perspective emerges. The widows who have no children to live with them find unexpected consolation from their grandchildren who visit them and "promise" to support and live with them when married. The extended family which will skip the middle generation, the parents, is not an unrealistic project in view of the everincreasing life expectancy.

*The pivotal role in the succession chain.* The *ie* as a jural unit transcending its individual members was oppressive to a young bride, and may be of no concern to a middle-aged woman. But the woman at a later stage comes to find her identity firmly anchored in the perpetuation of the *ie* or some part of it. Her sense of security transcends the "here and now," and is inseparable from a long chain of *ie* succession linking her to the preceding generations as well as to the following generations, precisely because she is now in a pivotal position to ensure the linkage. The *ie* being no longer legally institutionalized, informants mean different things when they say, "I want somebody to succeed the *ie* [*ie o tsuide hoshii*]"—the continuation of the family name, of occupancy of the dwelling (implying coresidence and care for the old parents), or succession to the house business. Understandably, the older and more prominent the *ie*, the stronger this desire is. Hiroe, mother of daughters only, wishes one of the daughters to keep on "this house of Tsuchiya which has continued over many, many generations."

In a household running a sizable business, the mother may try to have more than one married child stay on and bring in their spouses to be incorporated into a *dōzoku* enterprise. Kazuko, taking over the presidency of the lumber company upon her husband's death, has her eldest son (the company's vice-president) and his wife living with her, her daughter's accountant husband commutes, and her second son helps the first son. In this case, succession is not just in business, but in religion as well: all the children and children-in-law are converts to Sokagakkai, Kazuko's husband's faith. Harue, whose husband heads a construction material company, has also secured two sons-in-law, as successor and associate respectively, in business. A son-in-law may replace one's husband before the latter dies: Fuyuko has formed an alliance with her daughter's husband in running the house business, thus "promoting" her own husband, the originator of the business, to *"goinkyo-san"* (honorable retiree).

When the woman contemplates her responsibility for securing a successor, her son's "brilliant" career begins to look double-edged. Yoshimi did not expect her son to quit his career as an electronics engineer at a large corporation and was pleased with his success, but just recently she has begun to regret that she did not keep him with her to succeed to the house's business. She considers herself a failure in this respect.

A daughter-in-law could be a successor in business. Yaeko first planned to have her adopted son continue her beauty shop since she is a believer in the superiority of a male hairdresser. The son did not go along, so Yaeko searched for a bride for him who would be a successor. To her pleasure, this plan worked out.

For women, the *ie* succession also refers to the transmission of the domestic culture. When the woman comes into the position to teach the domestic tradition to her daughter-in-law, she becomes sensitized to the multigenerational chain of transmission. She begins to recall and reappreciate what her own mother or mother-in-law has taught her and feels responsible for handing it down to her daughter-in-law. As a key person in this chain, she identifies herself both with her late mother-in-law and with her successor daughter-in-law. She finds a mirror image of the former in her present self, and that of the latter in her younger self, and is emotionally moved by this chain of generational cycles.

Ayano is the best informant in articulating the affinally linked three generations of women:

> The in-law relationship is stronger than blood parenthood. Many aspects of Grandma [mother-in-law] are living within me. Uneducated, but she knew many proverbs. "One who does not appear to concern you actually does [*yō naki mono ni yō ari*]," she would say. She meant, you never know who your granddaughter is to marry, who is to be your grandson's wife, and therefore you should never be unfriendly to anybody. When you are about to go to bed at night, she would say, "Hard at night, then easy in the morning [*yoi no shinku asa no raku*]." Finish the work at night, says the lesson, however painful, so that you will have an easy time next morning. I repeated these proverbs to my daughter-in-law, and have found them living on in her. "Mother," she says, "as you told me, I finish up everything at night. Indeed, it's easy in the morning. *Yoi no shinku asa no raku*, isn't it?" So I say to her, "How nice! Now that all these have been transmitted to you, Grandma has finally come to bloom."

Again, not all mothers-in-law are so lucky or confident. A college-graduated daughter-in-law or daughter is so fussy that the granny is frightened to touch her grandchild. A circle of grannies, while busily moving their hands processing fish in their part-time work, all agreed that they preferred this work to caring for their grandchildren primarily because they were disqualified as child caretakers in the eyes of their daughters-in-law. Generational discontinuities seem keenly felt; the daughter-in-law instead of the mother-in-law seems to reign over the household, forcing the mother-in-law to be a loser to both the ascending and descending generations; an aged mother complains about her son having lost filial piety under his wife's influence; the *ie* is on the verge of extinction. A *mukoyōshi* son-in-law may threaten to break up the integrity of *ie*. Yone, upon her husband's death, was confronted with the outrageous demand of her *mukoyōshi* son-in-law for an immediate transfer of property to him. Stunned and enraged, the widow ousted this "impudent" *muko* from the successor status and severed the parent-child bonds. This meant the loss of her daughter, who stayed with her expelled husband. The property was divided in accordance with a court ruling. Yone now turned to her younger daughter already married out, and told her to return home to replace her elder sister, and if her husband refused to come along, to divorce him. To the surprise of both mother and daughter, the husband, a national civil servant, agreed to quit his secure job and to join his wife and mother-in-law. The two generations, thus reconstituted, live together harmoniously. Yone has not forgotten her elder daughter, however, and talks about her tearfully while still furious at her former son-in-law. Many mothers are less self-assertive. Eager to be accepted by the younger generation, and hesitant to overburden the successor, some mothers or mothers-in-law also express their indifference to the conservation of the *ie* legacy.

## KIN GROUPING

In the course of generational turnover, the senior woman is called upon to participate in the activities of kin groups (*dōzoku, shinseki*) with increasing frequency. As the members of older and peer generations diminish and are replaced by those of younger generations, the domestic identity expands beyond primary kinship.

*Death rites.* Most important of all such activities are funerals and death anniversary rites, where the host's kin comprise the core participants. While males play formal leadership roles, females perform indispensable functions. The death anniversary rite in which I participated in 1977 was a picturesque example of sex-role polarization. This particular rite, incidentally, combined several death anniversaries, as often happens for the sake of expediency: the fiftieth death anniversary of the host's grandparents, the thirty-third of his war-dead brother, and the twenty-fifth of his father. In the main hall of the temple, men and women were seated on opposite sides facing each other, segregated by the central space where the priests sat. Female attendants outnumbered the males two to one, totaling roughly fifty. Before the ceremony started, women greeted one another warmly, and chatted, commenting on changes in one another, inquiring about one another's family, expressing condolences for family losses, and so on. They were excited and looked rejuvenated by this reunion. The whole sector of women was thus full of lively sounds and voices. The men's sector was contrasting. Each attendant nodded his head slightly toward anyone who came in and sat down, but otherwise remained by himself without talking to others. As if to avoid being embarrassed by looking at one another, they looked upward or downward to signal that they were out of communication. Utter quietude prevailed on that side.

The ceremony began with the head priest's sutra recitation. It consisted, moreover, primarily of the endless chanting of more sutras by the priests, as joined by some women, and each attendant stepping forward in turn to offer silent prayer and burn incense in front of the altar. The whole procedure was perfunctory, unemotional, and boring; a break came, however, when a group of several women, by prearrangement, began to sing hymns on death. The words, melodies, and their voices sounded so sad that many participants, especially the closest female kin of the dead, became deeply moved and sobbed. I saw in these hymn singers a Japanese version of "wailers." It was clear to everybody present that this was the climax of the ceremony. In my view, this observation confirmed the assumption that women perform a primary role in maintaining and reactivating the human, emotional bond of kinship; they see a more social and emotional than a ritual and obligatory function in the ceremonial rites.

*Status in the kin group.* Aging is a process of climbing upward in kinship status for women as well as men. Emi, a widow of seventy-one, finds herself at the top of the *dōzoku* hierarchy, heading the *sōhonke* (the super-*honke*) in command of several *bunke*, and many *mago-bunke* (sub-*bunke*) (p. 22). This does not mean that all the satellite households will rush over to render aid whenever she needs it, but it does mean, to her satisfaction, that her eminence is confirmed by the seat arrangement in a ceremonylike death anniversary.

As the woman is blessed with children, grandchildren, and great-grandchildren, she becomes the focal point of kin solidarity and reunion. Not bound by traditional customs like death anniversaries, younger generations may plan reunions on behalf of the old grandma on her birthday, Mother's Day, or New Year's. Such a gathering is the greatest pleasure for Ai, who has nine living children, eighteen grandchildren, and eight great-grandchildren. To this figure, their spouses must be added. Fusa's offspring have formally organized an association to gather annually around her. The senior woman's top status is sustained by the appreciation and gratitude her offspring hold for the "long years" of her "hardship" and "suffering."

This privilege cannot be enjoyed by a childless widow. The funeral or other death rituals for a husband may occasion a dispute over property inheritance, as happened to two childless widows in the local sample. Toshiko never suspected her siblings-in-law to be so greedy until the forty-ninth-day mortuary rite for her husband. A younger brother, backed by the *shinseki*, demanded that the entire estate be "returned" to him, in total disregard of her "wifely right" and of the fact that she had earned and contributed "a lot" to the estate. This led to a lawsuit which dragged on for three years, costing her as much as 15 million yen in total. With a child, she would not have faced such a problem; childless, she was still looked upon as an outsider to her husband's family. This tragedy would have also been avoided if her husband had left a will, but he was one of a typical sort of Japanese who is unconcerned with such matters, a reflection of the cultural habit of accepting the *ie* legacy as a supraindividual entity.

## Extradomestic Engagements

Although domestic roles never come to an end, they do undergo some atrophy, primarily because of the children's maturation. The time, energy, and interest thus left to a woman are now devoted to extradomestic curricula. Not that women have had no extradomestic engagements earlier, but for most this is the time to intensify or resume such activities or to expand their old repertoires.

### Age-Peer Grouping

One of the most conspicuous phenomena in present-day Japan is age-peer grouping among middle-aged to elderly women.[2] Grouping varies in size, frequency of meeting, purposes, recruitment fields, and so on. Some groups are more formal and planned while others are more informal and spontaneous. Locally, the largest formal group is the *fujinkai* (women's association), organized through the reticulated neighborhood network and assisted by the city government. My informants tend to believe that a woman in her thirties and early forties is still busy as a PTA member, but that around her mid-forties she "graduates" to join the *fujinkai*. Most women at this or a later stage are, if not active, at least "nominal" dues-paying members. Around age sixty-five, the woman is likely to switch to the next age-group, *rōjinkai*, sometimes called *rōjin*-club (the association of the elderly), which is also organized by neighborhood units and financially and otherwise assisted by the government. The *rōjinkai* is heterosexual, though the longer-living women constitute a majority. Underlying the avoidance of simultaneous membership in more than one such group organized by the neighborhood principle is the idea that one household should be represented by one person. By the time the woman reaches sixty-five, her daughter-in-law may be ready to join the *fujinkai* as a "successor," requiring the senior woman to move into the *rōjinkai*. Note that in both the *fujinkai* and *rōjinkai* the local government is involved, as much as in the *chōnaikai* and *tonarigumi*. We have noted that a neighborhood group which appears spontaneous and "natural" is actually sustained by governmental authority and planning. What Ai said about the *rōjinkai* she belongs to is suggestive of this point: "You think you know everybody in your neighborhood, but I discovered I did not know some. Only when I joined the *rōjinkai*, I came to know them. We now greet each other."

Partially overlapping with the neighborhood grouping is the school affiliation which is mobilized for reunion in later years. Generally, both men and women begin in their forties to show more interest in alumni reunions. Women in particular form intimate groups of several former classmates, exchange telephone calls, and get together periodically.

The preservation or reactivation of "alumni identity" is not limited to one's school affiliation, but extends to occupational ties. Retirees from the same work place, whether co-workers, employer and employees, may form a sort of "alumni club"; Ayano, a career kindergarten teacher, now retired, has a group of other retirees—*senpai* and *kōhai*—meet in her house weekly. As mentioned in chapter 5, PTA retirees also continue to meet, no longer for their children but for themselves.

The activities of these and many other groups vary from dining and cathartic conversation to pursuit of hobbies or "studies" (music and dance, Buddhist hymns, calligraphy and painting, composition of haiku and *waka* poems, reading *The Tale of Genji*, tea ceremony, flower arrangement, leather handicraft, weaving, dyeing, carving, ceramics, plant growing, etc.). The government-initiated programs in particular tend to involve serious studies or "seminars" on such topics as food poisoning, the conflict of mother-in-law and daughter-in-law. Some belonging to nontraditional sects like Reiyūkai and Seichō-no-ie attend weekly or monthly branch meetings for rituals and study. Nor are athletic activities such as jogging and bowling entirely lacking. These activities crystallize into some form of product or performance to be exhibited to the public annually or more often. The *fujinkai* members, for example, entertain the *rōjinkai* members by displaying their repertoire of folk dances and songs on stage on the Revere-the-Elderly Day.

Sociability is a main motivation underlying these activities. Among other motivations are: wishes for emotional self-sufficiency to avoid being a burden on the family; diversion from routine domesticity; intellectual exercise to avoid senility; aspirations to recapture student days lost to the war; to master a skill and thereby, hopefully, to attain eminence (for example, having one's haiku published in a haiku club's magazine); to enjoy teaching one's peers in some art; to serve the community. Many informants regard these activities and group participation as their *ikigai*.

The following is a summary of three group meetings. The intention in describing them is to offer a flavor of what goes on in such a group.

*Diversion: A fujinkai group tour.* Traveling is the best diversion, and almost every group in Japan conducts an annual or semiannual trip as an essential part of the organizational plan. I participated in a five-day tour to northern Honshu along with about 120 women of the local *fujinkai*. Except for the initial and final parts of the trip, which were train rides, traveling was by bus: each morning, three buses swallowed all the participants, kept them all day, and released them into a hotel in the evening.

The first thing that struck me was the presence of (1) *neighborhood cliques*. While the *fujinkai* is a citywide organization linked hierarchically to higher levels, a strong solidarity was observed within a smaller unit, generally coterminous with the *chōnaikai* boundary. From the very beginning, when the co-travelers got on a train, I encountered unusual excitement over seating. Since only four could be seated in a booth, a five-member clique suffered a painful split. Seating arrangements in a bus, train, or dining room, and the assignment of hotel rooms were of great concern for both leaders and the rank and file. Though most of these were prearranged, there was always something unexpected. Once, two women were assigned to our room, which made them unhappy at being cut off from their group and at the same time guilty for intruding upon the privacy of our four-person group. They sat in a corner, quiet, reserved, and downcast. I was told that if one member of such a group decides not to join the trip, the rest tend to follow suit.

This clique segmentation was prevented, however, from disrupting the whole enterprise by the willing submission to (2) *regimentation*. The 120 women behaved almost exactly as expected whenever total group cooperation was required. Punctuality was one example. The time for departure from the hotel, for meals, for taking baths, and so on was rigidly kept. During supper, when we all met in a vast banquet room, almost everyone posed as an eager audience for stage shows, clapping hands (which kept them from eating), even though many were clearly bored. I could not imagine an American submitting to this degree of control.

The main purpose of the trip lay in recreation. To fulfill this purpose, the trip exhibited (3) a *liminal phase*, or what might be called counter-routine behavior. Raising the noise level was one such characteristic. The whole trip was, except for sleeping periods, an uninterrupted concatenation of noise, which would surprise those who hold a stereotype of quiet, reserved Japanese womanhood. The noise level reached maximum during the bus ride and suppertime. Most participants seemed to enjoy the noisy exchanges more than the sight-seeing: the bus guide's microphoned announcements and singing; riders' teasing of the young female guide; rotational or joint singing (or screaming) of folk songs, *shigin* (chanting famous poems composed in a Chinese style), and "pops"; listeners keeping rhythm by clapping hands or synchronized utterances; the guide teaching songs which were repeated over and over by the learners; exchange of jokes and loud laughter. At suppertime, the dance-and-song performances by hotel personnel, local folk-song groups, and the travelers were blasted through the PA system. I imagined these women to be "noiseholics," and sure enough, a couple of women who became sick during the bus ride recovered when the time came for joint singing. Obviously, noise was symbolic of a "good time."

One bus contained about forty passengers. In the course of co-riding a mini social evolution took place, differentiating primary performers from auxiliary performers and from passive audience. Performance eventually evolved into a one-woman show, reducing the rest to an appreciative, chuckling audience. This woman specialized in making erotic jokes and singing obscene songs which made the listeners laugh to their hearts' content. The songs referred bluntly to sex organs and copulation. Meanwhile, a candy which was shaped like a female sex organ was passed around. The joker then challenged the blushing guide:

Joker:   Listen, Miss Guide. This year our group of *fujinkai* took a trip to Jindaiji Temple. At its shop we found something called "Not to be told or shown to anybody else" [*hito ni yūnayo, miseru ja nai*]. I bought one. . . . What do you think I found there? . . . I bet you don't know. Okay, I'll let you know. Man and woman were sleeping.

Guide:   You saw dolls?

Joker:   Not dolls. Man's thing and woman's thing—the most important things. . . . I put it away in a secret place. If you want to see it, I will let you.

Another lewd joke went: "My birthplace is Ōhara-ken [Big-belly prefecture], Hesohita-gun [Below-navel county], Kemoja-mura [Hairy village], Tane Sanbanchi [Male-seed number three], Irereba Chinbee Kata [c/o Mr. If-penis-penetrates], Kimochi Yosaburo [Then-follows-ecstasy house]."

The bus driver and travel agent, the only males in the bus, were addressed primarily as sex objects.

Such obscenity is prohibited in the woman's domestic life. In fact, the above joker turned back into a straight, humorless housewife every time she got out of the bus; when I saw her again back home, I found her mindful of etiquette and modesty. Obscenity is another symbol of a temporary "good time." Also I could not help reading into this behavior of women—either as performer or laughing audience—the sexual inhibition and frustration imposed upon their domestic life-style. In the traveling "communitas" (Turner 1969) composed exclusively of later-year women, they could entertain themselves with what would be considered a male prerogative—raucous obscenity.[3]

A few more minor points of observation may be added. Bus riders occasionally engaged in childish games such as guessing the number of oncoming cars, guessing the total ages of the guide, driver, and the travel agent, and so on. Constant eating and food sharing was another striking feature. Each woman brought a variety of candies from home, and after consuming them they bought more at bus stops. All food was shared with neighboring riders, thus triggering an endless chain of reciprocity. Whenever there was no noise and no food to share, I found that most women were sound asleep, paying no attention to scenic views. Some admitted that this was the once-in-a-year chance for them to sleep freely in the day time. All these regressive characteristics of behavior seem part of the liminal phase.

Gift shopping is another feature. At every bus stop and hotel, the travelers rushed to buy gifts for their grandchildren, husbands, neighbors, nonparticipating *fujinkai* members, occupational associates, and customers, but nothing for themselves. Many talked about the stupidity of "us Japanese" being so concerned about gifts, and yet continued to buy until there was no space left in the bus. My impression was that gift shopping was the only occasion for the traveler to think about her home and family; it looked as if they were trying, by their extravagent buying, to redeem their guilt for enjoying this extraordinary diversion.

*Endeavors in self-improvement: a haiku meeting.* Along with diversions like traveling, groups of women engage in studies or in serious endeavors to improve themselves. The haiku meeting to be described here demonstrates such sober commitments. Walking toward the *sensei*'s house, the woman who had agreed to introduce me to the group stopped here and there to remind me of certain plants on the wayside as important for the world of haiku. The group is called Matsu-no-kai (a pseudonym, meaning the Pine tree club), and publishes a magazine, *Matsu*, to which the members contribute. The local chapter of this club meets in a different place every Friday. This time it was at the *sensei*'s residence, which is located on a hill in rural surroundings. At the house, my introducer and other members first went to the kitchen to present gifts to the *sensei*'s wife. In the main room, several women were seated around a table guessing the name of the plant floating in a jar which contained *medaka*, killifish, that day's theme. Two other women were gazing at garden plants, seriously trying to compose haiku phrases. One woman called my attention to a painting by a famous artist hanging on the wall. Everybody was serious by now, either looking at something, consulting a dictionary, or gazing into space. Faces were intent. No chatting.

The *sensei*'s wife brought in bowls of *yamamomo* (a wild fruit rarely found nowadays) which had been presented by a member, and suggested that it be eaten before haiku were composed about it. They then turned to the subject of *yamamomo*, all excited, and reflected about what things used to be like in the olden days. One remarked it would be difficult to make a haiku out of *yamamomo* only. Small slips of paper, *tanzaku*, were distributed; a question was raised about how to write the characters for *yamamomo*, and the answer given. By now eight women, ranging in age between the late fifties and late seventies, were present with the *sensei*, the only male, in the top seat. A woman remarked that "*natsukashii*" (fondly recalled) would be too commonplace a word to refer to the *yamamomo*. Another asked how to express "When the rainy season is over," to which the *sensei* answered, "Why not as is?" Attention was concentrated upon two things: *medaka* and *yamamomo*. Total silence. The *sensei* also was writing on the *tanzaku*, with his head bent over so that his near-sighted eyes almost touched on it. After one hour or so, the *sensei* asked, "Do you need more time, Fumie-san, Sumiko-san . . .?" The single-minded students did not even respond. One of them uttered, "I have given up on *yamamomo*, rather will concentrate on *medaka* since they move." Suddenly, the *fūrin* (windbell) tinkled and made all exclaim, "What a nice sound!" Then drum beating was heard, indicating that a group of young men nearby was practicing for the forthcoming ward festival. This triggered questions about festivals.

To an outsider or newcomer, the above sequence of utterances and actions would appear too fragmented to make any sense; but this behavior only demonstrated how well the students had internalized the lesson that a haiku composer should be keenly alert to every stimulus, however fleeting, from the surroundings.

Everybody finished writing ten haiku, each on one *tanzaku*, without identifying the composer. First, the *sensei* threw his completed slips into the basket, and the students followed him. One waited until last, commenting, "The sooner you put it in, the poorer the chance to win." The *sensei* called his wife, saying, "Ready!" The wife came in, shuffled the collected slips, and redistributed them to the authors at random, ten for each. A random collection of ten haiku was then copied by each participant on a single sheet of paper carefully to be passed on from one reader to the next. Through copying another's haiku writing, one came to learn new Chinese characters and beautiful penmanship. While circulating the completed sheets, the readers were supposed to select the ten very best haiku and write them down again, this time with the selector's name. Those who completed this task early began to chat, relaxing for the first time. A leading member read aloud one haiku after another from each list of selection, interrupted each time by the disclosure of authorship by the author herself. No counting was made and yet it was clear to everybody who won more than who. The *sensei's* selection weighted heaviest and was listened to most attentively; those whose poems were included in the *sensei's* list looked genuinely pleased and proud. The woman who had one of her poems selected by nearly all was praised and it was suggested by the leading member that she send that haiku in to *Matsu* for publication. Humbly, she denied that it was that good, but agreed to send it in.

After this climax, the *sensei* gave a lecture emphasizing the importance of faithful description of whatever is perceived without imposing one's preconceptions and ideas. Also he advised the audience to use correct Chinese characters. The same lecture must have been given many times before because the students began to show boredom and chat among themselves before the *sensei* was finished. The meeting ended with relaxed conversation over tea and cake. The sense of fulfillment after several hours of tension and endeavor was discernible on everyone's face.

*Organized aging: a* Rōjinkai *meeting.* While the *rōjinkai* groups are assisted by national and local governments, their meetings are conducted by the members themselves and their leaders emphasize the autonomy of age peers. The limitation of the aged in attention span and tolerance interferes with the programs, and yet, compared with the meetings of senior citizens' clubs I have seen in the United States, the Japanese *rōjinkai* exhibited more group discipline. The meeting I witnessed was of the group known as one of the best organized *rōjinkai* in Shizumi. It was one of the monthly meetings, held in a tatami-matted room of the community hall belonging to the *chōnaikai*. The sex ratio of participants—eighteen males and seventeen females—was unusual, and this relative overrepresentation of males is taken by many, including women, as the secret of the success of this group. Most of the male attendants were still married but did not bring their wives, "Because my wife is interested in other things" or "It would be embarrassing for both of us to attend." Female participants were mostly widowed. The age range was estimated as from the late sixties to the early eighties. Displayed on a blackboard in front was the meeting's program, above which hung the national flag with its rising sun. On a side wall were two banners with the words to the club song and the club's oath brush written on them.

The president introduced a new member who had brought sake and candy as an admission gift; he then introduced me. A leader signaled in a commanding tone and the attendants stood up, bowed to the flag, sang the national anthem in tune with an organ played by another leader, recited the oath, sang the *rōjin*-club song, and did a standardized exercise *(rajio taisō)* to a tape-recorded rhythm. Every action was in unison.

This regimented performance lasted for over an hour, and afterward these elderly people, exhausted, were allowed to sit down. The president announced the members who had received awards on the latest Revere-the-Elderly Day. The named man and woman stepped forward to receive the group's gifts to them, frames for their awards. By this time some members, especially women, had lost interest. The president then read aloud the certificate of commendation given to this group on the same Revere-the-Elderly Day. This was followed by a series of reports and announcements including those on: the forthcoming tournament in folk songs and folk dances sponsored by the citywide *rōjinkai* organization; a planned trip to stay at a local inn overnight, which triggered lively discussion on such problems as "how to encourage more members to join the trip"; the coming athletic meeting *(undō-kai)* of the city's *rōjinkai*, where each member was assigned to one race; cleaning up of the *chōnaikai* park (at this point a leader warned that everybody be aware of the fact that I was going to report to "all Americans" what was going on in this group—he was deeply concerned with the way the members' behavior might have appeared to me); the Tokyo trip taken recently by some members, covering the Imperial Palace, Diet Building, and Yasukuni Shrine. The last point stimulated a member to open up the question of whether Yasukuni Shrine (for the war dead) should not be recognized as a national shrine as it had once been, but the question was ignored. Unexpectedly, the president then turned to me, asking me to give a speech. My talk about older Japanese and older Americans did not receive a standing ovation. Throughout the meeting, several men, but no women, were taking notes.

The formal part of the meeting was over. Women distributed candy and drinks, which signaled the attendants to break up into smaller groups for intimate, relaxed chatting. A few men became drunk. In the midst of this, the accounting officer stood up and forcefully declared his resignation from that office. It should be staffed by new personnel, he said, for the interest of the group. It later turned out that he was upset that, despite his effort to reduce the hotel charge, the turnout for the club trip had been smaller than expected. The resignation was his retaliation.

Women, quiet so far, spontaneously started to sing folk songs. This "private" singing was followed by a long interval of regimented group singing meant to be more educational than recreational. The singing was joined in by all and led by a man. Three leaders kept singing tirelessly after everybody else was exhausted into silence.

The three-and-a-half-hour meeting was over, but the participants in the coming folk dance tournament stayed on to practice. A leader, watching the practice, encouraged them, "Well done! Keep going!"

In a meeting like this where sexes are mixed, exclusive male leadership stands out. Generally there tends to be more role differentiation in a mixed group than in a segregated female group, but I came to realize that this could not be attributed entirely to sex-role typing. Among male participants, there is a clear distinction between leaders and followers —much more so than in a women's group. Leadership derives from occupational expertise. The leaders in the observed *rōjinkai* group were retired school teachers and a former official of the prewar Ministry of the Interior. Another local *rōjinkai* group, also known as a model for other groups, is led by a retired career naval officer. Obviously, as an extension of their occupational status or competence, these men can lead the followers as if they were schoolchildren, docile citizens, or subordinates. Hence, I am inclined to generalize that a heterosexual or exclusively male group tends to evolve hierarchy and leadership primarily as a result of the differentiation among men of professionally developed attributes and capabilities, whereas a female group is more egalitarian because of the relative uniformity of domestic roles.

A few more observations of age-peer grouping may be added. All the groups I have observed were more or less diffuse in their purposes. Even a study group like Matsu-no-kai engages in group trips and plays. On the other hand, an apparently play-oriented group turns out to be study-minded, as indicated by such group names as "Minyō kyōshitsu" (Folk song class) or "Tenisu kyōshitsu" (Tennis class). There is a general tendency to stress an educational purpose either in actuality or appearance, probably because Japanese, women in particular, are compelled to justify any activity other than work as something beyond pleasure. Even travel is often designated *"kenshū ryokō"* (study tour), which explains why Japanese travelers are an eager audience to the travel guide's "teaching." Among educational purposes one witnesses the curriculum of spiritual education or character development. In a cooking class, for example, sponsored by the *fujinkai* and attended by roughly one hundred fifty middle-aged or older women, the male lecturer scolded a woman for chatting and told her either to listen or leave, which frightened the whole class into dead silence and attentiveness. He then went on to talk about his mother who, though uneducated, had instructed him not to tell lies—the lesson to which he owed, he believed, his success as a teacher and author in culinary art. The women received a full dose of moral education on filial piety. Half the class hour had been spent already, but nothing on cooking. When finally he came to cooking itself, he prefaced his lecture by saying that the most important clues to good cooking are upright posture, cleaning the kitchen quickly, and keeping the utensils clean. The women listened, nodding their heads in agreement.

### Public Recognition and Leadership

A woman at this life stage has accumulated social capital, acquires recognition for her ability and influence, and may assume leadership in the public domain, though in a less visible or formal way than in the case of a man.

*Backstage leadership.* While the *tonarigumi* headship is taken by every household in rotation, a higher-level leadership such as *chōnaikai* head is elected. As a man matures in his career, he is likely to be elected *chōnaikai-chō* or *ku-chō* (*chō* referring to head or leader), and then might run for a formal political office like the city assembly. In the course of further promotion in seniority status and retirement, he may be asked to be *ujiko sōdai* (leader of a ward's Shinto shrine congregation), and finally *danka sōdai* (leader of a Buddhist temple congregation). All this means that it is often his wife who, as his support staff, performs routine tasks in contacting the constituent member households, not only because the husband may be too busy with more important matters but also because the wife has become an expert in neighborhood management. Sometimes the wife's role is so important that the constituent members may first ask her to accept such leadership, and she may accept or reject it without consulting the husband, the leader in name. Among the most important activities of the local neighborhood communities are funerals and Shinto festivals. On both occasions, women are mobilized for backstage service, mainly for kitchen work. An elderly woman or the wife of a community leader must lead a group of women thus gathered.

More informally, younger women come to consult older, experienced women on a variety of personal problems. My informants accept such a consultant role as a sign of recognition and honor. Asked when they felt they had achieved *ichinimae* status, most women modestly denied they had yet attained it, but one said, "When people began to come to me for consultation [*sōdan*]."

*Marriage mediation.* This last point brings us to the woman's leadership in matching marriage candidates, for one of the most common problems for consultation is that of marriage. To be solicited to introduce a marriage candidate is certainly an honor for many women as it demonstrates a recognition of their "wide face" (*kao ga hiroi*—widely known), particularly among "good" people, as well as of their sound judgment. Indeed, the number of couples that have emerged through one's arrangement is a measure of one's maturity and reputation. One elderly woman would point to this couple and that couple as products of her arrangement (*matometa*) in much the same manner as a male contractor points to a highrise building as his creation.

Involvement in matchmaking may snowball. As a woman establishes herself as a successful matchmaker, more people will come for her help, which will result in a still greater number of applications since by now she has enough applicants to match one another instead of looking for other candidates. Toshiko is a good example. Having been a Tokyo resident, coming from a distinguished family, and skilled in social brokerage as part of her business, she began to "help" local residents. "I don't know why, but more and more people came over, believing I have a stock of candidates at hand." Now she has at least thirty applications at any given time. She is in a strategic position to link sons and daughters of prominent local families to those in Tokyo. In her talk, Toshiko referred frequently to outstanding people (e.g., hospital proprietor, foreign-university lecturer, Todai president, Kyoto University professor, Mitsubishi company vice-president, a "top man" in the business world, "coming from a Tokugawa vassal family") as fathers or uncles of the candidates or as candidates themselves whom she had handled. Just before my visit she had finished a one-hour telephone call in an attempt to match "an astronomer and son of a Todai professor with a Columbia University graduate." This claim was confirmed by a neighbor saying, "Mrs. Takeda knows so many prominent people, and we all ask her to find brides and grooms." The applicants are no longer limited to Toshiko's acquaintances. Strangers submit their pictures, vitae, and desirable qualifications of prospective mates, and Toshiko manages to match them by phone, without bothering to meet them. Obviously this is a business bringing her income, although she claims it is her "community service" or "mission."

To many women, a more important prestige lender than actual matchmaking is to be asked to be a ceremonial mediator (*tanomare nakōdo*). Admittedly, the husband's status counts most, but the wife still shares the honor fully.

*Keeper of social order.* A senior woman naturally identifies herself more with the existing social order in which her life has been invested than does a junior woman, and may try to exercise her influence to maintain that order. Being a consultant or marriage arranger gives her a legitimate opportunity to control younger people. Emi, who has matched twenty-five couples, is often asked to be an arbitrator for a quarreling couple. She tells them of her own regrets about having left her children with her divorced husband, to advise them against divorce. A daughter-in-law may be kept in her place under the influence of an elderly neighbor woman, although no informant explicitly admitted to playing such a role herself. A seventy-three-year-old widow has a number of her peers gather in her house regularly to chat over "such things as how to handle a daughter-in-law" and to criticize one another for being "too lenient" or "too strict." Typical gossip refers to "a lucky granny waited upon by her nice daughter-in-law" or to a household intimidated by a "bossy" daughter-in-law.

A senior neighbor woman's interference may get out of hand. When a neighbor friend praised her own daughter-in-law as "too good for my son," an informant in her mid-fifties said to her, "Don't be silly. How can you say that? She came because of your son." The informant warned the neighbor that with that kind of attitude, there would be trouble in that family soon. "As soon as a child was born, that *yome-san* began to claim her seat." When the child developed a skin eruption, the informant instructed the family on its treatment, but the child's mother resisted. Later, the informant was enraged to learn that the *yome* had left for her natal home because she could not stand the informant's interference. At a loss, the mother-in-law came and timidly asked the informant if she should go and ask the daughter-in-law to come back. " 'Absolutely not,' I said, 'That's the trouble with you. You are so lenient with your *yome-san*, that's why she gets such a big head. Don't ever beg her. Leave her alone until she comes back by herself.' " She also let the friend know that she, the informant, had a stronger voice in the neighbor's family matters because she had lived in the same neighborhood for many, many years, "not like that little bride who came here only yesterday." This incident ended with the young couple leaving the widow for a separate residence. Thus, a neighbor woman's self-appointed role as keeper of order went beyond the mother-in-law's expectation.

Gift-giving is another activity under a senior woman's control and is a way of maintaining social order and the human network. Gifts, as a sort of social currency, are circulated and exchanged to keep the rule of reciprocity alive. The senior woman gives and receives cash gifts as a primary participant in or a host for funerals and death anniversary rites, and the frequency of such occasions increases as she gets older. The reason Yuri refuses to move to Tokyo to live with her son's family is her sense of obligation to preserve the *ie*, which has been handed down "since the Tokugawa era," but this obligation boils down to her compulsion to fulfill all kinds of gift-giving obligations. Most of her pension is spent for this purpose, she said.

*Formal leadership.* In some activities where female participants predominate, women have opportunities to assume formal, frontstage leadership, particularly at a grass roots level of organization. Religion is one such area. In nontraditional sects especially, female leadership is conspicuous. In a branch meeting of the Seichō-no-ie, where a female *sensei* (sent from the headquarters) and six local members—all female —participated, I saw some aggressive leadership by the *shibu-chō* (branch leader) side by side with the *sensei*. A lengthy, repetitious series of rituals and the *sensei*'s lectures were followed by "study" discussion:

Sensei:      What is the purpose of religion?

[Mute Response]

Shibu-chō: Please say whatever you think. Don't worry about giving a wrong answer. . . . We were born with some mission. What is the mission?

Sensei:      This is a study meeting.

Shibu-chō: In order to study, you must not only listen to Sensei but express yourself. . . . How about you, Mrs. Hamada?

Hamada:    Thank you. . . . To improve our soul, isn't it?

Sensei:      That's one of them.

Another member volunteers:    It is to achieve *wa* [harmony].

Sensei:      That's also a wonderful idea.

Shibu-chō: What do you think, Mrs. Yoshioka?

Yoshioka:   I think it is to lead mankind to happiness.

Sensei:      That too.

Shibu-chō: Anything would do. All you have said is right.

Sensei:      To get rid of pain and to give pleasure, that is the real mission of religion.

The *shibu-chō* also took initiative in demanding my view of religion and in proselytizing me.

Mention has been made in chapter 1 of the Gedatsukai, another nontraditional sect, which is headed by elderly women. One of the

women leaders was witnessed giving instructions and reprimands to her
followers, better educated than she. She would then say, "It's not me
who says this, it's a god speaking through me." She was admired by
many for her "inspirational power."

In the mundane world, a woman can be elected the leader of the
*fujinkai* or other women's groups. Also many women, along with men,
are nominated to the local committee of the government-initiated welfare work *(minsei-iin)* and other such unpaid positions to serve as liaisons between the government and the residents. The maintenance of
local residents' welfare, whether it concerns an aged, bedridden person
left alone, a delinquent child, or a husbandless woman with children to
feed, requires that what is going on within each household be moni-
tored, and it is here that women's expertise in neighborhood monitoring
and management is called upon. These women may be called *sensei*.

Community leadership like this also tends to snowball around a
small number of women. My sample includes two such women. Naomi
is not only a *minsei-iin* but holds membership in the Child Welfare
Committee, Personal Problem Counseling Committee, Pension Committee, and Marriage Counseling Committee, all run by the local government or the local agents of the national or prefectural government.
She knows she can throw her weight around in the community, and
feels her talent and disposition really lies in leadership, not in running a
shop as she does. With some marital strain, Naomi looks upon herself as
malelike and pities her husband who "should have married a feminine
woman." Yasu's multiple leadership is based upon her activities as *fujinkai* member and leader. "As you engage in *fujinkai* activities," she says,
"all kinds of titles become attached to you." She held local leadership in
the Tuberculosis Prevention Women's Club, Japan Red Cross Volunteer
Group, Women's Rehabilitation Society. Also she was appointed *minsei-
iin*, Counselor for Mentally Retarded Children, and a member of the
Education Board. Considering all these as services for community welfare, her children call her "Welfare Granny." At her level, Yasu is no
longer a mere leader, but a leader of leaders, concerned with training
new leaders to succeed her generation.

Retired professionals may assume more specialized leadership
based on their career experience. Ayano, as a retired kindergarten
teacher, is invited to give lectures to adult education classes on childrearing. Maki, a retired midwife, takes a supervisory role in monitoring
the health of members of the *rōjinkai*, counseling and checking on their
blood pressures.

So far no mention has been made of politics. My local informants,
including community leaders, are strikingly indifferent to politics. No

one showed any interest in running for political office, and as voters, many said they would usually vote as asked to by kin, neighbors, or friends. The local women do not see much connection between their lives and politics. The only exception is when a local man runs for the National Diet. A businesswoman like Yoshimi gets involved with campaign work, particularly with the effort to increase the registered membership of the candidate's *kōenkai* (support group; see Curtis 1971 for a description of this system). When I returned to Shizumi in 1980, I found Yoshimi active in helping the *jimoto* candidate for the House of Representatives. She was hopeful that the candidate's patron politician, a faction leader of the Liberal Democrats in national politics, would be elected prime minister and would then pick the local candidate as one of the cabinet ministers. "That surely will promise prosperity for this city," which in turn would enhance local businesses including her own. To Yoshimi's disappointment, the candidate was a loser and his *oyabun* politician did not become prime minister.

A striking conservatism indeed! This local group of women may well be contrasted to the urban Japanese "political women" as observed by Pharr (1981) and to the radical women who appear on Japanese TV. At the same time, however, the local conservatism does reflect the postwar history of national politics wherein the Liberal Democratic party has maintained its supremacy.

General indifference to politics corresponds with similar indifference to volunteer work. A few young women like Harumi aside, no one expressed interest in spending leisure time in volunteer work. Most community services and leadership work mentioned above are initiated, guided, or funded by the government. Women's indifference to both politics and volunteer work seems to be rooted in their trust in and reliance upon governmental leadership, their habit of compliance, and their aversion to imposing their own will upon others. Even the leaders stressed how reluctant they were in accepting the requests to take leadership. As a reason for avoiding volunteer work, I was told by a woman that such activity would generate suspicion that you were seeking personal recognition.

## Preparation for Aging and Dying

However successfully a woman lives her later years, she must confront the final phase of life—senescence and death—which may involve the misery of terminal frailty and ailments. The prolonged life expectancy, general affluence and welfare shared by the aged, and some decades of active participation in extradomestic spheres—these blessings make this final transition all the more drastic and tragic. This is the dilemma faced by aging people in contemporary Japan (Lebra 1979b). The fear and misery of this phase is reflected in the suicide rate among older Japanese—particularly among women seventy-five or older, the Japanese had the highest rate in the world as of 1973 (*World Health Statistics Annual 1973*, cited in Koseishō 1976:116–17). While men can rely upon their wives, outliving them, for nursing, women have more reasons to worry.

## PERCEPTION OF THE AGING SELF

The first step of resocialization is to acquire an accurate perception of one's self in terms of the aging or aged status. A woman, like a man, may monitor her aging by using her family as a mirror reflecting her age: the aged husband, middle-aged children, maturing grandchildren and great-grandchildren would compel her to perceive her own age.[4] Exposure to her aged peers tends to be even more devastating. Further, culture provides patterned ways of internalizing one's age identity. In ordinary conversation Japanese ask one another's age, and when two people meet after a long separation one would frankly express his surprise at another having become "so old," "so white," or "so wrinkled," as well as being "still so youthful." Moreover, the age-specific terminology for address is encountered: not only the woman's grandchildren, husband, and all other family members but also outsiders, personally known or unknown, call her "Granny," no longer "Mommy" or "Auntie." Age symbols are further organized into aging ceremonies—in parallel with growth ceremonies like *shichigosan* for children—beginning with the sixty-first (by the old system of counting) year of life, which is called *kanreki* (completion of a life-calendar cycle), followed by seventieth, seventy-seventh, eighty-eighth, and so on. These age-transition ceremonies are celebrations but also are likely to facilitate the central celebrant to accept his/her age.

Aging and dying as a natural process may be learned in anticipation by nursing an old mother or a dying mother-in-law. Indeed, those who have had such experience are more confident than those who have not about their own aging, and have insight into how to be nursed. Bereavement is another occasion for anticipatory resocialization. The woman sees her parent, in-law, or husband die and, with the help of kin and neighbors, takes charge of the corpse (cleansing it, making it up, displaying it to mourning visitors, placing it in a coffin, waiting while cremation goes on, collecting the bones and ashes, etc.), unless she relies upon a professional mortician as is becoming a fad. With an overwhelming sense of the evanescence of life, she may see her turn approaching. Again, the death of her peers, close friends in particular, one after another, is most effective in preparing her for "her turn." When a woman says, "I am the only surviving one in my group," she usually adds, "I am waiting for *omukae* [a messenger from the next world to take her away]."

The woman's own deterioration is another reminder, of course. The menopause might be considered the initial phase of this process, but most of my informants claimed, in retrospect, having passed that transition without any trouble, except for *katakori*, stiff shoulder. Japanese in general, but more females than males, tend to have this problem and consider it as something inevitable. Local informants call it *shijū-kata* (stiff shoulder in the forties) or *gojūkata* (the same in the fifties), as if it were a stage inescapable for every person; hence a high frequency of massage or acupuncture treatments. Some local masseuses combine their "medical" therapy with religious instructions derived from supernatural communication.

The sensori-motor deterioration will eventually progress until the woman, no longer able to keep up social interaction, begins to stay home. With poor hearing, respiratory difficulty, an increasing propensity to trip, and finally paralyzed on one side, Rin at seventy-eight refrains from going out. During the interview, she took three pills, telling me, "This is for blood pressure, this is for calming down my feelings, and this one for my head." Withdrawal from outdoor life does not necessarily mean total "disengagement" (Cumming and Henry 1961). Under usual circumstances, the homebound person is likely to have visitors, perhaps more than when she was still going out, and if sick, even more visitors unless she is senile. A large number of sympathetic visitors would please the aged woman, but also may remind her that her life is coming to an end.

## Dependency Status

An accurate perception of one's own present or coming senescence does not necessarily mean an acceptance of one's dependency status. In reply to the question of what she is going to do when bedridden, a woman's typical response is: a refusal to answer, uneasy embarrassment, the claim that she has never thought about it, wishful prediction that she will die while healthy, or emphatic denial of expecting to be looked after by her children. Underlying these responses of dependency rejection is the reluctance to impose oneself as an unwelcome burden, or *meiwaku*, upon anybody, however helpless one may be. The woman's desire for self-reliance is interlocked with the ethic of *meiwaku* avoidance which she has been inculcated with since her childhood as noted in chapter 2.

Our youthful future-autobiographers share a similar attitude. They project their deaths at ages ranging from eighteen to ninety-three, but in average, at fifty-eight (males at fifty-four, and females at sixty-two), much earlier than the national life expectancy. Most premature deaths are caused by suicide or traffic accidents, and those who are to live beyond sixty tend to die suddenly from heart attack, cerebral apoplexy, and the like without a period of invalidism. These responses reveal their conscious or unconscious wish to skip the dependency period as much as our elderly informants do. Two girls projected the plight of an aged woman: one writing about becoming a nuisance for the children and dying in "ecstacy" at ninety-three, the other assuming the role of a sixty-year-old granny detested by people in the neighborhood before dying. Most Japanese, young and old, seem to have read or seen the film version of Sawako Ariyoshi's *Kōkotsu no hito* (The man in ecstacy), which depicts a victim of senile psychosis. "Going into ecstacy" (losing one's mind) is what they fear most. To die *pokkuri* (abruptly) is a sort of slogan, many old people pray for such luck, and according to the media reports, *pokkuri* temples are thronged with pilgrims. Nor are secular efforts neglected. Kayo, at eighty, keeps active, not only participating in a *rōjinkai* and the Health College led by a ninety-three-year-old former schoolteacher who "still can do *sakadachi* [standing on head]," but also jogging around the neighborhood block each dawn. Her wish is to die *pokkuri*.

Eventually, the granny, once fallen ill, must come under the care of somebody. While reluctant to talk about such expectations, an overwhelming majority of elderly informants seem to take for granted their children's willingness to care for them. Kuniko, a still very active businesswoman at sixty, would rather have a professional nurse, which she can afford, to live with her than bother her daughter-in-law as caretaker; women at their prime tend to opt for some such non-kin caretakers. But if pressed to choose between kin and an institutional care home *(rōjin hōmu)*, every respondent favored the former unequivocally. It is known to local residents that care homes, private or public, are now improving so in their facilities that the old image of a prisonlike *yōrōin* (institution for the aged) should be discarded. They also know, through media reports on care homes abroad as well as personal observation of their friends or distant kin living in such homes, that the best possible facility cannot make the inmates happy. Their aversion to *rōjin hōmu* is demonstrated by the fact that the city's *rōjin hōmu*, with a capacity for fifty inmates and funded by the national government, has failed to attract *jimoto* people; instead, it is filled with "outsiders," namely, recent settlers unknown to most residents.

It came to my attention that this resistance stems not only from the impersonal nature of the care afforded by such homes but from the sense of shame due to the likely publicity about being "abandoned" by their kin. Indeed, entry into a *rōjin hōmu* does mean abandonment in the eyes of locals, and is widely gossiped about. Many people told me of a ninety-four-year-old local woman, now bedridden, in a special public nursing home away from the city. This woman had worked all her life as a midwife, but her son turned out to be a bum. The mother tried to straighten out the household by bringing in a midwife as a bride for her son and successor to her business. Still, the son remained hopeless, and would steal the money that his wife earned. Finally, the wife ousted the delinquent husband, took all the house property into her possession, and stopped caring for the mother-in-law. It was precisely because of the rarity of such abandonment that this gossip circulated extensively.

The association of care home use with abandonment by the family is not unique to local residents. Those "outsider" inmates of the local care home revealed in interview bitter feelings toward their sons and daughters-in-law who had "abandoned" them. "It would be much better," I was told, "if I had no family at all." Truly, those who were really alone with no surviving kin looked less depressed, taking the life in a care home more for granted.

Dependency on one's offspring, specifically one's daughter or daughter-in-law, might be taken as a pay off for one's hard work and sacrifice in bringing up the next generation. But this is not enough for my informants to justify their acceptance of dependency status. The inner pressure to live up to the ideal of such a life-long reciprocity is not strong, especially in the case of a daughter-in-law who owes the mother-in-law only vicariously through the son/husband, unlike a daughter who *was* brought up by the mother. The mother-in-law must continue to work so that the daughter-in-law will really feel indebted. This sort of "bargain" is borne in mind by a number of grannies when they baby-sit their unruly grandchildren or do housework while their daughters-in-law engage in part-time jobs or attend classes. A lonely woman like Toshiko invests in neighborhood interdependency by, for instance, switching her patronage from reputable stores in Tokyo to neighbor shops.

Another way of preparing oneself for accepting dependency status is to act out an exemplary role of caretaker. The women who are nursing their mothers-in-law, some being in "ecstacy," tend to allude to this aspect of their work: "Helping the old people like this involves a sort of religious sentiment—if I work to help them, I might be helped too." The old caretaker is aware of a young, prospective caretaker watching her, hopefully to imitate her one or two decades later. A good rapport established at a later stage between a helpless mother-in-law and a helpful daughter-in-law may be understood in this triadic light with the youngest daughter-in-law as a possible emulator.

The accumulated credit or the memory of an exemplary model may eventually be exhausted or expire, and even a dedicated daughter-in-law may get tired of nursing, as the terminal sickness prolongs. It is common, therefore, for a sick old woman to desire death, even an artificial death. Coresponding with this demand is the general tolerance in Japan for what Americans call "mercy killing." A local doctor confided to me that he had done it three times against his own self-interest—by letting the hopeless patients live on, he could have made a lot of money. His primary concern was not so much for the patients as for their families burdened with nursing care and medical expenses. The Japanese term for euthanasia is *anrakushi* (peaceful death), stressing the dying person's state of mind rather than the "killer's" will.

Dependency on one's offspring for body care may be inevitable, if not desirable, but financial dependency, in my informants' view, must be avoided by all means as if economic autonomy is the minimum condition for self-esteem. At the time of interview, every informant had some source of income; widows and retirees had pensions of various sorts; low-income women at seventy or over were receiving the welfare pensions for the aged without having contributed toward them. This may be a local indication of "the pension age" *(nenkin jidai)*, brought about in the 1970s under the initiative of the national government (Soda and Miura 1980:74–75). My impression is that reliance upon a pension as a means of security in old age has taken deep root among Japanese across classes.

Two views were expressed regarding the welfare pensions.[5] Some receivers complained of the inadequacy of the amount; indeed it was far less than sufficient for minimum livelihood (thirteen thousand five hundred yen [sixty-eight dollars] per month as of 1977). But some others, including a city government employee in charge of the local and of the national pensions systems, pointed out that many of the beneficiaries, in fact being financially supported by their families, were either spending the pension as their allowances or saving it, that is, misusing it. What is important is, it seems, not so much whether one really lives on the pension or not but that a small amount of money affords the elderly woman symbolic autonomy and self-respect. As some of my informants told me, most of the pension goes to buy gifts for grand-children on their *shichigosan*, school admission day, graduation day, and so on. To retain the status of a giver while receiving substantial support from one's children, even though at the expense of public funds, seems to be essential to one's autonomy and mental health.

## OTHER-WORLDY ORIENTATION

The pain of confronting death is mitigated by the cultural recipe for other-worldly salvation, which for Japanese is deeply embedded in the cult of ancestors. The aged woman sustains herself by an intensified identification with the ancestors, or dead members, of the house. She waits for *omukae* to have "reunion" with the dead. No longer is an ancestor an object of worship, but rather the image of the worshipped and that of the worshipper come to overlap. A woman, resistant to coming under the care of her children, openly expects them to "take care of the ancestors" or has already transmitted the role of household priestess to her daughter-in-law, and is gratified to see her grandchildren imitate their mother. Her expectation is for the continued welfare of the ancestors, not for her own, but behind this avowed altruism creeps in an embarrassing insight into her egoistic motivation, since she herself is soon to become an ancestor. Emi is a devout Buddhist and ancestor worshipper (she is praised for faithfully tending her husband's first wife as well), "Probably because," she admitted, "I myself want to be worshipped." It may be that ancestor worship could serve as a culturally available metaphor or euphemism for signaling one's concern for premortem as well as postmortem dependency (Lebra 1979b:345).

An intensified identification with the dead may motivate the bereaved to conduct in a vicarious capacity what the dead would have been doing if alive. Motoko, assuming the role of successor to her dead mother, participates in the festivals of the Konkōkyō, a nontraditional Shinto-affiliated sect of which her mother was a devoted member, although Motoko is not a member herself. "Because that would make Mother happy, I believe," she reasoned. Motoko, uxorilocally married to a *mukoyōshi*, could continue her professional career thanks to her mother's home management.

In the course of a series of postmortem rites, the deceased person is purified and deified as *hotoke* (buddha), which means that whatever undesirable attribute he/she exhibited while in this world is reduced into oblivion. "Dying is a nice thing, isn't it?" says Yasu. "My children remember only good things about their father." Indeed, speaking ill of a dead person is taboo.

Such other-worldly beliefs and expectations may explain why my informants are loquacious regarding postmortem anticipations and at the same time reticent about the prospect of aging. One can understand the Japanese attitude toward euthanasia in this light.

Everything is not over yet even for a woman who is just waiting for other-worldly salvation. She has more to do in preparing for it. If there is any possibility of dispute over inheritance, she must see to it that the house estate will be handed down to a proper successor. One evening Yone discussed this matter with her son-in-law and told him how to divide the estate between her two grown-up grandchildren, apparently in an attempt to protect it from the other son-in-law who had been expelled. Most of my informants have never been titled owners of property, never claimed their right. "Everything that belongs to this *ie*, down to little things like telephones, is in my son's name," says Yoshimi, even though the son with a promising career in Tokyo is unlikely to return home to settle down. Many take pride in transmitting the house property from their fathers-in-law or husbands *directly* to their sons, daughters, or grandchildren. While conceding a little to the postwar civil code prescribing equal inheritance by all the children, they still tend to leave the bulk to a successor son or daughter, or any child who volunteers to stay home and care for the aged parents, which requires a formal renunciation of inheritance right by the other children. In any event, a dispute over inheritance is a scandal which local people would avoid by all means.

In addition to the economic assets, some women try to pass on tokens of their identities to posterity. Sayo, for example, is building up a collection of her brush written haiku, paintings, and handicrafts to be left behind.

The rites for other-worldly salvation are another matter of concern. Although some women dismiss death anniversary rites for themselves as unimportant or unnecessary, few are totally indifferent to the funeral rites. Informants' remarks, however, reflect their social concern, taking a funeral as an occasion for sociability more than for their own other-worldly interest. "I don't want an extravagant funeral. All I want is that all the attendants, some coming from remote areas, will be received well and treated with a feast." Festivity rather than mourning is looked forward to. Yasu wishes her children had been more fertile so that a crowd of her offspring would gather around her coffin. Instructions on how to conduct a funeral, as given to younger coresidents, also indicate the dying instructor's preoccupation with the survivors and attendants. Yone instructed her son-in-law to construct an altar upon her death on the first floor of the house so as to facilitate mourners to come in and out, and the coffin to be moved into a hearse parked a short distance away. Emi, when struck with liver cirrhosis, prepared for an imminent death. With no family in coresidence, she told her room tenants how to prepare for a funeral, whom to notify, and so on. On the forty-ninth day of the postmortem period which ends the uncertain status of the dead (belonging to neither this nor the other world), *dango* (starchy rice balls) should be offered, she instructed them, sutras should be recited, and guests fed. These instructions were to minimize the burden and inconvenience of the funeral hosts and guests. It may be that one's other-worldly salvation is inseparable from one's acceptability in the eyes of funeral participants.

In further preparation for death, one may build a grave for oneself on the compound of the *danka* temple, unless there is already a family grave one can join. Also, the postmortem "eternal care" *(eidai kuyō)* may be purchased in advance, often in response to the temple priest's suggestion or solicitation, by a woman who is alone, is unsure of her offspring's loyalty, or does not want to burden her children. Rin receives an "invitation" from the temple at least once year to make donations. "If I don't give money, I'll become *muen* [a homeless spirit] after death." She also showed me a receipt for two-hundred thousand yen (one thousand dollars) in payment for eternal care.

Self-help for other-worldly salvation may take a more extreme form. Two women in my sample went through a three-day religious training course in Zen temples, at the conclusion of which they were supposedly elevated, through a ritual simulating initiation into a nunnery (feigning head shaving), to the status of Gautama Buddha's disciple and awarded with a posthumous name and status *(kaimyō);* they both showed me the received *kesa* (surplice to be hung around the neck) inscribed with their respective *kaimyō*. Another woman who had done the same informed me to the effect that this practice is so popular that some temples, to process crowds of applicants, now engage in mass production of Buddha's instant disciples: one group of applicants after another line up and go through the ceremony en masse, climaxing in each group standing upon the central altar. "At that moment, you really feel you have become a buddha."

This chapter has covered the last but increasingly extending period of life when a woman, having accumulated experiences, gains retrospective insight into herself, the world, and the whole spectrum of life. This is the time when she, unless she is especially unfortunate, feels rewarded for the long years of hardship and energy investment.

The woman is still busy with her domestic responsibilities, but change has occurred in family relationships. She is in charge of the household unless she has already handed it over to her successor, her daughter or daughter-in-law. If her mother-in-law is still alive there has been status reversal coupled with the senior woman's physical dependency upon the junior woman. Typically, the husband and wife have rediscovered each other as the last companion as they were left alone. There are women still frustrated at this stage with their married lives, some contemplating a postmortem divorce. But by and large the wife or widow is glad she has persevered through the troubled marriage. Not only the living but dead members of the *ie* are cared for by the mature housewife, the custodian of the household altar and mortuary tablets.

Once becoming a mother, the woman does not cease to be one as long as she lives. Some children, now grown up and independent, have turned out well, meeting the mother's expectations and embodying her vicarious achievement. Some others have failed despite a costly educational investment, which makes the regretful mother realize that behind her *kyōiku mama* drive was a selfish urge on her part in disregard of the child's own propensity.

The child's marriage is another great challenge, but this is where the mother can demonstrate her expertise as a life professional. In choosing a husband for a daughter, the mother, at one time a daughter-in-law herself, will try to have the daughter avoid repeating the hardship she has gone through, and may insist on an uxorilocal marriage for her. The uxorilocal marriage is thus variously evaluated depending upon the evaluator's life stage, and most positively appreciated by the mother of a daughter. Quite another standard is applied to a son who will bring in a daughter-in-law for her. It is amusing to listen to a middle-aged woman, resentful of her parents' discrimination against the daughters and of her despotic husband, also admitting that she would hate to see her son pushed around by his wife. Implicit in her worry seems to be the fear that with such a weak son, the mother too will be pushed around by the newcomer. Maternal expertise is further mobilized in helping the daughter-in-law with childbirth, involving intimate body care, and in looking after the grandchildren.

The senior woman now holds a pivotal position in a chain of *ie* succession and comes to realize that the patrilineal principle of *ie* is in fact bolstered by the transmission of domestic culture from woman to woman. If fortunate enough, she will find something continuous in the midst of rapid change through the mother-in-law/self/daughter-in-law link. No longer is the *ie* the oppressor of the woman but something which should or does provide security for her. As older generations die out and younger generations augment, the woman is pushed upward in the kinship hierarchy, and may find herself at the top seat in a *dōzoku* assembly. This underscores the plight of a childless widow who remains an outsider to the *dōzoku*.

The children's independence does reduce the housewife's chores. She now engages in or resumes age-peer activities. Locally, a graduate from a PTA usually joins the women's association, and thereafter the association for the elderly. School affiliations are revived also, and many other study groups are formed and joined. Wherever the sexes are mixed, women at this stage still submit to male authority and leadership. But in an all-women group they relax, enjoy more equality, and, on occasion, feel free to violate the modesty code of femininity.

In the community, the senior woman assumes leadership in relation to the organized activities of the neighborhood, matchmaking, marriage counseling, social-order maintenance, religious proselytizing, and social work. Her qualifications are derived from her accomplishment as a neighborhood monitor and manager.

While thus active in and out of the domestic realm, every person must anticipate or face the tragedy of aging and dying, and this is more so for women than for men since the latter are likely to be cared for by their longer-lived wives. Even though one may perceive one's age identity accurately, the acceptance of one's dependency status is another matter. Even an eighty-year-old woman is disinclined to anticipate her dependency upon a caretaker, kin or non-kin. Hence the *pokkuri* (abrupt) death is a religious slogan among all the elderly. In this "independence" wish, one might detect an internalization of the old norm prescribing the avoidance of being a social burden. While rejecting the status of care recipient, most of the sampled women appear rather sure that they will be, if necessary, looked after by their daughters or daughters-in-law.

The ultimate salvation is embedded in the traditional cult of ancestor worship. The old woman now feels closer to the dead enshrined in the house altar and even looks forward to joining them. The idea of becoming a member of the ancestor group to be cared for by the descendants is indeed likely to mitigate the pain of aging. Even at this phase, one may be obsessed with self-help, as exemplified by the preparation for one's own funeral, the purchase of one's own grave and "eternal care," and the premortem attainment of buddhahood. Such self-help, however, usually goes hand in hand with the expectation that the descending generation will perpetuate ancestor worship.

# 8
## Conclusion

In the preface we raised some questions regarding the images of Japanese women, and the introductory chapter set forth the fourfold objective of this book—Japanese ethnography, sex polarity, life cycle, and self-fullfillment. With these tasks in mind, I shall attempt, first, to capture the main characteristics of *Japanese* life histories as presented in interview. Second, the role repertoire of Japanese *women* will be summarized along the scale of sex polarization and neutralization. Last, the changing life conditions that Japan, like many other countries, is facing today—changes involving women and men, young and old—will be tackled, and possible alternatives will be suggested for directing women to new forms of self-fullfillment.

### *Japanese* LIFE HISTORIES

As stated in the introduction, a comparative reference is necessary to portray something as "Japanese." Throughout this ethnography, I had in mind as such a reference those American women I happened to know. Now this comparison must be made more explicit. Over the years, while studying Japanese women, I have also been collecting written or oral autobiographies from American women—Caucasians living in Hawaii.

The two sets of life histories, Japanese and American, have much in common, reflecting a woman's concerns and role repertoire. What struck me as contrastive was, foremost, the way in which the life experience was recalled and coded. The American narrative tended to describe the recollector herself as the central "figure" at all phases of her life course, relegating everything else to the "ground." The general impression was that the American woman lived as an individual, no more or no less, throughout. This frustrated my intention to capture American social structure out of the individuals' biographies.

Meanwhile, I was learning about Japanese social structure through Japanese life histories. The Japanese woman would recall her experience often by placing herself in the social environment. It often appeared as if she could not begin to describe herself unless framed in interpersonal relationships or groups. The social units that provided frames varied with each autobiographer or by life stages: the natal family, *shinseki* and *dōzoku*, neighborhood, school, class, postmarital household, children's schools, occupational groups, peer groups, and so on. Whatever social units were singled out (or even when a unit was blurred into a "surrounding"), the autobiographers were productive of information on how Japanese social structure operated.

It is not that the Japanese individual always bends her personal will to social expectations or pressures. In fact, some of the life histories are, as shown from time to time in the preceding chapters, marked by the individual's strong determination toward self-fulfillment against social pressures. The point is that, whether in accepting or rejecting a social demand, one's decision or action is coded in such a way as to reflect some aspects of "social structure" or of the "role" which one is supposed to play.

With this experience behind, I interviewed or talked with American women. Particularly with regard to the events involving the woman's life transitions such as college entrance, employment, and marriage, I tried to prompt the interviewees to associate their decisions over these matters with some social concerns or expectations. I was confirmed that the decisions had been entirely their own.

The assertion that the woman has made her decision under no external influence presupposes freedom of choice available to her. Indeed, the American woman's life course appears blessed with a variety of alternatives and options. To state it more correctly, the oral autobiographer puts herself in a position to choose from among a number of alternatives, as if her identity is anchored in such freedom of choice. By contrast, the Japanese autobiographer emphasizes what little choice she had, how she was trapped into a course of action, as we have seen in this book. Her self-esteem seems to derive from the reflection on how she has persevered on a path not of her choice but of necessity. Recall how women, even in the case of love marriage, were trapped into a match under the pressure of the surrounding people. Even in choosing a professional career, anticipatory commitment was exceptional. More common, we found, was a haphazard, cumulative, *zuruzuru* involvement in what has in retrospect turned out to be a career.

It might be argued that the American woman, who presents herself as a free decision maker, has actually lived as restrained a life as a Japanese woman claims she has. Conversely, the Japanese woman, who portrays her life as beyond her control, may have had as much freedom as an American sister. The difference lies, so goes the argument, only in the cultural coding of experience, not necessarily in the experience as such. This argument cannot be totally rejected, since I myself wondered about the informants' exaggerations during interviews. But I must also ask, What is experience other than the coding? The difference in coding, I further believe, will in turn generate or reinforce the difference in the range of "actual" experiences.

Consider the site of domicile, for example, as an index of actual freedom or constraint. The majority of my American informants, young and old, turned out to be constant movers—constant by the Japanese standard. A woman born in Illinois moved to Michigan, Minnesota, Iowa, Arizona, and then to California. Retired and old, the widow again moved to Hawaii, and at interview time she was not sure that Hawaii would be her final "home." (I concede to the possibility that Hawaii attracts "nomadic" Americans more than do Mainland states.)

By contrast, the mobility of Japanese women in the same age range was found to be quite limited—typically only once or twice. Men may be transferred by their employers from place to place, but their wives are likely to stay "home" and the husbands' domiciles will be regarded as temporary. The Japanese sedentism could be partly imputed to Japan's population density, but it might also be traced to the sense of belonging to the house, be it a physical shelter or a symbolic unit like the house register, and to the community surrounding it. The woman, in particular, as a "housewife" seems to carry a sense of obligation to guard the fixed home base. Residential mobility or sedentism may well be taken as a concrete measure for social structure. Sedentism may give the Japanese woman either a sense of unshakable "fate" or that of stability, whereas the life-long "nomadism" may either bless the American woman with a sense of freedom or plague her with that of insecurity and isolation.

The structural embeddedness of the individual life implies the saliency of a triad rather than a dyad as a unit of social grouping. Through triadization, an individual becomes an integral part of social structure, whereas a dyad is likely to form an exclusive, autonomous unit. Illustrative of this is the role of a ceremonial mediator, holding a prestigious position, symbolizes not only a link between the marriage mates but a link between the couple and the community as a whole. Marriage itself is triadic in that it has meant admission of a spouse into a household, into a *dōzoku* or *shinseki*, into a neighborhood, into an occupational group, and so on. The traditional termlessness in addressing a childless spouse is symbolic of the structurally probational status attached to a purely sexual period of marriage.

The interlocking of the individual life history and the surrounding social structure is further demonstrated by the emotional gratifications that a woman derives from social support. Even when she pursues her own career, she tends to stress the pleasure she draws from the people around who benefit from her service, who help and encourage her, and who appreciate her dedication. This ties in with the general tendency of working women, particularly pioneer professionals, to stress their sense of mission to serve the community.

What is ruled out as an unacceptable motive is *wagamama*, selfishness. Even though a woman may be enjoying her career as the best way of fulfilling her personal wishes, this must not be confused with an approval of *wagamama*. Since pure play may be taken as a sign of *wagamama*, Japanese women tend to justify their play by attaching an educational function to it, as we have seen.

How do our informants evaluate their life experiences thus embedded in social structure (as compared with the American counterpart)? Their evaluations are, in a word, ambivalent: both negative and positive. As has been observed, a woman often presents herself as a victim of structural constraint, as a sufferer from her despotic father, promiscuous husband, domineering mother-in-law, as a loser in the patriarchical system, as a victim of the tyrannical *ie* mandate, and so on and so forth. Not infrequently, the interview aroused self-pity and resentment against the sources of the interviewee's frustrations. Several became teary. Some were determined not to have their daughters repeat the same miseries and mistakes. American women, visualized as independent and free, were often envied.

These negative evaluations are oddly mixed with positive ones. The same woman who depicts herself as a victim of the traditional structure turns around to appreciate her hardship as a good lesson, to feel rewarded for having persevered through her wretched marriage instead of following her impulse to divorce, to thank her mother-in-law for having trained her so severely. For the same reason, she takes a dim view of those women, including her own mother in some cases, who have had an easy life, and wishes the younger generation to replicate hardship like hers for their own benefit.

The negative appraisals are understandable, but the positive views need some explanation lest they be dismissed as a masochistic twist. The foregoing chapters have amply shown how a woman drew both frustrations and gratifications from the same source. A woman seemed to build her basis for life enjoyment upon the structural entrenchment she went through. Motherhood is an extreme example. Being a mother means being tied down to that role without respite; even the child-centered Japanese woman complains about the total loss of her autonomy. At the same time motherhood is the most commonly shared basis of satisfaction, *ikigai*, and fulfillment. One cannot choose one and abandon the other, since the hardship of mothering is the very essence of maternal identity.

The double function, negative and positive, of social structure, as it shows up in women's life histories, becomes more understandable if thrown into the life cycle perspective. The structurally entrenched sexual distance of a married couple, for example, may be gradually transformed into a congenial relationship as husband and wife age together. Even the conflict-ridden marriage, as seen in some cases, may evolve into a harmonious one in consequence of long cohabitation. More importantly, the woman's sexual identity, which predominated her earlier life stage, is overshadowed by her maternal preoccupation, from which she derives *ikigai*. Inherent in this cross-generational bonding is the development of a temporal perspective for her identity over and beyond here and now. As she further matures, she goes through a generational turnover whereby she comes to hold a pivotal role as a generalized caretaker for her old parents or parents-in-law as well as her offspring. Thus tied down as she is more heavily than ever, the now mid-aged woman begins to collect the pay off in terms of *ikigai* for her earlier endurance and role investment. The temporal perspective for her identity is further extended as her son marries and brings in her daughter-in-law. As an incumbent of the key position for transmitting the domestic culture from generation to generation, she begins to train her successor. In so doing, she becomes aware of her own image overlapping her mother-in-law's on the one hand, and mirrored in her daughter-in-law on the other. She may try to "recycle" or "counter-recycle" her accumulated experience in her daughter, daughter-in-law, or grandchildren so that the junior woman will repeat or avoid the senior woman's costly experience. The *ie* structure involving this cross-generational succession, which once appeared so oppressive, now becomes the very basis of the woman's security and comfort. Her son and daughter-in-law may refuse to go along, but such a heartbreaking turn of events will only intensify her conviction that tradition should be preserved. The cross-generational bonding, consanguineal or affinal, involves ancestor worship. The increasing identification with the dead and ancestors prepares the woman for her aging and death.

The *mukoyōshi* as part of the *ie* institution is evaluated differently at different life stages. A young daughter may not approve of her mother, married to a *mukoyōshi*, but a bride married to a *mukoyōshi* tends to feel herself lucky, and a mother may encourage her daughters to bring in their husbands instead of leaving her. This does not mean an increasing acceptance of female dominance as one ages. On the contrary, the norm of male dominance is sustained by a middle-aged or older mother. The wife who has suffered under a tyrannical husband may see to it that her daughter will choose a more considerate man for marriage, but when it comes to her son she tends to expect him to assert his male authority toward his wife. Implied here, of course, is the question of whether she, the mother, can control her daughter-in-law through her strong son or whether she will be pushed around by the young woman because of the son's weakness. This way the woman's role cycle repeats itself over generations, and the social structure underlying it is reinforced.

As the time perspective in terms of a cross-generational chain of succession as the structured basis of the woman's identity is extended to the past and future generations, the spatial basis, too, expands. The woman becomes increasingly incorporated into the *dōzoku* and *shinseki* network, age-peer groups, and community. The earlier childrearing activities are replaced by ritual roles, pursuits of studies and hobbies, recreations, community services. Involved here is not only the horizontal expansion of the social frame but vertical mobility in terms of leadership. Though limited and often backstaged, a woman can attain a position of power, leadership, or prestige as she gets older, to the extent that the seniority rule prevails. No longer merely a passive beneficiary of the social order, she may play an active role in maintaining that order.

This is a simplified picture—age does not always bring an expected reward—but it does explain why older women come to appreciate, in retrospect, the traditional structure under which they lived harsh lives. Indeed, living in Japanese society, compared with the American counterpart, has generally meant an accumulation of social capital. A housewife, let alone a working woman, as she circulates socially, builds up a social capital which only increases as she gets older. This may be credited to the Japanese proclivity to perpetuate any social relationship once formed, or to what might be termed the "alumni syndrome." Such relational durability seems to assure the woman's security in that, whenever in need, she can draw upon her "fellow-alumni" for help. Her insistence, by no means uncommon, on self-help vis-à-vis her children often turns out to be based upon the assurance provided by the social fund accumulated around her. The result is that the Japanese individual, in the course of life, becomes an increasingly integral part, and therefore citadel, of social structure. By comparison, the American individual, particularly a nonworking woman, seems to remain a relatively isolated individual no matter how long she has lived.

Nevertheless, the Japanese woman, like everybody else, must face the fate of aging and death, possibly including prolonged senility. The inevitable disengagement will be a blow to a Japanese woman who has thus far expanded her social space. One day, when she gets sick, she encounters an abrupt reversal of life-style—from gregariousness to isolation. The tragedy of aging is manifested by suicidal episodes. If there can be a peaceful way of aging and dying for the Japanese woman, it will be, again, an ultimate sense of lineal bonding both with the ancestors and with the succeeding generations.[1]

## SEX ROLES

The above characterization of Japanese life histories may hold not only for women but for men, though probably to a lesser degree. In this section we shall focus more on women's role repertoire in light of sex polarization and neutralization as defined in the introduction.

*Polarization.* First, let us consider in brief the structural support of polarization involving role specialization, status asymmetry, and segregation. The life histories have shown how the majority of women, especially of prewar and wartime generations, did not question the principle of *role specialization*, but found their primary role and identity in the domestic sphere. Education was geared, foremost, for feminine accomplishments for a wife and mother. Marriage was a necessary step for a woman toward her fulfillment, and in motherhood her personal identity was fused into a mother-child double identity. Though the American woman, too, is generally expected to marry, she can opt, in my impression, for a single career with greater impunity. The stigma of female singlehood in Japan is such that almost every woman over "the marriageable age" is eager to marry even without love. Once married, role division could so sharpen that husband and wife would have nothing in common.

The division of labor is structurally supported not only because this norm is shared by most people, irrespective of sex or age, but also in that the specialized sectors of the public domain of society depend upon it. Schools operate under the assumption that the students' mothers are homemakers always available to the children; companies expect their employees to be looked after by their homebound wives so that they, the husbands, will maintain their full-time or overtime dedication to the companies.

At this juncture, it should be realized that "role specialization" is not an appropriate label for the sexual division of labor. Men, indeed, "specialize" in their jobs, occupations, or work. But the woman's domestic role is characteristically diffuse, unpunctuated, multiple, or generalized. The male-female interdependence, then, is not between two specialized roles but a complementarity between the specialized role and the generalized role. The generalized role involves overall nurturance and body care, as typically supplied by a mother. This was very characteristic not just of the woman's domestic role, but, as seen in chapter 6, of her work assignment in the husband-wife team in the household occupation. It might be speculated that role specialization by one sector of a social system calls for role generalization by another; that the more technical specialization, the more need for overall human caretaking.

The generalized role is handicapped, first, in that it is reduced to a "residual" category consisting of whatever is left over after specialized industries have taken over what was formerly domestic labor. Because of this residual nature, housework is not appreciated as "work." Nonetheless, the housewife cannot enjoy as much leisure as expected, due to a second bind of the generalized role: the housewife cannot plan her work since her work often "emerges" haphazardly in contingency upon the unpredictable need of each family member. Thus, her work has no end; the time she has is the time which can neither be predicted nor scheduled. This imbalance between the specialist male and the generalist female is compounded by the inferiority of the generalized role. This is evidenced by the fact that, while women are assigned to generalized roles in a heterosexual group, in an all-male group such as the military or fishing crew the generalized, caretaking role is relegated to the lower-ranking personnel.

This brings us to *status asymmetry*. The structural embeddedness of sex roles stabilizes and rigidifies the sex-based hierarchy. Social structure as a whole dictates that women be inferior, submissive, more constrained, and more backstaged than men; that they be lower in status, power, autonomy, and role visibility. A man and woman as individuals might prefer to relate to each other in more equal terms or more flexibly, but in public, where the structural pressures for asymmetry are felt, they are likely to act as if the man were superior to the woman. A husband who appears henpecked disturbs a sense of social order and thus invites ridicule from women as well as male peers—hence pressures for onstage patriarchy. In this respect, one can safely assume that the Japanese woman is bound by the norm of sex asymmetry more rigidly than the American woman, who can mobilize her personal resources more freely in interaction with a man. As if to justify the existing asymmetry,

Japanese informants, both male and female, tend to accept the belief that men are smarter, more competent and foresighted.

Polarization by *segregation* is inherent in the structural embeddedness of sex roles in that sexual intimacy is inhibited by the public nature of sex roles. It has been observed, among older informants, that segregation was practiced even in primary schools. One might recall the instance where chaperonage for the daughter was required not so much to protect her as to advertise her seclusion as a bridal candidate. The structurally supplied mediators were necessitated by, and in turn also reinforced, segregation. Reference has been made to the feigned aloofness of a married couple as well. But aloofness was not only feigned in public, but sometimes penetrated the private sphere as was experienced by the frustrated wives who had had no chance to "burn" their love energies.

*Neutralization or reversal.* The same structure frees women from the polar stereotype, either by blurring the sexual boundaries or reversing sex roles. The first mechanism is *role monopoly* concomitant to role specialization. The clear-cut division of labor, while it deprives the woman of status and autonomy by tying her down to domestic drudgery, also empowers her to be a domestic matriarch. Her uncontested power and autonomy as a household treasurer, taken so much for granted that deprivation of this function may justify divorce, is part of her role monopoly. If one looks at the wife's complete control of the domestic realm apart from its structural context, one might be led to the conclusion that women are more powerful than men in Japan, or that Japanese women enjoy more power than American women, for whom the division of labor is not so clear-cut (Vogel 1978; Perry 1975).[2] What makes the housewife's role monopoly complete is the generalization of her role as an all-around caretaker. An extreme instance is found in the housemaid who emerged as the matriarch in the employer's household as a result of the all-around dependency of the family upon her caretaking. In American society, the cultural pressure for individual autonomy would check such overall dependency and therefore such role monopoly as well.

Role monopoly can be enjoyed in the professional world too. In a segregated occupation like nursing a woman can climb to the very top of the hierarchy, including an administrative position, instead of conceding leadership roles to her male colleagues. That segregation guarantees professional monopoly for women can be clearly shown in a more sex-segregated society: women preponderate in medicine and higher education, catering to female clientele, in Islamic societies (Papanek 1971; Cosar 1978).

To be recalled is the female entrepreneurship in hospitality businesses. These businesses are doubly or triply sex-segregated: in our sample it was the wife who took the primary charge of the operation of a brothel or bar, the husband being a nominal head; brothels and bars catered exclusively to male clients; such businesses thrived thanks to sex segregation in the larger society. Women who engage in this trade do take advantage of the constraint of segregation, even though they may do so reluctantly, or only because there are no other occupations available to them.

The second mechanism for sex-role neutralization is *structural asexuality* which allows the male prerogative to be shared by females. We have seen how the traditional *ie* as a corporate body, which has been a citadel of female subordination and inferiority, has also demanded that each member, male or female, represent it and substitute for another member if necessary. The primacy of the *ie*, then, could serve to blur sex boundaries so that a widow could engage in a conspicuously masculine enterprise; for example, a widow stepped in as a "successor" to her late husband, who had headed the house business, a lumber mill. We have also seen how the "succession syndrome" crossed over sex lines such that a daughter was expected and encouraged by her father to make a successful career. The institution of *mukoyōshi*, in which the male and female roles are reversed from the virilocal norm, can be understood in the light of *ie* primacy. Framed in the structural principle of the perpetuation of the *ie*, Japanese males do not show as much resistance to assuming their wives' names as the supposedly liberal-minded American males would. To be further recalled is the precedence of birth order over sex as well as the role of a daughter as a son substitute.

Likewise, the structural link between education and employment, while benefiting males, can also contribute to neutralization in that admission to a prominent university may remove gender stigma from a woman once and for all. The more "infernal" the examination, the more completely the woman can shed her femininity. The more heavily society relies upon universal, "sex-blind" examinations for screening candidates for education, licensing, and employment, the more opportunity she has to get into the traditionally male-dominant careers.

The rigidity of bureaucratic hierarchy can supersede sex hierarchy. Once a woman succeeds in launching an "elite course" in a seniority-based bureaucracy, she can hope to be promoted at the same pace as her male peers. The primacy of bureaucratic hierarchy also facilitates a woman to hold a managerial position vis-à-vis male subordinates. It looks as if the bureaucratic rank order makes the staff sex-blind, as if bureaucratic elitism nullifies sex elitism. In this respect, the Japanese career woman may be said to be better off than her American counterpart working in a large male-dominant corporation, as studied by Kanter (1977). Kanter imputes the plight of "token women" to their minority status, comparable to any minority group, but I presume that the American women in male-dominant careers suffer also because their sex identity is an inalienable part of their personalities which cannot be buried in the bureaucratic structure. Here is a paradox. American individualism and egalitarianism expose women's sex identity in a bureaucratic setup whereas Japanese "structuralism" and rank-order sensitivity neutralize women's sexuality in the eyes of males and females alike.

The third mechanism is what might be called *liminal transcendence*. "Liminal" is contrasted to "structural" as used by Turner (1969), and merges with such other concepts as "antistructure" and "communitas." The structurally defined sex norms may be lifted and license be indulged on special occasions. We have seen how middle-aged and older women, during the annual trip of the women's association, enjoyed the license of obscenity, a male prerogative, to their hearts' content and embarrassed the male audience. Such a periodic expression of structural moratorium may be analogous to cross-cultural instances of "rites of reversal" involving transvestism and women displaying male behavior (Gluckman 1954; Norbeck 1963; Bateson 1958).

Manipulation of "structural inferiority" or "outsiderhood" (Turner 1974:231–71) is another manifestation of liminal transcendence. Some career women, we recall, converted their sex-based disadvantage into resources to promote themselves; inferiority, peripherality, backstaged invisibility, or outsider status provided a woman the kind of freedom and opportunity from which a male colleague was barred: new prominent roles were created precisely due to a woman's structural inferiority.

The liminal reversal may be further rooted in the unconscious. Turner (1974:234) claims that the lowest class or outcast represents the "human total" and recognizes mystical power to be associated with the poor, weak, and rejected. This union of structural inferiority and liminal superiority may be embodied in a woman too, and all the more so in view of her "generalized role" symbolizing a total communion of "whole" persons. Such a view of womanhood holds best for motherhood. There are many Japanese men who despise women and look down upon their wives, but the same men may be unrestrained admirers of their mothers and motherhood in general. Japanese women as mothers could thus be promoted to what amounts to an object of religious worship.

The last point is not unrelated, in my view, to the rise of some women in the religious world—another form of liminal transcendence.

Sayo Kitamura, the foundress of Tensho-Kōtai-Jingu-Kyō, for instance, emerged right after World War II, as a host for a god speaking through her mouth. Though the god was identified as the host's "father," he was located in her womb—symbolic enough of the supernatural potency of motherhood. Furthermore, while she did shed her female identity by slipping into the role of a male god with masculine speech and dress, she also embodied the supreme female deity of Shinto, the Sun Goddess, as inseparably united with the male god (Lebra 1967). The Sun Goddess seems to be a culturally available symbol to be latched onto for a woman's liminal transcendence.

The overall social structure has been analyzed in terms of its support both of sex polarization and sex neutralization. This suggests a double function of structure for women's welfare. The structural embeddedness of sex roles, on the one hand, deprives women, and, on the other, protects them. Let me illustrate this double function by instances of domestic violence. Wife abuse may be understood as a naked, direct expression of male power, although ironically it tends to be a man lacking confidence as a husband who resorts to this extreme form of dominance. How does this phenomenon relate to social structure? On the one hand, the structural imperative of male dominance or superiority justifies and even demands its confirmation and reconfirmation in this unequivocal expression. We have observed a husband's concern with the maintenance of onstage patriarchy to be shown off to a third party, leaving a more equalitarian relationship or even matriarchy to the private life of husband and wife alone. Reference was made to a husband who was harsh and violent toward his wife only when guests were around, and who turned out to be gentle and loving when alone with his wife. Indeed, the Japanese audience tends to applaud a man who has the guts to slap his wife in the face. Male peers may advise one to beat one's wife now and then just to let her know her place. The same people in the "surrounding" will be upset to see a man putting up with his unreasonable wife or accepting a henpecked status. Wife abuse, then, is part and parcel of social structure with its formal, public nature. That being the case, it stands to reason that women would be better off in a private, informal, unstructured situation, and in this sense the American woman, whose society is less structured, might be said to be more free from abuse.

Nonetheless, we know American society is far from free of domestic violence; wife abuse appears equally, if not more, frequent in America than in Japan (Kumagai and O'Donoghue 1978). And we definitely know the incomparably greater frequency of rape among Americans than Japanese. This is where we must consider the other function of structure. Because sex roles are submerged in social structure, Japanese women may be more protected from sex abuse. We can draw evidence from our sample to support this proposition in a negative way. Recall those women who came into contact and married their husbands without mediators and without parental sanctions. These cases of unstructured marriage proved to be strikingly abuse-ridden, probably because the wives were directly exposed to the husbands' whims and physical aggression without the structural buffer which their natal families, mediators, or other third parties could have provided. To this we can add those cases of structured marriage which involve the husband's violence in a private encounter with the wife alone, shielded from public witnesses. This leads to the conclusion that the more structured the marriage, the more immune the woman is from her husband's violence.

### Toward Self-Programming in Changing Japan

Thus far, a woman's self-fulfillment has been viewed largely in conjunction with social structure, with emphasis upon how it was interlocked with and programmed by her structurally assigned roles. Her *ikigai*, if any, was bought, we saw, at a high cost of sacrifice, hardship, and endurance. The total picture drawn in this volume might indeed appear outmoded in the eyes of the change-minded reader. It should be remembered that our data derived from the life *histories* of the living individuals the oldest of whom were born in the 1890s. In an effort to correct whatever imbalance might have resulted, this final portion of the book will be devoted to new ways of attaining fulfillment in the face of the social change taking place at present and in the foreseeable future.

Some cautions must be taken in discussing social change. First, whether some social phenomenon is traditional or new depends upon the time span under consideration. The flexibility of marriage rules, including premarital sex, is indeed new if the old pattern is associated with the recent past, but it is a return in part, if not in entirety, to the pre- and early Meiji peasant way of life. Conversely, what looks like an outdated pattern such as the "full-time housewife" is actually a new phenomenon if viewed in longer-time perspective. One and the same phenomenon thus may be taken as a sign of linear change, curvilinear change, or cyclical change depending upon the viewer's time punctuation. Second, differences between an old and a young generation cannot be totally attributed to social change; life stages are partially responsible. I know many Japanese women who in their twenties were "swingers" living for no one but themselves, and who have since become unabashed *kyōiku mama*. Third, change is often exaggerated primarily due to our confusion between what is taking place among the majority and what is shown on TV or in popular women's magazines. Needless to say, what makes a phenomenon newsworthy is its novelty or uniqueness apart from the prevalent way of life. The exaggerated sense of change is often based upon blindness to the resistance to change on the part of those who have a vested interest in the "traditional" order. The United States, the country to which liberationists the world over look for a model to follow, has yet to pass the Equal Rights Amendment bill, obviously due to such a "backlash." It is a cliché that the worst enemy of women's liberation is women. This point leads to my last area of caution, an area which calls for a more lengthy discussion.

Change is not necessarily beneficial to women. The anthropological literature suggests that women's status is higher or sex equality is greater where the society is lower on the evolutionary scale in terms of subsistence, technology, and social structure. This is because the simpler society has less differentiated roles and statuses for males and females than does the more complex society. Thus, hunting and gathering societies allow more power or freedom for women than agricultural or more developed societies (Gough 1975; Lamphere 1974; Leacock 1975; Martin and Voorhies 1975; Sacks 1975). Recently, Leacock (1978) reasserted her Engelsian standpoint in this respect. Comparing the nomadic and sedentary !Kung, Draper (1975b) proposes that sedentism introduces greater sex differentiation in economic terms. This differentiation is reflected in the socialization process: sex difference between boys and girls is untapped among the nomadic !Kung for task assignment, while among the settled, only girls are available as easy targets of their mothers' commands for chores (Draper 1975a). Within the agricultural stage, shifting cultivation is seen to place women in a higher position than plow agriculture (Boserup 1970). For Reiter (1975), emergence of the state is a crucial variable that creates a distinction between the public and the private domain with women relegated to the latter. Bossen (1975) refutes the idea that modernization improves women's status.

But, of course, there are other views of change. (Even if the above views are entirely valid, how could we go back to the hunting-gathering stage?) To continue the survey of the literature, Divale (1976) demonstrates that low female status is found mostly among simpler societies while high female status cuts across all levels of complexities. Social, technological change may force men out of the traditionally male roles, such as the role of warrior, hunter, or initiator, which used to accord them a superior sex status but have now become obsolete. Meanwhile, new economic opportunities may open up for women, providing them free access to cash through marketing as in a Nigerian community

(McC. Netting 1969). This could not only devastate the ideal of male supremacy but plague men with a sense of sexual impotency (LeVine 1966). The introduction of motorized fishing equipment has turned women in Ghana into financiers to whom fishermen have become indebted (Christenson 1977). The increasing involvement of men in migratory wage labor intensifies matrifocality and increases women's autonomy (Olson 1977). Giele proposes a curvilinear model to correlate societal complexity and sex equality, and regards the "intermediate level" of complexity as "most deleterious to the status of women" (1977:9). The simplest and most complex stages are thus associated with a peak of women's status.

With these cautions in mind, let us look into the changing life conditions that the contemporary Japanese women are enjoying or struggling with. The technological and institutional change has caused the household to lose many of its productive functions to the specialized producers and manufacturers, not only in the procurement of raw materials but in their processing. Packaged instant foods and fast food industries are among the latest examples. What has been considered intrinsically the housewife's job, including housecleaning, is commercially available; ceremonies such as wedding and funeral are "sold" by "companies." The housewife may choose to retain responsibility for much of the housework, but even then automation has simplified the formerly skilled labor (notably rice cooking), and lightened the formerly heavy work (e.g., laundry). Schools have taken over the responsibility of educating children and are keeping them for an everincreasing period of time. Nursery care facilities for preschool children allow young mothers to devote their time to activities other than maternal chores. Moreover, nursing homes are being augmented for the aged who formerly had no place to turn but to the household. Birth control, owing to the diffusion of contraceptive techniques (and abortion), compounded by the prolongation of longevity, presumably due to improved nutrition and medicine, lengthens the "postparental" stage of women's life cycle and permits them to outlive their domestic role.

The result is twofold: the contraction of the housewifely role and denigration of its status, and increasing options for women to infiltrate or recapture the extradomestic sphere. The status of the full-time housewife thus loses its rationale and has to be transformed into something more. Further, once a woman is caught up in such change, she must realize that her long-range role investment through hardship and perseverance may not pay off, that the formerly structured reward system may go bankrupt. The skill she has acquired may soon become obsolete, her experience as a mother may be of no use from the point of view of her updated daughter-in-law, her heavily invested son may never return to her. Worse yet, a woman must be alert to pathological consequences of the mother-son bond in isolation from the public domain. The media disclose not only cases of mother-abuse, but sensational instances of mother-son incest. Moreover, women's mental health problems must be considered in conjunction with their educational achievements. In 1980, over one million women graduated from four-year colleges or universities. A follow-up study of a sample of university graduates discloses that 83 percent of those women who were jobless wished to obtain some kind of job (Fujitani 1980). A widening discrepancy between women's educational level and their occupational opportunities is likely to give rise to a large number of discontented, maladjusted women.

It goes without saying that solutions to these problems lie primarily in the legislative, institutional innovations toward equalization of sexes involving a fundamental social reorganization. This has been a subject discussed in public forums, written about in newspapers and journals, by many people with diverse backgrounds. I will not repeat it here, rather I will limit my concern to women's own choice and resolution in coping with the current change. It seems that a woman has little choice but to orient herself more toward her autonomy than toward relational dependency. Self-programming for life will replace structural programming. In this sense the Japanese woman is coming, whether she likes it or not, closer to the life-style of the American woman as I have described it here. This reminds us of another aspect of change. The media carry information on what is going on abroad, what Western women are up to, and what Westerners think about Japanese men and women. A newspaper article (*Asahi* 3/3/79), for example, quotes foreign correspondents likening Japanese women to a "folded accordion," something visible but not audible. According to the article, the correspondents say that women are found in every office and bring the tea, but no woman is present at the conference table. Why, they ask. Foreigners' reactions such as this will affect Japanese readers of both sexes, since they are as responsive to Western views of themselves as they were a century ago.

I shall suggest three directions of self-programming for women.[3] These are partially drawn from my impressions of what is already taking place among some women in Japan. However, much of the following discussion also reflects my value-laden judgement and speculations. Expressions like "should" and "must" will appear freely.

*Professionalized domesticity.* Despite the overall devaluation of housewifery, I suspect that there are and will be a large number of women who prefer to be wives and mothers above all else, and as many men who will choose such women as their spouses. What I suggest here is a strategic extension of the traditional division of labor. No longer resigned to her sex-bound fate, the woman should cultivate her feminine capacity toward her own fulfillment. With a college education, she is able to raise homemaking to a professional level of accomplishment.

Housewifery is to be looked upon as an occupation in its own right, and as such it should not be confined to one's own home but extended to the public domain. As a domestic expert, a woman may find a career in domestic counseling for instance. Instead of just losing domestic functions to the public, largely male-dominated industries, the domestic professional may well go out and sell her skill and knowledge to the public. Fujiwara (1979) reports on eighty-four women who have successfully converted their housewifely status into professions, many of which are based upon their domestic skills and experiences. Among such professions are: cook, dietician, instructor in Japanese cooking for foreign women, counselor or teacher on such matters as laundry, shopping, childrearing, health, housework in general, life management, and so on. One of the sampled women has become a home architect, Fujiwara reports, being awakened to the advantage of her domestic experience in designing homes. Prerequisite to these occupations are professional licenses, which are proliferating in present-day Japan, and schools to prepare candidates for licensing examinations are thriving. The occupations are generally of a free-lance type so that one's own home management does not have to be compromised. The women interviewed by Fujiwara expressed the joy and excitement brought them by these new "careers."

Group cooperation may be involved in the self-transformation of a housewife. The Volunteer Labor Bank led by an Osaka woman is a case in point (Lebra 1980). The main idea is that the housewife's resources— time and labor—could be pooled and exchanged according to each individual's life schedule. The underlying premise, enunciated by Teruko Mizushima, the organization's president, is that a woman's autonomy fluctuates during her lifetime. A woman loses her autonomy at the peak of her maturity due to her responsibility for childbearing and childrearing. In parallel with this is the variation in the availability of time and energy from one life stage to another. Early motherhood requires not only using up the mother's own but borrowing additional time and energy from others. From late motherhood on, a surplus of energy and time is restored, until finally energy goes down below the level of self-sufficiency in the course of aging. This fluctuation in the supply and demand of women's resources can be coped with, says Mizushima, by a system of depositing and withdrawing these resources like a savings account. The idea has been put into practice. If member A helps member B with three hours of ordinary labor, A's labor "passbook" has three points entered in its "deposit" column, and the same recorded in B's "withdrawal" column.

The revelations that members of this bank have undergone, as expressed in newsletters and interview, suggest more than just labor exchange. The exchange of domestic labor between women involving two unrelated households leads to a reassessment and revaluation of the work of a housewife. The domestic work, convertible into exchangeable points, ceases to be insignificant and unskilled. The housewife realizes that, far from being fed by her husband, she is contributing more than enough labor to feed herself. Revaluation thus induces a sense of autonomy to replace that of dependency. Furthermore, while domestic work within one's own household is nothing but routinized drudgery, working for another household amounts to a "performance" to be appreciated by an audience, and successful performance generates satisfaction and self-confidence about one's own uncovered competence. When she lacks confidence, the performer prepares herself by studying the job in advance. Further, interdomestic help exposes the housewife to a variety of housekeeping styles and brings into question her own habitual style. Since each member reserves certain days and hours in her weekly schedule for responding to labor demand, she must also plan her routine within her own household as well. All these factors contribute to a professionalization of housework. There is a tendency in fact emerging among the members to recognize themselves as "specialists" in "care for bedridden old people," "housecleaning," and so on. Another revelation is that the kind of labor which has been considered most intrinsic to housewifery is actually most scarce. The personal body care—postpartum care, nursing the sick, aged, and infants—is becoming less and less available in industrial societies, and this is what most people are concerned to secure when necessary. The housewife should be aware, members come to learn, that she is providing the most valuable kind of labor. Why should the male's work to produce "things" be looked upon more highly, they question, than the female's work to create, develop, and maintain human life, health, and safety?

The housewife may not have time to study for a professional license or may not be interested in joining a group like the Labor Bank. But as a professional housewife, she might offer some time for volunteer work.[4] Furthermore, her responsibility for monitoring the family health may induce her to be alert to health hazards like industrial pollutions, food poisoning, medical malpractices, which may involve her in consumer movements and ultimately in politics. These steps are being taken by some urban women, and probably it will not be too long before the conservatism of Shizumi women gives way to activism in the public arena.

*The double and quadruple career.* A woman, well-educated and discontented with the housewife role, will opt to work outside, not just as a part-timer but as a full career woman. She might choose such a career while giving up fulfillment as a wife-mother as did the career nurse in Shizumi. Most career women introduced in this book have chosen, however, to pursue both careers, occupational and domestic. Such a double career appears as the optimal, most satisfactory alternative for women.

Inherent in the woman's double career is the problem of overloads. Particularly if she wants to be a perfect professional as my informants did, her identity as a wife and mother tends to be sacrificed which means her career is not quite equally divided. Typically, our career women had their mothers or other female kin as surrogate housewives or baby-sitters, but even such fortunate career women were not totally free from guilt particularly toward their children. (Dependence upon female kin seems unfair, and too, the supply of such helpful kin may run out soon.) Is the double career in its full sense impossible after all?

Because of the social and emotional strain inherent in the double career, some of my informants who have chosen this alternative do not recommend it for other women. A public health nurse in Shizumi is a case in point. She declared in interview that mothers should stay home by all means. A double career woman herself, she was unable to explain to me why *she* would not stay home. From her adamant insistence on the "absolute" priority of motherhood, I could only surmise her insurmountable guilt as a neglectful mother. What stunned many people nationwide was a remark by Sumie Tanaka, a famous writer and mother, which appeared in a newspaper (*Asahi* 11/6/79). Tanaka reportedly said that her professional career had not fulfilled her, not even once, and that she had continued to work for no reason but to support her family. She condemned those women, the report continues, who find themselves "bored" with mothering and anxious to work outside, and advised them to rededicate themselves to their children. For weeks the newspaper carried excited responses from its readers, both for and against this Schlafly of Japan. These responses indicate the depth of the problem involved in a woman's career, and also reflect the overwhelming ambivalence of both supporters and opponents.

I have no novel solution to offer, but I do believe that the most viable and fair measure would be a reduction of the woman's overloads through her husband's participation in domestic work. A woman's double career should be matched by her husband's double career, together making a quadruple career. Among elite professional couples we did find such quadruple career cases. The implications of this proposal are far-reaching and by necessity involve institutional reforms. The organization employing the husband can no longer impose its despotic demand for his overtime; the absent father/husband syndrome cannot be justified. On the contrary, the rigid segregation between the work place and home, which is now maintained at the expense of the latter's autonomy, must be replaced by a flexible coordination of the two spheres for the husband as well as for the wife. While the husband is expected to internalize his identity as a domestic co-worker, the organizational autonomy of the employer must be shaken up. The mandatory transfers of employees away from home also need to be adjusted to the domestic cycles and needs of a family. In other words, many of the *Japanese* features of businesses and employment practices, which are often regarded as a clue to the success of Japan's economy, must be compromised by the need of the quadruple career couple. Such change may presuppose admission of women to "career positions" on equal basis within major corporations and government. A free-lance profession does away with the organizationally imposed strain, and many double career women tend to choose this alternative. But I do believe that the idea of double career will not be completely legitimized until organized employers accept double career men and women.

The expansion and quality improvement of nurseries and other facilities for children help a double career woman, and should be made. But her self-blame for parental neglect will not be mitigated unless her husband assumes a co-parental role to complement hers.

*Maximal freedom.* The first two types accept the conventional roles of women as wife and mother, although they both aspire beyond them as well. But is it so mandatory for a woman to be married and become a parent? Particularly if she has her own life goal, why should she bind herself to seemingly unavoidable domestic chores? Is there much sense in seeking a double career when it is so fraught with conflicts? A woman may opt to enjoy freedom, instead, by denying the conventional sex-specific role to herself. Remaining single is the first manifestation of this choice.

Women's experience as described in the foregoing chapters suggests that singlehood is one of the most unlikely options a woman might take. Aversions to a single life do not seem, however, to stem so much from a young woman's real desire for marriage as from her fear of stigma attached to an "Old Miss." An overaged single woman, unless she is an established career woman, is discriminated against as abnormal or otherwise unreliable, and is left more vulnerable to male abuse, as we have seen in Shizumi. But new trends are emerging. Tolerance of premarital sex and unwed motherhood entails the lessened social sanctions against singlehood. Such value change is necessary partly because a single life is not always by choice. However elaborate the networks for matchmaking may be, there are always some men and women who are unable to find suitable spouses for one reason or another. Many wartime women were found to be living alone (Shiozawa and Shimada 1975). Why should these women carry the stigma all their lives? It is time that Japanese of both sexes relinquished the rigidly sex-typed role images for man and woman and recognized full citizenship for single persons.

Freedom from sex typing involves more. Marriage, if found a mistake, should be reversible. Many deplore the rising divorce rates in Japan, but endurance of a miserable marriage may be more regrettable. Whether divorce and widowhood should be followed by remarriage or not is to be decided by the woman herself. Parenthood is another matter of choice, with childless marriage or foster parentage to be accepted as options. Roles of husband and wife may well be reversed: older wife, better-educated wife, breadwinner wife, and house-husband, absentee-mother and *kyōiku papa*, masculine wife and feminine husband, and so on. The fixed reversal goes against the principle of maximal freedom, so these dichotomous roles should be freely exchanged in accordance to each party's schedule.

Sex is something either to be enjoyed or to be rejected, not something binding. Women who reject heterosexual involvement may anchor their emotional stability in "sisterly love."

The maximization of role options and individual decision making, free from conventional norms, would ultimately lead to the random distribution of roles between men and women, and sex would become insignificant as a determining variable. All that is left would be difference in physical features, and even here the difference could be buried beneath the unisex type of adornment, hairstyle, and cosmetics.

I am hesitant to go too far in advocating this direction of self-programming for several reasons. First, I am not sure that women really want to transcend their sexual identity. Feminism has often included erotic liberation for the sake of romantic love, freedom to make love, and maximization of heterosexual indulgence. This aspect of liberation would be contradictory to the ideology embracing sex reversal and sex neutrality as implicated in this third type. A staunch liberationist is likely to want to retain her sexual attractiveness. Second, what appears or is claimed to be an expression of a woman's choice or autonomy may turn out to be a consequence of a male partner's tyranny. Divorce may be forced upon a woman; the unwed mother may remain unwed because the father refuses to marry; the breadwinner's role may be imposed upon the wife by a parasitic, exploitative husband. Freedom, individuation, and desexualization—all these may provide an ideological camouflage for male aggression, abuse, and lawlessness from which women ought to be protected. Recall my argument that the structural norm protects as well as constrains women. Third, preservation of maximal freedom may mean a refusal to make any social commitment (not to marry, not to have a child, etc.) or, if any commitment is made, a readiness to reverse the commitment (divorcing, for example). Without making a commitment, one will not be able to build one's life for the future. Finally, it is not quite certain whether this kind of individualistic freedom, if realized, promises happiness for women, let alone happiness for all. This conservative reservation stems from my observation of those American women who are enjoying much more freedom than my Japanese friends and yet do not look as contented as the latter. Some of them indeed have declared to me that women are much better off in other societies including Japan.

I am proposing this third alternative only as a reminder of a possible range of options available to women, in order to counter the culturally conditioned willingness of Japanese women to submit to their "fate." The three directions of self-programming suggested here are far from mutually exclusive: a woman might switch from one to another. Given a long healthy life, a woman might be able to enjoy a second or even third life in sequence, covering the whole spectrum of the three alternatives. It is conceivable that a housewife might undergo a career mutation in her early forties to become a double career woman, and further turn into a widow and retiree enjoying maximal freedom.

Whatever option one decides to take, whatever course of life one regards as most promising, it would be advisable to take into consideration what older people have to say about their life experiences. I hope that this book has conveyed some of the hindsights gained by older women, often at a cost of hardship and sacrifice.

# Notes

CHAPTER 1. *Introduction*

1. The methodological problem involved here was identified by Kracke (1980), who argues that the complementarity of the sociocultural system and the individual's psychological system is analogous to that of the position and velocity of an electron. "As one brings the individual into sharper focus, the social context recedes from focus and is blurred, and vice-versa" (p. 274). In search of an explanation for a certain behavioral response, Kracke illustrates, one may thus either explore the outer landscape of the sociocultural milieu or look inwardly into the individual's feelings, which might be traced to his childhood. "Whichever direction is taken, the pursuit of one set of reasons progressively closes access to the other set, for the explanation already given will color the terms of the subsequent one" (p. 275).

2. For this section, I rely, in addition to the information gathered directly from local residents, upon five publications of Shizumi City Government, which are designated as SC plus roman numerals. Years of publications are: SCI, 1960; SCII, 1958; SCIII, 1975; SCIV, 1976; SCV, 1975.

3. There is an interesting report on the use of community bathhouses as centers of intimate ("naked") interaction (Hashimoto 1978).

4. Among Japanese folklorists who were led by the late Kunio Yanagita there is general consensus that peasants had followed their own domestic mores until recently while increasingly exposed to the totally different jural principles developed by the warrior class. Class difference seems to manifest itself in matrimonial culture in particular, as will be detailed in the following chapters.

5. The idea borrowed from Williamson, Putnam, and Wurthmann (1976).

CHAPTER 2. *Premarital Constraints and Options*

1. These stimulus fragments were borrowed from Phillips (1965).

2. Doi (1971), who is most responsible for the wide circulation of this term among students of Japan, encompasses a much broader spectrum of phenomena under it.

3. Before 1907, when the six-year education became compulsory, it had fluctuated between sixteen months and four years (Passin 1965b:73).

4. This was only thirty years after the promulgation of the first "School Act" by the Meiji government. It would be difficult to understand this speed of progress in compulsory universal education without knowing its historical background. The new educational system of Meiji Japan was actually grafted

upon the old educational condition of the Tokugawa era, where a large number of commoners, not to mention samurai, court nobles, and priests, had been trained at least in the three Rs primarily at *terakoya* (private schools available to commoners). This historical continuity was stressed by Karasawa (1968:164), Dore (1965), Passin (1965b). Historical discontinuities were not entirely lacking, needless to say: the theoretical removal of class barriers in the choice of schools; greater sex equality in school attendance replacing the pre-Meiji male bias.

5. There was class variation in the degree to which schools were mobilized into the wartime policy of the government. Education among the upper class since the late Tokugawa era has emphasized transmission of Western culture and Western languages in particular, and this tradition was kept throughout the war both at home and at school. Gakushuin (Peers' School) students continued to receive excellent training in English or French.

6. The persisting prejudice against *hinoeuma* women is shown by the birth control in a *hinoeuma* year as illustrated in the following table of births in three years:

| Year | Number of Births |
|------|------------------|
| 1965 | ca. 1,820,000 |
| 1966 | 1,360,000 |
| 1967 | 1,930,000 |

The year 1966 was the latest *hinoeuma* year, revealing a drop by 26 percent from the previous year. *Asahi* (11/5/78) also reports this drop was sharper than the drop in 1906, the previous *hinoeuma*, which was by 5 percent.

CHAPTER 3. *Marital Transition*

1. Suenari (1972) demonstrates the relatively high frequency of *anekatoku* (succession by the elder daughter) on the basis of house register records, and claims that first-child inheritance, instead of eldest-*son* inheritance, has been a norm rather than simply an economic necessity.

2. The premarital inaccessibility of the spouses to each other evinces the diffusion of the samurai matrimonial culture among the commoners, whereas the latter, practicing village endogamy, permitted young boys and girls to meet prior to a ceremonial sanction of the match, as suggested by the custom of *yobai* (a boy's nocturnal, clandestine visit with a girl at home). Nor was the mediator's role as significant among the peasants as it has become (Yanagita 1963). In view of this background, the greater sexual freedom enjoyed by the younger generation today cannot be attributed simply to postwar change.

3. The lack of subjective commitment in mate selection is exemplified as follows. A television program "Wide Show" (8/29/78)—one of the most popular programs for the housewife audience—introduced a married couple. The husband and wife met while they were working in the same building, one as a security guard, the other as a typist, and then married. Asked if he chose the woman from among many candidates, he said, "Not that I chose, but it so happened."

The interviewer turned his question to the wife, "Were you attracted to this guy?" Her answer was, "I was only anxious to marry because I was past twenty-five."

4. A detailed description of marriage rites in a village is given by Hendry (1981).

5. *Ashiire* was a customary form of engagement or tentative marriage which, according to Omachi (1949), allowed sexual union while maintaining duolocal residence and thereby ensuring the supply of labor of each party for his/her natal family. Omachi further speculates that it "may represent a transitional form from the matrilocal to the patrilocal marriage system and can still be observed in the Izu Islands, especially in To-shima" (1963:252). According to my fifty-one-year-old informant, in her day *ashiire* marriage was "most common." "Without a formal ceremony, you live together, only with a tentative rite [*karishūgen*]. Only after a while of co-living, you hold a formal wedding." This is another flexible aspect of peasant culture, distinct from the rigid samurai rule.

6. This is another point of class difference since, for samurai, marriage began with only the *yomeiri* ceremony. For the peasants, the customs of *yuino* and *ashiire* may have been all in one with the *mukoiri* ceremony (Yanagita 1963).

7. This custom may be a symbolic vestige of "bride-stealing" which could be interpreted in various ways: the spouse-giver was expected to show reluctance partly as a matter of propriety and partly because daughter-giving meant the loss of labor; "stealing" was a collusive ritual to dispense with an expensive wedding on the part of the bride-giver; the traditional form of marriage being *mukoiri*, the bride's departure called for ritual stealing (Yanagita 1963:82–104). Omachi makes reference to the ritually acted out reluctance to give away the bride, as observed in Iwate Prefecture (1949:232–233).

CHAPTER 4. *Postmarital Involvement*

1. Conversational terms are different from nonconversational (such as written or legalistic/formal) terms, and within the conversational usage there is a distinction between regular and crude forms. Further, the husband or wife of someone other than the speaker (altercentric) is referred to respectfully with another term:

| | Husband | Wife |
|---|---|---|
| Conversational | | |
| Regular | shujin | kanai, nyōbō |
| Crude | teishu, oyaji, etc. | okā, kakā, etc. |
| Nonconversational | otto | tsuma |
| Altercentric terms in conversation | goshujin, danna-san | oku-san |

See Passin (1965a) for a comprehensive analysis of Japanese "intra-familial" terms.

2. Keizai Kikakuchō, Kokumin Seikatsukyoku, Kokumin Seikatsu Chōsaka, ed. *Seikatsu jikan no kōzō bunseki*, 1975, pp. 28–29.

3. The in-law conflict is a favorite, and uniquely Japanese, theme of soap operas in Japan. This is in comparison to American soap operas (Maykovitch 1975).

4. This is another illustration of how one's mother is addressed "Grandma" from the standpoint of the youngest member of the house, in this case, the speaker's nephew.

5. *Hana no shita ga nagai* (long under one's nose) is a common expression for teasing someone for being smug with love for a spouse or lover. In this particular case, the mother's tone of voice was evidently more accusatory than teasing.

6. This is the other side of the coin dealt with by Perry (1976), who postulates that the daughter-mother alliance, as observed among Senri Town residents strengthens the daughter's autonomy against her husband and in-laws. Since alliance is mutual, the same alliance may strengthen the mother's position against her own daughter-in-law. It all depends on whose ox is being gored. I am saying that the mother-daughter alliance is not necessarily detrimental to the *ie* system and bride hazing as proposed by Perry.

CHAPTER 5. *Motherhood*

1. *Naien* may actually refer to the same state of tentative marriage as *ashiire*, but the Japanese tend to differentiate these terms, attaching the legal meaning to the former (as legally unsanctioned) and the social/ritual meaning to the latter (as prior to the full-fledged wedding).

2. The mother's guilt toward the aborted fetus is captured by religious establishments. I saw an advertisement sponsored by a number of local Buddhist temples urging guilty mothers to be concerned with their *mizugo*, water child, namely, the aborted fetus, and to save its spirit through religious service. On the one hand it appealed to their guilt by describing the plight of the "pitiable child" whose life was suspended, and on the other it threatened the guilty mother by referring to the troubles caused by the suffering fetus's spirit such as illness, family discord, delinquency. The final message of the advertisement was that such a woman buy a stone-built buddha statue for the fetus spirit to hang onto. One statue cost ¥18,500 ($93 as of 1978).

3. A masochistic version of the "linear transference" of reciprocity (Lebra 1975:559–60).

4. One of the twelve animal signs associated with calendrical cycles. The dog here symbolizes fertility and easy delivery.

5. For the *tsukisoi* system and the Japanese value system underlying it, see Caudill (1961).

6. Hara and Wagatsuma (1974) warn us that the idea of an around-the-clock caretaker for a child is far from the traditional pattern which was preva-

lent among peasants until recently. The farming family, for example, unable to afford a full-time mother, left its infant alone while all the adults were working in the field. In the northeastern region, the child was placed in a basket called *ejiko* which served as a substitute for a baby-sitter.

7. For a rigorous study of co-sleeping alignment, see Caudill and Plath (1974).

8. This judgement by mothers is reciprocally validated by children, particularly by boys, as shown in the drawing test conducted in classrooms. The children were asked to draw their families, including themselves, as they were doing something, and to identify who they were. The primary school third graders (eight and nine years old), both male (n = 20) and female (n = 19), drew their mothers without one exception (!) while less than a third (30 percent of the boys, 26 percent of the girls) also drew their fathers, and some even forgot to include themselves. This almost exclusive attention to the mother by both sexes radically changes as the child grows to the junior high school level. The junior high second-year students (thirteen and fourteen years old) responded differently by sex, each sex paying more attention to the parent of the same sex. Thirty-eight percent of the boys (total = 21) drew their fathers and 9.5 percent their mothers only, whereas of the girls (total = 19), 47 percent described their mothers only, 5 percent fathers only. Both parents were depicted by 10 percent of the male and 5 percent of the female respondents. In both samples, there is a tendency to choose one parent, but change does occur from unconditional preference for the mother to the same-sex parent. To reinforce this finding it may be added that the older children drew their siblings much along the same pattern of sex preference: boys tended to choose brothers, girls to describe sisters.

These children are similar to the sample of adult women in producing the imbalanced pictures of parents. The difference is that for the adults imbalance is distributed at random between fathers and mothers whereas it is systematic for the children either in favor of mother or of the same-sex parent.

9. Accounts of such home medicine are included in Lock's (1980) work.

10. Dore (1978:177) parallels the child's school identity with the salaryman's occupational identity in terms of its entirety.

11. The high school enrollment sharply increased nationwide from 43 percent in 1950 to over 90 percent (91 percent for boys, 93 percent for girls) in 1975 (Monbushō 1976:17). Higher education, including both the four-year university and the two-year junior college levels, also rose in enrollment from 10 percent in 1960 to 38 percent in 1975 (Monbushō 1976:30), indicating that higher education has ceased to be for the privileged class only. The increase in enrollment meant the mushrooming of high schools, colleges and universities. This expansion of the school population and facilities has not altered the hierarchical structure of the educational institutions, however, in association with entrance examinations and employment. As a matter of fact, democratization of educational opportunites has intensified competition among candidates for top institutions.

12. I have no objective evidence either to support or refute this widespread prejudice against women teachers. I have observed several first-grade classes

including one taught by a woman. I was most impressed by the woman's performance in terms of her total commitment and skill. All the women teachers I met in the same school agreed that they are like *kōya no shirabakama* (a dyer wearing an undyed skirt), too busy with their occupation to teach their own children.

13. According to a 1976 report by the Ministry of Education, 74 percent of the students admitted to private medical schools were found to have paid "backdoor admission fees" of as much as 16 million yen (over sixty thousand dollars) per person on the average (*Asahi* 2/18/77).

14. I owe Thomas Rohlen, who in personal conversation shared his insight into this discrepancy in the present Japanese education.

CHAPTER 6. *Occupational Careers*

1. As of 1979, women comprised 38.6 percent of the labor force, which was broken down into self-employment (13.9 percent), family-employed (24.0 percent), and other-employed (61.9 percent), showing an increase over the years in the last category (Sōrifu 1980:43–44).

2. The significance of the father's role in a woman's career aspirations was underscored by Hennig and Jardim (1977) in their observation of American "managerial women." The success of these women in the traditionally masculine careers is attributed in part to their internalization of masculine values through a strong identification with and support from their fathers.

3. The content of this section is further elaborated in Lebra (1981b).

4. Among American dual career families, too, role strain for the wives is generally centered on "childrearing problems mainly in terms of their own guilt and fatigue" (Johnson and Johnson 1977:393).

CHAPTER 7. *Later Years*

1. Women's sex-role transcendence and power acquisition at this life stage have been cross-culturally observed: Antoun (1968), Sangree (1969), Harper (1969), Paul and Paul (1975), Hayes (1975), Jopling (1947), Meigs (1976), Scrimshaw (1978).

2. Part of this section was presented in Lebra (1979b).

3. The obscene performance of older women at drinking parties was observed by Embree (1939:176) in prewar Suye Mura, and interpreted by Norbeck (1953:381) as an age-graded privilege.

4. A similar kind of age identity derived from the perceived change of family members rather than self was noted by Neugarten (1975:96) for American women: the onset of middle age for a woman is marked by the launching of her children; likewise, she does not do "body-monitoring" for herself but for her husband and thereby does "rehearsal for widowhood."

5. Of all kinds of old-age pension beneficiaries, welfare pension receivers nationally comprised 35.7 percent (nearly 4 million people), as of 1979 (Soda and Miura 1980:79).

CHAPTER 8. *Conclusion*

1. The foregoing view of the Japanese woman's life as "structurally embedded" may not be shared by other observers of Japan. Plath (1980) chose to characterize the Japanese biographies from an individualistic point of view in opposition to the social structure frame of reference. I am presenting my point of view, believing that it is valid as far as Japanese women are compared with American women in the same age bracket (Lebra 1981a).

2. The structural paradox is found across cultures. Under the overarching patrilineal and patriarchical system of Chinese society, the Taiwanese woman is able to build up her "uterine family" around herself within the domestic sanctuary (Wolf 1972). For Rogers (1975), the domestic-extradomestic polarization puts women into "real" power while reducing men to a symbolic authority figure.

3. A similar theme was presented in a different context in Lebra (1976d).

4. When I returned to Shizumi in 1983, I learned of dedicated *borantia* (volunteer) workers, who help the bedridden elderly and who draw genuine admiration from my local informants.

# References

Antoun, Richard T.
　1968　On the Modesty of Women in Arab Muslim Villages: A Study in the Accommodation of Traditions. *American Anthropologist* 70:671–706.

Bateson, Gregory
　1958　*Naven.* Stanford, Calif.: Stanford University Press.

Befu, Harumi
　1963　Patrilineal Descent and Personal Kindred in Japan. *American Anthropologist* 65 (6):1328–1341.

Blood, Robert O., Jr.
　1967　*Love Match and Arranged Marriage: A Tokyo-Detroit Comparison.* New York: Free Press.

Boserup, Ester
　1970　*Woman's Role in Economic Development.* London: George Allen and Unwin.

Bossen, Laurel
　1975　Women in Modernizing Societies. *American Ethnologist* 2:587–601.

Brown, Judith K.
　1970　A Note on the Division of Labor by Sex. *American Anthropologist* 72:1073–1078.

Brown, Keith
　1966　Dozoku and the Ideology of Descent in Rural Japan. *American Anthropologist* 68 (5):1129–1151.

Caudill, William
　1961　Around the Clock Patient Care in Japanese Psychiatry Hospitals: The Role of the *tsukisoi. American Sociological Review* 26:204–214.

Caudill, William, and David W. Plath
　1974　Who Sleeps by Whom? Parent-Child Involvement in Urban Japanese. In *Japanese Culture and Behavior: Selected Readings*, ed. T. S. Lebra and W. P. Lebra. Honolulu: University Press of Hawaii.

Caudill, William, and Helen Weinstein
　1974　Maternal Care and Infant Behavior in Japan and America. In *Japanese Culture and Behavior: Selected Readings*, ed. T. S. Lebra and W. P. Lebra. Honolulu: University Press of Hawaii.

Chodorow, Nancy
    1974    Family Structure and Feminine Personality. In *Woman, Culture, and Society,* ed. M. Z. Rosaldo and L. Lamphere. Stanford, Calif.: Stanford University Press.

Christenson, James B.
    1977    Motor Power and Woman Power: Technological and Economic Change Among the Fanti Fishermen of Ghana. In *Those Who Live From the Sea,* ed. M. E. Smith. St. Paul: West Publishing Co.

Cosar, Fatma Mansur
    1978    Women in Turkish Society. In *Women in the Muslim World,* ed. L. Beck and N. Keddie. Cambridge: Harvard University Press.

Craig, Albert M.
    1975    Functional and Dysfunctional Aspects of Government Bureaucracy. In *Modern Japanese Organization and Decision-Making,* ed. E. F. Vogel. Berkeley and Los Angeles: University of California Press.

Cumming, Elaine, and W. E. Henry
    1961    *Growing Old: The Process of Disengagement.* New York: Basic Books.

Curtis, Gerald L.
    1971    *Election Campaigning Japanese Style.* New York: Columbia University Press.

Divale, William Tulio
    1976    Female Status and Cultural Evolution: A Study in Ethnographer Bias. *Behavioral Science Research* 11:169–211.

Doi, Takeo
    1971    *Amae no Kozo* [The structure of *amae*]. Tokyo: Kōbundo.

Dore, Roland P.
    1965    *Education in Tokugawa Japan.* Berkeley and Los Angeles: University of California Press.
    1978    *Shinohata: A Portrait of a Japanese Village.* New York: Pantheon Books.

Draper, Patricia
    1975a    Cultural Pressure on Sex Differences. *American Ethnologist* 2:602–616.
    1975b    !Kung Women: Contrasts in Sexual Egalitarianism in Foraging and Sedentary Contexts. In *Toward an Anthropology of Women,* ed. R. Reiter. New York: Monthly Review Press.

Durkheim, Emil
    1960    *The Division of Labor in Society.* Glencoe: Free Press.

Embree, John F.
    1939    *Suye Mura: A Japanese Villago.* Chicago: University of Chicago Press.

Epstein, Cynthia Fuchs
1970    *Woman's Place*. Berkeley and Los Angeles: University of California Press.

Fischer, John L.
1964    Words for Self and Others in Some Japanese Families. *American Anthropologist* 66 (6):115–126.

Friedl, E.
1967    The Position of Women: Appearance and Reality. *Anthropological Quarterly* 40:97–108.

Fujin ni Kansuru Shomondai Chōsakaigi [The Council for Investigating Women's Problems], ed.
1974    *Gendai Nippon josei no ishiki to kōdō* [The mentality and behavior of the contemporary Japanese women]. Tokyo: Ōkurashō Insatsu-kyoku [Finance Ministry Press].

Fujitani, Atsuko
1980    Daisotsu josei hyakuman-nin jidai [The age of one million women graduating from university]. *Asahi Jānaru* (7/11):82–87.

Fujiwara, Fusako
1979    *Shufu ga shūgyō suru toki* [The housewife's occupation]. Tokyo: Tentetsusha.

Giele, Janet Zollinger
1977    Comparative Perspectives on Women. In *Women: Roles and Status in Eight Countries*, ed. J. Z. Giele and A. C. Smock. New York: John Wiley and Sons.

Gluckman, Max
1954    *Rituals of Rebellion in South-East Africa*. Manchester: Manchester University Press.

Gough, Kathleen
1975    The Origin of the Family. In *Toward an Anthropology of Women*, ed. R. Reiter. New York: Monthly Review Press.

Hara, Hiroko, and Hiroshi Wagatsuma
1974    *Shitsuke* [Child discipline]. Tokyo: Kōbundo.

Harper, Edward B.
1969    Fear and the Status of Women. *Southwestern Journal of Anthropology* 25:81–95.

Hashimoto, Toshiko
1978    Sentō ni kansuru ichi kōsatsu [A reflection on public bathhouses]. In *Seikatsugaku* [Life Science], vol. 4, ed. Nippon Seikatsu Gakkai [Japanese Life Science Society]. Tokyo: Domesu Shuppan.

Hayes, Rose O.
1975    Female Genital Mutilation, Fertility Control, Women's Roles and the Patrilineage in Modern Sudan: A Functional Analysis. *American Ethnologist* 2:617–633.

Hendry, Joy
1981     *Marriage in Changing Japan.* New York: St. Martin's Press.

Hennig, Margaret, and Anne Jardim
1977     *The Managerial Woman.* Garden City, N.Y.: Anchor Press/Double-day.

Hirai, Kiyoshi
1974     *Nihon jūtaku no rekishi* [A historical review of Japanese residential housing]. Tokyo: Nippon Hōsō Shuppan Kyōkai.

Ito, Tomonobu
1977     Oya to ko no genjitsu [Parents and children]. *Asahi Shinbun,* 2/1.

Ito, Toshiyuki, Hideo Sato, and Hajime Hisahara
1967     Shotō kyōiku [Elementary education]. In *Gakkō seido* [The school institution], ed. Arata Naka and Eiichi Mochida. Tokyo: Daiichi Hōki Shuppan.

Johnson, Colleen Leahy, and Frank Arvid Johnson
1977     Attitudes Toward Parenting in Dual-Career Families. *American Journal of Psychiatry* 134 (4):391–395.

Johnson, Erwin H.
1964     The Stem Family and Its Extensions in Present-Day Japan. *American Anthropologist* 66 (4):839–851.

Jopling, Carol F.
1974     Women's Work: A Mexican Case Study of Low Status as a Tactical Advantage. *Ethnology* 13:187–195.

Kanter, Rosabeth Moss
1977     Some Effects of Proportions on Group Life: Skewed Sex Ratios and Responses to Token Women. *American Journal of Sociology* 82 (5): 965–990.

Karasawa, Tomitaro
1968     *Kindai Nippon kyōiku shi* [The modern history of Japanese education]. Tokyo: Seibundo Shinkosha.

Keizai Kikakuchō, Kokumin Seikatsukyoku, Kokumin Seikatsu Chōsaka [The National Life Condition Research Section, National Life Bureau, Economic Planning Agency], ed.
1975     *Seikatsu jikan no kōzō bunseki* [The structural analysis of time expenditure for daily life].

Kiefer, Christie W.
1974     The Psychological Interdependence of Family, School, and Bureaucracy in Japan. In *Japanese Culture and Behavior: Selected Readings,* ed. T. S. Lebra and W. P. Lebra. Honolulu: University Press of Hawaii.

Kitaoji, Hironobu
1971     The Structure of the Japanese Family. *American Anthropologist* 73: 1036–1057.

Koseishō [Ministry of Health and Welfare], ed.
  1976   *Kōsei hakusho: fujin to shakai hoshō* [White paper on health and welfare: women and social security].

Kracke, Waud H.
  1980   The Complementarity of Social and Psychological Regularities: Leadership as a Mediating Phenomenon. *Ethos* 8 (4):273–285.

Kumagai, Fumie and G. O'Donoghue
  1978   Conjugal Power and Conjugal Violence in Japan and the U.S.A. *Journal of Comparative Family Studies* 9 (1):211–222.

Lamphere, Louise
  1974   Strategies, Cooperation, and Conflict Among Women in Domestic Groups. In *Woman, Culture, and Society*, ed. M. Z. Rosaldo and L. Lamphere. Stanford Calif.: Stanford University Press.

Leacock, Eleanor
  1975   Class, Commodity, and the Status of Women. In *Women Cross-Culturally: Change and Challenge*, ed. R. Rohrlich-Leavitt. The Hague: Mouton.
  1978   Women's Status in Egalitarian Society: Implications for Social Evolution. *Current Anthropology* 19 (2):247–275.

Lebra, Takie Sugiyama
  1967   An Interpretation of Religious Conversion: A Millennial Movement Among Japanese-Americans in Hawaii. Ph.D. dissertation, University of Pittsburgh.
  1974a  Interactional Perspective of Suffering and Curing in a Japanese Cult. *International Journal of Social Psychiatry* 20:281–286.
  1975   An Alternative Approach to Reciprocity. *American Anthropologist* 77 (33):550–565.
  1976a  Taking the Role of the Supernatural 'Other': Spirit Possession in a Japanese Healing Cult. In *Culture-Bound Syndromes, Ethnopsychiatry, and Alternate Therapies*, ed. W. P. Lebra. Honolulu: University Press of Hawaii.
  1976b  Ancestral Influence on the Suffering of Descendants in a Japanese Cult. In *Ancestors*, ed. W. H. Newell. The Hague: Mouton.
  1976c  *Japanese Patterns of Behavior.* Honolulu: University Press of Hawaii.
  1976d  Sex Equality for Japanese Women. *Japan Interpreter* 10:284–295.
  1978   Japanese Women and Marital Strain. *Ethos* 6:22–41.
  1979a  Tōgōteki josei kenkyū o mezashite [Toward an integrative study of women]. *Minzokugaku Kenkyū* [Japanese Journal of Ethnology] 44:105–132.
  1979b  The Dilemma and Strategies of Aging Among Contemporary Japanese Women. *Ethnology* 18:337–353.
  1980   Autonomy through Interdependence: The Housewives Labor Bank. *Japan Interpreter* 13:133–142.

1981     Japanese Women in Male-Dominant Careers. *Ethnology* 20 (4):291–306.

1982     Self-Reconstruction in Japanese Psychotherapy. In *Cultural Perceptions of Mental Health and Therapies*, ed. A. Marsella and G. White. Dordrecht, Holland: D. Reidel.

LeVine, Robert A.
1966     Sex Roles and Economic Change in Africa. *Ethnology* 5:186–193.

Lock, Margaret M.
1980     *East Asian Medicine in Urban Japan: Varieties of Medical Experience.* Berkeley and Los Angeles: University of California Press.

Martin, M. Kay, and Barbara Voorhies
1975     *Female of the Species.* New York: Columbia University Press.

Maykovich, Minako K.
1975     Comparison of Soap Opera Families in Japan and the United States. *International Journal of Sociology of the Family* 5 (2):135–149.

McC. Netting, Robert
1969     Marital Relations in the Jos Plateau of Nigeria. *American Anthropologist* 71:1037–1045. Unpublished manuscript.

McCoy, Sharon
1979     The Japanese Kimono School: A Contemporary Institution for Female Study of Traditional Adornment.

Meigs, Anna S.
1976     Male Pregnancy and the Reduction of Sexual Opposition in a New Guinea Highlands Society. *Ethnology* 15:393–407.

Monbushō [Ministry of Education], ed.
1976     *Shōwa 50 nendo, waga kuni no kyōiku suijun* [The 1975 educational level of our nation].

Morioka, Kiyomi
1967     Life Cycle Patterns in Japan, China, and the United States. *Journal of Marriage and the Family* 29 (3):595–606.

Nadel, Siegfried
1957     *The Theory of Social Structure.* London: Cohen and West.

Naikaku Sōridaijin Kanbō Kohōshitsu [Publicity Section, Prime Minister's Secretariat]
1973     *Fujin ni kansuru ishiki chōsa* [The states of consciousness regarding women]. Vol. 1.

Nakane, Chie
1967     *Kinship and Economic Organization in Rural Japan.* London School of Economics Monographs on Social Anthropology, no. 32. London: Althone Press.

Neugarten, Bernice L.
1975     The Awareness of Middle Age. In *Middle Age and Aging*, ed. B. L. Neugarten. Chicago: University of Chicago Press.

Norbeck, Edward
    1953    Age-grading in Japan. *American Anthropologist* 55 (3):373–384.
    1963    African Rituals of Conflict. *American Anthropologist* 65:1254–1279.

Olson, Jon L.
    1977    Women and Social Change in a Mexican Town. *Journal of Anthropological Research* 33 (1):73–88.

Omachi, Tokuzo
    1949    Kon'in [Marriage]. In *Kaison seikatsu no kenkyū* [The life conditions in coastal villages], ed. Kunio Yanagita. Tokyo: Nihon Minzoku Gakkai [The Japanese Folklore Society].
    1963    Ashiire-kon, Putting-One's-Feet-In Marriage. In *Studies in Japanese Folklore*, ed. R. Dorson. Bloomington: Indiana University Press.

Papanek, Hanna
    1971    Purdah in Pakistan: Seclusion and Modern Occupations for Women. *Journal of Marriage and the Family* 33:517–530.

Passin, Herbert
    1965a   Intrafamilial Linguistic Usage in Japan. *Monumenta Nipponica* 21: 97–113.
    1965b   *Society and Education in Japan*. New York: Teachers College Press.

Paul, Lois, and Benjamin D. Paul
    1975    The Maya Midwife as Sacred Specialist: A Guatemalan Case. *American Ethnologist* 2:707–726.

Perry, Linda L.
    1976    Mothers, Wives, and Daughters in Osaka: Autonomy, Alliance and Professionalism. Ph.D. dissertation, University of Pittsburgh.

Pharr, Susan J.
    1981    *Political Women in Japan: The Search for a Place in Political Life*. Berkeley and Los Angeles: University of California Press.

Phillips, Herbert P.
    1965    *Thai Peasant Personality: Thai Patterns of Interpersonal Behavior in the Village of Bang Chan*. Berkeley and Los Angeles: University of California Press.

Plath, David W.
    1964    Where the Family of God . . . Is the Family: The Role of the Dead in Japanese Households. *American Anthropologist* 66:300–317.
    1980    *Long Engagements: Maturity in Modern Japan*. Stanford Calif.: Stanford University Press.

Quinn, Naomi
    1977    Anthropological Studies on Women's Status. *Annual Review of Anthropology* 6:181–225.

Rapoport, Rhona, and Robert N. Rapoport
    1976    *Dual-Career Families Re-Examined.* London: Martin Robertson and Co.

Reiter, Rayna R.
    1975    Men and Women in the South of France: Public and Private Domains. In *Toward an Anthropology of Women*, ed. R. Reiter. New York: Monthly Review Press.

Rogers, Susan C.
    1975    Female Forms of Power and the Myth of Male Dominance: A Model of Female/Male Interaction in Peasant Society. *American Ethnologist* 2:727–756.

Rohlen, Thomas P.
    1974    *For Harmony and Strength: Japanese White-Collar Organization in Anthropological Perspective.* Berkeley and Los Angeles: University of California Press.

Rosaldo, Michelle Zimbalist
    1974    Woman, Culture and Society: A Theoretical Overview. In *Woman, Culture, and Society*, ed. M. Z. Rosaldo and L. Lamphere. Stanford, Calif.: Stanford University Press.

Sacks, Karen
    1975    Engels Revisited: Women, the Organization of Production, and Private Property. In *Toward an Anthropology of Women*, ed. R. Reiter. New York: Monthly Review Press.

Salamon, Sonya
    1974    In the Intimate Arena: Japanese Women and Their Families. Ph.D. thesis, University of Illinois.
    1975    "Male Chauvinism" as a Manifestation of Love in Marriage. In *Adult Episodes in Japan*, ed. D. W. Plath. Leiden: E. J. Brill.

Sangree, Walter H.
    1969    Going Home to Mother: Traditional Marriage Among the Irigwe of Benue-Plateau State, Nigeria. *American Anthropologist* 71:1046–1056.

Schlegel, Alice ed.
    1977    *Sexual Stratification: A Cross-Cultural View.* New York: Columbia University Press.

Scrimshaw, Susan C. M.
    1978    Stages in Women's Lives and Reproductive Decision-Making in Latin America. *Medical Anthropology* 2 (3):41–58.

Sekiguchi, Reiko W.
    1973    Joshi kōtō kyōiku shūryō-sha no shakai-teki ichi: sono shokugyō ni tsuite Nippon to Nishi-Doitsu to no hikaku kenkyū [The social positions of women with higher education: occupational distributions in Japan and West Germany]. *Shakaigaku Hyōron* [Japanese sociological review] 23 (4):83–100.

1975 Raifu saikuru to josei no ikikata [The life cycle and women's life pattern]. In *Gendai josei no ishiki to seikatsu* [The mentality and life conditions of today's women], ed. Noboru Yoshida and Michiko Kanda. Tokyo: Nippon Hōsō Shuppan Kyōkai.

Shimbori, Michiya
1965 *Nippon no daigaku kyōju shijō* [The academic market in Japan]. Tokyo: Tōyō Shuppansha.

Shiozawa, Miyoko, and Tomiko Shimada
1975 *Hitori gurashi no sengoshi* [Living alone in the postwar era]. Tokyo: Iwanami.

Smith, Robert J.
1966 *Ihai:* Mortuary Tablets, the Household and Kin in Japanese Ancestor Worship. *Transactions of the Asiatic Society of Japan*, 3d. ser., 9:83–102.

Soda, Takemune, and Fumio Miura, eds.
1980 *Zusetsu rōjin hakusho* [The white paper on the elderly with illustrations]. Tokyo: Sekibunsha.

*Sōgō Nihon Minzoku Goi* [Encyclopedia of Folk Vocabulary]
1955 Comp. Minzokugaku Kenkyūjo [Folklore Research Institute]. 5 vols.
–1956 Tokyo: Heibonsha.

Sōrifu [Prime Minister's Office], ed.
1978 *Fujin no genjō to shisaku* [The present life conditions of women and governmental policies]. Tokyo: Gyōsei.
1980 *Fujin no genjo to shisaku: Kokunai kōdō keikaku dainikai hōkokusho* [The present life conditions of women and governmental policies: the second report on the National Action Program]. Tokyo: Gyōsei.

Sōrifu Seishōnen Taisaku Honbu [The Youth Policy Headquarters, Prime Minister's Office]
1973 *Seishōnen hakusho* [White paper on youth].

Spradley, James P., and Brenda J. Mann
1975 *The Cocktail Waitress.* New York: John Wiley and Sons.

Suenari, Michio
1972 First Child Inheritance in Japan. *Ethnology* 11:122–126.

Takiuchi, Taizo
1972 Oyako shinjū to Nihonjin no kodomokan [Parent-child double suicide and the Japanese view of children]. *Kyoto Furitsu Daigaku gakujutsu hōkoku: jinbun* [The scientific reports of Kyoto Prefectural University: the humanities] 24:47–60.

Turner, Victor W.
1969 *The Ritual Process: Structure and Anti-Structure.* Chicago: Aldine.
1974 *Dramas, Fields, and Metaphors: Symbolic Action in Human Society.* Ithaca: Cornell University Press.

Vogel, Ezra F.
   1971    *Japan's New Middle Class: The Salary Man and His Family in a Tokyo Suburb.* Berkeley and Los Angeles: University of California Press.

Vogel, Suzanne H.
   1978    Professional Housewife: The Career of Urban Middle Class Japanese Women. *Japan Interpreter* 12 (1):16–43.

Whiting, John W. M., and Irvin L. Child
   1953    *Child Training and Personality: A Cross-Cultural Study.* New Haven: Yale University Press.

Williamson, Nancy E., Sandra L. Putnam, and H. Regina Wurthmann
   1976    *Future Autobiographies: Expectations of Marriage, Children, and Careers.* Papers of the East-West Population Institute no. 38 February 1976.

Wolf, Margery
   1972    *Women and the Family in Rural Taiwan.* Stanford, Calif.: Stanford University Press.

Wolff, Kurt H., ed.
   1950    *The Sociology of Georg Simmel.* Glencoe: Free Press.

Yanagita, Kunio
   1963    Kon'in no hanashi [On marriage]. In *Yanagita Kunio shū* [Collected works by Yanagita Kunio], vol. 15. Tokyo: Chikuma Shobō.

# Glossary

*Aisatsu.*  Formal greeting.

*Amae.*  The behavior or attitude expressive of dependency wishes.

*Amayakasu.*  To indulge another person's *amae*.

*Ashiire.*  A "stepping in"; tentative or pre-nuptial marriage.

*Atotori.*  An heir, successor.

*Bonyū.*  Mother's milk.

*Bunke.*  A branch house of a *dōzoku*.

*Butsudan.*  The household altar that enshrines the ancestors and dead members of the family; symbolic of Buddhist affiliation.

*Chōnaikai.*  A residential district; a division in a *ku-chōnaikai-tonarigumi*.

*Chōnan.*  The eldest son.

*Chūgakko* (or *chūgaku*).  The noncompulsory middle or intermediate school for boys in the prewar era; but compulsory for both sexes in the postwar school system.

*Daimyō.*  The lord of a feudal domain.

*Dakine.*  Co-sleeping with the child embraced.

*Danka.*  A household affiliated with a Buddhist temple.

*Demodori.*  The "once-married-out-and-returned" woman, namely, a divorcée.

*Dōki.*  Colleagues who joined an organization or were employed in the same year.

*Dōzoku.*  A cohesive group of households consisting of the *honke* (main house) and its *bunke* (branch houses); analogous to a patrilineage.

*Fujinkai.*  A women's association.

*Furo.*  A deep bath often large enough for two or more persons to cobathe.

*Futon.*  The bedding spread on the floor.

*Geta.*  Wooden footwear.

*Giri.*  Social obligation.

*Goinkyo-san.*  An honorable retiree.

*Gonin-gumi.*  Units of five or so households in villages of the Tokugawa era (1603–1867) which shared joint responsiblity vis-à-vis higher units of village administration.

*Gyōgi.*  Manners and comportment.

*Gyōgi-minarai.*  An apprenticeship in *gyōgi* learning.

*Haha.*   Mother; used in reference to one's own mother or mother-in-law.

*Hakoiri-musume.*   A "boxed-in daughter"; an overprotected daughter.

*Han.*   The feudal domain controlled by a *daimyō* in the Tokugawa era.

*Hanayome-gakkō.*   A bridal school.

*Hangyoku.*   An assistant geisha.

*Haori.*   A knee-length coat worn over the kimono.

*Hara.*   Belly or womb.

*Heimin.*   Commoners.

*Hinoeuma.*   A certain year of the horse in the Chinese zodiac system which returns in a sixty-year cycle.

*Hirōen.*   A publicity banquet.

*Honbyakushō* (or *osameshi*).   A tax-paying, full-fledged peasant in Tokugawa era, who was distinguished from the *komae* (partial tax payer) and *mizunomi* (the untaxable "water drinker") .

*Honke.*   Main house of a *dōzoku.*

*Honne.*   An undeclared actual feeling or opinion.

*Hotoke.*   The Buddha or the dead.

*Ichininmae.*   Full adulthood.

*Ie.*   The stem-family household.

*Iemoto.*   The founding house of a school of art or its headmaster.

*Ihai.*   A mortuary tablet.

*Ikigai.*   Life's worth or the purpose of life.

*Inkyo.*   Retirement from the headship of a household; also the retired head.

*Ippon.*   A fully qualified, independent *geisha.*

*Ironaoshi.*   The change of bridal costumes during the wedding banquet.

*Jikka.*   The natal household; used by a married-out daughter in reference to the house of her birth.

*Jimoto.*   A local or insider.

*Jinko-eiyō.*   "Artificial nutrition"; refers to animal milk and all baby foods other than *bonyū.*

*Jogakkō.*   The four- to five-year girls' high school under the prewar system; equivalent of the boys' *chūgakko.*

*Juku.*   A wide range of private, extracurricular schools or classes. In contemporary usage, *juku* refers primarily to a cram school preparatory for entrance examinations.

*Kachō.*   Section chief; a crucial position in a bureaucracy.

*Kafū.*   The domestic style or tradition of a household.

*Kagyō.*   Household occupation.

*Kaimyō.*   The posthumous name and title inscribed on the *ihai.*

*Kamidana.*   The household god shelf symbolic of Shinto affiliation.

*Kanreki.*   The sixtieth birthday marking a completion of the Chinese calendrical cycle.

*Karishugen.*   A tentative wedding.

*Kawaigarareta.*   Fondled or indulged.

*Kazoku.*   The nobility reorganized in Meiji era (1868–1912) which was composed of old aristocrats (*kuge, shōgun, daimyō,* and administrative chiefs) and new aristocrats (lower ranking *samurai* and commoners whose meritorious services were recognized).

*Ken.*   A prefecture; it replaced the pre-Meiji *han*.

*Kōden.*   The funerary (usually monetary) gift given to the bereaved.

*Kōden-gaeshi.*   A return gift in kind for *kōden*.

*Kōhai.*   A junior graduate or member of an organization.

*Kojūto.*   A spouse's sibling, particularly one's husband's sister.

*Komae.*   A partial tax payer as distinguished from the *honbyakushō*.

*Koseki.*   The house register.

*Kōshō.*   The two-year school supplementary to the six-year primary school under the prewar system.

*Ku-chōnaikai-tonarigumi.*   The reticulated system of a residential community in which the city is divided into a number of *ku* (wards). The latter are broken down into *chōnaikai* (districts), which are further divided into the smallest clusters of households called *tonarigumi* (neighborhood associations), reminiscent of *gonin-gumi*.

*Kuge.*   Imperial court nobles of the *kazoku*.

*Kurō.*   Hardship or suffering.

*Kyōiku-mama.*   The mother who relentlessly drives her child to study.

*Mago-bunke.*   "Grandchild" *bunke*; refers to a branch house of a branch house (see *dōzoku*).

*Mama-haha.*   Step-mother.

*Marumage.*   The traditional hair style of a married woman.

*Meiwaku.*   Trouble or burden imposed upon another person.

*Mekake.*   A concubine.

*Miai.*   In general, an arranged marriage; but specifically, the ceremony in which the man and woman intended for marriage are introduced.

*Mikoshi.*   A palanquin shrine containing the god body temporarily removed from the regular ward shrine, or *ujigami*.

*Mizugo.*   Aborted or miscarried fetus.

*Mizunomi.*   "Water drinker"; the untaxable as distinguished from the *honbyakushō*.

*Mizushōbai.*   A variety of service-oriented businesses—restaurants, teahouses, bars, brothels, and other hospitality businesses—characterized by an unpredictability of income.

*Moraikko.*   A child given away by a family with too many children to be fed and picked up by a family that needs cheap labor; sometimes also refers to an adopted child.

*Muko.*   A groom or adopted husband/son-in-law; *mukoyōshi*.

*Muko-iri.*   A groom's entry into the bride's household; uxorilocal marriage.

*Muko-tori.*   Receiving the *muko* into the bride's household.

*Mukoyōshi.*   An adopted son-in-law who moves to live with his wife's family and assumes its name.

*Mura.*   A hamlet or village which may or may not be an administrative unit.

*Mushi.*   "Bugs" believed to reside in the body and cause physical or mental disturbances.

*Naien.*   Privately married; without legal sanction.

*Naishoku.*   A private, unreported job.

*Nakōdo.*   A go-between for a marriage, actual or ceremonial.

*Nigō.*   A concubine or mistress.

*Obiiwai.*   The "belly-band" ceremony held for a woman in her fifth month of pregnancy.

*Ochikobore.*   "Dropped debris"; refers to a schoolchild who is unable to keep up with a standard of academic performance.

*Ohyakudo.*   A form of religious commitment; one walks up to a shrine a hundred times usually in order to appeal to the shrine god for a successful attainment of a goal.

*Omoiyari.*   Empathetic kindness.

*Omukae.*   A messenger or invitation from the next world.

*Osameshi.*   See *Honbyakushō*.

*Otonashii.*   Subdued.

*Oyakata.*   A master or boss.

*Oyashiki-bōkō.*   An apprenticeship in a mansion for *gyōgi-minarai*.

*Pokkuri.*   "Abruptly"; it has come to refer to an abrupt death.

*Rajio-taiso.*   A standard exercise done in tune with the nationally broadcast radio program.

*Ren'ai.*   Heterosexual love in general; specifically, love marriage as distinguished from *miai* marriage.

*Rōjin hōmu.*   A care home for the aged.

*Rōjinkai.*   The association of the elderly.

*Rōnin.*   The examination candidate who, having failed in the last exam, is no longer enrolled in a regular school; a position analogous to the masterless *samurai*.

*Satogaeri.*   The bride's return visit to her *jikka* soon after the wedding.

*Seken.*   The surrounding world or community consisting of neighbors, kin, colleagues, friends, and other significant persons whose opinions are considered important.

*Sekentei.*   The honorable appearance as viewed by the *seken*.

*Senpai.*   A senior (relative to the *kōhai*) graduate or member of an organization.

*Sensei.*   A master, teacher, or esteemed person.

*Senzo.*   Ancestors.

*Shamisen.*   A three-stringed lute.

*Shichigosan.*   The rites-of-passage ceremony for three-, five-, and seven-year-old children.

*Shinbō* (or *gaman*).   Perseverance.

*Shin heimin.*   A new commoner or former outcast.

*Shinjū.*   Plural suicide or, more commonly, a parent killing him/herself after killing his/her child.

*Shinseki* (or *shinrui*).   Kin beyond the primary family unit.

*Shizoku.*   The gentry below the *kazoku* class composed predominantly of common-ranking former samurai.

*Shōgun.* An overlord of the pre-Meiji warrior government (A.D. 1192–1867).

*Shufu.* A housewife.

*Shujin.* The house master or husband.

*Sōhonke.* The grand main house from which a number of lesser main houses (*dōzoku*) have branched out.

*Soine.* Sleeping by a child.

*Sunao.* A mixture of personality attributes such as straightforwardness, honesty, pliancy.

*Tanomare-nakōdo.* The ceremonial mediator who did not actually arrange the marriage but who plays a primary role in the wedding.

*Tatemae.* The declared principle.

*Teishu kanpaku.* A tyrannical husband.

*Tekireiki.* Marriageable age.

*Terakoya.* Private schools made available to commoners prior to the Meiji educational reform.

*Tonarigumi.* See *Ku-chōnaikai-tonarigumi.*

*Tsukisoi.* A personal nurse who stays with the patient around the clock at the hospital.

*Tsuwari.* Morning sickness.

*Uchi.* Household, *ie;* inside, private, personal.

*Ujigami.* The community shrine or its god(s) to which the residents of the locality, a ward for example, belong as *ujiko.*

*Ujiko.* Shrine members belonging to an *ujigami.*

*Ukemochi.* The Japanese version of a homeroom teacher, who teaches most subjects to the same group of students.

*Uwaki.* Fickleness or infidelity.

*Wagamama.* Selfish.

*Wakamono-gumi.* Young men's association.

*Yagō.* The house name; it is legally unrecognized but often better known than the legally registered family name.

*Yasashii.* Tender or considerate.

*Yobikō.* The exclusively examination-focused *juku.*

*Yōkan.* A sugared bean paste candy.

*Yome.* A bride or daughter-in-law.

*Yome-iri.* The bride's entry into the groom's household; that is, virilocal marriage.

*Yosomono.* A new settler or outsider (see *Jimoto*).

*Yuinō.* An engagement gift from the spouse-receiving family to the spouse-giver.

*Yuinō-gaeshi.* The return gift for *yuinō.*

*Zabuton.* A floor cushion.

*Zuruzuru.* One step of commitment slipping to another step.

# Index

Abuse: child, 49; during courtship, 96–97; daughter-in-law, 141–144, 162 (*see also* In-law relationship); mother, 310; and rape, 306; wife, 130, 135, 157, 162, 306, 316

Adoption and fosterage, 38, 49, 73, 88, 190–191, 315. See also *Moraikko*

Aged, the: and dependency status, 285–289; nursing, 254, 287–288; and pensions, 281, 288, 322; Revere-the-Elderly Day for, 270, 276; and rites of aging, 284; self-esteem of, 288; senility, 270, 301; and status promotion, 268. *See also* Life cycle, the; *Omukae*; Retirement; *Rōjin hōmu*; *Rōjinkai*

*Aisatsu*, 44, 45, 227

*Amae*, 40, 133, 145, 153, 178, 180, 186, 187, 263

American(s), 163, 271, 276; husbands, 131; lives of, as compared to Japanese lives, 295–297, 300–301, 302, 303, 304–305, 306, 323; women, 1, 124, 295, 298, 308, 310, 316, 322

American/Japanese: courtship, 78; marriage, 260

Americanization, 106

Ancestors, 22, 120, 257–259; memorial rites (death anniversaries) for, 11, 18, 146, 154, 259, 267–268, 280, 290; worship of, 289, 293–294, 299. See also *Butsudan*; *Ihai*

*Ashiire*, 106, 319, 320

*Atotori*, 84, 85, 90, 257

Birth order, 40–41, 90, 182–184, 198

*Bonyū*, 173, 174

Bridal arts: professionalization, 233–234; training, 58–60. See also *Iemoto*

*Butsudan*, 19, 181, 204, 205, 257, 258, 259

Career(s): compatibility of, with domestic roles, 247–250; and counter-socialization, 238; double, 313–314; and expertise, 238–240; female advantage in, 246–247; male dominant, 241–247, 304; promotion and achievement in, 240–241, 248; revocation of, 228–229; and socialization, 235; unfolding of, 230–238. *See also* Work experiences (extradomestic)

Change: in the domestic institution, 23–24; in education, 71–72, , 236, 321; in fertility rates, 166; in in-law relationship, 148, 157, 266; in life expectancy, 253; in marriage, 84, 102, 104, 110, 114, 140, 157; in postmarital residence, 262–263; in premarital sex, 122, 318; in residential architecture, 136; in self-fulfillment, 307–316

Child-birth: hazards of, 170; helping a daughter or daughter-in-law with, 263; the Lamaze method of, 173; and "natural" delivery, 168. See also *Tsukisoi*

Child-care: and bathing, 175, 176, 177, 180; father's role in, 179–181, 193; and feeding, 173–174; grandparent's role in, 178–179; and sleeping, 174, 176, 177, 180 (see also *Soine; Dakine*). *See also* Health care; Mother-child bonds; Socialization

*Chōnaikai*. See *Ku-chōnaikai-tonarigumi* system

Class identity, 73–74

Community: and children's associations, 17, 227; and motherhood, 209–213; and insider-outsider boundary, 7–9, 12, 87, 225, 227, 283, 287 (see also *Jimoto; Yosomono*); leadership, 283, 293; neighbors, 79, 83, 111–112, 125, 149, 172, 191, 192, 202, 209, 214, 225, 227, 280, 282, 283,

professional, 63, 80, 91, 230, 240; dietician, 61, 66, 239; fish processor, 225; food saleswoman, 64, 67; food shop keeper, 226–227; *geisha*, 64, 67–69, 70, 80; hairdresser, 55, 61, 80, 230, 239; hotel maid, 66–67, 70, 225; hotel management, 226; housemaid, 64; insurance saleswoman, 225; judge, 231–232; journalist, 245; kindergarten teacher, 230, 231, 239, 240, 282; midwife, 65, 239, 240, 282; national government official, 236, 237, 241, 243; nurse, 55, 60, 61, 237, 238, 248–249, 303, 313; nursery school teacher, 65; pharmacist, 54, 61, 66, 239; public corporation official, 243; research assistant, 232; research corporation president, 246, 247; restaurant management, 226; restaurant kitchen worker, 225; schoolteacher, 61, 86, 229; seamstress, 224; store clerk, 225; teacher of bridal arts, 190, 233, 234

*Yagō*, 21, 22
Yanagita, 317, 318, 319
*Yasashii*, 42, 123, 126, 130, 131, 137, 186
*Yōkan*, 41, 184, 231
*Yome*, 77, 85, 91, 105, 107, 141, 142, 208, 280
*Yosomono*, 7, 8, 9, 12, 87
*Yuinō*, 105, 106, 110, 111, 262, 319

*Zuruzuru*, 232, 296

**Production Notes**

This book was designed by Roger Eggers. Composition and paging were done on the Quadex Composing System and typesetting on the Compugraphic 8400 by the design and production staff of University of Hawaii Press.

The text and display typeface is Compu-graphic Caledonia.

Offset presswork and binding were done by Vail-Ballou Press, Inc. Text paper is Writers RR Offset, basis 50.

| | | | |
|---|---|---|---|
| OCT 1 3 87 | APR 0 7 1997 | | |
| OCT 1 3 87 | APR 1 6 1997 | | |
| | APR 2 8 1997 | | |
| OCT 2 5 88 | | | |
| NOV 8 1998 | APR 1 8 | | |
| JUL 3 1991 | MAR 0 5 1999 | | |
| MAR 1 0 1995 | OCT 1 6 2000 | | |
| MAR 3 1 | 1 5 2003 | | |
| | APR I 0 | | |
| DEC 0 8 1996 | | | |
| MAR 2 1 1997 | | | |